SOURCE BOOK OF SUBSTANCE ABUSE AND ADDICTION

SOURCE BOOK OF SUBSTANCE ABUSE AND ADDICTION

edited by

Lawrence S. Friedman, M.D.
Associate Professor of Pediatrics
Chief, Division of Adolescent
  Medicine
University of California,
  San Diego
School of Medicine
San Diego, California

Nicholas F. Fleming, B.A.
Class of 1996
Harvard Medical School
Class of 1996
John F. Kennedy School of
  Government
Boston, Massachusetts

David H. Roberts, M.D.
Intern in Internal Medicine
Massachusetts General Hospital
Boston, Massachusetts

Steven E. Hyman, M.D.
Associate Professor of Psychiatry
Director, Division on Addictions
Harvard Medical School
Director of Research
Department of Psychiatry
Massachusetts General Hospital
Boston, Massachusetts

Editor: David C. Retford
Managing Editor: Kathleen Courtney Millet
Production Coordinator: Kimberly S. Nawrozki and Anne Stewart Seitz
Copy Editor: Margaret D. Hanson, R.N.
Designer: Julie Burris
Illustration Planners: Academy ArtWorks, Inc., Mario Fernandez, Wayne Hubbel
Typesetter: Automated Graphic Systems
Printer: Victor Graphics
Binder: Victor Graphics

Copyright © 1996

Williams & Wilkins
351 West Camden Street
Baltimore, Maryland 21201-2436, USA
(800)638-0672

Rose Tree Corporate Center
1400 North Providence Road
Building II, Suite 5025
Media, Pennsylvania 19063-2043 USA

Accurate indications, adverse reactions, and dosage schedules for drugs are provided in this book, but it is possible that they may change. The reader is urged to review the package information data of the manufacturers of the medications mentioned.

Printed in the United States of America

Library of Congress Cataloging-in-Publication Data

Source book of substance abuse and addiction / edited by Lawrence Friedman . . . [et al.].
    p.   cm.
    Includes index.
    ISBN 0-683-03364-6
    1. Substance abuse. 2. Drugs of abuse. I. Friedman, Lawrence
    (Lawrence S.), 1951–
    [DNLM: 1. Substance Abuse. WM 270 C7974 1996]
    RC564.C6826   1996
    616.86—dc20
    DNLM/DLC
    for Library of Congress   95-10767
                                                 CIP

The publishers have made every effort to trace the copyright holders for borrowed material. If they have inadvertently overlooked any, they will be pleased to make the necessary arrangements at the first opportunity.

98 99
3 4 5 6 7 8 9 10

Preface

Abuse of and addiction to alcohol, nicotine, opiates, cocaine, and drugs may represent the greatest public health problem currently facing the United States. Drug abuse and addiction cause physical and mental illness, individual suffering, destruction of families, and lost productivity. All of this is at great societal and health care cost. They are also key contributors to domestic violence, accidents, crime, the spread of HIV, and diminished civility in our society. Given the pervasiveness and cost of substance abuse and addiction, especially in medical settings, it is extremely troubling that usually capable physicians and other health care providers often fail to identify these problems or intervene effectively if they do. This "blind spot" for abuse and addiction has been documented in many studies, and multiple reasons for it have been adduced. In some cases, physicians and other health care providers are inappropriately concerned about alienating valued patients; in others, they are concerned that a diagnosis of addiction will be harmfully stigmatizing. Often, physicians are inappropriately pessimistic about efficacy of treatment, and relapses are considered absolute failures in contrast to other disorders, where relapse is considered an expected feature of the illness. Health care providers are often uncomfortable broaching the subject with patients and don't know how to proceed if a diagnosis is made. It is not altogether surprising that physicians and other health care providers react to addicts and substance abusers in the way they do.

Only in recent years have medical schools begun to change curricula so that these topics are given the same recognition and emphasis that other subjects receive. One of the primary missions of the Division on Addictions, when it began in 1992 at Harvard Medical School, was to increase medical student and medical community awareness, understanding, inquiry, and discovery about this problem. Recognizing that there was a "blind spot" in their training, this book was the vision of medical students who were interested in learning how to approach substance abusing patients but were frustrated at the lack of teaching materials aimed at students. Decisions about content and organization were made by students who worked gallantly together for over two years.

Two students, editors David Roberts and Nicholas Fleming, took a leadership role, and with their colleagues and faculty advisors have produced a superb text. This book is accurate, practical, and easy to use. While it was written with the medical student in mind, it should be of great utility to those in postgraduate training, and any physician in the practice of primary care medicine and other disciplines, such as social work and counseling. We commend all of the authors on a job well done, and believe that this text should go a long way toward curing physicians of their unfortunate "blind spot" about drug abuse and addiction.

Lawrence S. Friedman, M.D.
Steven E. Hyman, M.D.

Contributors

Rini Banerjee, M.D.
Intern in Obstetrics and
  Gynecology
Brigham and Women's
  Hospital
Boston, Massachusetts

Manish Bhandari
Class of 1996
Harvard Medical School
Boston, Massachusetts

David Brendel
Class of 1997
Harvard Medical School
Boston, Massachusetts
Doctor of Philosophy
  Candidate
University of Chicago
Chicago, Illinois

Danielle Brook
Class of 1997
Columbia University College of
  Physicians and Surgeons
New York, New York

John T. Brooks, M.D.
Intern in Internal Medicine
Brigham and Women's
  Hospital
Boston, Massachusetts

Melissa Bush
Class of 1996
Harvard Medical School
Boston, Massachusetts

Thomas Cappola, M.D.
Intern in Internal Medicine
Brigham and Women's Hospital
Boston, Massachusetts

Elizabeth B. Caronna
Class of 1997
Harvard Medical School
Boston, Massachusetts

Deborah Cohan
Class of 1996
Harvard Medical School
Boston, Massachusetts

Gail Cohen, M.D.
Intern in Pediatrics
Medical College of Virginia
Richmond, Virginia

Sherry Tziporah Cohen, M.D.
Intern in Psychiatry
The Cambridge Hospital
Cambridge, Massachusetts

Sarah E. Dick, M.D.
Intern in Internal Medicine
University of Washington
  Affiliated Hospitals
Seattle, Washington

Nicholas F. Fleming, B.A.
Class of 1996
Harvard Medical School
Class of 1996
John F. Kennedy School of
  Government
Boston, Massachusetts

Benny Gavi
Class of 1996
Harvard Medical School
Boston, Massachusetts

Kathryn A. Glatter, M.D.
Cardiology Fellow
University of California,
   San Francisco
San Francisco, California

Douglas B. Haghigi
Class of 1997
Harvard School of Dental
   Medicine
Boston, Massachusetts

Jeremy Halberstadt
Class of 1997
Harvard Medical School
Boston, Massachusetts

David Hirsch
Class of 1996
Harvard Medical School
Boston, Massachusetts

David L. Kaufman
Class of 1996
Harvard Medical School
Boston, Massachusetts

B. Price Kerfoot
Class of 1996
Harvard Medical School
Boston, Massachusetts

Gordon Leung, M.D.
Intern in Internal Medicine
Johns Hopkins Hospital
Baltimore, Maryland

Triste Lieteau
Class of 1998
Harvard Medical School
Boston, Massachusetts
University of Chicago Law School
Chicago, Illinois

Eugene Lit, M.D.
Intern in Ophthalmology
Massachusetts Eye and Ear
   Infirmary
Boston, Massachusetts

Albert Losken
Class of 1996
Harvard Medical School
Boston, Massachusetts

Jim MacDonald, M.D.
Intern in Family Practice
Maine-Dartmouth Family Practice
   Residency
Augusta, Maine

Saverio Maviglia, M.D.
Intern in Internal Medicine
Brigham and Women's Hospital
Boston, Massachusetts

Kathleen B. McHugh, M.D.
Intern in Internal Medicine
Brigham and Women's Hospital
Boston, Massachusetts

Jeffrey Paley, M.D.
Intern in Internal Medicine
Massachusetts General Hospital
Boston, Massachusetts

Arun J. Ramappa
Class of 1996
Harvard Medical School
Boston, Massachusetts

Chandrajit P. Raut, M.D.
Intern in General Surgery
Massachusetts General Hospital
Boston, Massachusetts

Sarath Reddy
Class of 1996
Harvard Medical School
Class of 1996
Harvard School of Public Health
Boston, Massachusetts

David H. Roberts, M.D.
Intern in Internal Medicine
Massachusetts General Hospital
Boston, Massachusetts

George Sakoulas, M.D.
Intern in Internal Medicine
New England Deaconess Hospital
Boston, Massachusetts

Susan E. Spratt, M.D.
Intern in Internal Medicine
Beth Israel Hospital
Boston, Massachusetts

Antonia Stephen
Class of 1996
Harvard Medical School
Boston, Massachusetts

Edward C. Sun
Class of 1996
Harvard Medical School
Boston, Massachusetts

Shelley L. Sylvester
Class of 1996
Harvard Medical School
Boston, Massachusetts

Wilson W.H. Tang
Class of 1996
Harvard Medical School
Boston, Massachusetts

Elizabeth M. Twardon, M.D.
Intern in Family and Community
   Medicine
St. Paul Ramsey Medical Center
St. Paul, Minnesota

Howard West
Class of 1996
Harvard Medical School
Boston, Massachusetts

Stephen D. Wiviott
Class of 1996
Harvard Medical School
Boston, Massachusetts

Lori Wiviott-Tishler, M.D., M.P.H.
Resident in Internal Medicine
Brigham and Women's Hospital
Boston, Massachusetts

Suzanne Wong, M.D.
Intern in Obstetrics and
   Gynecology
Brigham and Women's Hospital
Boston, Massachusetts

Contributing Editors

JudyAnn Bigby, M.D.
Assistant Professor of Medicine
Harvard Medical School
Brigham and Women's Hospital
Boston, Massachusetts

Booker Bush, M.D.
Assistant Professor of Medicine
Harvard Medical School
Associate Physician in Internal
  Medicine
Beth Israel Hospital
Boston, Massachusetts

S. Jean Emans, M.D.
Associate Professor of Pediatrics
Harvard Medical School
Co-Chief, Division of Adolescent/
  Young Adult Medicine
Children's Hospital
Boston, Massachusetts

Lawrence S. Friedman, M.D.
Associate Professor of Pediatrics
Chief, Division of Adolescent
  Medicine
University of California, San
  Diego
School of Medicine
LaJolla, California

John A. Fromson, M.D.
Director, Physician Health
  Services
Massachusetts Medical Society
Waltham, Massachusetts
Clinical Instructor in Psychiatry
Harvard Medical School
Boston, Massachusetts

Steven E. Hyman, M.D.
Associate Professor of Psychiatry
Director, Division on Addictions
Harvard Medical School
Boston, Massachusetts

Cynthia Kettyle, M.D.
Clinical Instructor in Psychiatry
McLean Hospital
Belmont, Massachusetts
Director
Medical Student Education in
  Psychiatry
Harvard Medical School
Boston, Massachusetts

Barry Kosofsky, M.D., Ph.D.
Assistant Professor of Neurology
Harvard Medical School
Assistant in Neurology
Massachusetts General Hospital
Boston, Massachusetts

David Potter, Ph.D.
Robert Winthrop Professor of
  Neurobiology
Harvard Medical School
Boston, Massachusetts

John A. Renner, Jr., M.D.
Associate Professor of Psychiatry
Boston University School of
  Medicine
Veterans Administration
  Outpatient Clinic
Substance Abuse Treatment
  Center
Boston, Massachusetts

Nancy A. Rigotti, M.D.
Assistant Professor of Medicine
Harvard Medical School
Director, Quit Smoking Service
Massachusetts General Hospital
Boston, Massachusetts

Howard J. Shaffer, Ph.D.
Associate Professor of Psychology
Associate Director of Division on
  Addictions
Harvard Medical School
Boston, Massachusetts

Michael Shannon, M.D., M.P.H.
Associate Professor of Pediatrics
Harvard Medical School
Associate Chief and Fellowship
  Director
Division of Emergency Medicine
Children's Hospital
Boston, Massachusetts

Roger Weiss, M.D.
Associate Professor of Psychiatry
Harvard Medical School
Boston, Massachusetts

Alan Woolf, M.D., M.P.H.
Associate Professor of Pediatrics
Harvard Medical School
Director, Massachusetts Poison
  Center
Associate in Medicine
Children's Hospital
Boston, Massachusetts

Contents

Introduction

Substance abuse and addiction are topics that pervade the practice of medicine and challenge our understanding of diverse fields, ranging from neuroscience to human behavior. Despite this pervasiveness and its impact on patients and physicians, medical education continues to teach the concepts of substance abuse medicine in a piecemeal fashion. Aspects of substance abuse medicine are found in most disciplines taught in medical school, including pharmacology, neurobiology, psychiatry, and general internal medicine, but a unifying perspective is required to integrate the many pieces together.

This book is designed to present a much-needed synthesis of available, but often widely scattered, information about substance abuse and addiction. It brings together themes, issues, and concepts from the four years of medical school and residency by simultaneously addressing the basic pharmacology and history-taking skills of the first two years, and the more clinical treatment and management decisions of the third year, fourth year, and beyond.

Four major themes provide the basic organizational framework:

1. The patient-doctor relationship: This concept includes history-taking skills, interactions with the substance-using patient, and physical diagnosis of abuse and addiction.
2. The neurobiological and pathophysiological effects of substance abuse and addiction on the human body and mind.
3. An epidemiological evaluation of the impact of substance abuse and addiction on the individual, the family, and society.
4. A practical approach to the treatment and management of substance abusing patients in general, and specifically in reference to particular drugs.

In exploring these themes we have tried to construct an invaluable reference for medical students and physicians who need quick, easy-to-find, accurate, and focused information. To this end we have concentrated on the areas of substance abuse medicine where there are adequate data on effective strategies for management and treatment. Other areas with more limited data, such as general prevention strategies, are discussed in individual drug chapters where applicable. Additionally, each chapter includes further reading that provides the reader with more detailed reading of specific areas of substance abuse medicine.

This book represents the culmination of a collaboration between 45 medical students and 16 faculty members at Harvard Medical School, many of whom have close associations with the HMS Division on Addictions. Support for the project was provided by the HMS Division on Addictions, its faculty and administration, and the HMS Cannon Society. We particularly thank Drs. Larry Friedman and Steve Hyman for their clear vision of the project's potential and their unfailing humor and support; Christine Thurmond and the rest of the Division on Addictions staff for their unlimited administrative resourcefulness, patience, and ability to handle crises, as well as our neuroses; and Neal Baer, Michelle Finkel, Jesus Rame, Roger Meyer, and Larry Holmes for their contributions to this project. Finally, the editors thank the many medical residents and faculty members currently working with substance-abusing patients. In addition to providing their experience, knowledge, and advice, these physicians also demonstrated the many ways to have positive, satisfying, patient-doctor relationships within substance abuse medicine.

Nicholas F. Fleming, B.A.
David H. Roberts, M.D.
Boston, Massachusetts

SECTION I

GENERAL CONCEPTS
AND APPROACHES

Chapter 1

What Are Substance Abuse and Addiction?

Nicholas F. Fleming with David Potter and Cynthia Kettyle

Definitions of addiction, substance abuse, and substance dependence must encompass the multifactorial dimensions and variable presentations of these conditions. Defining the terms of substance abuse is difficult because certain aspects, including how abuse or addiction happens and why it happens, or what causes people to become addicted, are not adequately understood. Additionally, addiction is frightening to each person because everyone seems susceptible—whether the addiction is to substances, gambling, food, or sex—and, socially, the label "addict" or "abuser" is devastating to both position and self-esteem.

Various perspectives on substance use, including psychological, physiological, pharmacological, neurobiological, social, and political, enrich attempts to understand these disorders. The use of psychoactive substances produces a spectrum of consequences, with overlapping characteristics. This chapter explores the current neurobiological mechanisms of addiction, abuse, and dependence and the individual risk factors for addiction to drugs of abuse.

TERMS RELATING TO SUBSTANCE ABUSE

The terms addiction, substance abuse, and substance dependence describe the current understanding of the body's, particularly the brain's, adaptive responses to repeated drug exposure.

Substances *are chemicals, like alcohol, drugs, or food.* In this book the term "substance" will be used interchangeably with the term "drug." **Drugs** *belong to a more specific category, which encompasses substances with specific effects on the brain and the body.*

Tolerance *is a diminished biological or behavioral response to repeated administration of the same amount of a drug; or, the need for an increased amount of the drug to achieve the same, desired level of effect.*

While the exact mechanisms of tolerance are not fully understood and differ from drug to drug, tolerance reflects the body's homeostatic adaptations to counter the effects of a drug. The body makes pharmacokinetic and pharmacodynamic adaptations.

Pharmacokinetic adaptation occurs at the level of drug distribution and metabolism. For example, in response to alcohol ingestion, the liver produces increased amounts of alcohol dehydrogenase, the enzyme that begins ethanol metabolism. Consequently, for a given alcohol ingestion, the peak blood level is reduced by the more rapid breakdown of ethanol.

Pharmacodynamic modifications occur at the level of the drug's biologic or cellular targets. For psychoactive substances, these targets are neurons. Opiates, for instance, induce an up-regulation of a cyclic AMP (cAMP) 2nd messenger system in target cells exposed to chronic administration. These affected cells reside in several places, including the locus ceruleus and the periaqueductal gray (Fig. 1.1). This up-regulation acutely diminishes opiate-induced inhibition of Na^+-dependent inward current and activates a K^+ channel. Figure 1.2 describes the mechanisms in more detail.

Cross-tolerance *is the decreased pharmacological and behavioral effects of a drug that occurs secondary to the use or abuse of a second drug.* This phenomenon has both metabolic and functional aspects. Metabolic cross-tolerance develops when one drug increases the metabolism of a second drug. For example, use of a sedative-hypnotic will cause tolerance to this entire drug class and necessitates the administration of higher doses to achieve a desired effect. By contrast, functional cross-tolerance occurs when habitual use of a drug causes decreased psychoactive effects in response to administration of a different drug. For example, the brain's neuroadaptive response to alcohol diminishes the effects of sedative-hypnotics on the brain, again necessitating a higher dose to achieve a desired effect. In some cases, ethanol does not alter the metabolism of the sedative-hypnotic at all, it only diminishes its effects on the brain.

Sensitization *is an adaptive process in which a constant drug dose causes increasing effects.* This process is often referred to as "reverse-tolerance" and may mask a simultaneous process of tolerance. Some aspects of cocaine or amphetamine use demonstrate this phenomenon. **Desensitization**, an effect often seen with tolerance, *is the decreased effect that a drug has on a cell in response to chronic administration.* The interactions between a neurotransmitter and its synaptic receptor, including the cell up-regulating the receptor (sensitization) or the receptor becoming insensitive in the continued presence of a drug (desensitization), illustrate these concepts.

Withdrawal *(Abstinence Syndrome) is a syndrome of physical and/or psychological disturbances that follows the abrupt discontinuation of a drug or pharmacological blockage of the actions of a drug.*

While tolerance reflects the body's compensation for the drug's effects, withdrawal results from these same adaptive processes, unopposed when the drug is discontinued. The discontinuation causes physical and psychological disturbances (Table 1.1). Central nervous system (CNS)

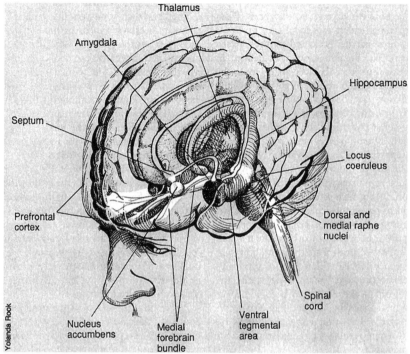

Figure 1.1. Anatomy of addiction. While psychoactive substances cause systemic effects, studies of neural processes of addiction have focused on several anatomically discrete regions in the brain, including the periaqueductal gray (PAG), the locus ceruleus (LC) and the mesolimbic dopamine system. Evidence points to these regions as important areas for addiction, but they are not the proven common pathway in all forms of substance abuse.

Located in the anterior pons on the floor of the fourth ventricle, the LC and the PAG are involved in physical dependence and withdrawal of opiates. By contrast, the positive reinforcing properties of opiates, cocaine, nicotine, amphetamine, alcohol, and cannabinoids map to the ventral tegmental area (VTA), located in the anterior ventral midbrain, and NAc, located in the ventral forebrain. This network of neurons is often called the "reward circuitry." Drug activation of the VTA-NAc pathway may alter motivational state, stress responses, and locomotor activity.

The neuroanatomic locations of withdrawal and addiction appear to be distinct. Direct stimulation of the LC with opiates will produce a withdrawal syndrome upon administration of naloxone, but not compulsive self-administration of opiates. By contrast, drug stimulation of the VTA-NAc causes compulsive drug administration, but no withdrawal syndrome if the drug is discontinued.

depressants, such as alcohol, barbiturates, and opiates, have physical withdrawal symptoms such as muscle cramps, nausea, convulsions, and sweating, that reflect the compensatory hyperexcitability of the CNS. By contrast, the withdrawal syndromes of CNS stimulants, such as nicotine, cocaine, and amphetamines, involve a general hypoexcitability of the

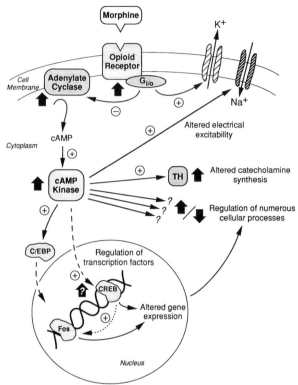

Figure 1.2. Effects of chronic opiate administration in the locus ceruleus. Chronic opiate administration produces multiple effects in the locus ceruleus as indicated by the *arrows*. It increases the levels of the $G_{i/o}$, adenylate cyclase, cAMP-dependent protein kinase, and several phosophoproteins, including tyrosine hydroxylase. These neuroadaptations contribute to the altered phenotype of the opiate-addicted state. For example, the intrinsic excitability of locus ceruleus neurons is increased via enhanced activity of the cAMP pathway and enhanced Na^+-dependent inward current. These changes contribute to opiate tolerance, dependence, and withdrawal. Although the mechanisms of opiate tolerance are not fully established, they can serve as a paradigm for other neuroadaptations by other drugs. Tolerance to opiates represents a relative decrease in the ability of μ opiate receptor agonists to regulate K^+ channels and a Na^+-dependent inward current, which may occur via several mechanisms:

Mechanism 1: The up-regulated cAMP system in the locus ceruleus would contribute to tolerance by making it more difficult for opiates to inhibit the Na^+-dependent inward current and to activate a K^+-dependent outward current via inhibition of the cAMP system.

Mechanism 2: It is possible that the up-regulated cAMP system also contributes to tolerance in locus ceruleus neurons by enhancing desensitization of the μ opioid receptor.

As another example of the effects of chronic opiate administration, the capacity of the neurons to synthesize catecholamines is increased via induction of tyrosine hydroxylase. This altered phenotypic state may be maintained in part by persisting changes in transcription factors (e.g., CREB, c-FOS, and C/EBP).

TABLE 1.1. FLOW CHART OF DRUG ACTIONS

Step 1: Administration of a drug
↓
Adaptive processes in the brain that diminish the effects of drugs (tolerance)

Step 2: Removal of the drug
↓
Adaptations that persist when the drug is removed/cleared
↓
Unopposed compensation processes
↓
Unpleasant symptoms (withdrawal)
↓
Continued drug use to ward off psychological and physical symptoms (dependence)

central nervous system secondary to chronic overstimulation by these drugs.

Dependence *is persistent drug intake to prevent or diminish the physical or psychological disturbances of withdrawal.* The definition of dependence includes tolerance and withdrawal, but has an additional behavioral component.

Traditionally, dependence has had physiological and psychological components. *Physical dependence* refers to physical tolerance and withdrawal symptoms. Several molecular mechanisms have been discovered that allow neurons to adapt intracellularly and induce dependence. These mechanisms include: (*a*) regulation of protein turnover; (*b*) regulation of RNA translation and turnover; (*c*) regulation of gene transcription; (*d*) posttranscriptional mechanisms; and (*e*) modifications of proteins and glycoproteins. Many of these mechanisms are illustrated by chronic opiate administration (Fig. 1.2). Chronic administration produces an up-regulation of the cAMP pathway in the locus ceruleus neurons. When opiate administration stops, this up-regulation causes an increased intrinsic excitability of the neurons by enhancing certain Na^+ channel activity, reducing the phosphorylation of μ receptors, thereby inhibiting them, and diminishing certain K^+ channel activity. The hyperexcitability, revealed when opiate administration stops, presumably accounts for some of the withdrawal symptoms. Users respond to these symptoms by wanting to administer more drug.

Psychological dependence refers to the "non-physical" symptoms that occur upon termination of drug use, including craving, agitation, anxiety, and depression. Drug administration relieves the withdrawal symptoms, both physiological or psychological, and produces an elevation of mood, unless the user is very tolerant. Inclusion of psychological dependence extends the dependence syndrome to all classes of drugs, even those without pronounced "physical" withdrawal syndromes, like cocaine. However, both physiological and psychological dependence have underlying physiological mechanisms.

Substance Abuse (drug abuse) is frequently used in two very different manners. First, as a diagnostic term, *it is intermittent impaired control of substance use and represents a stage in the spectrum of substance use disorders* , (described in detail later in this chapter). Second, in the more common, colloquial use of the term, *it describes drug use that violates social standards or causes self-harm.* Addiction and dependence are aspects of this second definition.

Addiction *is the compulsive use and impaired control of intake of a drug despite its adverse consequences.* Characteristics of addiction include preoccupation with the acquisition of the drug, compulsive use of the drug, propensity to relapse, loss of control, and denial. Specific areas of the brain account for each of these features of addiction. The definition of addiction incorporates tolerance, dependence, and two other important elements—compulsive drug use and loss of control.

Initially, addictions were considered manifestations of a fear of physical withdrawal. However, the addictive drug category now includes substances like cocaine, which produce limited physical withdrawal syndromes—cocaine addicts use the drug to avoid the psychological withdrawal symptoms. The most addictive drugs are opiates, cocaine, amphetamines, alcohol, and nicotine. These drugs activate the brain's reward circuitry, which leads to positive reinforcement and further drug use (Fig. 1.1).

The reward circuitry connects with many areas of the brain including those parts having to do with memory and context. For many drugs the ventral tegmental area (VTA) and the nucleus accumbens (NAc) appear to serve as reward "coordinator" sites for other regions of the brain. Certain actions, such as drug administration, will activate the reward system, leading to modifications in other brain regions. Consequently, processes, such as memory, are linked to drug administration. The reinforcing actions of cocaine, opiates, and amphetamines clearly depend on mesolimbic dopamine projections from the VTA to the NAc. For example, lesions of the NAc reduce or diminish the reinforcing actions of these substances. However, a lesion of the VTA does not eliminate self-administration of opiates to the NAc, demonstrating that the VTA is essential to cocaine and amphetamine reward, but not to opiate reward.

VTA and NAc cells undergo plastic changes after chronic drug administration. In response to opiates, the NAc up-regulates its cAMP system (increased adenylate cyclase and cAMP-dependent protein kinase) and the G-α_i protein, a regulator of phosphorylation, decreases its activity, further enhancing the cAMP levels. In contrast, VTA cells demonstrate no cAMP changes in response to chronic drug administration. Instead, cocaine, opiates, and alcohol cause decreased levels of neurofilament proteins. However, documentation of these cellular changes has greatly outpaced the understanding of the relation of these events to behavioral changes.

Translating these biochemical adaptations into functional significance presents several problems:

1. The NAc and VTA contain several cell types, and these cells may respond differently to different drugs;
2. Little is known about chronic drug effects on the electrophysiology of VTA and NAc neurons;
3. Controversy remains as to whether the primary site of action of particular drugs is the VTA, the NAc, or both;
4. The VTA-NAc system is involved in drug preference and in actions relevant to use of drugs, but these behaviors are complex.

In summary, addiction is complex. It involves tolerance and dependence, but out-of-control, compulsive drug use is also a key element. The reward circuitry of the mesolimbic dopamine system is apparently important in this compulsive use, but connections between the biochemical changes and behavioral modifications remain unclear.

RISK FACTORS AND THEORETICAL MODELS OF SUBSTANCE ABUSE

Numerous risk factors for substance use disorders have been studied. This section defines risk factors and introduces concepts that will be described in detail in later chapters.

Genetic Vulnerability

Disproportionate findings of substance abuse in particular families appears to signal a genetic susceptibility to these disorders. Alcoholism, much studied in this respect, shows a 50% correlation with a positive family history. Adoption studies and studies of twins have separated environmental influences from genetic factors. They have provided strong evidence for a genetic component of alcoholism. When compared to nonalcoholic adoptees, more alcoholic adoptees had alcoholic biological parents. Furthermore, the alcoholism of foster parents did not correlate with adoptees' alcoholism, suggesting that environment had less influence. Studies of twins demonstrate a higher concordance for alcoholism among identical twins than among fraternal twins.

Genetic variations exist in the neuronal mechanisms for addiction; the most dramatic at this time is the mesolimbic system. The differences in this system may account for the responsiveness of a subset of abusers to drugs of abuse. These differences could account for different levels of susceptibility to abuse of certain drugs among different ethnic groups found on epidemiological studies. Chapter 7 details more fully the genetic propensity to alcoholism.

Environmental Factors

While less clearly involved in the studies above, environmental stimuli and access to drugs can predispose people to substance abuse. For example, glucocorticoid treatment and environmental stress may augment the reinforcing properties of opiates, cocaine, and amphetamines. As a result, drug use is much more "rewarding," leading to a higher vulnerability to addiction. On the molecular level, this exposure enhances the reinforcing properties of the VTA-NAc pathway.

Returning to an environment associated with previous substance use after many years of abstinence can induce withdrawal symptoms and initiate drug-seeking behavior, especially if the reformed drug user is under stress. Thus, cues in an environment may renew the cycle of addiction even after years of abstinence; it is impossible to "detoxify" long-term memories of the context of use. Chapters 9 and 11 give good descriptions of environmental factors and their relation to use of cocaine and opiates.

Pain and Self-Medication

Self-medication ascribes drug use and misuse to underlying consequences of a disease process, like feelings of frustration, depression, anger, or physical aspects of pain. Conscious and unconscious denial, rationalization, and minimization play a role in advancing substance use to substance abuse. Chronic pain, as exemplified by sickle cell crises, represents an example of a physical cause of substance abuse. Patients with sickle cell disease may receive chronic opiate treatment for sickle cell crises and develop intermittent dependence on these drugs. However, dependence does not imply addiction. In this case the risk of development of addiction, though real, is low. Although self-medication based on a fear of withdrawal occurs, this level of distress does not usually compel a person to take a drug. Chapter 19 addresses the issue of pain management and substance abuse.

"Addictive Personality" and Psychiatric Comorbidity

Recognition of high levels of psychiatric comorbidity in the substance abuse population has fueled a search for an "addictive personality." Alcoholism is the most thoroughly studied substance-related disorder in this regard; affective disorders like depression, sociopathy, and border-line personality are the major psychiatric illnesses associated with alcoholism. Personality traits often thought to accompany alcoholism include impulsiveness, narcissism, dependence, anxiety, hypochondria, and ambivalence. However, these associations rely on retrospective studies in which it is difficult to determine which disorder is primary. Prospective studies have established that no specific profile predisposes to alcoholism. Nevertheless, the possibility of a comorbid psychiatric disorder should always be considered when treating patients afflicted with substance-related disorders. Similarly, psychiatric patients should be screened for substance abuse. Chapter 18 continues this discussion in more depth.

Sociocultural Factors

The sociocultural influences on substance abuse include ethnic background, culture, gender, age, occupation, social class, subcultures, and religious affiliation. For instance, young, single, unemployed urban men have a high incidence of alcoholism. Some individuals, especially adolescents, initiate drug use due to peer pressure. Cultural groups also establish characteristic patterns of use. For example, in Irish and Native American communities men more often drink away from home. Other factors that influence choice of drug include the legality and availability of a drug, for instance, cigarette smoking or drinking alcohol versus heroin use. Finally, the alternative activities available in communities can affect the initiation of drug use. On Native American reservations, for example, some communities believe that drinking has become a pastime, due to a lack of opportunities. Certain professional groups, such as physicians, are also a vulnerable population. Chapters 2, 3, and 5 discuss this topic in more detail.

CLINICAL DIAGNOSIS OF SUBSTANCE-RELATED DISORDERS

Since the first Diagnostic and Statistical Manual (DSM I) appeared in 1951, substance use disorder diagnoses have undergone an interesting transformation. The evolution of the diagnostic criteria reflects changing perceptions of substance use by the medical and psychiatric communities. In DSM I, "Addiction" was classified as a personality disorder, listed immediately after Sexual Deviation. It stated that "drug addiction is usually symptomatic of a personality disorder. . . the proper personality classification is to be made as an additional diagnosis." Alcohol was the only specific substance listed.

In DSM II, personality disorders included "Drug Dependence" and a separate category for Alcoholism. Tobacco and caffeine-containing beverages were not discussed. Diagnosis required "evidence of habitual use or a clear sense of need for the drug," but "withdrawal symptoms are not the only evidence of dependence." Cocaine was cited as a drug without withdrawal symptoms.

In 1980, DSM III included "Substance Use Disorders" as a new diagnostic class that "deals with behavioral changes associated with regular substance use that affects the central nervous system." The severity of these disorders became classified as either Substance Abuse or, in more severe cases, Substance Dependence. Distinguishing the two diagnoses required evidence of tolerance or withdrawal, hallmarks of substance dependence.

The publication of the DSM IIIR clarified some of the problems with the prior definitions. Under DSM III certain ambiguities or diagnostic dilemmas existed. For example, surgical patients requiring opiates for pain, who then experienced tolerance, withdrawal, and dependence on these drugs, rarely experienced disruptions in their lives secondary to the drug use. On the other hand, cocaine users experience major life disturbances with drug-craving and drug-seeking behaviors without classical "physical" withdrawal symptoms.

The DSM IIIR renamed the diagnostic class as Psychoactive Substance Use Disorders. These disorders consisted of "symptoms and maladaptive behavioral changes" associated with the use of psychoactive substances. The behavioral changes, viewed as "undesirable in almost all cultures," represent "the continued use of a drug despite the presence of a persistent or recurrent social, occupational, psychological, or physical problem that the person knows may be exacerbated by that use and the development of serious withdrawal symptoms following cessation of or a reduction in the use of a psychoactive substance."

In 1994, the DSM IV again renamed the class as Substance-Related Disorders, which include "disorders related to the taking of a drug of abuse, to the side effects of a medication, and to a toxin exposure." This book focuses on the Substance Use Disorders—Substance Dependence and Substance Abuse—and Substance-Induced Disorders, such as substance intoxication and substance withdrawal. The specifics of each disorder are described in relation to particular drugs in the individual drug chapters. Tables 1.2–1.4 list the current criteria for Substance Dependence, Substance Abuse, and Substance Withdrawal.

CONCLUSION

Defining and diagnosing substance-related disorders has been and continues to be problematic. The interplay of tolerance, withdrawal, psychosocial dysfunction, and neurobiological mechanisms make pathognomonic diagnostic criteria a challenge. In many ways, the diagnostic

TABLE 1.2. DSM IV DIAGNOSTIC CRITERIA FOR SUBSTANCE DEPENDENCE

A maladaptive pattern of substance use, leading to clinically significant impairment of distress, as manifested by three (or more) of the following, occurring at any time in the same 12-month period:

tolerance, as defined by either of the following:

  a need for markedly increased amounts of the substance to achieve intoxication or desired effect

  markedly diminished effect with continued use of the same amount of the substance

withdrawal, as manifested by either of the following:

  the characteristic withdrawal syndrome for the substance (refer to Criteria A and B of the criteria sets for Withdrawal from the specific substances)

  the same (or a closely related) substance is taken to relieve or avoid withdrawal symptoms

the substance is often taken in larger amounts or over a longer period than was intended

there is a persistent desire or unsuccessful efforts to cut down or control substance use

a great deal of time is spent in activities necessary to obtain the substance (e.g., visiting multiple doctors or driving long distances), use of the substance (e.g., chain-smoking), or recover from its effects

important social, occupational, or recreational activities are given up or reduced because of substance use

the substance use is continued despite knowledge of having a persistent or recurrent physical or psychological problem that is likely to have been caused or exacerbated by the substance (e.g., current cocaine use despite recognition of cocaine-induced depression, or continued drinking despite recognition that an ulcer was made worse by alcohol consumption)

dilemma reflects changing perceptions toward addiction and substance use. However, as the correlation between behavior and neurobiological adaptations to substance use becomes more apparent, two central challenges remain: understanding why the use of a substance becomes uncontrolled and how to develop effective ways of bringing the use under control.

TABLE 1.3. DSM IV DIAGNOSTIC CRITERIA FOR SUBSTANCE ABUSE

A maladaptive pattern of substance use leading to clinically significant impairment or distress, as manifested by one (or more) of the following, occurring within a 12-month period:

> recurrent substance use resulting in a failure to fulfill major role obligations at work, school, or home (e.g., repeated absences or poor work performance related to substance use; substance-related absences, suspensions, or expulsions from school; neglect of children or household)
>
> recurrent substance use in situations in which it is physically hazardous (e.g., driving an automobile or operating a machine when impaired by substance use)
>
> recurrent substance-related legal problems (e.g., arrests for substance-related disorderly conduct)
>
> continued substance use despite having persistent or recurrent effects or interpersonal problems caused or exacerbated by the effects of the substance (e.g., arguments with spouse about consequences of intoxication, physical fights)

The symptoms have never met the criteria for Substance Dependence for this class of substances

---

TABLE 1.4. DSM IV CRITERIA FOR SUBSTANCE WITHDRAWAL

The development of a substance-specific syndrome due to the cessation of (or reduction in) substance use that has been heavy and prolonged

The substance-specific syndrome causes clinically significant distress or impairment in social, occupational, or other important areas of functioning

The symptoms are not due to a general medical condition and are not better accounted for by another mental disorder

---

FURTHER READING

Diagnostic and Statistical Manual. Ed. I, II, III, IIIR, IV. Washington, DC: American Psychiatric Association. I, 34–39; II, 45–46; III, 163–179; IIIR, 165–185; IV, 175–190.

Donovan JM. An etiologic model of alcoholism. Am J Psychiatry 1986;143:1–11.

Gawin FH. Cocaine addiction: psychology and neurophysiology. Science 1991;251:1580–1986.

Hyman SE. Molecular and cell biology of addiction. Curr Opin Neurosci Neurosurg 1993;6:609–613.

Jenke MA. Drug abuse. In: Rubenstein E, Dale DC, Federman DD, eds. Scientific American Medicine. New York: Scientific American Publishers, 1991.

Koob GF, Bloom FE. Cellular and molecular mechanisms of drug dependence. Science 1988;242:715–723.

Nestler EJ, Hope BT, Widnell KL. Drug addiction: a model for the molecular basis of neural plasticity. Neuron 1993;11:995–1006.

Wise R. Opiate reward: sites and substrates. Neurosci Biobehav Rev 1989;12:129–133.

Wise RA, Bozarth MA. A psychomotor stimulant theory of addiction. Psychol Rev 1987;94:469–492.

Chapter 2

Epidemiology of Substance Use

Gail Cohen, Nicholas F. Fleming, Kathryn A. Glatter, Douglas B. Haghigi, Jeremy Halberstadt, and Kathleen B. McHugh with Alan Woolf

Substance use is ubiquitous—it occurs in all age groups, both genders, all ethnic groups, and all socioeconomic groups. Epidemiological surveys have identified the prevalence rates of use among the different groups, the trends of use over the years, and the most popular substances among different groups. This chapter explores the epidemiological data on aspects of substance use including initiation of use, current trends of drug use among adolescents, adults, and the elderly, and data on treatment modalities.

INITIATION OF SUBSTANCE USE

As a normal consequence of development adolescents attempt to assert their individuality while conforming to peer norms. Separation from family, membership within a social group, and peer-sanctioned illicit activities are issues that require adolescents to balance individuality and a sense of belonging. These conflicting influences make the adolescent and young adult population particularly susceptible to the initiation of the drug use. On average, initiation of the use of all substances occurs before the age of 23, with most use beginning before the age of 20 (Table 2.1). Furthermore, initiation of licit substance use often precedes

TABLE 2.1. AVERAGE AGE OF INITIATION OF DIFFERENT SUBSTANCES

Drug	Age
Cigarettes	15.0
Inhalants	16.4
Alcohol	17.0
Hallucinogens	18.5
Marijuana/Hashish	18.2
Stimulants	18.8
Sedatives	19.6
Heroin	20.1
Analgesics	21.7
Cocaine	21.4
Tranquilizers	23.8

illicit substance use. This use includes cigarettes, which while legal for adults, are theoretically illegal for teens.

Social forces strongly affect the initiation of substance use. The influences and effects of these forces are described below:

- **Peer** norms, modeling, and use are the most salient predictors of substance use for adolescents. Same sex friends most commonly introduce illicit drugs to each other.
- **Parents** enforce rules, champion values, and can have a profound positive or negative effect on the child's risk of substance use initiation. Parental substance use correlates with substance use by their children. Some studies have shown that adolescents who live in homes where parents are either heavy users or *strict* abstainers—the polarized extremes of the spectrum—have higher use rates.
- **Siblings** can also act as positive and negative role models or as providers of substances. Particularly for males, older siblings are a strong positive or negative influence on younger siblings' drug use in the context of concurrent parental or peer drug use.
- **Family dynamics,** and the quality of family interactions, powerfully influence adolescent substance use, positively correlating with inconsistent rule enforcement, a lack of parent-child intimacy, a lack of parental interest, and a lack of control. Adolescents may attempt to cope with domestic unrest through substance abuse. Finally, there is a disproportionately higher incidence of substance use among children from single and stepparent families.
- **Psychological profile,** including low self-esteem, susceptibility to peer pressure, and mental illness (especially depression, mania, and attention deficit disorder), correlate with earlier substance use.
- **Physicians** can also act as positive role models, but unfortunately, they can also prescribe potentially abusable drugs, such as anabolic steroids, benzodiazepines, and opiates.
- **Drug dealers** have not been shown to factor much into substance use initiation.
- **Popular culture** has created several images of drug use. This culture is driven by advertisements, television, movies, and music videos.

Evaluation of these social forces and the young age of initiation has resulted in three theories designed to explain the initiation of substance use:

- **Problem Behavior Theory:** A lack of respect for authority, mores, and social standards forecasts delinquent behavior, substance use, and sexual promiscuity.

- **Stage Theory:** Substance use is a progressive process, beginning with alcohol and cigarettes, progressing to recreational licit and illicit drug use, marijuana, and then to hard-core drug use. However, each stage is not invariably followed by the next.
- **Peer Cluster Theory:** The adolescent's family dynamics, religious identification, school adjustment, and friends influence the initiation of substance use.

Social forces interact with the addictive qualities of the drugs themselves to determine the prevalence rates of use for different substances.

PREVALENCE TRENDS IN SUBSTANCE USE

Adolescent Population (Tables 2.2 and 2.3)

Possession, purchase, and use of all drugs, including alcohol and tobacco products, are illegal for adolescents. Nevertheless, initiation of most drug use begins during this stage of life. The epidemiology of adolescent substance use demonstrates the relevance of and need for early education, prevention, and intervention.

Studies Examining the Adolescent Population

Two major studies have examined patterns of drug use in adolescents: the National Institute on Drug Abuse (NIDA), or "Monitoring the Future" study, and the National Household Survey on Drug Abuse (NHSDA).

Since 1975, NIDA has annually used questionnaire responses of 12th graders from both public and private high schools to estimate the prevalence (lifetime, annual, 30-day, and daily) of substance use. In addition, NIDA has retrospectively tracked the prevalence of substance use in earlier grade levels by asking the high school seniors to report on their substance use practices in grades 6–12 (these data cover the 23-year period from 1969–1992). The associations of demographic factors, such as gender, ethnicity, geographic region, and educational goals, with drug use have been analyzed.

The NHSDA study is a cross-sectional study of drug use among the noninstitutionalized, civilian population from 1972–1991, which uses in-home interviews of randomly selected participants to assess the prevalence of substance use. Like the NIDA study, these data depend on self-reported drug use. This study covers the 12–17-year-old age groups (in addition to the 18–25, 26–34, and >35 age groups to be discussed below) and uses demographic factors similar to the NIDA study to analyze the data. However, this study has no longitudinal component as individuals received no follow-up interviews.

TABLE 2.2.   TRENDS IN SUBSTANCE USE—ADOLESCENTS

Drug	Trends	
	NIDA data: High School Seniors only	**NHSDA: Combined 7th–12th Graders (Ages 12–17)**
Any illicit drug use	• Steady increase in annual prevalence until 1978, when it peaked at 54%—consistent with the simultaneous increase in marijuana use	
	• Prevalence rates:	
	NIDA: (1979–1992):	NHSDA (1979–1991): 12–17
	lifetime: 65.1% to 40.7%	34.3% to 20.1%
	annual: 54.2% to 27.1%	26% to 14.8%
	monthly: 38.9% to 14.4%	17.6% to 6.8%
	daily: not available	
Alcohol	• Use peaked in the early 1980s and has declined since then	
	• Prevalence of occasional heavy drinking (five or more drinks in a row during past 2 weeks) fell by approximately 25% since its peak in the early 1980s	
	• In early 1980s, increased prevalence of use for grades 6–9 (marks a trend wherein alcohol use was initiated at an earlier age, and more commonly by girls)	
	• In contrast to peer pressure, major reasons for drinking include:	
	41% drink when they are upset because it makes them feel better;	
	25% drink because they are bored;	
	25% drink to feel high	
	• Prevalence rates:	
	NIDA: (1979–1992):	NHSDA (1979–1991): 12–17
	lifetime: 93.2% to 88%	70.3% to 46.4%
	annual: 88.1% to 76.8%	53.6% to 40.3%
	monthly: 70% to 51%	36.9% to 28.2%
	daily: 6.9% to 3.4%	

Cigarettes

- Decline in use since late 1970s
- Compared to rates of decline of other substances, cigarette use has decreased proportionately less despite taxes and heightened awareness of associated health risks
- For grades 8–12, rates peaked in the mid 1970s, declined until 1983, and have since increased
- Prevalence rates:

NIDA:	(1977–1992):	NHSDA (1982–1991): 12–17
lifetime:	75% to 62%	49.5% to 37.9%
annual:	not available	24.8% to 20.1%
monthly:	39% to 28%	14.7% to 10.8%
daily:	29% to 17%	

Marijuana

- During 1970s, use rates increased for all grade levels. A decline began in 1980 for grades 9–12 and in 1981 for grades 7 and 8
- Initiation of use most commonly occurred after the 8th grade
- Decline attributed to concerns of adverse health effects and increased peer disapproval
- Prevalence rates:

NIDA:	(1979–1992):	NHSDA (1979–1991): 12–17
lifetime:	60.4% to 32.6%	30.9% to 13%
annual:	50.8% to 21.9%	24.1% to 10.1%
monthly:	36.5% to 11.9%	16.7% to 4.3%
daily:	10.7% to 2%	

Cocaine

- Decreased use since 1985
- Greater than 50% of initiation occurs in grades 9–12
- In late 1970s, largest increases in use were in grades 11–12, with a decline after 1986
- Prevalence rates:

NIDA:	(1985–1992):	NHSDA (1982–1991): 12–17
lifetime:	17.3% to 6.1%	6.5% to 2.4%
annual:	13.1% to 3.1%	4.1% to 1.5%
monthly:	6.7% to 1.3%	1.6% to 0.4%
daily:	0.4% to 0.1%	

(continued on next page)

TABLE 2.2. TRENDS IN SUBSTANCE USE—ADOLESCENTS, *continued*

	Trends	
Drug	**NIDA data: High School Seniors only**	**NHSDA: Combined 7th–12th Graders (Ages 12–17)**
Crack	• Annual use rates have fallen 60% since 1986 • There is little regional variation among high school seniors • Use now lower in large cities and nonmetropolitan areas (both at 1.3%) than in smaller cities (1.6%) • Prevalence rates: NIDA: (1987–1992): lifetime: 5.4% to 2.6% annual: 4.1% to 1.5% monthly: 1.3% to 0.6% daily: 0.1%	
Hallucinogens/Psychoedelics	• Gradual decline from 1975 to 1992, with a plateau in 1984 • LSD declined since the 1970s, but has slightly increased for all grades since 1987 • Prevalence rates: NIDA: (1975–1992): lifetime: 16.3% to 9.2% annual: 11.2% to 5.9% monthly 4.7% to 2.1% daily: 0.1%	NHSDA (1982–1991): 12–17 7.1% to 3.3% 4.7% to 2.1% 2.2% to 0.8%
Inhalants	• Increase in popularity from 1976 to 1990, with subsequent decline in 1992 • Since 1984, rates for grades 8–12 increased dramatically (rise attributed to an artifact of data gathering—nitrite inhalants were inappropriately excluded in previous years) • Prevalence rates: NIDA: (1976, 1990, 1992): lifetime: 10.3%, 18.0%, 16.6%	NHSDA (1979–1991): 12–17 9.8% to 7.0%

annual:	3.0%, 6.9%, 6.2%		4.6% to 4.0%
monthly:	0.9%, 2.7%, 2.3%		2.0% to 1.8%
daily:	0.0%, 0.3%, 0.1%		

Stimulants

- Decline since peak in early 1980s for grade levels 7–12
- Prevalence rates:

	NIDA: (1975 to 1992):	NHSDA (1982–1991): 12–17
lifetime:	32.2% to 13.9%	6.7% to 3.0%
annual:	26% to 7.1%	5.6% to 1.9%
monthly:	15.8% to 2.8%	2.6% to 0.5%
daily:	1.2 to 0.2%	

Heroin

- Overall decline since 1975 with plateau between 1979 to 1990, until 1992 when use increased
- Prevalence rates:

	NIDA: (1975, 1990, 1992):	NHSDA (1977–1991): 12–17
lifetime:	2.2%, 0.9%, 1.2%	1.1% to 0.3%
annual:	1.0%, 0.4%, 0.6%	0.6% to 0.2%
monthly:	0.4%, 0.2%, 0.3%	0.1%
daily:	0.1%, 0.0%, <0.05%	

Sedatives

- Steady decline in use from 1975 to 1992 for grades 10–12; consistently low use rates for grades 6–9
- Methaqualone use increased for all grade levels in the late 1970s and early 1980s; since 1982, use has fallen to almost 0% because Quaaludes are no longer legally manufactured in the U.S.
- Prevalence rates:

	NIDA: (1975 to 1992):	NHSDA (1982–1991): 12–17
lifetime:	18.2% to 6.1%	5.8% to 2.4%
annual:	11.7% to 2.9%	3.7% to 1.3%
monthly	5.4% to 1.2%	1.3% to 0.5%
daily:	0.3% to 0.1%	

(continued on next page)

TABLE 2.2. TRENDS IN SUBSTANCE USE—ADOLESCENTS, *continued*

Drug	Trends	
	NIDA data: High School Seniors only	**NHSDA: Combined 7th–12th Graders (Ages 12–17)**
Tranquilizers	• Use has decreased dramatically since 1977 • Since the early 1980s, rates for grades 9–12 have declined with stable low use rates for grades 6–8 • Prevalence rates: NIDA: (1975 to 1992): lifetime: 17.0% to 6.0% annual: 10.6% to 2.8% monthly: 4.1% to 1.0% daily: 0.1% or less	NHSDA (1982–1991): 12–17 4.9% to 2.1% 3.3% to 1.3% 0.9% to 0.4%
Steroids	• Rates of use have declined from 1989 to 1992 • 4.4% of students in grades 9–12 admitted use • Athletes showed higher usage (5.5%) than nonathletes (2.4%) • Prevalence rates: NIDA: (1989 to 1992): lifetime: 3.0% to 2.1% annual: 1.9% to 1.1% monthly: 0.8% to 0.6% daily: 0.1%	

TABLE 2.3 VARIABLES IN SUBSTANCE USE—ADOLESCENTS

Variables	Trends
Gender differences (past year prevalence)	• Any illicit drugs: girls 12.5% > boys (11.0%) • boys: higher rates of marijuana, smokeless tobacco, PCP, steroids, heroin, and needles • girls: higher rates of cocaine, crack, inhalants, hallucinogens, stimulants, tranquilizers, analgesics • Alcohol: boys (33.7%) > girls (31.4%) • Cigarettes: boys (19.2%) > girls (17.1%)
Regional differences	• South: highest rates of inhalants, stimulants, tranquilizers, analgesics, and smokeless tobacco • West: highest rates of cocaine, marijuana, PCP, heroin, and needles • Alcohol: North Central (34.3%) > West (33.8%) > Northeast (31.9%) > South (31.0%) • Cigarettes: North Central (19.3%) > South (18.8%) > West (17.6%) > Northeast (16.0%)
Socioeconomic status	• Adolescents of lower socioeconomic status have drug use rates well above the national average • Increased life stresses—poverty, unemployment, lack of education—turn adolescents to drugs to cope • Socioeconomic status, independent of race, appears to affect rates of adolescent drug use. A study comparing drug use rates in private, suburban, and urban pediatric practices found similar rates of overall drug use among a mainly (89%) white, suburban practice and a mainly (95%) black, urban practice despite the marked racial differences. Both populations were predominantly middle class adolescents from largely intact, working families. The prevalence of drug use in these groups was well below the average national use rates.
Educational goals	• College and noncollege-bound seniors have nearly equal rates of substance use • An association among substance use, truancy, and crime exists: Truants were more often males, exhibited three times more marijuana use, and four times more cocaine, heroin, LSD, amphetamine, and other illegal drug use. Furthermore, they were more likely to smoke cigarettes, drink alcohol, and engage in fights and vandalism. • Substance use in this population is associated with domestic discord, risk-taking behavior, truancy, poor academic performance, sexual promiscuity, and crime.

(continued on next page)

TABLE 2.3 VARIABLES IN SUBSTANCE USE—ADOLESCENTS, *continued*

Suicidality	• Suicide attempts and suicidal ideation occur more frequently with the use of many drugs, such as cocaine, marijuana, LSD, PCP, MDMA, heroin, and alcohol. Acute and chronic substance use most likely leads to suicide via two mechanisms: 1) increased impulsiveness/recklessness, or 2) a result of psychiatric disturbances and reduced serotonin levels, both sequelae of chronic drug use.
	• From 1950 to 1980, the adolescent suicide rate increased by 31% for males and by 67% for females
Perception of harmfulness of substance use	• A smaller proportion of younger students perceived smoking at least a pack of cigarettes a day as a very risky behavior
	• Since 1986, there has been a constant increase in the perceived risk of using most illicit drugs, consistent with a concurrent general decline in adolescent drug use. In particular, perceived harmfulness of marijuana and cocaine has increased significantly in comparison to a concomitant decline in the prevalence of use.
	• Interestingly, the perceived harmfulness of almost all substances, with the exception of cigarettes, is less among seniors in high school than among younger students. This trend correlates with increased prevalence of use among the older high school students.
	• More than one-third of high school seniors did not understand the intoxicating effects of alcohol.
	• More than one-third believed that drinking coffee, getting some fresh air, or taking a cold shower can "sober you up."

Study Limitations

Validity of Self-Reported Data

Although the accuracy of self-reported data on actual substance use behavior remains questionable, respondents to the surveys have shown remarkable consistency in reporting their own behavior, making the trends found in these anonymous surveys seem valid.

Extrapolation of Data to All Adolescents

In-school surveys exclude certain segments of the adolescent population, namely absentees and dropouts. This exclusion has caused concern about the generalizability of the data, given that these unsurveyed groups may have substantially different drug use patterns.

TABLE 2.4 ESTIMATES OF THE U.S. POPULATION THAT USES VARIOUS SUBSTANCES, 1993

Drug	Number of Users (in millions)	
	Lifetime	Past Month
Alcohol	173.3	102.8
Cigarettes	147.5	50.1
Any illicit drug	77	11.7
Marijuana/Hashish	69.9	8.9
Cocaine	23.5	1.3
Crack	3.7	.42
Inhalants	10.4	.89
Hallucinogens	18	.52
Heroin	2.3	.08
Nonmedical use of:		
Psychotherapeutics	23.0	2.6
Stimulants	12.5	.72
Sedatives	7.1	.53
Tranquilizers	9.5	.57
Analgesics	11.9	1.4
Anabolic steroids	.75	.08

NIDA found that, on the day of the survey, absentees accounted for nearly all of the nonrespondents. Correcting the data for them showed that absentees had significantly higher drug usage rates. The correction was small, though, averaging 1.4%, because of the relatively small number of absentees. Similarly, other studies, including the NHSDA, have shown consistently higher drug use rates among dropouts when compared to those who finish high school. Although the omission of dropouts and absentees from the calculations may alter the prevalence of drug use, the trends reported over the years should not be affected. The proportion of students who drop out of school has remained at 15% over the last 20 years. Consequently, the trends elicited over time can be assumed valid reflections of adolescent drug use.

Adult Population

Both the NIDA and the NHSDA survey cover adult populations. For the NIDA study, the high school seniors receive questionnaires annually to follow changes in drug use patterns over time. Consequently, the study provides longitudinal data about changing drug use practices as the cohort ages, and cross-sectional data about college student and young adult drug use patterns among different cohorts.

The NHSDA survey examines substance use in the 18–25, 26–34, and >35 age groups. The data that it receives from this cross-sectional survey have been extrapolated to estimate the number of people using substances in the United States. The most recent estimates are presented in Table 2.4. The combination of these two studies offers both a cross-sectional and, in some cases, a longitudinal perspective of the trends of substance use among adolescents and adults (Tables 2.5 and 2.6).

Study Limitations

The studies for the adult population have limitations similar to those of the adolescent population discussed above. In addition, although the NHSDA survey covers only the noninstitutionalized, civilian population, it excludes less than 2% of the population from its estimates. Consequently, the trends of drug use may not apply to the excluded populations, and thus, can only be generalized to the noninstitutionalized, civilian population.

Elderly Population

Currently, individuals aged 65 and older account for 12% of the population, and that number is expected to increase to 14% by the year 2010, and to 20% by 2030. The rapid growth of this sector of the population makes it an increasingly important group to study. However, studies assessing the drug use patterns have been difficult.

Studies of Drug Use (and Their Limitations) in the Elderly Population

The studies of drug use in the elderly population comprise mostly anecdotal reports without the broad scope of the NIDA or NHSDA studies. Consequently, good estimates of the prevalence of substance use and abuse among the elderly are unavailable for two main reasons:

First, at least 80% of elderly persons have at least one chronic illness (about twice the rate of those under age 65) and the average elderly person has three diseases, for which he or she is prescribed an average of eight medications. Although they comprise 12% of the population of the United States, elderly patients consume 30% of prescribed drugs and 70% of over-the-counter medications.

Second, the aging process involves changes that make those who are at least 65 years old or older particularly prone to misuse prescriptions and over-the-counter medications. Furthermore, the effects of alcohol and other drugs are often more severe and complex in the elderly, due to physiologic aging, underlying pathology, or the co-administration of other medications. Experts estimate that 15% of the 25 million elderly have drug addictions.

In the elderly population, the line between therapeutic use, misuse, and abuse is narrow and can obscure good approximations of inappropriate drug use patterns. There is a ready availability of licit drugs—anxiolytics, narcotics, sedatives, alcohol—and rare use of illicit drugs. Furthermore, the use of drugs that alleviate pain and anxiety often develop into physiological dependence, a state expected with therapeutic administra-

TABLE 2.5 TRENDS IN SUBSTANCE USE IN ADULTS

Drug	Trends	
	NIDA data: College Students and Young Adults	**NHSDA: 18–25, 26–35, and >35 year old age group**
Any illicit drug use	• Use peaked in early 1980s then declined until 1992, when annual use increased • Most individuals initiate drug use before age 20 • Lifetime prevalence has increased in the 26+ group due to aging of cohorts with higher rate of past drug use • 26–34-year-olds have 2–3 times the prevalence rate of drug use than the ≥ 35 year olds: annual (18.4% vs. 6.4%) • Prevalence rates: NIDA: (1986, 1991, 1992): lifetime: 70.5%, 62.2%, 60.2% annual: 41.9%, 27%, 28.3% monthly: 25.8%, 15.1%, 14.8%	NHSDA (1979–1991): 18–25 26 and older ≥35 (1991) 69.9% to 54.7% 23.0% to 36.0% 27.3% 49.4% to 29.1% 37.1% to 15.4% 6.4% 10.0% to 9.4% 6.5% to 4.6% 3.1%
Alcohol	• Use peaked in the early 1980s and has remained relatively stable (within 2%) • Decline of the 1980s are due in part to raising the minimum drinking age • Individuals 3–4 years after high school graduation show small decline in rates of binge drinking; college students showed no downward trend • Prevalence rates: NIDA: (1986 to 1992): lifetime: 94.8% to 93.4% annual: 88.6% to 86.2% monthly: 75.1% to 69% daily: 6.1% to 4.5%	NHSDA (1979–1991): 18–25 26 and older ≥35 (1991) 95.3% to 90.2% 91.5% to 88.6% 87.4% 87% to 82.8% 72% to 69% 64.9% 75.9% to 63.6% 61.3% to 52.5% 49.5%

(continued on next page)

TABLE 2.5 TRENDS IN SUBSTANCE USE IN ADULTS, *continued*

Drug	NIDA data: College Students and Young Adults	Trends — NHSDA: 18–25, 26–35, and >35 year old age group
Cigarettes	• Decline since late 1970s • Following the same cohort of young adults shows that they continued similar use rates until they were 30, and then use decreased (discontinuation of smoking) • Sex differences: female > male by 3% in 1980 among 19–22 year olds. Difference has disappeared in 1992 with prevalence for both at 20% • Prevalence rates:	
	NIDA: (1986 to 1992): lifetime: not available annual: 40.1% to 37.9% monthly: 31.1% to 28.3% daily: 25.2% to 20.9%	NHSDA (1979–1991): 18–25 18–25 26 and older ≥35 (1991) 82.8% to 71.2% 83% to 77.6% 78% 47.2% to 41.2% 40% to 32% 30% 49.4% to 32.2% 39.1% to 28.2% 27%
Marijuana	• After years of decline, annual use increased slightly in 1992 • High school seniors have higher usage rates than graduates • Prevalence rates:	
	NIDA: (1985–1992): lifetime: not available annual: 36.5% to 25.2% monthly: 32% to 13.3% daily: 4.1% to 2.3%	NHSDA (1979–1991): 18–25 26 and older ≥35 (1991) 68.2% to 54.7% 20% to 32.7% 24% 47% to 24.5% 11% to 6.6% 4% 35% to 13% 6.6% to 3.3% 2%

Cocaine

- Annual cocaine use rate decreased since 1986
- Annual use rate has dropped more quickly for males (15.5%) than females (12.1%), but prevalence in males still higher
- Prevalence rates:

	NIDA (1986 to 1992):	NHSDA (1979–1991): 18–25	26 and older	≥35 (1991)
lifetime:	32% to 19.5%	28.3% to 18%	4.3% to 12%	6.8%
annual:	19.7% to 5.7%	19.6% to 7.7%	4.2% to 2.3%	1.4%
monthly:	8.2% to 1.8%	9.3% to 2.0%	2.0% to 0.8%	0.5%
daily:	0.2% to ≤ 0.1%			

Crack

- Decline in use rate from 1987 to 1992
- Use most common among young and middle-aged adults, males, blacks, residents of metropolitan areas, residents of the West, those with less than a high school education, and the unemployed
- Prevalence rates:

	NIDA (1987 to 1992):
lifetime:	6.3% to 5.1%
annual:	3.2% to 1.4%
monthly:	1.0% to 0.4%

Heroin

- Prevalence rates for heroin use have declined since 1986, with a plateau of the decline of rates in the last three years
- Prevalence rates:

	NIDA (1986 to 1992):	NHSDA (1972–1991): 18–25	26 and older	≥35 (1991)
lifetime:	1.3% to 0.9%	4.6% to 0.8%	1.0% to 1.5%	1.5%
annual:	0.2% to 0.2%	1.3% to 0.3%	0.2%	0.1%
monthly:	0.1% to 0.1%	0.1%	low precision, unable to estimate	

Hallucinogens

- Increasing use rate since 1990 (NIDA study).
- Greater decline in older population than among high school seniors until 1989.
- Prevalencee rates:

(continued on next page)

TABLE 2.5 TRENDS IN SUBSTANCE USE IN ADULTS, continued

Drug	NIDA data: College Students and Young Adults			Trends		NHSDA: 18–25, 26–35, and >35 year old group		
	NIDA:	(1975, 1990, 1992):				NHSDA (1979–1991):		
				18–25		26 and older		≥35 (1991)
	lifetime:	20.1%, 16.5%, 16.0%		25.1% to 13%		4.5% to 7.8%		5.2%
	annual:	4.9%, 4.2%, 5.1%		9.9% to 4.7%		0.8% to 0.5%		0.2%
	monthly:	1.4%, 1.0%, 1.6%		4.4% to 1.2%		0.1%		0.1%
	daily:	not available						

- Increasing prevalence until late 1970s, then rates have shown variability.
- With increasing age use drops significantly.
- Marked decline in nitrite use from 1986 to 1992: annual (2.0% to 0.1%), and thirty-day (0.5% to 0.1%).

Drug	NIDA data			Trends		NHSDA		
Inhalants	• Prevalence rates:							
	NIDA:	(1986 to 1992):				NHSDA (1988–1991):		
				18–25		26 and older		≥35 (1991)
	lifetime:	not available		12.5% to 4.2%		5.0% to 4.2%		2.5%
	annual:	12.3% to 13.5%		4.1% to 3.5%		0.8% to 0.5%		0.4%
	monthly:	both 1.9%		1.7% to 1.5%		0.5% to 0.3%		0.2%
	daily:	0.4% to 0.6%						

- Long-term decline since mid 1980s, plateau in 1992.
- Rise in lifetime prevalence due to aging cohort with high prevalence of past drug use.

Drug	NIDA data			Trends		NHSDA		
Stimulants	• Prevalence rates:							
	NIDA:	(1986 to 1992):				NHSDA (1985–1991):		
				18–25		26 and older		≥35 (1991)
	lifetime:	32.3% to 20.2%		21% to 9.4%		5.8% to 7.1%		5.4%
	annual:	10.6% to 4.1%		10.8% to 3.3%		2.6% to 0.9%		0.5%

monthly: 4.0% to 1.5% 0.7% to 0.2% 0.1%
daily: 0.2 to 0.1%

Sedatives (Barbiturates and Methaqualone)

- Steady decline from 1975 to 1992.
- Prevalence rates:

	NIDA: (1975 to 1992):	NHSDA (1986–1991):		
		18–25	26 and older	≥35 (1991)
lifetime:	11.1% to 7.4%	18% to 4.3%	5.2% to 4.5%	3.5%
annual:	2.3% to 1.6%	9% to 1.9%	2.0% to 0.9%	0.7%
monthly:	0.7% to 0.5%	2.8% to 0.7%	0.5% to 0.3%	0.3%
daily:	not available			

Tranquilizers

- Highest prevalence in late 1970s and early 1980s, then decline that has stabilized in 1990s.
- Prevalence rates:

	NIDA: (1986 to 1992):	NHSDA (1979–1991):		
		18–25	26 and older	≥35 (1991)
lifetime:	17.6% to 11.3%	16% to 7.4%	2.6% to 5.7%	4.2%
annual:	5.4% to 3.4%	7.1% to 2.6%	2.8% to 1.5%	1.2%
monthly:	1.8% to 1.0%	2.6% to 0.6%	1% to 0.5%	0.5%
daily:	0.1% or less			

Steroids

- Lifetime rates of use have increased from 1989 to 1992, while annual and thirty day use rates fell.
- Prevalence rates:

	NIDA: (1989 to 1992):
lifetime:	1.1% to 1.9%
annual:	0.5% to 0.4%
monthly:	0.2% to 0.1%

TABLE 2.6. VARIABLES IN SUBSTANCE USE—ADULTS

Variables	Trends
Gender differences (past year prevalence)	• Gender differences have narrowed and for any illicit drugs: male (31%) > female (27%) for ages 19–22. Faster rates of decline for males than females, though more males actually use substances. • males: higher use rates of marijuana, LSD, and other hallucinogens, stimulants, cocaine, inhalants, steroids, and heroin use • Similar use rates of cigarettes, tranquilizers, analgesics • Alcohol: men (73%) > women (62%), more heavy drinking among males • Women obtain drugs of abuse via licit, medical channels more often than men. Nearly 70% of all psychotropic drugs are prescribed by physicians for female patients
Educational differences	• College students have lower drug use rates for all drugs except marijuana and MDMA (ecstasy) • College students have a higher monthly use rate for alcohol (71% versus 62%), but a lower daily prevalence (3.7% versus 4.0%) • The most striking difference is in the difference in smoking cigarettes—college students have 14% daily rate versus a 28% daily rate for non-college high school graduates
Regional differences	• Declines in almost all drug categories for all of the regions since 1987 • South: highest use rates of inhalants, stimulants, tranquilizers, analgesics, and smokeless tobacco • West: highest use rates of marijuana, cocaine, PCP, heroin, nonmedical use of psychotherapeutic drugs (stimulants, tranquilizers, etc.) • Alcohol: Northeast (56%) > West (56%) > North Central (50%) > South (41%) • Cigarettes: North Central (28%) > South (27%) > Northeast (27%) > West (25%)
Population density	• Farm, country, and small towns have lower use than larger-size communities; large cities tend to have the highest rates • General decline for all community sizes since the mid-1980s • Alcohol: slightly positive relationship of size of city and increased rates of alcohol use • Negative association of cigarette smoking with urbanity for all ages; little difference in trends for the different community sizes

(continued on next page)

TABLE 2.6. VARIABLES IN SUBSTANCE USE—ADULTS, *continued*

Variables	Trends
	• Crack use bears little association to community size except that very large cities have shown lower than average rates in 1991 and 1992
Perception of harmfulness of substance use	• General increased perception of harmfulness since mid-1980s • Increased perception of harmfulness with increasing age for hallucinogens, cocaine, crack, heroin, amphetamines, barbiturates, and cigarette smoking. This trend correlates with declines in use of all substances with increasing age. • There is increased perception of harmfulness among high school seniors for the use of marijuana and alcohol, a trend reflected in the substantially lower use rates of alcohol among this younger group, but this group has a similar prevalence of marijuana use.
Impact of drug use and abuse on the Justice System	• In 1990 drug arrests made up 8% of all state and local arrests • 7% of all referred delinquency charges are for drug violations—an increase over the time period from 1985–1988 • Large metropolitan areas have the highest drug arrest rates, while rural areas have the lowest • The West has the highest drug arrest rate, followed by the Northeast, South, and Midwest • Percentage of arrestees with positive urinalysis at time of arrest:

	Positive for any drug (%)	
Arrest charge	Male	Female
Drug sale possession	79	81
Burglary	68	58
Robbery	66	66
Larceny-theft	64	59
Stolen property	59	59
Homicide	52	49
Prostitution	49	81
Assault	48	50

tion of a drug, which is distinct from an addiction. Alterations in absorption, distribution, metabolism, and excretion of drugs can enhance the effect of the drugs and increase their levels. Table 2.7 details general trends in drug use among the elderly and special populations requiring more attention from the physician.

TABLE 2.7. TRENDS IN SUBSTANCE USE—ELDERLY

Category	Data/Trends
Abuse of individual substances	• Substances that are commonly abused and misused include alcohol, prescription drugs, and over-the-counter medications, as opposed to illicit drugs
Illicit substances	• There is little information on the prevalence of illegal drug use suggesting limited rates • Younger individuals who are street addicts tend to "die out" or "mature out" of their addictions and lifestyles. For example, many individuals who begin to abuse illicit substances die as a result of violence, trauma, or drug overdose. Other persons will change their drugs of choice to legal medications.
Alcohol	• It is generally accepted that alcohol is the most popular drug abused among the elderly • Estimates report that 2–10% of the elderly population abuse alcohol • Older women are more likely to abuse alcohol than younger females • The aged alcoholic is more likely to be part of a higher socioeconomic stratum than individuals who develop alcoholism earlier in life. • Older abusers of alcohol are less likely to have a positive family/genetic history of alcoholism since the disease usually manifests itself earlier in life if there is a positive family history. • The elderly have a more promising rate of recovery than younger adults.
Drugs other than alcohol	• The most prominent nonalcoholic drugs abused include barbiturates, benzodiazepines, opioid analgesics, and tranquilizers.
Issues of poisoning	• The elderly are more prone to suffer from morbidity and mortality from both accidental and intentional poisoning. Although hospital intervention occurred nearly twice as often, death from poisoning was nearly 12 times that of younger groups. • A 1-year retrospective study of poisoning in all age groups demonstrated that the intoxication was nearly twice as likely to be intentional (21% versus 11%).
Nursing home patients	• Over half of the drugs prescribed for residents of nursing homes in the state of Massachusetts were psychoactive in nature • Side effects from certain medications are often confused with the normal aging process. Addictions may develop to medication initially begun for anxiety or sedation

Treatment of Substance Abuse

Although few precise quantitative data exist about the treatment of substance users, the National Drug and Alcoholism Treatment Unit Survey (NDATUS) has attempted to measure the location, scope, and characteristics of privately and publicly funded drug abuse and alcoholism treatment and prevention facilities, services, and activities in the United States.

The study obtained prevalence data by evaluating the number of individuals receiving active care in ambulatory and outpatient settings in a 1-month period, and the patients receiving inpatient, 24-hour detoxification, and rehabilitation/residential care on a single given day. In 1991, the most recent NDATUS survey received responses from 82% of all known treatment and prevention units (11,277 units), roughly 80% of which were treatment units. While the response rates are good, these data do not represent the characteristics of the unreported units. However, they do provide substantial data about the general characteristics of treatment units. Data from previous NDATUS studies are not comparable to the most recent data because of variability in the reporting level of the different units, alterations in the format for reporting data on client diagnoses and type of care in each of the last two surveys, and changes in unit orientation (inpatient to ambulatory). Table 2.8 presents the most recent data.

TABLE 2.8. TRENDS IN TREATMENT DATA OF CLIENTS

Characteristic	Data/Trends		
Demographic data	Diagnosis	No.	% of total
	Drug abuse	237,008	29.2
	Alcoholism	365,147	45.0
	Both diagnoses	209,664	25.8
	All	811,819	100

• A total of 1.82 million clients were reported in an unduplicated client count in a 12-month period; California, New York, and Texas accounted for one-quarter of these clients.
• Demographic data based on treatment setting

Age	No.	%
18	43,698	5.9
18–20	38,544	5.2
21–24	95,718	13.0
25–34	260,184	35.2
35–44	197,165	26.7
45–64	71,315	9.7
65 & over	7,464	1.0
unknown	73,448	

• Over one-third of all clients were aged 25–34 and another quarter was aged 35–44. Treatment programs service these individuals much more than the younger groups despite lower prevalence rates.

Gender differences

• Gender differences in client population:

Gender	Drug abuse	Alcoholism	Both problems	All
Female	29.1	20.5	23.6	24.3
Male	70.9	79.5	76.4	75.7

• Nearly three-quarters of all clients were male (72.5%)
• Female clients were more likely to be drug abuse clients and less likely to be alcoholism candidates
• Female clients slightly more likely to be treated in private nonprofit units and far less likely than male clients to be treated in Federal units and in correctional facilities
• 4.9% of female clients were reported to be pregnant
• Women enter treatment at a later stage in their addiction
• Three barriers prevent a woman from seeking treatment: 1) personal denial of addiction problems by women themselves; 2) responsibility of care for dependent children, aging parents, and other family members, and 3) family denial of women's addiction problems and/or family opposition to treatment.

(continued on next page)

TABLE 2.8. TRENDS IN TREATMENT DATA OF CLIENTS, *continued*

Characteristic	Data/Trends
Type of care	• 87.8% of total patients received ambulatory[a] care • 10.8% received 24 hour rehabilitation/residential[b] care • 1.4% of clients received 24-hour detoxification[c]
Population density information	• Over 50% of clients (54.4%) resided in urban areas • 23.7% resided in suburban areas • 21.9% resided in rural areas
Special population groups	• Almost one-quarter (23.6%) of all clients were IV drug users at the time of admission • 8.4% of clients in units were reported as HIV positive
Methadone clinics	• 6.7% of 9057 units provided methadone maintenance for 95,286 clients • Females account for 12% of patients on methadone maintenance

[a]Services provided on an outpatient basis, which may not include detoxification.

[b]3 levels: 1) ambulatory has service rendered in less than 24 hours that provide for safe withdrawal in an ambulatory setting; 2) freestanding residential provides 24 hours per day services in a nonhospital setting that provides for safe withdrawal and transition to ongoing treatment; 3) hospital inpatient provides 24 hours per day medical acute care services for detoxification for persons with severe medical complications associated with withdrawal.

[c]Includes 10 hospital (other than detoxification), 24 hour/day medical care in a hospital facility in conjunction with treatment services for alcohol and other drug abuse and dependency; 20 short-term residential, typically 30 days or less of nonacute care in a setting with treatment services for alcohol and other drug abuse and dependency; and 3) long-term residential, typically over 30 days of nonacute care in a setting with treatment services for alcohol and other drug abuse and dependency (may include transitional living arrangements such as halfway houses).

FURTHER READING

Adolescents

Farrow JA, Schwartz RH. Adolescent drug and alcohol usage: a comparison of urban and suburban pediatric practices. J Natl Med Assoc 1992;84:409–413.

Garrison CZ, McKeown RE, Valois RF, Vincent ML. Aggression, substance use, and suicidal behaviors in high school students. Am J Public Health 1993;83:179–184.

Johnson V, Pandina RJ. Effects of the family environment on adolescent substance use, delinquency, and coping styles. Am J Drug Alcohol Abuse 1991;17:71–88.

Khavari KA. Interpersonal influences in college students' initial use of alcohol and drugs—the role of friends, self, parents, doctors, and dealers. Int J Addict 1993;28:377–388.

National Household Survey on Drug Abuse: 1972–1991 (Ages 12–17). Rockville, MD: US Department of Health and Human Services, 1993.

National Institute on Drug Abuse "Monitoring the Future Study" 1975–1992 (High School Seniors). US Department of Health and Human Services, National Institutes of Health publ. no. 93-3597. Washington, DC: US Government Printing Office, 1993.

Rogers P, Silling SM, Adams LR. Adolescent chemical dependence: a diagnosable disease. Psychiatric Annals 1991;21:91–97.

Adults

Bureau of Justice Statistics: Drugs, Crime, and the Justice System, 1992. Washington, DC: US Department of Justice, 1992;7:158–159, 173.

Clayton RR, Voss HL, Robbins C, Skinner WF. Gender differences in drug use: an epidemiological perspective. In: Ray BA, Braude MC, eds. Women and drugs: a new era for research. Rockville, MD: National Institute on Drug Abuse, 1986:80–99.

National Institute on Drug Abuse and National Institute on Alcohol Abuse and Alcoholism. National Drug and Alcoholism Treatment Unit Survey (NDATUS) 1991 Main Findings. Rockville, MD: US Department of Health and Human Services, 1993.

Elderly

Alcoholism Services of Cleveland, Inc. Fact Sheet, 1993.

Avorn J, Dreyer P, Conelly K, Soumerai S. Use of psychoactive medications and the quality of care in rest homes. N Engl J Med 1989;320:227.

Finch J, Barry KC. Substance abuse in older adults. In: Fleming MF, Barry KC, eds. Addictive Disorders. St. Louis: Mosby Year Book, 1982.

Pasarelli EF. Drug abuse and the elderly. In: Lowinson J, Ruiz P, eds. Substance Abuse: Clinical Problems and Perspectives. Baltimore: Williams & Wilkins, 1981:752–757.

Solomon K. Alcoholism and prescription drug abuse in the elderly: St. Louis grand rounds. J Am Geriatr Soc 1993;41:57–59.

Chapter 3

Cultural Perspectives on Substance Abuse

Wilson W.H. Tang with JudyAnn Bigby

DEFINING CULTURE IN A HEALTH CARE CONTEXT

Traditionally, culture has described populations sharing a common set of values, norms, traditions, customs, arts, history, folklore, and institutions. In recent years, a much more sophisticated idea of culture has emerged. Culture is shaped by, and in turn shapes, local worlds of everyday experience. In these local worlds, life experience becomes an interpersonal flow of communication, interaction, and negotiation connecting families, work settings, networks, and communities. For illness behavior, culture constructs unique mental states that influence the interpretations of both normal and pathological experiences, and the strategies for dealing with such experiences.

CULTURAL IMPACTS ON SUBSTANCE ABUSE

Culture affects how substance abuse is perceived, experienced, and expressed, how help is sought, and what treatments succeed or fail. Heavy drinking among some Hispanic males, for example, may be accepted as a sign of "machismo," that is, equating manhood with the ability to hold one's liquor. Consequently, toleration of alcohol abuse in this community exists and help is not sought unless a man can no longer provide for his family.

The choice of drugs of abuse, their patterns of use, and their health implications are also culturally salient. For example, the apparent preference of intravenous heroin and cocaine use in minority communities correlates with an increased risk of contracting hepatitis B or HIV. However, casual explanations based on value judgments or stereotypes preclude the understanding of each person with substance use problems.

DIAGNOSTIC AND THERAPEUTIC IMPLICATIONS OF CULTURE

Cultural patterns affect both the diagnosis and the treatment of substance abuse. In the United States, mental health professionals use formalized diagnostic criteria (DSM-IV) to interpret and diagnose the illness behavior of persons abusing substances. Despite expanding these Western criteria with each new edition, the DSM-IV is limited due to the lack of discussions of the cultural variations of substance abuse presentation. Consequently, appropriate diagnoses may be difficult to make.

Furthermore, institutions and cultures affect patient perceptions of medical problems. Under cultural influences, patients may deny or even refuse to seek help for substance abuse problems. In treating substance-related disorders in different cultural groups, the long-term lifestyle reorientation, behavioral changes, and medical therapy characteristic of substance abuse programs should include families and familiar groups, organizations, institutions, and political systems.

The development of cultural competency requires clinicians to acquaint themselves with their patients' culture and heighten their own awareness of patients' culturally salient illness behavior. This chapter attempts to establish a culturally sensitive approach to substance-related disorders. This approach encompasses an understanding of different cultural perceptions of substance abuse, interpretation of current research, and treatment strategies.

ETHNIC PATTERNS OF SUBSTANCE ABUSE IN THE UNITED STATES

Cross-cultural and ethnic-specific drug abuse research is an important and rapidly growing field. Researchers have struggled to understand the biological role of race in the origins of substance abuse. For example, certain minority groups have differences in lactate dehydrogenase levels, but these differences do not demonstrate a clear clinical significance. Similarly, early links between distinct dopamine (D_2) receptor allelic gene frequency and substance abuse among White Americans and African Americans have not been supported by subsequent research. Nevertheless, these genetic differences could reflect other characteristics that predispose certain populations to addictions.

Without a clear role of race in the origin of substance abuse, socially defined ethnicity and its effects on the prevention and treatment of substance abuse rise to the forefront of the discussion. The data on the ethnic patterns of substance abuse in the United States are derived mainly from the National Household Survey on Drug Abuse (NHSDA). Although trends of interactions between various sociodemographic variables change over the years, the major points are summarized in Tables 3.1–3.3.

Alcohol

White Americans have slightly higher rates of alcohol use among the categories compared. In different non-White groups, there are more

TABLE 3.1. 1991 NATIONAL HOUSEHOLD SURVEY ON SUBSTANCE ABUSE: LIFETIME, NONMEDICAL SUBSTANCE USE BY RACE/ETHNICITY

	Alcohol	Cigarette	Tobacco	Marijuana	Cocaine	Crack	Inhalants	PCP	Sedatives	Tran-quilizers	Analgesia	Stimulants	Ice	Heroin	Anabolic Steroids	Overall (any)
White	86.7	75.8	15.7	33.8	11.8	1.5	5.6	8.9	4.6	6.1	6.5	7.9	0.5	1.2	0.6	37.7
Black	79.0	65.3	9.5	35.7	11.2	4.3	3.8	4.1	3.0	3.1	4.7	3.3	0.8	1.9	0.4	39.2
Hispanic	77.4	60.6	6.5	27.2	11.1	2.1	4.8	6.4	3.0	3.9	3.9	4.8	0.4	1.5	0.4	30.9

TABLE 3.2. TRENDS IN ILLICIT DRUG USE PREVALENCE BY RACE/ETHNICITY (1990–1991)

	Ages 12–17		Ages 18–25		Ages 26–34		Ages ≥35		Total	
	1990	1991	1990	1991	1990	1991	1990	1991	1990	1991
Drug use in Lifetime										
White	24.0	20.6	59.3	59.1	67.6	65.7	26.0	26.9	38.1	37.7
Black	20.5	20.4	47.6	46.4	53.7	58.0	28.9	34.6	36.1	39.2
Hispanic	21.1	17.9	47.3	40.1	45.0	42.2	22.8	24.9	32.6	30.9
Drug use in Past Year										
White	16.9	15.1	30.2	31.4	22.4	18.3	5.7	6.0	13.1	12.4
Black	12.7	15.2	24.4	25.6	24.0	23.0	8.3	9.6	14.9	15.9
Hispanic	17.0	15.3	27.3	20.9	20.1	13.1	5.5	7.0	14.8	11.9
Drug use in Past Month										
White	8.9	6.6	16.0	16.0	9.5	8.7	2.5	2.7	6.2	5.9
Black	6.7	7.0	13.7	16.9	13.7	13.7	5.1	5.8	8.6	9.4
Hispanic	6.5	7.9	11.4	11.6	9.4	5.9	3.0	3.8	6.6	6.3

TABLE 3.3. SUBSTANCE USE AND ABUSE AMONG ETHNIC GROUPS

	Black	Hispanic	Native American	Asian American/ Pacific Islanders
Cultural background	More than 12% of the U.S. population The majority of these 28 + million blacks live in urban areas, with a disproportionately large number of youth.	More than 6% of the U.S. population. Presently the fastest growing minority group and predicted to be the largest minority community by the year 2000. Includes Mexican-Amerians, Puerto Ricans, Central/South Americans, and "others of Spanish origin."	0.6% of the U.S. population. Consists of a total of 1.5 million people representing over 500 Native American tribes and Alaskan Native villages. Common issues confronting Native Americans include dislocation, economic development, relationship with Federal government and urban migration.	3% of the population in the U.S., mostly settled in dense populations in California, New York, and Hawaii. Early immigrants as workers or small business owners concentrated in Chinatowns. Recent immigrants include professionals, students, and refugees.
Prevalence and epidemiology	Estimation from arrest and treatment records, the proportion of African-Americans among drug abusers is above 22%. Increased rates of alcohol abstention (63% women/ 37% men) Men less likely to be heavy drinkers than whites Women who do drink are more likely to be heavy	Increased rates of alcohol abuse and/or dependence among men (highest rates found in Mexican-Americans) Increased abstention (45–60%) and decreased abuse/dependence among women Increased alcohol use among women in 40s and 50s	High substance abuse related mortality: 4 of top 10 causes of death are alcohol related: accidents, cirrhosis, suicide, homicide. High lifetime prevalence and current use in all drug categories (except cocaine). Alcohol and marijuana are the most widely used drugs by Native American youth.	Generally low levels of alcohol (except native Hawaiians) and drug use, though increasing especially in adolescents with use rates comparable to national average. Relatively more heavy alcohol drinking in Japanese and Koreans Among S.E. Asian immigrants/refugees. Laotian male had higher

	drinkers compared to whites Use sharply increases among men in 30s Drinking frequency rises among men with increasing income Alcohol problems correlate with unemployment	Increased alcohol use among men in 30s Increased use and alcohol problems with higher education/income and acculturation Increased problem drinking among women in 20s and 30s Increased alcohol-related arrests among men	Inhalant use is still highest among all minority groups Other stimulants and cigaretts also popular in Native American youth substance abuse. High prevalence of Fetal Alcohol Syndrome (33 times higher than White Americans).	rates of alcohol and opium abuse that Hmong, Khmer and Vietnamese. Reasons may include their common use of opium in their native countries.
Common substances of abuse	Increased use of heroin, cocaine, illicit methadone, marijuana (New York City data) More dangerous routes of administration (IV, smoking, freebase)	Increased use of marijuana, alcohol, cocaine, and illicit methadone; narcotic addictions at younger ages in Chicanos Increased inhalant abuse, especially among adolescents More dangerous routes of administration (IV, smoking, freebase)	Alcohol primary drug of abuse among adults Increased rates of marijuana use (88%) and inhalants (34%) among high school seniors	Cigarettes and alcohol as primary drug of abuse Increased cocaine and heroin abuse
Rate of progression, severity, and complications	Lower rates of adolescence/early adulthood illicit drug abuse and lifetime experience under 35yrs old; high rates over 35 yrs old	Less guilt associated with drinking Over-represented among IV drug abuse-related AIDS (14% Hispanics)	Highest reported rates of adolescence/early adulthood illicit drug abuse Much higher cirrhosis mortality rates, among both men and women	Lowest reported rates of adolescence/early adulthood illicit drug abuse Highest risk of developing abuse-related programs

(continued on next page)

TABLE 3.3. SUBSTANCE USE AND ABUSE AMONG ETHNIC GROUPS, *continued*

	Black	Hispanic	Native American	Asian American/ Pacific Islanders
	Increased alcoholism-related morbidity and mortality among men, especially hepatitis, fatty liver, cirrhosis (2x), esophageal cancer (10x for age group 35–44 yrs old)	Reach treatment later due to increased family cohesion ("enabling"); in the Hispanic culture emphasis is placed on the family as the primary source of support	Higher rates of Fetal Alcohol Syndrome/Effects Mortality 3–4x national average Deaths occur at earlier ages	
	Increased drug-related homicide (70% black homicide drug abuse related between 15–35 yrs old)	Mexican-Americans (and probably Hispanics in general) have been reported to underutilize health care services compared with non-Hispanic white and black reference groups in the United States; thus, this may have severe consequences for their health.		
	Increased IV drug abuse-related AIDS (26% black, 50% of heterosexual IV drug abuse-related AIDS occurs in blacks)			
	More likely to persist in cocaine use and develop problems after initiation, though rate of initiation is lower			
Treatment & preventive issues (Special needs & general misconceptions)	2–3 × more likely to enter treatment than whites	Use family strength to initiate/enhance treatment	Use Native American staff, culturally appropriate interventions	Social pressure, traumatic life events (especially refugees), and life stress

Enter treatment at younger age (peak age 35–44)

Use cultural supports to initiate/enhance treatment (church/family)

therefore treatment should consider the participation of the entire family

Prevention programs must be bilingual since many Hispanics prefer to speak their native languages; it is important to ensure that the patient understands his/her condition and treatment

Be aware of folk beliefs and practices that may result in self-treatment; often traditional Western medicine is the last resort

The level of acculturation and intracultural variation may hinder/facilitate progression and treatment of substance abuse

may predispose to substance abuse

Outreach necessary to detect substance abuse problems

Western medical knowledge poorest in Hmong, bad in Laotian and Cambodian (Khmer), followed by Vietnamese and other S.E. Asians; good in Chinese, Japanese and Koreans

Use Asian or bilingual staff, possibly in same language and culture. Family oriented approach useful, although patient and family often prefer being anonymous

Social support (75% lost extensive family network in the U.S.)

heavy drinkers among African Americans, especially in older age groups. Alcohol is the main substance of abuse for Native Americans and Asian Americans.

Marijuana

In contrast to a nationwide drop in marijuana use over the years, the use rates in the African American community continue to rise. Use rates for marijuana are highest among African Americans and lowest among Hispanic Americans.

Cocaine

Cocaine use has remained stable among Hispanic Americans despite a national decline. Use in White Americans is still slightly greater than in minority groups. Lifetime crack (and heroin) use did not differ significantly across young groups, but more prevalent use is reported in older African Americans ($\geq$35 years old).

Psychotherapeutic and Other Drugs

While African Americans had the lowest prevalence of psychotherapeutic drug use in 1985, in 1990 they had the highest of the three major minority groups cited. White Americans are the most likely to use hallucinogens and inhalants among the 18–34-year-old age group.

From these data, one cannot conclude that substance abuse is a minority problem. Although these national surveys illustrate a substantial reduction in the prevalence of most types of substance abuse, the data contribute only a partial description of cross-cultural drug use. They focus on comparative prevalence rather than the patterns and problems associated with specific ethnic populations and specific substances of abuse.

CULTURALLY SENSITIVE APPROACH TO THE PATIENT USING SUBSTANCES

The ultimate goal of a culturally sensitive approach to patients is to create a construct within which the physician can both learn to understand more about other cultures and provide the best medical care possible. This construct will help generate perspectives on the problem of substance abuse by synthesizing medical knowledge, personal experience with other cultures, research and reading, and consultations with members of specific ethnic groups.

Fundamentals of Cultural Sensitivity

First, ethnicity is described as a **risk marker** rather than a risk factor. Ethnicity-associated differences are often presented as self-evident explanations. For example, the belief that an African American is more likely to smoke marijuana than crack can lead to false assumptions about African American patients. In studies that control for social and environmental conditions, differences in prevalence of crack cocaine smoking among ethnic groups disappear. Using similar criteria, the drug use patterns of Mexican American youths correlate with levels of poverty better than with cultural factors. Similarly, studies of Native American alcoholism reflect economic deprivation factors including poverty, poor housing, and poor health care, rather than an "Indian-ness." These statistics give clinicians a better picture of the patient population's social dynamics, thus serving as risk markers, rather than risk factors.

Second, **vague definitions of race and ethnicity** produce broad, generalized categories that may be misleading. The NHSDA classifies groups only as Black, White, Hispanic, and Other. Such categories generate misleading information since skin characteristics are used to create an arbitrary distinction among ethnic groups. For example, a patient from Puerto Rico with an African American origin may have difficulty identifying himself as simply either "Hispanic" or "Black." Additionally, data from all other minority groups (Native Americans, Asian Americans, Alaskan Americans) appear lumped together as "other." These definitions cause problems when trying to draw conclusions from study data and they reflect a lack of cultural sensitivity.

Third, the **heterogeneity within ethnic groups** limits racial and ethnic definitions. While the "homogeneous, white" population includes a variety of ethnic groups—English, French, German, Italian, Swedish, Irish—there are over 450 identifiable American Indian tribal units and over 32 distinct ethnic and cultural groups among Asian Americans/ Pacific Islanders. Similar variations in "Hispanic" (which includes Mexicans, Puerto Ricans, Cubans, Dominicans, Chileans, and others) and "Black" populations (heterogeneous in their socioeconomic background and their origins of descent—Caribbean, Central or South America, and Africa) make generalizations difficult. Within these broad categories, each group differs significantly in cultural values, languages, norms, acculturative orientations, and drug use patterns.

On the other hand, the **exclusion of ethnic groups** from such categorical groupings can also occur. The Alaskan American group falls outside of the classifications mentioned above since none of the minority groupings seems appropriate.

Stereotyping of ethnic groups can hinder the acquisition of an accurate picture of the patient. For example, the stereotypical assumption that Asian Americans are successful, model minorities with substance abuse problems limited to alcohol and cigarettes disregards the rising illicit drug problem in Asian youths.

Acculturation describes the process of incorporating ethnic culture into mainstream culture, and the loss of ethnic culture as groups adopt mainstream culture. Acculturative status varies as a function of degree of contact with the host culture, the amount of change a person is willing to accommodate, and the level of pressure and stress exerted. Age at immigration is an important predictor of subsequent cultural incorporation into the host society—the younger the age, the greater the acculturation. A newly arrived middle-aged Vietnamese immigrant has a set of risk factors for substance abuse and an illness behavior totally different from those of either an American-born Vietnamese adolescent or a newly immigrated Vietnamese adolescent.

In addition, immigration itself brings new substances of abuse into the country. For instance, "khat" is a drug now encountered in urban areas with high concentrations of Somali emigres. Initially only found in Somalia, khat leaves are chewed to produce a euphoric state.

Ethnicity is a product of both self-designation and labeling and identification by other groups in a multicultural society. Structural features of the host society determine the acceptance of an ethnic person into the different institutions of the society, a process called structural **incorporation**. Racial discrimination denies equal access to opportunities in the economic, political, and health spheres. Ethnic identity and cultural support become important sources of psychological security, self-esteem, and solidarity within a discriminatory and impersonal society.

Application of the Culturally Sensitive Approach

Despite abundant literature describing specific ethnic variations in beliefs, treatment expectations, and illness behaviors, the most important element in providing a culturally sensitive framework of medical care is a careful, sensitive medical history.

Determining the importance of cultural differences is always a difficult part of providing care for substance abusing patients. The assessment of a **patient's ethnicity model** is critical. The ethnicity model can be behavioral—the ethnic background profoundly conditions daily behavior and personal beliefs are often incongruent with those of Western-trained providers—or ideological—ethnic identification is nominal. Given the extent of intra-ethnic variations and stereotyping, practitioners must avoid generalizations whenever possible. Never assume that similarly appearing patients have the same cultural backgrounds.

The degree of adherence to ethnic standards of health behavior depends on educational level, previous exposure to the health care system, generation removal from the immigrant status, urban versus rural location, income, occupation, religion, and family. These factors all affect how a patient perceives, experiences, and copes with substance abuse, creating an **explanatory model of substance abuse**. A culturally

TABLE 3.4. QUESTIONS FOR ELICITING PATIENT'S EXPLANATORY MODEL

- I know that patients and doctors sometimes have different ideas about diseases, so I'd like to know more about your idea of the problem..(open-ended)
- What do you call your problem? or Do you think it is a problem?
- What do you think caused your problem?
- Why do you think it started when it did?
- What is going on in your body?
- How has this problem affected your life?
- What frightens or concerns you most about this problem and treatment?
- How is your problem viewed in your family? Is it acceptable?
- How is your problem viewed in your community? Is it acceptable? Is it considered a disease?
- How does your problem affect your stature in the community?
- What has been your experience with the health care system?

sensitive approach to eliciting the explanatory model is provided in Table 3.4.

Unfortunately, racism persists in our society. Most ethnic groups have had previous negative experiences attributable to racism and/or racial insensitivity. Practitioners must be aware that patients bring these experiences and expectations to interactions with providers. Potential cultural, institutional, and professional biases on the practitioner's part should also be identified and discussed with other providers.

The overall goal of culturally sensitive care for substance users should focus on empathic understanding of the relationships among symptoms, distress, and the personal life of the patient. An understanding of the patient's illness, constructed from separate pieces of information about the relationship of symptoms to work, family life, and self-esteem, is difficult, but effective care demands these measures. Interpreters and family members can help elicit this information. Practitioners then use this information to determine the seriousness of symptoms and disability and to plan strategies for reducing distress through appropriately focused counseling, rehabilitation, joint problem solving, and social service interventions. Interventions have greater efficacy when integrated into the patient's lifestyle and social surroundings. Fears, ignorance, lack of explanation, and cultural taboos affect expectations about treatment and influence patients' compliance with treatment goals.

Treatment and Prevention

The prognoses for minorities in standard substance abuse treatment programs are worse than for the overall population. For example, confrontational techniques rarely work for patients with language and cultural barriers, and some minority groups may view methadone maintenance as a way of keeping minorities addicted and dependent. Difficulties

TABLE 3.5. CROSS-CULTURAL ISSUES IN SUBSTANCE ABUSE

Risk factors
  language barriers: non-English speaking, unable to present accurate history
  financial barriers: lack of insurance
  cultural barriers; difficulty in adapting to Western culture
  knowledge barriers: lack of knowledge about health care systems and legal
    services
  social barrier: return to adverse living conditions after rehabilitation
Role of the physician
  paternalistic model: physician is supposed to be fully responsible for curing the
    patient
  "one-stop services": seeking help for medical, socioeconomic, and other social
    problems
Role of the patient
  passive and expected "quick-fixes": Western medicine viewed as last resort
    upon failure of traditional medicine
  substance abuse not viewed as medical problem but a habit unresolved by pill
    prescriptions

in gaining access to substance abuse treatment centers, and physicians overlooking the importance of traditional healing concepts, hinder the efficacy of such programs. These perspectives illustrate the frequent complaints among minorities with substance abuse treatment. Table 3.5 outlines some of the cross-cultural issues that must be addressed in order to have a successful treatment or prevention program for minorities or immigrants.

Treatment programs have attempted to address these issues through minority hiring and cultural sensitivity training for all health care professionals. However, these solutions must comply with the needs of the community to be effective. For example, hiring specially trained interpreters for a particular Asian community may be more effective than recruiting Asian American practitioners, since different Asian cultures have drastically different languages and values. An Asian American practitioner may still need an interpreter for a patient who does not speak the native language.

Concerns over adolescent and immigrant drug problems have emerged in almost all minority groups. In most cases, a lack of knowledge secondary to cultural and language barriers, and access to the legal and health care systems, have limited the extent of help given to those in need. Consequently, health care coverage remains sporadic and insufficient. Community outreach for adolescents and immigrants could provide a crucial advance toward solving part of the problem, though more effort is needed to coordinate and optimize the available resources.

CONCLUSIONS

Despite a recent increase in awareness of the substance abuse problems in minority groups, no consensus unites major issues of drug and alcohol use and treatment in minority groups. Prevalence, etiology, and treatment outcome data involving ethnic and cultural differences are sparse, especially in Native American and Asian American groups. Incorporating culturally sensitive approaches to diagnosis and treatment helps ensure a better understanding of the patient's illness experience, increases the patient's trust, comfort and compliance, identifies the relevant sociodemographic factors, and guides the delivery of efficacious and successful treatment.

RESOURCES

African Americans

Black Children of Alcoholic and Drug Addicted Persons (BCOADAP)
c/o National Black Alcoholism Council
417 Dearborn Street
Chicago, IL 60605
Phone: (312) 663-5780

Institute on Black Chemical Abuse
2614 Nicollet Avenue
Minneapolis, MN 55408
Phone: (612) 871-7878

Asian Americans

Association of Asian Pacific Community Health Organizations
310 Eighth Street, Suite 310
Oakland, CA 94607
Phone: (415) 272-9536

National Asian Pacific American Families Against Substance Abuse (NAPAFASA)
420 East Third Street, Suite 909
Los Angeles, CA 90013-1647
Phone: (213) 617-8277

General

Multicultural Training Resource Center
1540 Market Street, Suite 320
San Francisco, CA 94102
Phone: (415) 861-2142

National Clearinghouse for Abused Drugs and Information (NCADI)
Phone: (800) SAY-NOTO

Office of Minority Health Resource Center (OMHRC)
PO Box 37337
Washington, DC 20013-7337
Phone: (800) 444-6472

Hispanic Americans

National Coalition of Hispanic Health and Human Services Organization
1030 15th Street NW, Suite 1053
Washington, DC 20005
Phone: (202) 371-2100

National Hispanic Family Against Drug Abuse
1115 K Street NW, Suite 1029
Washington, DC 20005
Phone: (202) 393-5136

Native Americans

Indian Health Service (IHS):
Alcoholism and Substance Abuse Programs Branch
Rm 6A-53A, Parklawn Bldg
Rockville, MD 20857
Phone: (301) 443-4297

National Association for Native American Children of Alcoholics (NANACoA)
Seattle Indian Health Board
PO Box 3364
Seattle, WA 98114

National Center for American Indian and Alaska Native Mental Health Research
  (NCAIANMHR)
Department of Psychiatry, University of Colorado, Health Sciences Center
4200 East Ninth Avenue, C-249
Denver, CO 80262
Phone: (303) 270-4600

FURTHER READING

African Americans

Harper FD. Alcoholism and Blacks: an overview. In: Watts TD, Wright R Jr, eds. Alcoholism in Minority Populations. 1989:17–31.
Lillie-Blanton M, Anthony JC, Schuster CR. Probing the meaning of racial/ethnic group comparisons in crack cocaine smoking. JAMA 1993;269:993–997.
Nobles WW, Goddard LL. Drugs in the African-American Community: Clear and Present Danger. In: Dewart J, ed. The State of Black America 1989. 1989:161–182.

Asian Americans

Austin GA, Prendergast ML, Lee H. Substance abuse among Asian American youth. Prevention Research Update No. 5, Winter 1989. Western Center for Drug-Free Schools and Communities.

Flaskerud JH, Liu PY. Influence of therapist ethnicity and language on therapy outcomes of Southeast Asian clients. Int J Soc Psychiatry 1990;36(1):18–29.

Ja DY, Aoki B. Substance abuse treatment: cultural barriers in the Asian-American community. J Psychoactive Drugs 1993;25:61–71.

General

Adlaf EM, Smart RG, Tan SH. Ethnicity and drug use: a critical look. Int J Addict 1989;24:1–18.

Bachman JG, Wallace JM, O'Malley PM, et al. Racial/ethnic differences in smoking, drinking, and illicit drug use among American high school seniors 1976–1989. Am J Public Health 1991;81:372–377.

Cheung YW. Ethnicity and alcohol/drug use revisited: a framework for future research. Int J Addict 1990–1991;25:581–605.

De La Rosa MR, Recio Adrados JL. Drug Abuse Among Minority Youth: Advances in Research and Methodology 1993. National Institute on Drug Abuse Research Monograph 130. Rockville, MD: US Department of Health and Human Services, 1993.

Lawson GW, Lawson AW. Alcoholism and Substance Abuse in Special Populations. Rockville, MD: Aspen Publishers, 1989.

Orlandi MA, Weston R, Epstein LG. Cultural Competence for Evaluators: A Guide for Alcohol and Other Drug Abuse Prevention Practitioners Working With Ethnic/Racial Communities. Rockville, MD: Office of Substance Abuse Prevention, 1992.

Trimble JE, Bolek CS, Niemcryk SJ. Ethnic and Multicultural Drug Abuse: Perspectives on Current Research. Harrington Park Press, 1992.

Wright R, Watts TD. Alcohol Problems of Minority Youth in America. Lewiston, NY: E. Mellen Press, 1989.

Hispanic Americans

De La Rosa MR, Khalsa JH, Rouse BA. Hispanics and illicit drug use: review of recent findings. Int J Addict 1990;25:665–691.

Mayers RS, Kail BL, Watts TD. Hispanic Substance Abuse. Springfield, IL: Charles C Thomas, 1993.

Morales A. Substance abuse and Mexican American youth: an overview. J Drug Issues 1984;14:297–311.

Native Americans

Beauvais F, Oetting ER, Wolf W, Edwards RW. American Indian youth and drugs, 1976–1987: a continuing problem. Am J Public Health 1989;79:634–636.

Fisher AD. Alcoholism and race: The mis-application of both concepts to North American Indians. Can Rev Sociol Anthropol 1987;24:81–98.

Moncher MS, Holden GW, Trimble JE. Substance abuse among Native American youth. J Consult Clin Psychol 1990;58:408–415.

Schinke SP, Orlandi MA, Schilling RF, Botvin GJ, Gilchrist LD, Landers C. Tobacco use by American Indian and Alaska Native people: risks, psychosocial factors and preventive intervention. J Alcohol Drug Educ 1990;35:1–12.

Walker RD, Benjamin GA, Kiviahan D, Walker PS. American Indian Alcohol Misuse and Treatment Outcome. National Institute on Alcohol Abuse and Alcoholism Research Monograph 18: Alcohol Use Among US Ethnic Minorities. Washington, DC: US Government Printing Office, 1989.

Young TJ. Native American drinking: a neglected subject of study and research. J Drug Educ 1991;21:65–72.

Chapter 4

Substance Abuse and Family Dynamics

Melissa Bush, Elizabeth B. Caronna, and Susan E. Spratt with JudyAnn Bigby

Substance abuse can play many roles in a family system: as a catalyst for violent or abusive acts, as an excuse for the violence and abuse, and as a defensive response to violence and abuse. Cycles of violence and substance abuse often recur across generations with one family member's substance abuse causing direct or indirect emotional and physical harm to other family members. As families become isolated from the community and social services, clinicians may be the only ones to detect the signs of family dysfunction or sexual and physical abuse. Dysfunctional family interactions resulting from the family's response to the drug or alcohol problem can deeply scar family members' growth and development. This chapter outlines the effects of substance abuse on family systems, with particular emphasis on family violence, the "symptom" that often brings family dysfunction to the attention of the physician.

DYSFUNCTIONAL FAMILY PATTERNS CAUSED BY SUBSTANCE ABUSE

Since alcoholism is the most common form of substance abuse affecting families, its disruptive effects on family systems have received the most intense investigation. However, the effects described below are not limited to alcohol. They can serve as a paradigm for other drugs of abuse. Clinicians need to be aware of these patterns because alcohol dependence may present through direct or indirect contact with the addicted individual (Table 4.1). The manifestations of alcoholism in any member of the affected family are the following:

- **Financial/job-related:** The substance-abusing family member becomes less reliable and less efficient at work, missing more days of work, forcing other employees to cover, and even stealing from employers to support a habit. These habits ultimately lead to missed promotions, rare raises, or even dismissal. Financial problems include poor money management or the use of funds to buy drugs.

TABLE 4.1. PRESENTATIONS OF SUBSTANCE ABUSE IN FAMILY MEMBERS

Problem Type	Examples
Medical	• headaches • back pain • ulcers • difficulty sleeping
Family violence	• spouse abuse • child abuse
Adolescent	• runaways • early marriage • juvenile delinquency • suicide attempts
School performance	• absenteeism • poor grades • behavioral problems in class
Financial	• poor financial management • depletion of family resources
Employment	• frequent job changes • difficulties with punctuality and coworkers
Psychiatric symptoms	• depression • anxiety
Sexual dysfunction	• impotence • precocious sexual behavior

- **Emotional:** Chemically-dependent individuals may experience feelings of guilt, depression, and other stress-related illnesses.
- **Medical problems:** Chronic and often acute abuse of a substance may have significant, though nonspecific, medical consequences. The individual drug chapters (Chapters 7–16) discuss these problems.
- **Disruption of family rituals:** Family rituals, such as daily supper, can be interrupted when the substance-abusing patient misses dinner due to intoxication or forgets to bring dinner home. Major holidays such as Thanksgiving, Christmas, or birthdays generate increased tension, increased consumption of alcohol, and increased potential for crisis.
- **Physical and sexual abuse:** Physical and sexual abuse is more prevalent in families with a history of substance dependence. The relationship between physical or sexual abuse and substance abuse is intertwined, but highly variable. The connection between cause and effect is not clear (discussion of this topic occurs later in this chapter).

- **Marital discord:** The financial, medical, and emotional problems discussed above cause tension within the family, which can manifest itself as physical and sexual abuse of a spouse or child. These actions create an environment in which the non-abusing parent must either support and protect a child, which often provokes the abuser, or abandon the child to temporarily soothe the relationship with the abuser.
- **Isolation from the community:** As substance abuse continues, the family becomes increasingly isolated from its previous community of extended family, friends, and social clubs. Isolation may begin with the exhibition of socially disruptive and inappropriate behavior by the substance abuser. Children of substance-abusing parents may avoid bringing friends home because of the unpredictable nature of their parents' behavior.

Defense Mechanisms of Family Members

Substance-abusing people and their families are prone to the following defense mechanisms, which enable them to escape from painful and difficult feelings.

- **Denial:** Behaving as if a problem does not exist. Substance abusers and their families deny that use is out of control. Actions that signify substance abuse, to an outsider, are not recognized as unusual by family members.
- **Rationalization:** When the substance abuse is recognized as a potential problem, but its magnitude is discounted because of extenuating circumstances, such as stress at home or work.
- **Projection:** When the abuser attributes the cause of his or her chemical dependency to others. For example, an alcoholic may blame a "nagging spouse" or "wild children" for excessive alcohol intake.
- **Minimization:** Belittles the extent of the problem and its consequences. People with substance abuse problems may say "I only drink on weekends," or "I may drink a lot, but I don't drink as much as. . .," or "I'm a happy drunk."

Children are more profoundly affected by substance-abusing parents than other adults since the children can no longer trust a parent to provide a safe, stable home. Children of chemically-dependent parents must learn unspoken rules that exist in their homes—not to discuss what happens at home with outsiders and to conceal a parent's habits. These unwritten rules inhibit the emotional development of a child. Furthermore, children use the same defense mechanisms discussed above to conceal their feelings.

Stereotypical Roles in Substance-Abusing Families

Stereotypical roles in a substance-abusing family have been described in popular literature to help family members understand the role each may play and, thus, help break the cycle of substance abuse and dysfunctional family environments. Clinicians need to have an awareness of these roles since patients may describe themselves accordingly. The roles listed below allow the family to achieve a delicately balanced existence in a chaotic environment, and act as defense mechanisms. Often the roles evolve or change as family dynamics change. Family members who allow their roles to define their behaviors display limited personal growth.

Roles in the Substance-Abusing Family

- The *substance abuser* is the central figure of the family drama. The rest of the roles are defined in response to his or her actions.
- The *chief enabler* protects the substance abuser from confrontations with the consequences of chemical dependency. Behaviors include taking on responsibilities neglected by the substance abuser and covering up for mistakes and adverse actions. Although appearing outwardly strong and responsible, an enabler may neglect personal and family needs. Stress- and anxiety-related illness are common in enablers secondary to the frustrations of controlling and fixing the damage caused by the substance abuse.
- The *family hero* is an overachiever who strives for success in work and school, makes the family proud, and tries to escape from the family's problems. In addition, the hero may take on some of the enabler's role in the home. The hero experiences similar stress-related illnesses as the enabler.
- The *scapegoat* acts out in anger to draw attention away from the substance abuser's actions, often giving the substance abuser an excuse for destructive behavior. The scapegoat may represent the only family member unable to suppress their anger. Unfortunately, this anger may be self destructive. Scapegoats are often children who are at high risk for substance abuse and injuries resulting from risk-taking behavior.
- The *lost child* becomes forgotten by avoiding family and social situations to escape the problems caused by the substance abuse. This child may withdraw by reading, watching television, playing video games, or by always appearing content. These children do not learn how to interact with peers and are prone to eating disorders.
- The *family clown* attempts to divert the attention away from the substance abuse and disguise inner pain by providing comic relief. This child is often the youngest and most immature in the family. These children may have trouble succeeding in school.

Addiction is a chronic, all-consuming disease that affects the entire family. Co-dependency refers to the physical, psychological, and social effects of substance abuse on other family members. Family behavior and roles may revolve around the substance abuse, although the problem may never be mentioned. These elaborate coping mechanisms create a fragile family reality that is damaging to every member of the family, and does little to address the problem of the addiction. Any of the co-dependents may require attention and treatment.

SPECIFIC EFFECTS OF SUBSTANCE ABUSE ON FAMILY DYNAMICS

Compromised Parenting and Depletion of Family Resources

Chemically-dependent parents may be unable to ensure a child's physical well-being, stimulate academic interests, or offer emotional support. Additionally, substance abuse can divert family resources from necessities, such as food, money, shelter, and time, to substance abuse. As a model for resource depletion and detrimental effects on parenting, inner city drug users diverted resources as follows:

- *Food:* Many addicts spend money allocated for food to purchase drugs. Some addicts trade, barter, or sell on the black market an entire monthly allotment of food stamps in 1–2 days. In crack houses that accept food stamps, it has been estimated that at least 40% of the customers use food stamps to buy drugs. People sell children's milk formula to obtain money for drugs. Withholding basic resources from children, such as food, constitutes child abuse.
- *Money:* While people may initially have money to spend on an addiction, once heavy use begins, savings, then salaries, and finally all sources of income are exhausted. Addicts may resort to criminal activity, such as stealing, selling drugs, and prostitution, to support their habit.
- *Housing/homelessness:* Diversion of money from rent can cause the loss of a family's home. Once homeless, substance abuse interferes with the ability to compete for scarce housing, employment, or services.
- *Time:* The time a substance abuser spends obtaining and using drugs reduces the time available for care and raising of children. Heroin abusers report that play with their children requires more attention than they are capable of giving while under the influence of heroin. Stimuli, such as walking by a certain shop, seeing an old drug-using friend, or even certain smells, which may trigger intense arousal and drug craving, can cause parents to leave their children unattended.

Immediate Effects on Family Dynamics

As suggested above, children raised in homes affected by substance abuse commonly suffer from some neglect. In fact, the 1989 Child Fatality Review Panel of New York City recommended that proof of parental substance abuse alone should incite a presumption of abuse or neglect.

In families affected by substance abuse, children growing up with discordant atmospheres have a higher risk of developing childhood problems. Consequences of a discordant family atmosphere include the following:

- *Inconsistent discipline:* Discipline is inconsistent ranging from lax to strict, and consequently, children are unable to equate actions with a predictable outcome. These children learn that punishment is random and that any action is allowed, as long as it remains undiscovered. These children have difficulty distinguishing appropriate from inappropriate behavior and do not envision having control of their future.
- *Neglect:* Neglect is common. One study found that children in homes affected by substance abuse are left at home alone beginning at an average age of 6 years, while children of non-substance-abusing families were not left alone until 11 years of age.
- *Role reversal:* Older children must often assume responsibility for both younger siblings and for the parents themselves. They care for their siblings without adequate adult supervision, often causing them harm. This situation may lead older children to abuse younger siblings since it is the only form of discipline they know. Older children are also vulnerable to physical abuse for inadequately fulfilling the parental role thrust upon them. Finally, children may be forced into the difficult role of parental confidante, receiving emotionally charged confessions.
- *Bonding:* Poor child-to-parent bonding can lead to family discordance throughout development. Observation of the following behaviors and situations should alert the clinician to possible substance abuse in the child's family:

  Substance abuse in pregnancy correlates with early separation of mother and child after delivery. Separation occurs due to the need for medical treatment for substance withdrawal, prematurity, intrauterine growth retardation, and infection.

  Postpartum stress often causes increased risk for drug use and decreases quantity and quality of parent-child bonding, a phenomenon manifested in the extreme by the abandonment of the baby in the hospital ("boarder babies").

Toddlers of substance-abusing mothers showed insecure attachments—abnormal affect and weak feelings of anger, pleasure, or distress at separation. Furthermore, they exhibit low developmental scores and abnormal play with scattering, batting, or picking up and putting down toys without sustained play.

Older children displayed hyperactivity, short attention span, developmental delay, retardation, aggressive conduct disorder, and difficulty learning from experience. These traits, along with family and parental stresses, can contribute to lowering the threshold for child abuse.

Sequelae of Altered Family Dynamics

In a family system, substance abuse may lead to a multi-generational cycle of substance abuse and altered family dynamics. Children in these families have increased risks for anxiety disorders, substance abuse, and depression in adulthood. As a result, they are more likely to have difficulties parenting and propagate a cycle of substance abuse and physical/emotional abuse. Long-term effects of substance abuse on families include:

- *Abuse/neglect:* Adults who as children were raised in violent households are more likely to abuse or neglect their own children. Of people currently using substances, substance abuse occurred in 83% and physical abuse occurred in 55% of the households in which they were raised.
- *Communication:* Life in a substance-abusing home often involves a complicated network of lies and denial. Consequently, many children of chemically-dependent parents have difficulty developing a well-integrated self-image and establishing meaningful relationships.
- *Mental health:* In dysfunctional families, adolescents with mood disorders may turn to alcohol and drugs in an effort to cope with their depression or anxiety.
- *Substance abuse:* Parental substance abuse and alcoholism are strong predictors of a child's drug and alcohol use. Adolescents with family histories of substance abuse are more likely to report problems/consequences related to substance abuse.
- *Sexual abuse:* Adolescents with family histories of substance abuse may be more likely to report a history of sexual abuse.
- *Family hardships:* Family members who accept the responsibility for children whose parents are absent because of substance use, most often the grandmother, suffer adverse health consequences such as: insomnia, back and stomach pain, and exacerbation of previously

TABLE 4.2. SELF-HELP GROUPS FOR CHEMICALLY-DEPENDENT PATIENTS AND FAMILIES

Group Name	Targeted Population
Alcoholics Anonymous (AA)	Individuals with alcohol dependency
Al-Anon	Friends and family of alcoholics
Alateen	Adolescents in families with alcoholism
Adult Children of Alcoholics (ACOA)	Adults who were raised by alcoholic parent(s)
Narcotics Anonymous (NA)	Individuals with drug dependency
Nar-Anon	Friends and family of those with drug problems
Cocaine Anonymous (CA)	Individuals with cocaine dependency
Families Anonymous	Parents of children with chemical dependency

controlled chronic conditions, such as hypertension and arthritis, because of the added responsibility of child care.

Effects of Substance Abuse on Interventions in Families

Family therapy specifically addresses the relationships between family dynamics and substance abuse. Substance abuse influences each of the following aspects of intervention.

- *Treatment:* The treatment of substance-abusing families must take into account the needs of each member of the family. Table 4.2 lists the names of self-help groups for chemically-dependent individuals and their families. Families living in poverty need a variety of concurrent interventions, such as housing, welfare, etc., beyond those directed at the risk for abuse and neglect.
- *Prognosis:* When addicted parents who abuse or neglect their children refuse drug treatment or help from agencies, the prognosis is poor. Furthermore, substance-abusing parents involved with the criminal justice system may also be less compliant with treatment.
- *Hope:* The postnatal environment can mitigate the damage caused by drug and alcohol exposure in utero. Drug treatment for mothers improves the outcome for their children in many ways. Enrollment of women in methadone treatment programs leads to improved care for their children postnatally and improved prenatal care with future pregnancies.

SUBSTANCE ABUSE AND FAMILY VIOLENCE

Although the correlation between family violence (including child physical and sexual abuse, spouse abuse, and elder abuse) and substance abuse has been documented, few causal mechanisms have been postulated. Regardless of which problem occurs first, clinicians need to con-

TABLE 4.3. PREVALENCE OF PHYSICAL ABUSE AND NEGLECT IN SUBSTANCE-ABUSING FAMILIES

Group/Category	Prevalence
Temporal associations between substance use and physical or sexual abuse	• In a study of 200 families in which one or more family member was addicted to alcohol or heroin, abuse (physical or sexual) or serious neglect was present 41% of the time. • In a study with a sample of 550 child abusers, 43% of the men and 30% of the women were substance abusers. • 51% of women treated in an emergency department for domestic violence and 88% of their assailants consumed alcohol heavily. • In a sample of 104 lesbians, 39 reported experiencing physical abuse in a past or present relationship. 64% said that drugs or alcohol were used before or during the battering. • One study showed that 49% of child molesters were drinking at the time of the offense and that 48% of fathers who committed incest were alcoholics.

sider coexistence of substance abuse and physical or sexual abuse in a family with either problem and screen accordingly.

Prevalence of Physical Abuse

Children, spouses or partners, and elderly people may be victims of physical abuse. Health care providers should always watch for warning signs of victimization in their patients, regardless of age, class, race, or sexual orientation (Table 4.3).

Prevalence of Sexual Abuse

Sexual abuse can occur concurrently with physical abuse of children or spouses, or without additional forms of violent behavior. If one child in a family is found to be a victim or survivor of current or past sexual abuse, it must be determined whether other children are also at risk. Since the disclosure of sexual abuse has only recently become socially acceptable, and because survivors may become aware of their victimization many years after it occurred, the statistics cited in Table 4.3 may represent underestimates of prevalence rates due to underreporting.

SCREENING FOR DOMESTIC VIOLENCE AND ITS SEQUELAE

Domestic Violence as a Public Health Issue

Health professionals are urged to screen all women for domestic violence. In cases of child abuse and neglect, the clinician relies extensively on physical signs, such as multiple fractures, contusions, abrasions, or malnutrition. Readers should be aware of their individual states' mandates for physicians about reporting suspicions of physical or sexual abuse. In contrast to abuse against children, an adult must be willing to report the violence for action to occur in domestic violence cases. The Massachusetts Medical Society recommends that physicians screen for violence as part of the routine history, especially when substance abuse is also suspected.

When screening patients, avoid derogatory terms like "abused." Many survivors of violence do not see themselves as victims or as abused. Additionally, screening for violence may not detect all patients living in fear. A person may not recognize isolation, intimidation, and financial control as abuse. The following questions illustrate a line of inquiry designed to detect violence:

- At any time, has a partner hit, kicked, or otherwise hurt or frightened you?
- Do you feel that there is inequality in your relationship with your partner?
- Who controls the family finances? How do you pay for groceries and school clothes?
- What happens when you disagree? What happens when you disagree and your partner has been drinking?

Presentations of Domestic Violence

- *Physical injury:* Physical injury is the most concrete manifestation of domestic violence. One study of women with physical injuries treated in emergency departments found a paucity of information about who harmed the patient. Medical records filled with such phrases as "hit by a lead pipe," "blow to head by stick with nail in it," and "hit on left wrist with jackhammer," neglected to mention who had performed these violent acts. In these cases, the physicians treated only the symptoms without addressing the cause of the problem. Although physical injury may be the most visible display of violence in the home, its treatment does not guarantee discovery or disclosure of domestic violence.
- *Psychiatric and somatic presentations:* Common primary care complaints of battered women include chronic headaches, abdominal pains, complaints of sexual dysfunction, recurrent vaginal infections, joint pains, muscle aches, sleep disorders, and eating disorders.

Assessing the Level of Violence in Homes

In assessing the level of violence in the home of a person who has indicated that there is violence, one must consider the following questions:

TABLE 4.4. DOMESTIC VIOLENCE SCREENING/ASSESSMENT

How were you hurt?
Has this happened before?
When did it first happen? How badly have you been hurt in the past?
Was a weapon involved/is there a weapon in the house? What kind?
Who lives at home? Childrens' ages? Are the children in danger?
Have they been hurt or hit by him? How badly?
What have you done in the past to protect yourself?
What have you done in the past to get help?
Have you ever called the police? Reported the incident to the police?
What was their response?
Have you ever obtained a protective order?
Have you ever tried to press charges?
Does your partner have a criminal record?
Has he beaten up or hurt other people?
Has he threatened to kill you?
Has he tried to kill you? What did he do?
Are you afraid to go home?
Where can you go?
Have you left in the past? What happened when you left?

- *What is the nature of the violence? Are weapons involved?* If the perpetrator is impulsive and has access to a lethal weapon, the risk of injury and death is higher than if no weapon is involved.
- The history of the violent person. *Is he/she violent to other people or animals? Does he have a criminal record?*
- Where can the survivor go for help or protection. *Has she called the police? Have they been helpful or have they failed to arrive? Does she have a place to stay if she were to leave (a shelter or a friend or relative's house)?*
- *Who else lives in the home?* One must assess the risk of violence to other dependents in the house: children and elders. If a child is at risk of being harmed, the mother should be informed that she can be held responsible for failure to protect her children and that her children can be taken away from her. Knowledge that she may lose her children often forces a woman to leave a batterer.
- *Is there a repetitive cycle to the violence?* In order to help survivors of violence, health providers must understand the cycles of violence. The violent act is followed by a honeymoon period of apology and promises never to repeat the violence. Rising tensions inevitably culminate in renewed violence after the period of calm ends.

Each positive answer raises the risk of increasing or continued violence and should raise the concern of the clinician enough to try to intervene in the cycle of violence. Table 4.4 presents more specific screening questions modeled on the general guidelines above.

What to Do Next

Ultimately, the goal of intervention is to eliminate violence from the patient's life. However, the health professional should remember that simply telling a woman or man to leave is not always the appropriate response. Assessing whether the patient has a place to go is critical since leaving is the most dangerous time for a person living in a violent relationship. The health provider often feels powerless to help the patient change the circumstances after recognizing a pattern of violence. The most important roles a health care provider can fill are:

- Detect the violent situations by asking the screening questions.
- Affirm that the patient does not deserve the violent treatment.
- Investigate the patient's options for leaving the violent situation.
- Inform the patient of her options (shelter/social services).
- Become a source of support for the patient even if the patient is not willing to act immediately on the clinician's advice.
- *Please Note:* In most circumstances it is unwise for an inexperienced clinician to confront the physical or sexual abuser. This act may lead to increased violence. These matters are best brought to the attention of and left to the criminal justice system and experienced clinicians.

The following represent some important ideas to remember when treating families with concurrent substance abuse and domestic violence:

- Attributions of blame for domestic violence against the woman tend to vary according to the gender of the intoxicated person; the disinhibiting power of alcohol provides an excuse for men to explain their actions (even the victims of the violence may excuse the perpetrator in this way). On the other hand, women who are disinhibited by alcohol, thereby challenging gender stereotypes, are seen to be "asking for" their battering.
- Domestic violence occurs with or without substance abuse. Research has suggested that substance-abusing, battering men are violent both when they are and are not under the influence of substances. Subsequently, substance abuse must not be viewed as the sole cause of family violence, but as a possible catalyst. In a family where substance abuse and violence coexist, the family cannot be considered free of risk for further violence even after the addicted individual is known to be abstinent.

CONCLUSION

Substance abuse by even a single family member can have a wide range of effects on the entire family. These effects include dysfunctional family patterns and coping, deleterious defense mechanisms, and physical and sexual abuse. The health care provider can play a critical role in detecting domestic violence, child abuse, and substance abuse. It is the provider's responsibility to report cases when suspicion of danger to a child or spouse is high. Although the causal effects of substance abuse and physical and sexual abuse are not firmly established, they are strongly correlated and the presence of one raises the probability that the other is present as well. Because of the strong correlation, the two problems must receive concurrent attention and treatment.

FURTHER READING

Bays J. Substance abuse and child abuse: impact of addiction of the child. Pediatr Clin North Am 1990;37.

Gorney B. Domestic violence and chemical dependency: dual problems, dual interventions. J Psychoactive Drugs 1989;21:229–238.

Graham AV, Berolzheimer N, Burge S. Alcohol abuse: a family disease. Prim Care 1993;20:121–130.

Hernandez JT. Substance abuse among sexually abused adolescents and their families. J Adolesc Health 1992;13:658–662.

Miller BA. The interrelationships between alcohol and drugs and family violence. National Institute on Drug Abuse Research Monograph Series no. 103. Drugs and Violence: Causes, Correlates, and Consequences. 1990;177–207.

Velleman R. Intergenerational effects—a review of environmentally oriented studies concerning the relationship between parental alcohol problems and family disharmony in the genesis of alcohol and other problems. I. The intergenerational effects of alcohol problems. II: The intergenerational effects of family disharmony. Int J Addict 1992;27:253–280, 367–389.

RESOURCES

The following information includes phone numbers of shelters and support services for survivors of domestic violence and child abuse in Boston. We have provided a skeleton for you to write out local information for the Coalition for Battered Women, Victim Services, Adult Protective Services, or Domestic Violence Services. The Department of Social Services or Child Welfare of each state can provide information on how child abuse reporting is mandated.

Boston, Massachusetts

24-Hour Hotline (A Project of Casa Myrna Vasquez):
(800) 992-2600

Massachusetts Coalition of Battered Women Services Groups:
(617) 426-8492

Victim Compensation and Assistance Division, Dept. of Attorney General:
(617) 727-2200

Asian Women's Project of Boston
(617) 739-6696

Department of Elder Affairs:
(800) 922-2275

Disabled Person Protection Commission:
(800) 426-9009

Department of Social Services (Child Abuse):
(800) 792-5200

Battered Women's Shelters in Boston Area:
Casa Myrna Vasquez (617) 262-9581
Renewal House (617) 566-6881
Transition House (617) 661-7203
Harbor Me (617) 889-2111
FINEX House (617) 288-1054
Elizabeth Stone House (617) 522-3417
Respond (617) 623-5900

List of Phone Numbers and Addresses Important for Physical and Sexual Abuse Cases

City:

Department of Social Services (Child Abuse):

Department of Elder Affairs:

Battered Women Services Groups:

Victim Compensation and Assistance Division, Dept. of Attorney General:

Disabled Person Protection Commission:

Battered Women's Shelters:

Chapter 5

Substance Abuse Within the Health Care Community

Danielle Brook, Triste Lieteau, Kathleen B. McHugh, and Sarath Reddy with John A. Fromson

The topic of substance abuse among health care workers conjures up the image of an impaired physician or nurse making decisions, performing procedures, or administering medications that could seriously harm a patient. In 1972 the American Medical Association (AMA) Council on Mental Health published a report defining physician impairment as "the inability to practice medicine with reasonable skill and safety to patients by reason of physical or mental illness, including alcoholism or drug dependence."

Stressful work conditions, access to psychoactive drugs, and the ability to self-prescribe are some of the risk factors that contribute to substance abuse in the health care community. Fortunately, over the last two decades, increased public attention and self-policing by professional organizations have helped address substance abuse in the health care community. As a result, monitoring, treatment, and advocacy programs for chemically-dependent health care professionals have been established.

EPIDEMIOLOGY

Public Perceptions

For some time, the general public believed that substance abuse was widespread among health care professionals, with some reports suggesting that physicians and nurses were 30 to 100 times more likely than the general population to become addicted to psychoactive substances. These unsupported estimates were based solely on assumptions like this one: unrestricted access to prescription drugs and the high stress of the medical field must, naturally, amplify the likelihood of abuse, thereby making drug addiction "an occupational hazard" for both nurses and physicians.

Population Survey Data

Physicians in General

Recent studies have challenged these long-held assumptions about rampant substance abuse among members of the health care community. Studies of alcohol and drug abuse among physicians indicate that the prevalence of chemical dependency ranges between 8–12%—the same prevalence rate found in the general population.

Several of the predisposing risk factors for substance abuse among health care professionals include: family history (positive in 85.6% of cases), environmental factors, lack of coping mechanisms, lack of preventive measures, denial, and availability of drugs.

Medical Students and Resident Physicians

Heavy substance abuse patterns have not been documented among medical students or resident physicians. One would expect that the stresses of medical school and residency, combined with the new privilege of prescribing drugs, would place these individuals at high risk for drug abuse. However, medical students have consistently had psychoactive drug use rates comparable to peers in the general population. Additionally, when compared to their peers in the general population, residents have had significantly *lower* use rates for all psychoactive substances except benzodiazepines and alcohol—two substances often associated with abuse at later stages of a physician's career.

Subspecialty Data

Analysis by subspecialty established that certain groups of physicians are at greater risk for chemical dependency. Based on the higher representation of anesthesiologists in treatment programs for impaired physicians, anesthesiologists have been considered one of these groups. In a survey at the Medical College of Wisconsin, 15.8% of anesthesiology residents had abused controlled substances during their residencies. Anesthesiologists may be at greater risk because of availability of drugs such as meperidine, fentanyl, and other anesthetic agents. Moreover, drugs may be more readily obtained in the operating room because of lax control during crisis situations. On the other hand, individuals at risk for substance abuse may self-select to train in anesthesiology.

Female Physicians

Most studies examining rates of substance abuse among physicians have excluded women. Consequently, rates or patterns of substance abuse among female physicians are difficult to assess. Women comprise 3–6% of physicians treated in substance abuse treatment programs. From these statistics, it has been concluded that female physicians suffer from chemical dependency at lower rates than their male colleagues. However, the increasing numbers of women entering medicine may alter these statistics. Further studies will determine the rates and patterns of chemical dependency for female physicians.

Other Health Care Professionals

Although most nonphysician health care workers are not authorized to prescribe drugs, they are often involved in drug administration or distribution. By withholding patient medication, obtaining prescriptions from unsuspecting physician colleagues, or stealing drugs from hospital supply rooms, health care workers find access to the drugs.

Nurses are no more likely to have engaged in illicit drug use or experienced problems with alcohol abuse than the general population. Analysis of the use rates for a number of substances, including the more accessible sedative-hypnotics, revealed that rates were consistently lower for nurses than for the general population.

In a retrospective study of 1352 impaired health care professionals, physicians showed the highest rates of substance abuse in proportion to their numbers in the health care community. Nurses were underrepresented in the sample, and dentists and pharmacists were represented proportionately.

Summary

While the health care community does have a unique set of risk factors, health care workers become addicted to psychoactive substances at rates approximately similar to the general population.

COMMON DRUGS OF ABUSE

Each branch of the health care profession has a propensity for abusing a unique selection of psychoactive substances. In addition to the drugs of choice, the classification of substance abuse, the number of drugs abused, and the route of administration appear to be related to profession more than to age or gender. The substance most commonly abused by physicians, pharmacists, dentists, nurses, and other health care professionals is alcohol. Nurses most often report single-drug abuse, while physicians and pharmacists commonly suffer from polysubstance abuse.

In a recent survey, senior medical students who reported recreational drug use most commonly used alcohol (87.5%), followed by marijuana (10%), cigarettes (10%), and cocaine (2.8%).

SUBSTANCE ABUSE PATTERNS

Health care professionals abuse an eclectic and distinct variety of drugs, based on their knowledge of psychopharmacology and their access to certain drugs. Despite their knowledge of the side effects, clinical effects, and the addictive potential of drugs, health care professionals sometimes turn to substance use for the answers to unaddressed emotional problems or a way to maintain a high level of function. The rigorous physical and emotional stresses associated with balancing the care of patients and a personal life can initially provoke an occasional escape or short-term self-treatment, which may then progress to dependency.

The impairment and addiction of health care professionals can be divided into three categories of drug use: (*a*) self-treatment of pain, anxiety, or depression (the most common); (*b*) recreational use—drugs for pleasure, euphoria, or experimentation; and (*c*) performance-enhancing use.

Self-Treatment

This pattern of drug use is especially prevalent among physicians over age 40. In this age subgroup, self-treatment far exceeds recreational use of psychoactive substances and poses the greatest risk for impairment and addiction. In contrast, among medical students and physicians between the ages 26–30, recreational use exceeds self-treatment.

Despite warnings within the medical profession, self-treatment with prescription drugs continues to occur. A study of physicians training in the Boston area found that 36% of physicians had treated themselves with one or more psychoactive drugs, most commonly opiates and sedative-hypnotics. Although some state medical boards have stringent policies concerning self-medication, this practice appears to be widespread and may represent the major mode by which addiction begins in the health care community.

Recreational Use

While rates of drug use for self-treatment or instrumental use have remained stable or declined, recreational drug use among physicians has reflected current trends in recreational drug use in American society. Although young medical professionals may limit their recreational drug use to substances such as marijuana, which is associated with lower rates of impairment and addiction, such recreational use may progress to use of higher-risk drugs, such as sedatives, cocaine, and opiates.

Performance-Enhancing Use

Substance abuse may also originate in the form of instrumental or performance-enhancing drug use. Such drugs may be used to stay awake or facilitate work. Amphetamines are the major class of drugs employed in this category, and the use of these drugs has declined since the mid-1960s, when federal laws restricted their usage.

TABLE 5.1. RECOGNITION OF SUBSTANCE ABUSE IN HEALTH CARE WORKERS

Changes in personal behavior
- disheveled personal appearance
- emotional crises
- poor eating and sleeping habits
- alcohol on breath
- inappropriate behavior
- drunkenness, euphoria, anxiety, depression, or hallucinations
- prescriptions for self and family

Other personal difficulties
- financial problems
- neglect of social commitments
- legal problems
- arrests for driving under the influence or while intoxicated

Changes in relationships with children or spouse
- absences from home
- less time spent with children
- extramarital affairs
- impotence
- separation or divorce

Changes in the office
- deterioration of relationship with staff and patients
- frequent office absences
- complaints by patients regarding behavior
- excessive orders for drug supplies

Impaired hospital performance
- inappropriate clinical decision making
- inappropriate orders
- not available at night
- conflicts with hospital personnnel

Alterations in career stability
- increased frequency of job change
- greater likelihood of filling temporary positions
- increasing malpractice incidents
- vague letters of reference

RECOGNIZING SUBSTANCE ABUSE

In order to assist the health care professional with a substance abuse problem, other health care workers must watch for signs of substance abuse. In broad terms, the health care professional with a substance abuse problem exhibits changes in manner and personal appearance, isolates himself from friends and family, and displays altered behavior in the office or hospital (Table 5.1) (see Chapter 6).

The psychological profile of the substance-abusing physician is that of a person in distress, attempting to cope with the rigors of the medical profession and often lacking education about substance abuse. Workload, fatigue, and physical illness are often rationalizations for drug abuse. Self-medication with alcohol or drugs also may represent attempts to alleviate depression, fatigue, or tension.

For the health care professional, substance abuse is often a solitary and clandestine activity. This reclusiveness leads to emotional isolation and fosters a sense of helplessness among family members. Additionally, the feeling that physicians can take care of themselves may impede intervention on behalf of an addicted colleague. Physicians will often attempt to conceal these signs in order to maintain their status and position. The motivation for denial is perhaps greater in medicine than for any other profession.

The isolation of the substance-abusing health care professional is further reflected in altered relationships with family and friends. In fact, professional impairment often does not occur until the very late stages of drug dependency and is preceded by disruption in relationships with spouse and children. The chemically-dependent health care professional proceeds from isolation from friends and social commitments to, ultimately, neglect of professional duties, disorganization, and poor clinical judgment.

TREATMENT STRATEGIES

In spite of the statistics detailed above, both the public and health care community have adopted a *zero tolerance* approach with regard to substance abuse among health care workers. Physicians and nurses impaired by substance abuse pose a risk to the patients. Moreover, substance abuse in the health care community undermines the public's trust in the health care system.

The need to safeguard patient well-being and public trust prompted the AMA Council on Mental Health to issue its 1973 report entitled "The Sick Physician," which called on organized medicine to police itself with regard to substance abuse, and to establish treatment and rehabilitation programs for impaired physicians.

Identifying substance abuse as a treatable illness allows enlightened institutions to abandon severe punitive measures and to adopt a more compassionate approach. Every effort should be made to create an atmosphere that is nonaccusatory and nonjudgmental. Nevertheless, confrontation of a health care worker with a substance abuse problem will undoubtedly be uncomfortable and will evoke denial. The following recommendations for approaching a professional with suspected chemical dependency refer to physicians, but could be applied to anyone in health care.

An intervention team consisting of at least two physicians should approach its substance-abusing colleague: one preferably from the same specialty as the abuser, someone who shares common professional stresses; the other, a specialist in substance abuse, or a recovering physician. The meeting should be confidential and private.

The topic of suspected substance abuse should be directly and openly discussed. The immediate goal, the evaluation of the affected physician for treatment, must be stated from the beginning. It should be clearly explained that the meeting has been prompted by concerns about the health, professional credibility, and reputation of their substance-abusing colleague. Admission is often accompanied by an overwhelming sense of failure, lack of control, anger, embarrassment, and fear. This emotional stress has led to suicide in some cases. Therefore, appropriate and reliable emotional supports should be identified before and during the meeting.

All 50 states have physician health programs, most of which are affiliated with state medical societies. For example, in Massachusetts, the physician with a drug or alcohol problem can be referred to the Physician Health Services (PHS), a corporation of the Massachusetts Medical Society. In Massachusetts, a mandated reporter is exempt from filing a report to the Board of Registration in Medicine if there are no allegations of patient harm and if the reporter receives confirmation within 30 days that the physician is in compliance with the PHS program. PHS and the contracting physician sign a 3-year, renewable contract.

Several of the stipulations are as follows:

- The physician must agree not to use "illegal, mind-altering drugs" and alcohol and to suspend medical practice voluntarily until drug-free.
- The physician will have a support system consisting of a PHS associate director (also a physician), a therapist, and a physician-monitor at the workplace who can attest to abstinence, and a primary care physician. Attendance at support group meetings, including groups specifically designed for physicians, is required.
- Random urine samples will be obtained twice a week for the first 3 months of the PHS contract and once per week for the remainder of the contract.
- If the physician relapses, he will immediately cease caring for patients, enter into treatment, and is encouraged to re-contract.

In the event that the physician fails to meet the terms of the contract, PHS is required to notify the chief of service and the Board of Registration in Medicine. If the Board takes a disciplinary action against the physician, then the physician's chemical dependency becomes a matter of public record.

INSTITUTIONAL PREVENTION STRATEGIES

Medical Education

Medical schools are required by the Higher Education Act of 1965 to establish policies and programs that address the problem of substance abuse among their students. However, surveys during the late 1980s indicated that the majority of United States medical schools violated these federal guidelines. In 1988, only 16% of all United States medical schools had a formal policy for the identification and treatment of substance abuse problems. This study also indicated a clear lack of student knowledge about their institution's policy regarding substance abuse.

These data could result either from the absence of such policies or from the ineffective dissemination of such guidelines to students. Additionally, less than 1% of curriculum time is devoted to substance abuse education in United States medical schools, relegating substance abuse to a less important role. Unfortunately, even in the presence of elaborately organized, well-intentioned, and publicized guidelines, the lack of enforcement and monitoring procedures makes the guidelines more symbolic than effective.

Physician Health Programs

As previously mentioned, all 50 states have physician health programs that address the problem of substance abuse. Their aim is to provide conferences and workshops that acknowledge the problem of physician substance abuse, outline the means of obtaining help, and provide monitoring and advocacy for physicians in recovery.

REHABILITATION PROGRAMS

The promise of confidentiality and the availability of effective treatment programs have prompted substance-abusing physicians to address their illness. The prognosis for substance abuse treatment among health care professionals is good, especially with early detection and early institution of treatment. If the physician successfully recognizes the problem in the context of a treatment plan, outcomes are generally more favorable than in the general population. In a recent prospective study of 73 addicted physicians, 83% had good outcomes—either complete abstinence or a brief relapse, lasting less than 1 week, with no subsequent return to use. By comparison, only 62% of a population of 185 middle class controls achieved favorable outcomes.

Furthermore, physicians with severe addiction problems achieved similar rates of success to those with milder substance abuse problems. These promising results among physicians were attributed to the stringent follow-up requirements of hospital review boards and state licensing committees. These organizations promote abstinence while behavioral and other therapies hasten the healing process. Maintaining social standing and professional status may further compel the physician to discontinue drug or alcohol abuse. Most physicians resume their medical practice with supervision after the use has definitively ceased. Success depends on both the motivation of the substance abuser and continued follow-up that includes monitoring and support. Some physicians with multiple relapses choose to retrain in a branch of medicine with reduced access to drugs.

Less favorable outcomes occur when substance abuse goes unidentified and the benefits of early detection and treatment are lost. Poor prognoses are observed in physicians who have taken large quantities of highly addictive drugs over extended periods of time. In some instances, psychiatric conditions, such as neuroses, personality disorders, depression and, less commonly, schizophrenia, compound the substance abuse problem. Thus, the identification of accompanying psychiatric illness mandates the need for adjunctive psychiatric treatment during rehabilitation.

LEGAL RESPONSIBILITIES OF PHYSICIANS

Prescription Medications

The privilege of prescribing potentially addictive medications gives physicians a powerful and vital role in this country's drug control infrastructure. Consequently, physicians must undertake three tasks: (*a*) understand state and federal regulatory policies regarding prescription and dispensation of controlled substances; (*b*) prevent diversion of controlled substances to illicit markets; and (*c*) avoid attempts by those with chemical dependency to obtain controlled substances illegally or unnecessarily.

Individual state licensing boards determine which physicians practice within their borders. Additionally, under the Federal Controlled Substances Act of 1970, physicians must register themselves and their offices with the Drug Enforcement Administration (DEA), obtain a personal license and registration number, and administer and dispense controlled substances according to the DEA regulations.

A schedule of commonly encountered controlled substances is presented in Table 5.2. Substances are classified according to medical utility and abuse potential. DEA regulations do not require physicians to keep a record of prescriptions of Schedule II, III, IV, and V controlled substances as a part of normal professional practice. (NOTE: state laws vary and may impose additional requirements). However, regulations require

TABLE 5.2. SCHEDULES OF CONTROLLED SUBSTANCES

The drugs and drug products that come under the jurisdiction of the Controlled Substances Act are divided into five schedules. Some examples in each schedule are outlined below. For a complete listing of all the controlled substances contact any office of the Drug Enforcement Administration.

Examples of drugs in these Schedules are as follows:

Schedule I Substances

The substances in this schedule are those that have no accepted medical use in the United States and have a high abuse potential. Some examples are heroin, marijuana, LSD, MDMA, peyote, mescaline, psilocybin, N-ethylamphetamine, acetylmethadol, fenethylline, tilidine, dihydromorphine, and methaqualone.

Schedule II Substances

The substances in this schedule have a high abuse potential with severe psychic or physical dependence liability. Schedule II controlled substances consist of certain narcotic, stimulant, and depressant drugs. Some examples of Schedule II narcotic controlled substances are: opium, morphine, codeine, hydromorphone (Dilaudid), methadone, pantopon, meperidine (Demerol), cocaine, oxycodone (Percodan), and oxymorphone (Numorphan). Also in Schedule II are amphetamine (Dexedrine), methamphetamine (Desoxyn), glutethimide (Doriden), phenmetrazine (Preludin), methylphenidate (Ritalin), amobarbital, pentobarbital, secobarbital, fentanyl (Sublimaze), sufentanil, etorphine hydrochloride, phenylacetone, dronabinol and nabilone.

Schedule III Substances

The substances in this schedule have an abuse potential less than those in Schedules I and II, and include compounds containing limited quantities of certain narcotic drugs and non-narcotic drugs such as: derivatives of barbituric acid except those that are listed in another schedule, nalorphine, benzphetamine, chlorphentermine, chlortermine, phendimetrazine, paregoric and any compound, mixture, preparation or suppository dosage form containing amobarbital, secobarbital or pentobarbital.

Schedule IV Substances

The substances in this schedule have an abuse potential less than those listed in Schedule III and include such drugs as: barbital, phenobarbital, chloral hydrate, ethchlorvynol (Placidyl), meprobamate, (Equanil, Miltown), paraldehyde, methohexital, fenfluramine, diethylpropion, phentermine, chlordiazepoxide (Librium), diazepam (Valium), oxazepam (Serax), chlorazepate (Tranxene), flurazepam (Dalmane), clonazepam (Clonopin), alprazolam (Xanax), halazepam (Paxipam), temazepam (Restoril), triazolam (Halcion), lorazepam (Ativan), midazolam (Versed), Quazepam (Dormalin), mebutamate, dextropropoxyphene dosage forms (Darvon) and pentazocine (Talwin-NX).

Schedule V Substances

The substances in this schedule have an abuse potential less than those listed in Schedule IV and consist primarily of preparations containing limited quantities of certain narcotic and stimulant drugs generally for antitussive, antidiarrheal, and analgesic purposes. Some examples are buprenophrine and pyrovalerone.

TABLE 5.3. TIPS FOR PRESCRIBERS OF CONTROLLED SUBSTANCES

1. Keep all prescription blanks in a safe place where they can't be stolen easily. Minimize the number of prescription pads in use.
2. Write a prescription order for Schedule II controlled substances in ink or indelible pencil or use a typewriter. The order must be signed by the physician.
3. Write out the actual amount prescribed in addition to giving an Arabic number or Roman numeral—to discourage alterations of the prescription order.
4. Avoid writing a prescription order for a large quantity of controlled substances unless it is absolutely determined that such a quantity is necessary.
5. Maintain only a minimum stock of controlled substances in the medical bag.
6. The medical bag should be taken by the physician while away from the automobile, or locked in the trunk.
7. Be cautious when a patient mentions that another physician had been prescribing a controlled substance for him/her. Consult the physician or the hospital records—or else examine the patient thoroughly and decide if a controlled drug product should be prescribed.
8. A prescription blank should only be used for writing a prescription order—and not for notes or memos. A drug abuser could easily erase the message and use the blank to forge a prescription order.
9. Never sign prescription blanks in advance.
10. Maintain an accurate record of controlled substance products dispensed—as required by the Controlled Substances Act and its regulations.
11. Assist the pharmacist when he/she telephones to verify information about a prescription order. A corresponding responsibility rests with the pharmacist who dispenses the prescription order.
12. Phone the nearest DEA field office to obtain or to furnish information. The call will be held in the strictest confidence.

detailed record keeping if a physician is regularly dispensing, maintaining an inventory of, or actually performing the administration of controlled substances.

Unfortunately, physicians must be vigilant about attempts by patients to obtain controlled substances under false pretenses or to divert them to illicit markets. The DEA publishes a list of common sense guidelines for physicians prescribing controlled substances (Table 5.3). In addition to common sense and cautious prescription practices, new policies to prevent fraud and abuse are in varying stages of implementation across the country. In some regions of the country, physician and state regulatory agencies have created efforts in Multiple Copy Prescription Programs. Under such programs, prescriptions for controlled substances are generated in triplicate. One form is taken by the patient to the pharmacist; one copy remains filed in the physician's office; and the final copy is sent to the state agency. Other innovative programs will perhaps include electronic data transfer systems, which create a permanent electronic record of physician transactions.

Self-Prescription of Medications

Physicians need to be aware of and abide by state self-prescribing guidelines. In Massachusetts, for instance, licensing regulations prohibit a physician from prescribing controlled substances in schedules II, III, and IV for their own use. Additionally, physicians are prohibited from prescribing Schedule II controlled substances (except for emergencies) to immediate family members, to relatives permanently residing in the same residence, or to spouse "equivalents."

Reporting of Chemically-Dependent Professionals

While the possession and distribution of illicit drugs is illegal, physicians are not mandated to report the use or abuse of such drugs, except in one situation. This situation occurs when a physician learns of another health care professional's substance abuse. State laws vary widely in their mandates for reporting of chemically-dependent colleagues. According to the 1972 American Medical Association House of Delegates, it is the "physician's ethical responsibility to take cognizance of a colleague's inability to practice medicine adequately by reason of mental illness, including drug and alcohol dependence."

At this time, only 8 of the 50 states have passed laws mandating that physicians report their colleagues' substance abuse. In Massachusetts, for instance, the Mandatory Reporting Statute extends to any physician who is habitually drunk, dependent on drugs or alcohol, or who practices medicine while impaired by alcohol, drugs, physical disability, or mental instability. Such health care providers must be reported to the state Board of Registration in Medicine, or as described earlier, to the Physician Health Services of the Massachusetts Medical Society. All physicians should know their state's policy regarding reporting substance abuse within the health care community.

Additionally, a hospital has the legal right and duty to suspend a physician who poses an immediate threat to patient welfare. Hospitals can be held accountable for the actions of an impaired and/or incompetent health care worker. Thus, to protect themselves from malpractice and to assure quality care, hospitals must conduct peer reviews and supply treatment referrals when necessary.

CONCLUSIONS

By establishing policies regarding substance abuse, state agencies and medical societies have sought to insure that patients continue to receive the highest standards of care. Effective outreach, education, and treatment programs for chemically-dependent physicians have promoted an atmosphere conducive to the rehabilitation rather than the penalization of the health professional who seeks to free himself from chemical dependency. In addition, it is important that nonimpaired health care workers recognize the signs of substance abuse, and know the policies and procedures in their respective institutions and states, so that they may identify, approach, and assist their chemically-dependent colleagues.

FURTHER READING

Baldwin DC Jr, Hughes PN, Conard SE, et al. Substance use among senior medical students: a survey of 23 medical schools. JAMA 1991;265:2074–2078.

Brewster JM. Prevalence of alcohol and other drug problems among physicians. JAMA 1986;255:1913–1920.

Drug Enforcement Administration. Physician's manual—an informational outline of the controlled substances act of 1970. 6th Ed, publ. no. 275-114. Washington, DC: US Government Printing Office, 1990.

Gallegos KV, Lubin BH, Bowers C, Blevins JW, et al. Relapse and recovery: five- to ten-year follow-up study of chemically dependent physicians—the Georgia experience. Md Med J 1992;41:315–319.

Hughes PH, et al. Resident physician substance use in the United States. JAMA 1991;265:2069–2073.

Hughes PH, et al. Patterns of substance use in the medical profession. Md Med J 1992;41:311–314.

McAuliffe WE, et al. Psychoactive drug use by young and future physicians. J Health Soc Behav 1984;25:34–54.

McAuliffe WE, et al. Psychoactive drug use among practicing physicians and medical students. N Engl J Med 1986;315:805–810.

Morse RM, Martin MA, Swenson WM, Niven RG. Prognosis of Physicians Treated for Alcoholism and Drug Dependence. JAMA 1984;251:743–746.

Chapter 6

Clinical Evaluation

Rini Banerjee, Deborah Cohan, Thomas Cappola, Sarah E. Dick, Benny Gavi, Triste Lieteau, and Edward C. Sun with Booker Bush and S. Jean Emans

This chapter presents a general overview of history, physical examination, and screening techniques that can identify patients with substance-related disorders. Factors such as age, gender, socioeconomic background, known drug history, and level of intoxication will steer the physician in different directions. The interviewer must pursue a line of questioning relevant to the patient and follow up on any affirmative or vague answers during the interview. The physical examination then complements the history by revealing the characteristic signs and symptoms of substance use and abuse. Screening techniques help develop a differential diagnosis, assess the degree of the patient's substance-related disorders, and suggest courses of action for treatment. A summary flow chart of screening questions is included in Appendix 1.

SUBSTANCE USE AND ABUSE HISTORY-TAKING

Language

Language is the medium through which the medical encounter unfolds—it can "make or break" an interview. Remaining nonjudgmental during this interaction is particularly important—using labels, diagnoses, and generalizations will only impede the process of eliciting a potentially embarrassing and difficult history. Familiarity with drug terminology is also helpful to the provider (see Substance Abuse Jargon).

Patient-Doctor Interactions

Ideally, an addiction history is elicited once a sense of trust is established. Ironically, many practitioners justify *not* screening their patients because they do not want to disrupt the therapeutic alliance between provider and patient. However, reports estimate that between 50 and 90% of addiction problems go undiagnosed by their primary care providers. In general, a discussion of substance use should proceed only after the patient's chief complaint has been addressed. Interactions in which a

TABLE 6.1. PHYSICIAN APPROACH TO IDENTIFYING SUBSTANCE ABUSE

Knowledge Requirements

- Basic pharmacology, physiology, and clinical presentation of substances of abuse
- Local, state, and federal resources for those with addictions or in recovery
- In-hospital addiction/substance abuse consultation services

Skills to Practice and Utilize

- Substance use/abuse history questions
- Screening questions about risky behaviors
- Open-ended questioning and active listening
- Offer alternatives to substance abuse
    Availability of treatment/detoxification options
    Document benefits to ceasing substance use
    Encourage construction of new social relationships

Positive/Productive Attitudes

- Openness to substance abuse diagnosis
    Investigating nonspecific complaints
    Overcoming personal biases
    Development of nonjudgmental style

- Preparation for patient's denial, hostility, distrust
    Create safe environment
    Establish supportive role
        Listening and accepting
        Confidence-building, rewarding responses
    Patiently repeat attempts to discuss substance abuse

- Preparation for (physician's) frustration, disappointment, and failure
    Set reasonable goals
    Respect patient autonomy
    Recognize failures/mistakes as patient's own
    Plan for repeat attempts to achieve goals

- Plan and prepare for relapse
    Identify anxiety-provoking situations
    Develop strategies for resisting temptations
    Accept, learn from, overcome failures

provider's agenda dominates the discussion almost always fail. Table 6.1 presents a general approach for the physician when substance abuse may be a concern.

Asking screening questions can prove difficult and uncomfortable. The provider may want to inform the patient that information about drugs and alcohol are routinely elicited from all patients. Several options exist for the timing of questions during an interview. One can incorporate them as part of the medical history, the medication history, or a habits history—questions of nutrition, exercise, and cigarette use.

Another option is to ask about a family history of addictions and the drugs of abuse, and follow up with questions about the patient's own use. Patients may find it less threatening to speak first about past use or another person's use before talking about their own current use.

Furthermore, initiating a line of questioning by asking about more socially acceptable substances, such as caffeine, and then moving on to tobacco, alcohol, marijuana, sedatives, cocaine, amphetamines, hallucinogens, and narcotics can provide a smooth, progressive line of questioning.

History Screening Tools for Use and Abuse

The history is by far the most important tool for the evaluation of substance use. Routine history-taking can often provide evidence of substance use even before asking about drug and alcohol use specifically. Different screening tools can identify certain types of substance users. Although it may be impossible to incorporate each of these into every interview, they should be kept in mind when developing a history-taking technique that adapts to patient responses.

Adolescent Patients

Establishing a nonjudgmental environment is also crucial when working with children and adolescents. Taking notes during the interview or labeling patients with diagnoses could easily preclude the development of a trusting relationship between patient and provider. It is reasonable to begin seeing children alone by the age of 11 or, if tobacco, alcohol or other drug use is suspected, even earlier. Providers can assure confidentiality if a patient is not clearly putting him/herself or someone else's life at risk. At some point, however, it is usually important to include the parents or guardians because maintaining abstinence will usually require their involvement.

Prior to discussing the drug and alcohol history, it is important to remind the patient that you are asking out of concern for his/her health and for no other reason. As obvious as this may seem to the physician, many patients do not realize that the physician has this goal. Providers should also let teenagers know that they are available to answer questions and to provide information about drugs and alcohol. The following guidelines will help build a framework for interviewing adolescents:

Psychosocial Assessment

The provider may want to first address the patient's general psychosocial functioning.

1. Ask about *school*: Do you like school? What are your grades this year? versus last year? Have you ever gotten in trouble at school? Ever suspended?

TABLE 6.2. SIGNS OF ONGOING SUBSTANCE USE IN ADOLESCENTS ELICITED FROM THE HISTORY

- Recent change in peer groups
- Rebelliousness
- Avoidance of parents upon returning home
- Curfew violations
- Truancy
- Poor grades
- Low self-esteem

- Long periods of time spent away from home
- A sense of alienation
- Anxiety
- Sensation-seeking behavior
- Depression
- Less interest in extracurricular activities
- Delinquency

2. Ask about *extracurricular activities*: What do you do outside of school? Do you participate in any activities or sports? Do you work? Have you dropped any of your activities in the past year? What do you do at night and on weekends?

3. Ask about *friends*: Do you have friends? How do you know them? How long have you been friends with them? Have you recently changed your group of friends? What do your parents think of your friends?

4. Ask about *family life*: How do you get along with your family? Are there family rules about curfew? Driving?

5. Ask about *legal involvement*: Have you ever been in trouble with the law?

General Questions

Then the interviewer asks general questions about alcohol and drug use, eventually leading up to direct questions about the patient's personal experience, which can be introduced in the context of the patient's health (Table 6.2).

1. *General:* Do you know anyone who smokes? Drinks alcohol? Uses drugs? What do other students at school or in your neighborhood do for fun?

2. *Family and friends:* Does anyone in your family smoke? Drink? Use drugs? How about your friends? What do you and your friends do to have fun? How much smoking/drinking/drug use do you see at parties? Does anyone in your family go to Alcoholics Anonymous?

3. *Past personal use:* A provider can convey a nonjudgmental attitude if questions about drug and alcohol history are inquisitive rather than condemnatory: Tell me about your experiences with drugs and alcohol. Have you ever smoked? Drunk alcohol? Smoked marijuana? Sniffed glue? Used cocaine or crack? Popped pills? Injected steroids? Used heroin or other drugs?

4. *Current personal use:* Try to determine what drugs the adolescent is currently using, keeping in mind that there may be polysubstance

use. Also, ask about the methods, amount, frequency, and duration of drug use.

Follow-up Questions
Ask about the consequences of tobacco, alcohol, and drug use not already discussed.

- Health—including suicidal ideation, suicide attempts, sexually transmitted diseases (STDs);
- Family/Social relations—including sexuality, domestic violence;
- School/Employment—including time away from school, job loss;
- Financial/Legal—including selling drugs, prior arrest, driving (or riding with others) while intoxicated or under the influence of drugs.

The RAFFT screening test (see below) organizes inquiries about substance use in the adolescent population.

- Do you drink or use drugs to RELAX, feel better about yourself, or to fit in?
- Do you ever drink alcohol or use drugs while you are ALONE?
- Do you or any of your closest FRIENDS drink or use drugs?
- Does a close FAMILY member have a problem with alcohol or drug use?
- Have you ever gotten into TROUBLE from drinking or drug use?

Sexually Transmitted Diseases and Substance Abuse

Several studies have investigated and documented an association of alcohol and/or illicit drug use with sexual risk taking. Many adolescents experiment with various sexual behaviors and recreational drugs, consequently placing themselves at an increased risk for STDs, unintended pregnancy, and addiction. A recent study of risk behaviors among United States high school students and out-of-school youth (1992 Youth Risk Behavior Study) documented the following:

- 45.4% of in-school and 70.1% of out-of-school 14–19-year-olds reported ever having sexual intercourse. For these two populations, 14.0% and 36.4%, respectively, reported sexual intercourse with four or more partners.
- Condom use during most recent intercourse was less variable with 59.8% (in-school) and 50.2% (out-of-school) reporting a positive response.
- By comparison, lifetime substance use of in-school respondents included alcohol (55.2%), cigarettes (50.9%), marijuana (15.9%),

cocaine (2.1%), and injection drugs (2.1%). Greater percentages of positive responses were found in the out-of-school populations for all substances listed.

- Students who drank heavily (>4 drinks/occasion) were much more likely to have had sexual intercourse than non-heavy drinkers (0–4 drinks/occasion).
- Heavy drinkers were also less likely to have abstained from intercourse and were more likely to have had two or more partners (of those sexually experienced).
- Substance use was associated with less condom use among sexually active responders (substance use before sex—48% condom use; no substance use before sex—58% condom use).

Taking a Sexual History

Clinicians must tailor their questions to the individual patient, but assumptions about patients may lead to failure to recognize and counsel about risky sexual behaviors. Key points for clinicians to remember when taking an adolescent's sexual history include:

- Patients must understand all questions—misunderstandings arise when patients either do not understand English or when scientific terms are used instead of lay terms.
- Until a trusting and nonjudgmental relationship is established, patients may fabricate "acceptable" sexual histories. Such fabrications can hinder and delay accurate diagnosis and compromise disease intervention.
- It is often helpful to discuss behaviors that occur with the patient's peer group first, as this may lead into a discussion of the patient's own behaviors.
- Flexibility and patience are essential.
- Patients need to understand issues around confidentiality. While conversations about confidential issues should not be initiated in front of parents, occasionally personal issues do need to be discussed with parents to protect the health and safety of the adolescent. In this case, tell the adolescent that his/her parents will be informed and explain the necessity of this action.

The following questions more specifically address the issues of substances in relation to sexual activity:

- Do you drink or use drugs when you are out with your partners?
- Have you ever used intravenous drugs? Any partners ever use drugs?
- Have you ever had sex for drugs or money?
- Are you more likely to have sex when you are drinking or when using drugs?

- Are you less likely to use condoms/contraception when you drink or use drugs?
- Have you ever not remembered having sex with someone because you were high?

The spread of HIV and other STDs, particularly among the 15–29-year-old age group, has prompted increased attention on risky sexual behaviors and strategies for their prevention. Substance use plays a pivotal role in placing individuals at higher risk for STDs. Clinicians can play a multifaceted role in terms of prevention and treatment of STDs by opening lines of communication for education, support and advice, by eliciting a history of sexual activities and substance use, by assessing the risks of the patient for STDs, and by treating any diagnosed STDs.

Adult Patients

Tobacco
Inquire about current use:

- Do you smoke?
- Do you use tobacco in any other form? (i.e., chewing tobacco)?
- Are you exposed to secondhand smoke?

If patient denies current use, ask:

- Have you ever smoked?
- When did you quit? How long and how much did you smoke?
- How did you quit? How hard was it to quit? Do you consider restarting?

If patient acknowledges current use, ask:

- How much do you smoke? How often? For how many years?
- Have you ever tried to quit? How long did you abstain?
- What made you return to smoking? What role does smoking play in your life?
- Do you need a cigarette shortly after awakening in the morning?

Alcohol and Other Drugs
Two-Question Test. A very fast means of screening for alcoholism. Ask:

- Have you ever had a drinking problem?
- When was your last drink?

Answering "yes" to the first question and "within the past 24 hours" to the second is considered a positive test of alcoholism with a sensitivity of 91.5%. While this is a fast tool, it is limited to alcohol.

CAGEAID (CAGE (see below) questions Adapted to Include Drugs). A more thorough method of detecting alcohol and drug use with a sensitivity of 85–94% and specificity of 79–88% with 2 of 4 positive responses.

1. One may begin by asking a very *general question,* as "Have you had anything to drink during the past year?" then "What about drug use in the past year?"
2. If the answers are "no," follow up by asking an open-ended question as to whether there is a specific reason why they have not and whether they have ever drunk alcohol or used drugs. This, in turn, can be followed by:

   • Do you have a family history of substance use?
   • Are you in recovery?
   • Have you had problems with alcohol or drugs in the past?

Any positive response warrants follow-up as to which substance was used, the method of use, the amount and duration of use, and the role the substance played in the patient's life. Any vague response may be addressed by asking a more directed question, such as "Did you drink a case of beer a week?" or "Did you smoke the cocaine or use it nasally?"

3. If the answer is "yes," follow-up with the CAGEAID questions:

   • Have you ever thought about CUTTING down on your drinking? On your drug use?
   • Have you ever been ANNOYED by peoples' criticism of your drinking? Of your drug use?
   • Have you ever felt GUILTY about your drinking? About your drug use?
   • Have you ever drunk alcohol to get you going in the morning or to treat a hangover (EYE OPENER)? Have you used drugs to get you going?

T-ACE for women. Alternatively, women may be more effectively screened for alcoholism using the T-ACE questions. Women are more likely to feel guilty about their drinking and drug use leading to a false positive result on the "guilt" question in CAGEAID. It has been suggested that women, instead, be screened based on their level of tolerance; the ACE questions are identical to the CAE of the CAGE questions. Thus, the "guilt" question is replaced by:

TABLE 6.3. STANDARD ALCOHOL DRINK EQUIVALENTS

A standard drink includes any of the following:

- 12-oz can of beer or ale
- 12-oz bottle of wine cooler
- 6-oz glass of wine
- 6-oz glass of sherry or liqueur
- 1.5-oz shot of spirits (whiskey, gin, vodka)

- How many drinks does it TAKE to make you feel high?

An answer of three or more drinks is positive. Like CAGEAID, 2 of 4 affirmative responses count as a positive screen. A disadvantage of the T-ACE is its usefulness only in relation to alcohol use.

Whether using CAGEAID or T-ACE, the patient should be encouraged to speak more about any positive responses. For instance, a provider may ask:

- What made you want to cut down?
- What sort of comments do you find annoying?
- What do you think you feel guilty about?
- How often do you use alcohol or drugs to get you going in the morning?

With a positive CAGEAID or T-ACE (2 of 4 affirmative), try to understand the extent of the substance use and its impact on the patient's life.

1. Ask about the *method* of use (drinking, sniffing, inhaling, smoking, oral ingestion, intravenous injection, subcutaneous injection, intramuscular injection, nasal ingestion).
2. Try to learn about the *amount* of substances used in order to gauge potential medical complications for which the patient may be at risk. Keep in mind, however, that substances affect individuals differently, and no standard amount places a patient at risk. Nonetheless, as mentioned, some suggest that a woman who requires more than three drinks to feel intoxicated is experiencing tolerance. Other studies have argued that four or more alcoholic drinks a day for a 70-kg individual is a positive sign of alcoholism. Table 6.3 lists the standard equivalent doses of alcohol.
3. Try to understand the *context* in which a person uses substances and the *consequences* of their substance use by asking such questions as:

- How do you deal with stress in your life?
- Do you think that your drinking/drug use has made an impact on your life? On your family? On work or school performance?

- Have you had any problems with the law?
- Have you ever had financial problems as a result of your drinking/ drug use?
- Has your drinking/drug use had an impact on your health?
- Have you been involved in an accident or experienced any trauma or other injury as a result of drinking or drug use?

The individuality of each patient is important when asking these follow-up questions, since the consequences of drinking alcohol for a homeless or unemployed elderly man are different from those of a college student.

Elderly Patients

Evaluating older patients for drug and alcohol use can be particularly difficult. Providers often have biases about who uses drugs. Drug use in the elderly population may manifest itself as an exacerbation of an underlying illness rather than a new problem. Chronic disease processes, such as alcoholism, hepatitis, congestive heart failure, and poor nutrition tend to increase the effect of these drugs. The physician must closely monitor the effects of drug-drug interactions in a patient on multiple medications and the increasing effects that drugs of abuse have on the elderly. As people age, changes in absorption, distribution, metabolism, and excretion are common.

Traditional tools, such as the CAGE questions, have not been demonstrated to adequately identify elderly patients with such problems. The CHARM questions have been suggested as a better screen for the elderly.

Psychosocial Assessment

One may first want to do a psychosocial assessment of the patient's sources of stress and means of coping with such stress. Common stresses include: declining health, loss of independence, functional impairment, pain, and illness or death of family, partner, or friends.

Recent Alcohol or Drug Use

Since elderly patients who abuse alcohol may present in three different patterns (Table 6.4), inquiring about past use as well as present use is important. If the patient states that he or she has not used any substances in the past year, inquire about past problems. If the patient states that he or she has used substances in the past year, move onto the CHARM questions:

- Have you ever thought about CUTTING down?
- HOW: Do you have rules about drinking alcohol or drug use? Has your pattern of drinking or drug use changed recently?
- Has ANYONE expressed concern about your alcohol or drug use?

TABLE 6.4. TYPES OF ELDERLY ALCOHOLIC PRESENTATIONS

1. *Survivors* have a long-time history of alcohol abuse and have survived into old age. Alcohol-related medical problems, such as cirrhosis, pancreatitis, hypertension, or diabetes, may be present.

2. *Intermittents* may have been drinking sporadically for a long time, but the drinking has never presented a problem. When faced with the stresses of old age they try to cope again with alcohol and may move unknowingly into dependency.

3. The *Late Onset* group become addicted later in life. Often, increased drinking is precipitated by loneliness, loss, financial insecurity, boredom, or loss of self-esteem.

- What ROLE does alcohol/drugs play in your life?
- Have you ever drunk/used drugs MORE than intended?
- Have you ever had problems with your MEDICATIONS or taken more than prescribed?

Questions about the amounts of alcohol and drugs used may not be as valuable in older adults, because the threshold at which substances have a negative impact may decline with increasing age.

Other Screening Tools

- MAST (Michigan Alcoholism Screening Test)—a set of 24 questions with a sensitivity of 90% and specificity of 80%, and SMAST (Short MAST)—a set of 13 questions with a 70% sensitivity and 80% specificity (Table 6.5).
- AUDIT (Alcohol Use Disorders Identification Test) is a screening test for problem drinking (Table 6.6).

Other Sources of Information

Relatives and friends may be valuable sources of information. After granting consent, the patient may or may not choose to be present during the discussion. Either way, such meetings can yield valuable information about the impact that substance use has had on a patient and his or her environment.

MANIFESTATIONS OF SUBSTANCE ABUSE

General Comments

Since the presentation of substance abuse is often quite nonspecific, it can be mistaken for other medical or psychiatric conditions. Likewise chemical dependency can mask or be masked by underlying medical or psychiatric disease. Therefore, it is important to have a low threshold

TABLE 6.5. THE MICHIGAN ALCOHOLISM SCREENING TEST QUESTIONNAIRE

Question	Scoring	
1. Do you feel you are a normal drinker (meaning you drink less than or as much as most other people?)	No	2[a]
2. Have you ever awakened the morning after drinking the night before and found you could not remember a part of the evening?	Yes	2
3. Does your spouse, parent, or other near relative ever worry or complain about your drinking?	Yes	2
4. Can you stop drinking without a struggle after 1 or 2 drinks?	No	2
5. Do you ever feel guilty about your drinking?	Yes	1
6. Do friends or relatives think you are a normal drinker?	No	2
7. Are you always able to stop drinking when you want to?	No	2
8. Have you ever attended a meeting of Alcoholics Anonymous?	Yes	5
9. Have you gotten into physical fights when drinking?	Yes	1
10. Has drinking ever created problems between you and your spouse, parent, or other near relative?	Yes	2
11. Has your spouse, parent, or other near relative ever gone to anyone for help about your drinking?	Yes	2
12. Have you ever lost boyfriends or girlfriends because of your drinking?	Yes	2
13. Have you ever gotten into trouble at work because of your drinking?	Yes	2
14. Have you ever lost a job because of drinking?	Yes	2
15. Have you ever neglected your obligations, your family, or work for 2 or more days in a row because you were drinking?	Yes	2
16. Do you drink before noon fairly often?	Yes	1
17. Have you ever been told you have liver trouble? Cirrhosis?	Yes	2
18. After heavy drinking, have you ever had delirium tremens or severe shaking, or heard voices or seen things that were not really there?	Yes	2
19. Have you ever gone to anyone for help about your drinking?	Yes	5
20. Have you ever been in a hospital because of drinking?	Yes	5
21. Have you ever been a patient in a psychiatric hospital or ward where drinking was part of the problem that resulted in hospitalization?	Yes	2
22. Have you ever been seen at a psychiatric or mental health clinic or gone to any doctor, social worker, or clergy for help with any emotional problem where drinking was part of the problem?	Yes	2
23. Have you ever been arrested for drunken driving, driving while intoxicated, or under the influence of alcoholic beverages?	Yes	2
24. Have you ever been arrested, even for a few hours, because of drunken behavior?	Yes	2
	Total	

[a]SCORES: 0–4 = nonalcoholic; 5–6 = suggestive of alcoholism; 7 = alcoholism.

TABLE 6.6 ALCOHOL USE DISORDERS IDENTIFICATION TEST (AUDIT)

Please circle the answer that is correct for you

1. How often do you have a drink containing alcohol?

| Never | Monthly or less | Two to four times a month | Two to three times a week | Four or more times a week |

2. How many drinks containing alcohol do you have on a typical day when you are drinking?

| 1 or 2 | 3 or 4 | 5 or 6 | 7 to 9 | 10 or more |

3. How often do you have 6 or more drinks on one occasion?

| Never | Less than monthly | Monthly | Weekly | Daily or almost daily |

4. How often during the last year have you found that you were not able to stop drinking once you had started?

| Never | Less than monthly | Monthly | Weekly | Daily or almost daily |

5. How often during the last year have you failed to do what was normally expected from you because of drinking?

| Never | Less than monthly | Monthly | Weekly | Daily or almost daily |

6. How often during the last year have you needed a first drink in the morning to get yourself going after a heavy drinking session?

| Never | Less than monthly | Monthly | Weekly | Daily or almost daily |

7. How often during the last year have you had a feeling of guilt or remorse after drinking?

| Never | Less than monthly | Monthly | Weekly | Daily or almost daily |

8. How often during the last year have you been unable to remember what happened the night before because you had been drinking?

| Never | Less than monthly | Monthly | Weekly | Daily or almost daily |

9. Have you or someone else been injured as a result of your drinking?

| No | Yes, but not in the last year | Yes, during the last year |

10. Has a relative or a friend, or a doctor or other health worker, been concerned about your drinking or suggested you cut down?

| No | Yes, but not in the last year | Yes, during the last year |

(continued on next page)

Procedure for Scoring AUDIT

Questions 1–8 are scored 0, 1, 2, 3, or 4. Questions 9 and 10 are scored 0, 2, or 4 only. The response coding is as follows:

	0	1	2	3	4
Question 1	Never	Monthly or less	Two to four times per month	Two to three times per week	Four or more times per week
Question 2	1 or 2	3 or 4	5 or 6	7 to 9	10 or more
Questions 3–8	Never	Less than monthly	Monthly	Weekly	Daily or almost daily
Questions 9–10	No		Yes, but not in the last year		Yes, during the last year

The minimum score (for nondrinkers) is 0 and the maximum possible score is 40.

A score of 8 or more indicates a strong likelihood of hazardous or harmful alcohol consumption.

for considering a diagnosis of substance abuse. Table 6.7 provides a list of presentations which, though nonspecific, should raise the index of suspicion for substance abuse.

In general, the psychiatric and behavioral manifestations appear first, making a good history the most important part of a substance abuse evaluation. In acute intoxication or chronic abuse, physical and laboratory abnormalities can appear and are useful in assessing the severity of the abuse and its sequelae. A diagnosis of substance abuse does not rule out the presence of other disease, and one should avoid the tendency of attributing every abnormality to substance abuse.

Specific Manifestations of Abuse

Although the abuse of many different substances share common clinical manifestations, substances can produce more specific symptoms and sequelae. Familiarity with these symptoms helps diagnose and assess the severity of the abuse of particular substances. Table 6.8 presents some of the more common manifestations of substance abuse by substance and system. This organization of the manifestations of substance abuse may be useful during a "review of systems" and physical examination on a patient whom you suspect is abusing a particular substance. Refer to Chapters 7–16 for a more complete listing and discussion of each substance's medical consequences.

TABLE 6.7. PRESENTATIONS OF SUBSTANCE ABUSE

Psychiatric/Behavioral	Trauma	Medical
Acute psychosis	Assault/unusual	Acute abdominal pain
Anxiety	injury	AIDS
Child abuse/neglect	Drowning	Ascites
Delirium	Falls	Cardiomyopathy
Depression	Accidents, especially	Cirrhosis
Mania	motor vehicle	Early myocardial
Panic attack	accidents (MVAs)	infarction or
Suicide attempt		cerebrovascular
Addictive behaviors		accident
requests for pain medication		Encephalopathy
for common complaints		GI bleeding
such as lower back pain,		Hyperventilation
migraine, or renal colic		Infections
claims that the patient lost		Abscess
his or her prescriptions		Aspiration
patients who travel from		pneumonia
clinic to clinic		Endocarditis
patients who are willing to		HIV infection
negotiate for other		Sepsis
medications if their initial		Soft tissue infection/
requests for potent opiates		cellulitis
are refused		Tetanus
Patients who are allergic to		Tuberculosis
all pain medication except		Viral hepatitis
opiates		Hepatitis
		Pancreatitis
		Poisoning
		Seizure

FURTHER READING

American Medical Association Chicago. Guidelines for Adolescent Preventive Services. Chicago: American Medical Association, 1992. Publ. by AMA; Chicago IL.

Centers for Disease Control. 1993 Sexually transmitted diseases treatment guidelines. Atlanta: Morbidity and Mortality Weekly Report, vol. 42. Sept. 24, 1993.

Cyr MG, Wartman SA. The effectiveness of routine screening questions in detection of alcoholism. JAMA 1985;267:51–54.

Farrow JA, Deisher R. A practical guide to the office assessment of adolescent substance abuse. Pediatr Ann 1986;15:675, 678–689, 682–684.

Lane PA, Burge S, Graham A. Management of addictive disorders in women. In: Addictive Disorders. St. Louis: Mosby-Year Book, 1992;265.

Maly R. Early recognition of chemical dependence. Prim Care 1993;20:34.

Schuckit MA, Irwin M. Diagnosis of alcoholism. Med Clin North Am 1988; 72:1133–1153.

TABLE 6.8. SPECIFIC MANIFESTATIONS OF ABUSE OF CATEGORIES OF DRUGS

System	Alcohol	Tobacco	Cocaine	Marijuana	Opiates	Hallucinogens (LSD, PCP)	Sedative/hypnotics	Amphetamines	Inhalants	Anabolic Steroids
Psychiatric/behavioral	Chronic anxiety, dysphoria, insomnia, job loss/trouble in school, financial problems, absenteeism		Euphoria, elevated mood, depression, irritability, restlessness, anxiety, panic attack, acute psychosis with hallucinations, paranoia, violent behavior	Elevated mood, euphoria, agitation, confusion, disturbing hallucinations, panic reactions, Paranoia, decreased concentration, amotivational syndrome	Pain out of proportion to physical findings, drug-seeking behavior, euphoria, dysphoria, drowsiness, impaired attention	LSD: euphoria, psychotic reactions, flashbacks. PCP: delirium, psychosis, schizophrenia, depression	Disinhibition, mood lability, decreased attention, insomnia, anxiety, amnesia, "shopping bag sign": patient's family brings in a large bag of different sedatives upon requesting the patient's medication	Euphoria, increased self-esteem, grandiosity, suspiciousness, hypervigilance, anxiety, paranoia, delirium, hallucinations, delusions	Acute organic brain syndrome, acute psychotic reaction, euphoria, disinhibition	Increased aggression
General	Weight gain		Weight loss		Hyperthermia, diaphoresis		Diaphoresis	Hyperthermia, diaphoresis	Chemical-soaked clothing	
Skin	Folliculitis, rosacea, seborrheic dermatitis, psoriasis, porphyria cutanea tarda. Stigmata of liver disease: palmar erythema, spider angiomata	Tobacco stains, wrinkling			Hyperpigmentation over veins, abscess, skin popper lesions, jaundice				Dermatitis, chemical, and thermal burns	Peripheral edema, acne, gynecomastia
Head, Eye, Ear, Nose, Throat	Facial erythema, facial edema, parotid swelling, Nasopharyngeal cancer	Oral cancer, pharyngeal cancer	Chronic sinusitis, unilateral nasal edema, septal perforation	Conjunctival injection, dry mucous membranes, dilated pupils	Miosis	PCP: increased salivation, dysarthria, nystagmus		Lacrimation, tinnitus, diplopia, halitosis, epistaxis	Facial edema ("moon face"), male-pattern alopecia, deepened voice	

Respiratory	Upper respiratory infection (URI) pneumonia (especially aspiration, *Klebsiella*, *Haemophilus*, *influenzae*) asthma exacerbation	Chronic obstructive pulmonary disease (COPD) pneumonia (especially *H. influenzae*) asthma exacerbation Lung cancer	(when smoked) Black sputum, cough, dyspnea, hypersensitivity pneumonitis spontaneous pneumothorax	Dry cough, lung cancer, COPD, asthma exacerbations, nasal congestion, sore throat	Respiratory depression	PCP: respiratory depression	Respiratory depression		Airway freezing, laryngospasm, pneumonitis
Cardiovascular	Hypertension (especially labile hypertension) Arrhythmia (especially atrial fibrillation "holiday heart") Ischemic heart disease (at high doses) Cardiomyopathy	Ischemic heart disease Peripheral vascular disease	Coronary vasospasm leading to angina or myocardial infarction, arrhythmia (sinus tachycardia, ventricular fibrillation)	Tachycardia, increased supine systolic blood pressure, decreased standing systolic blood pressure	Hypertension, tachycardia, endocarditis (especially right-sided endocarditis)	PCP: cardiogenic shock	Hypotension, tachycardia	Tachycardia, hypertension, arrhythmia	Arrhythmia
Gastrointestinal (GI)/Abdominal	*Esophagus:* reflux, Barrett's rupture, cancer, esp. in smokers *Gastric:* acute and chronic gastritis, exacerbation of peptic ulcer disease *Pancreas:* acute and chronic pancreatitis *Intestinal:* malabsorption leading to diarrhea, rectal fissure, and pruritis *Liver:* acute hepatitis, liver failure, and cirrhosis, ascites, hepatic cancer *Splenomegaly,* hypersplenism, ascites	Esophageal reflux Esophageal cancer Pancreatic cancer			Nausea, hepatic dysfunction, constipation		Nausea	Abdominal pain, nausea, vomiting, hepatitis	Hepatic dysfunction jaundice

TABLE 6.8.   SPECIFIC MANIFESTATIONS OF ABUSE OF CATEGORIES OF DRUGS, *continued*

System	Alcohol	Tobacco	Cocaine	Marijuana	Opiates	Hallucinogens (LSD, PCP)	Sedative/hypnotics	Amphetamines	Inhalants	Anabolic Steroids
Genitourinary (GU)	*Male:* decreased arousal, pleasure; increased impotence, ejaculatory latency, testicular atrophy *Female:* decreased libido, lubrication, irregular menses, especially with concomitant eating disorder	Renal cancer, Bladder cancer *Pregnancy:* low birth weight baby, miscarriage, stillbirth, abruptio placenta, placenta previa, preterm rupture	Cervical cancer *Pregnancy:* abruptio placenta, stillbirth, miscarriage, abstinence syndrome in neonate	Male infertility, impotence, decreased libido, abnormal menstruation	Irregular menses, decreased libido				Clitoral hypertrophy, amenorrhea, dysmenorrhea, testicular atrophy	
Musculoskeletal	Gout, myopathy (esp. in shoulders), Dupuytren's contracture, rhabdomyolysis						Rhabdomyolysis		Rhabdomyolysis	Rapid increase in weight and muscle mass, stress fractures, muscle strains
Neurological	Seizures, loss of consciousness, hemorrhagic cerebrovascular accident, especially in young, subdural hematoma; Headache: migraine or chronic undefined headache	Cerebrovascular accident	Seizure, cerebrovascular accident, diffuse small vessel ischemia		Analgesia, stupor, coma, peripheral neuropathy, dysarthria		Dysarthria, ataxia, hyperreflexia, tremor	Autonomic hyperactivity, seizures	Painful peripheral neuropathy, ataxia, dysarthria, tremor, paresthesia	Abrupt onset of temporary hyperkinesia with rapid speech pattern

	Sleep disorder: can persist for 2 years postabstinence; Wernicke's encephalopathy, Korsakoff's syndrome, Neuropathy: first sensory, then motor; polyneuropathy			
Laboratory	*Thrombocytopenia:* down to 30,000–50,000 range, recovery with 1 week of abstinence. *Anemia:* microcytic (secondary to iron deficiency of GI bleeding), macrocytic (secondary to direct alcohol effect and folate or B12 deficiency). *Enzyme levels:* • Elevated ALT and AST with AST:ALT ratio > 1.5–2.0 • Elevated GGT in chronic abuse. Elevated PT/PTT and decreased albumin in liver failure • Elevated CPK in rhabdomyolysis • Elevated amylase/lipase with acute pancreatitis • Hyper or hypoglycemia	Elevated AST/ALT, decreased globulins	Elevated AST, ALT, BUN, creatinine, elevated lead levels (with gasoline), methemoglobinemia (with nitrites)	Elevated AST/ALT, decreased HDL and increased LDL cholesterol

Comparison of laboratory screening tests

TABLE 6.8. SPECIFIC MANIFESTATIONS OF ABUSE OF CATEGORIES OF DRUGS, *continued*

System	Alcohol	Tobacco	Cocaine	Marijuana	Opiates	Hallucinogens (LSD, PCP)	Sedative/ hypnotics	Amphetamines	Inhalants	Anabolic Steroids
	Comparison of laboratory screening tests									
	test abnormal	**comment**								
	GGT >40 u/L	First to increase with chronic abuse Recovers with 1–2 weeks of abstinence								
	MCV >90 +/− 7	Sign of chronic abuse. Takes weeks/ months to develop and recover due to lifespan of RBCs								
	AST >40 u/L	AST:ALT >2.0 ALT consistent with acute alcohol abuse								

SECTION II
ABUSED SUBSTANCES

Chapter 7

Alcohol

Jim MacDonald and Elizabeth M. Twardon with Howard J. Shaffer

For nearly 10,000 years, beer and wine have been daily thirst quenchers. In ancient times, water was avoided because it carried illness. Fermented liquids, on the other hand, maintained fluid balance and provided calories. Although moderation guided most ancient consumptive practices, festivals like the Bacchanal, a Greek religious ritual, promoted the consumption of large amounts of alcohol. Introduced to the West by Arabic civilizations in the 12th century, distillation allowed the purification and isolation of ethanol from fermented beverages. This new process marked the transition from the consumption of beer and wine as nutrients to the consumption of alcohol in quantities sufficient to be harmful.

In 1795 the United States physician Benjamin Rush published the Inquiry into the Effects of Addictive Spirits upon Body and Mind, in which he labeled the excessive use of distilled liquor a disease. To this day, the disease model has maintained dominance in mainstream thought over other explanatory models of alcoholism, because it incorporates components of the social, psychological, and biological models (Tables 7.1 and 7.2).

A doctor's movement organized by Rush lobbied Congress for the imposition of heavy duties on all distilled spirits. These efforts represent one of the first public health initiatives in United States history. Later, in the late 19th century, perceptions that the poor and the working class experienced most alcohol-related problems led paternalistic organizations, such as the Women's Christian Temperance Union and the Anti-Saloon League, to promote temperance education and to push for outright prohibition of alcohol. By 1917, 26 states had laws prohibiting the sale of alcoholic beverages. In October 1919, Congress passed the Volstead National Prohibition Act over President Wilson's veto, thereby implementing the 18th Amendment. The "noble experiment" of prohibition had begun. Prohibition lasted until the 21st Amendment repealed the 18th in 1933. Soon thereafter, official alcohol help groups made their appearance. In 1939, an alcoholic physician founded Alcoholics Anonymous (AA), establishing the most successful and widespread support group to promote sobriety.

TABLE 7.1 ETIOLOGIC MODELS OF ALCOHOLISM

Psychological model: Personality/psychopathology predispose to alcohol abuse
- Self-medication
- Symptom of psychiatric disease

Social model: Environment/social pressures reinforce alcohol abuse
- Underemployment
- Poverty
- Marital discord
- Job stress
- Children model adult behavior
- Children conform to peer pressures to drink

Biological model: Biology/genetic differences predispose to alcohol abuse
- Disproportionate alcoholism in men (5:1)
- Increased risk for sons/brothers of male alcoholics
- Twin/adoption data indicate increased risk in families with alcoholic parents (up to 4×)

Disease model: Alcoholism results from the interplay of biology, psychology, sociology
- Disease has typical signs and symptoms and a usual course
- Abstinence is the only effective recovery
- Biochemical predispositions include:
  Genetic/congenital (**Table 7.2** lists several possible genetic links to alcoholism)
  Nutritional deficiencies
  Dysfunction in CNS/endocrine system
- Psychosocial predispositions include:
  Feelings of inadequacy and alienation
  Alcohol as an accepted relief from pain/problems

EPIDEMIOLOGY

Alcoholism crosses gender, race, age, and socioeconomic strata. Although 95% of people have consumed alcohol in their lifetime, no survey has adequately quantified the percentage of people who abuse or become dependent on alcohol. Most alcoholics do not fit the homeless, "skid row" stereotype nor do they differ from the general population in their initial experiences with alcohol. Chapter 2 presents more detailed statistics about alcohol use in the United States among different age groups.

PHARMACOLOGY

Structure and Mechanism of Action

Ethanol, CH_3CH_2OH, is a small, amphiphilic organic molecule without isomeric carbons. The absence of chirality and the molecule's small size

TABLE 7.2. GENETIC DISORDERS ASSOCIATED WITH ALCOHOLISM

Genetic Disorder	Evidence
Alcogene—gene responsible for alcoholism	• Strong association between the A1 allele of the Dopamine 2 Receptor (D2DR) gene and severe alcoholism. The A1 allele is associated with an overall reduction in the number of D2 receptors. Decreased numbers of D2 receptors have been correlated with a number of pleasure-seeking behaviors • The B1 allele is also associated with severe alcoholism
Deficiency of serotonin	• Lower blood:plasma ratio of tryptophan (the amino acid precursor of serotonin) to other amino acids occurs more in familial, early-onset alcoholics than in nonfamilial, late-onset alcoholics • Alcohol's biphasic effect temporarily increases serotonergic activity, but later suppresses this neurochemical system; thus, creating a craving for more alcohol • New antidepressant drugs that selectively block re-uptake of serotonin help decrease the amount that individuals drink
Defective capacity of the brain to oxidize aldehydes	• The spinal fluid of alcoholics has more aldehyde condensation products than the spinal fluid of nonalcoholics following alcohol ingestion

reduce the likelihood that ethanol activates specific recognition sites. Instead, ethanol's amphiphilic property allows it to dissolve in water and lipids, and thus interact with neuronal membrane lipids. In fact, alcohol's anesthetic effect results from an ethanol-induced disorganization of the membrane lipid bilayer, impairing normal neuronal function.

Although this model is the most frequently accepted, a number of investigators have noted that the alterations in membrane fluidity that occur at usual doses may be too small to have pharmacological effects. Particular proteins (receptors, ion channels, enzymes) may be differentially sensitive to ethanol. A perturbation of these protein systems may cause the intoxicating effects of ethanol. This receptive element theory may account for alcohol's effects at physiological levels.

The best studied receptive element is the γ-aminobutyric acid (GABA) receptor/chloride channel (see Chapter 12). GABA is the major inhibitory neurotransmitter in the brain. The effectiveness of benzodiazepines and barbiturates in the treatment of alcohol withdrawal suggests that alcohol may cross-react with GABA receptors. Although ethanol's interactions with GABAergic systems seem to only partially explain its pharmaco-

TABLE 7.3 CNS SYMPTOMS ASSOCIATED WITH BLOOD-ALCOHOL CONCENTRATIONS

Concentration (g/dL)	Sporadic Drinker	Chronic Drinker
0.050 (party level)	Congenial euphoria	No observable effect
0.075	Gregarious, garrulous	Often no notable effect
0.100 (legally intoxicated)[a]	Uncoordinated	Minimal signs
0.125–0.150	Unrestrained behavior, episodic lack of control	Pleasure, euphoria begins, lack of coordination
0.200–0.250	Alertness lost, lethargy	Requires effort to maintain emotional/motor control
0.300–0.350	Stupor to coma	Drowsy, slow
>0.500	Can be fatal, may require hemodialysis	Coma

[a]In some states, like California, .080 is considered legally drunk.

logical properties, it does potentiate native GABA's actions at the GABA receptor/chloride channel.

Pharmacokinetics

Absorption of alcohol occurs primarily in the small intestine and colon. The small intestine absorbs alcohol completely and independently of the presence of food. Alcohol usually reaches maximum concentrations in the blood within 30 to 90 minutes of the last sip. Once absorbed, ethanol is almost uniformly distributed throughout all tissues and fluids of the body. Negative effects, such as increased reaction time, diminished fine motor control, and impaired critical faculties, appear when blood alcohol concentration reaches 0.20 to 0.30 g/dL (Table 7.3). Alcohol concentration in urine (about 130% of that in blood) and expired air (about 0.05% that in blood) can estimate blood alcohol levels. Measurement of the alcohol concentration in expired air forms the basis of the well-known "breathalyzer" tests used by law enforcement officials.

As the blood alcohol concentration increases, an individual feels euphoria. However, as the blood alcohol concentration decreases, the drinker usually feels dysphoric—even at levels that initially caused euphoria. Chronic, excessive ingestion of ethanol is associated with increased tolerance, requiring larger doses to reproduce the original effects. At moderate degrees of intoxication, another form of tolerance, called tachyphylaxis, occurs. Tachyphylaxis is a phenomenon of diminished effects at a given blood alcohol concentration as the body rapidly adapts to its presence over time.

Metabolized principally by the liver, 90–98% of alcohol is ultimately converted to carbon dioxide and water. The remainder is excreted in sweat, urine, saliva, and tears. Ethanol is metabolized at a relatively constant rate, independent of its blood concentration. Two key enzymes catalyze the oxidation of alcohol: alcohol dehydrogenase (ADH), found primarily in the liver and stomach; and aldehyde dehydrogenase (ALDH), found throughout the body (see below).

A microsomal mixed-function oxidase system found in the smooth endoplasmic reticulum of hepatocytes converts alcohol to acetaldehyde. In chronic users of alcohol this system has an increased role. It consists of an NADPH-cytochrome P-450 reductase induced by chronic ethanol exposure. This induction helps explain the increased rate of alcohol elimination in heavy drinkers, and the interactions between ethanol and other drugs, which the cytochrome P-450 system metabolizes.

In people with normal hepatic function, alcohol is metabolized at a rate of about 120 mg/kg/hour. A popular rule of thumb recommends waiting at least 1 hour for every 1 to 2 drinks consumed before attempting to drive. On average, ingestion of 44 g (4 oz) of whisky on an empty stomach results in maximum blood concentrations of 0.07 to 0.09 g/dL compared to 0.03 to 0.05 g/dL after a mixed meal.

Alcohol Dehydrogenase (ADH)

ADH catalyzes the conversion of alcohol to acetaldehyde, a toxin. ADH accounts for metabolism of low to moderate doses of ethanol. Its dependence on NAD, a coenzyme of limited supply, accounts for the zero-order kinetics of ethanol metabolism. Gender differences in vulnerability to alcoholic liver disease have been noted for many years and, recently, attributed in part to lower gastric ADH levels in women. The resulting decreased gastric oxidation of alcohol in women increases its bioavailability. People of different races have been found to differ in their ADH isozymes. People with ADH_2 (Asians) metabolize alcohol about 30% faster than those with ADH_1 (Caucasians).

Aldehyde Dehydrogenase (ALDH)

Acetaldehyde, the toxic byproduct of ADH and cytochrome metabolism of alcohol, is rapidly converted normally to acetate by aldehyde dehydrogenase (ALDH). Of the two types, cytosolic ($ALDH_1$) and mitochondrial ($ALDH_2$), $ALDH_2$ oxidizes the majority of the acetaldehyde produced. Nearly half of Asians have an $ALDH_2$ deficiency. Individuals with this mutation experience a flushing reaction due to increased accumulation of acetaldehyde and more intense adverse symptoms after the acute ingestion of ethanol.

Normally, about 2% of ingested alcohol escapes oxidation. But when large amounts of alcohol are consumed, as much as 10% bypasses oxidation and is excreted by the kidneys and lungs. The energy released or stored per gram of alcohol amounts to 7 kilocalories.

Consumption of Other Alcohols

Methanol, or "wood" alcohol, is a common industrial solvent often found in gasline antifreeze, windshield washer fluid, shellac, solid/canned fuels, some paints, varnishes, and paint removers. Alcoholics unable to obtain alcohol sometimes consume methanol-containing products, or ingestion may be accidental (e.g., by a child). Methanol, metabolized to formaldehyde by ADH and then to formic acid by ALDH, can cause severe acidosis, retinal damage and blindness, coma, and death. Consumption of as little as 15 ml of methanol has caused blindness; ingestion of 70 to 100 ml is usually fatal unless treated promptly. Diagnosis can be made by suggestive ingestion history, ocular complaints, wide anion gap acidosis, and methanol level.

Exposure to *ethylene glycol* and *diethylene glycol,* products commonly used in auto antifreeze and windshield de-icer, by inhalation, skin absorption, or consumption can also lead to severe acidosis, renal damage, and CNS depression from their metabolites. ADH metabolizes ethylene glycol to glycoaldehyde, which is then metabolized by ALDH to glycolic acid, which is further broken down to glyoxylic and oxalic acids. Both initial reactions produce NADH from NAD, shifting the reduction-oxidation potential to favor lactate production. Lactate with glycolic acid is responsible for most of the damaging, even deadly metabolic acidosis. Initial symptoms resemble those of alcohol intoxication with vomiting predominating. Congestive heart failure and pulmonary edema may occur 12–36 hours after ingestion. Oliguric renal failure from oxalate crystal deposition, with associated flank pain, can be seen 36–72 hours after ingestion. Crystalluria, wide anion gap acidosis, and wide osmolar gap suggest ethylene glycol ingestion.

Isopropyl alcohol is usually ingested as commercial rubbing alcohol. Individuals intoxicated with isopropyl alcohol present similarly to those intoxicated with ethanol with dizziness, confusion, and ataxia. The diagnosis can be made by a positive acetone test of the blood or urine, the absence of a metabolic acidosis, and an isopropyl alcohol level. Table 7.4 summarizes the acute toxicity of the different alcohols.

Guidelines for Treatment

Rational treatment of methanol and ethylene glycol ingestion is based on the understanding that the metabolites, *not* the substances themselves, are toxic. Metabolism of both methanol and ethylene glycol to toxic metabolites is initiated predominantly by ADH, although at slower rates than that for ethanol. Prompt intravenous administration of ethanol, a preferred substrate for ADH (with a 100-fold greater affinity for ADH),

TABLE 7.4. ACUTE TOXICITY OF THE ALCOHOLS

	Ethanol	Methanol	Ethylene Glycol	Isopropanol
CNS depressant	+	+	+	+
Convulsion	+	+	+	+
Odor	+	−	−	+ (acetone)
Blood gases	respiratory acidosis ketoacidosis	severe metabolic acidosis	severe metabolic acidosis	mild metabolic acidosis
Anion gap	+	+ + +	+ + +	+
Osmolar gap	+	+	+	+
Oxalate crystalluria	−	−	+ +	−
Symptom onset	30 min	12–48 h	30 min–12 h	rapid
Lethal dose	5–8 g/kg	1–5 g/kg	1.5 g/kg	3–4 g/kg
Lethal blood level (mg/dL)	350–500	80	200	400
Special treatment	HD[a]	ETOH; HD	ETOH; HCO$_3$, HD	HD; HCO$_3$

[a]HD, hemodialysis

competitively inhibits the oxidation of methanol and ethylene glycol, allowing each to be excreted directly without undergoing metabolism to their toxic byproducts. Ethanol should be administered for peak methanol or ethylene glycol levels greater than 20 mg/dL, for a suspicious anion gap metabolic acidosis, or for any symptomatic patient suspected of ingesting methanol or ethylene glycol.

- The ideal blood ethanol concentration (100–150 mg/dL to saturate available ADH), can be achieved with a loading dose of 0.6 g/kg in D$_5$ W intravenously (or by mouth) over 30–45 minutes, followed by infusion of about 10 g/hour in an adult.
- Ethanol infusion should continue until methanol or ethylene glycol levels fall below 10 mg/dL and formate levels reach less than 1.2 mg/dL, acidosis resolves, a normal anion gap is restored, and CNS symptoms abate.
- Ethanol administration can continue for 3 to 5 days without dialysis or 1 day with dialysis until clinical findings resolve.
- Dialysis is indicated for methanol or ethylene glycol levels greater than 50 mg/dL, severe/resistant acidosis, renal failure, visual symptoms, or congestive heart failure.
- Infusion with 10% ethanol intravenously should continue even if hemodialysis is begun. As dialysis also removes the ethanol, its infusion rate should increase to about 16 g/hour.

Nonbeverage Alcohols

A variety of consumer products containing ethanol, or related alcohols, in concentrations that equal or exceed those found in traditional alcohol beverages (e.g., beer, wine, spirits) is also abused. Typically, nonbeverage alcohol consumers are persons who, for a variety of reasons (such as imprisonment, poverty, or alcoholism) have insufficient access to usual alcohol beverages. Notably, the practice may be as high as 50% among prisoners and has been reported as high as 20% among inpatient alcoholics at Veterans Aministration hospital alcoholism treatment units. However, nonbeverage alcohol abuse is not limited to these groups. In a study of Kentucky high school students, 6% reported having consumed Sterno (solid alcohol cooking fuel). Consumption of weapons fuels containing large concentrations of high-grade alcohol has been reported among military personnel.

The substances most frequently consumed are typically related to health care or cooking, such as mouthwash, aftershave lotions, cough syrups, cold remedies, solid alcohol cooking fuels, flavoring extracts, and cooking sherry.

Alcohol and Polypharmacy

Acute and chronic alcohol use has distinct effects on the metabolism of drugs. Acutely, ethanol inhibits drug metabolism by: (a) interfering with therapeutic actions of drugs by altering their metabolism, or (b) prolonging and enhancing drug effects by competing for common microsomal detoxification pathways. Chronic alcohol consumption accelerates drug metabolism of certain drugs, such as warfarin, diphenylhydantoin, tolbutamide, and isoniazid, and usually produces cross-tolerance. Despite an increased tolerance to a variety of drugs when sober, chronic alcoholic patients exhibit increased susceptibility to the same drugs when intoxicated.

A previous history of alcohol abuse influences prescribing decisions. Even after withdrawal, alcoholics require different doses to achieve therapeutic levels. Half-lives of each of these drugs tend to be 50% shorter in abstaining alcoholics than in nondrinkers. Table 7.5 lists important drug interactions with alcohol.

CONSEQUENCES OF USE

Most of the information about the effects of alcohol on various systems appears in Tables 7.6–7.8. However, a few important disease states receive additional consideration below.

Central Nervous System

The central nervous system is the most susceptible to serious damage by excess alcohol ingestion. Most importantly it is a CNS depressant, which accounts for most of its acute effects. Furthermore, it has chronic effects. 50–70% of detoxified alcoholics exhibit mild cognitive impair-

TABLE 7.5. DRUG INTERACTIONS WITH ALCOHOL

Drug	Interactions with Ethanol
CNS depressants	• Augmentation of effects
Barbiturates	• The lethal dose for barbiturates is nearly 50% lower in the presence of alcohol than when it is used alone • Blood levels of secobarbital or pentobarbital as low as 0.5 mg/100 ml combined with blood alcohol levels of 0.1 g/100 ml can cause death from respiratory depression
Benzodiazepines	• No effect on clearance of long-acting benzodiazepines (chlordiazepoxide and diazepam) • Inhibition of metabolism when they are taken orally, by decreasing first-pass effects
Phenothiazines	• Competitive inhibition of hepatic metabolism with decreased clearance and enhanced sedative effects— impaired coordination, severe, even fatal, respiratory depression, and hypotension
Tricyclic antidepressants (TCAs)	• The ratio of sedative to stimulant activity in the different TCAs determines whether they have synergistic or antagonistic interactions • They can cause hypotension and use should be monitored closely in alcoholic patients
Phenytoin	• Acute alcohol ingestion reduces the clearance of phenytoin • In chronic drinkers, alcohol's enzyme induction enhances phenytoin clearance rates, reduces phenytoin levels, and thus, leaves a patient susceptible to possible seizures
Opiates	• Alcohol and opiates potentiate each other's effects • Users of illicit methadone often use alcohol to experience a "high" that methadone alone does not provide
Warfarin	• Acute alcohol intoxication reduces the metabolism of warfarin, leading to higher blood warfarin levels and resulting in increased anticoagulant effects and risk of hemorrhage • Chronic alcohol abuse can enhance metabolism leading to decreased anticoagulant effects
Acetaminophen	• Acetaminophen hepatotoxicity is enhanced by regular ethanol intake, presumably because of a depletion of hepatic glutathione and the increased production and decreased clearance of its hepatotoxic metabolite • Acetaminophen should be avoided in alcoholic patients
Antimicrobials	• Consumption with metronidazole, cephalosporins, sulfonylureas, chloramphenicol, furazolidine, griseofulvin, quinacrine, or oral hypoglycemics causes flushing, headache, nausea and vomiting, and dizziness—symptoms similar to those triggered by disulfiram
MAO inhibitors	• Tyramine, found in some beers and wines, can act as a pressor amine that releases norepinephrine from tissues, and interacts with monoamine oxidase inhibitors to cause a hypertensive crisis
Miscellaneous	• Additive hypotensive effect in combination with reserpine, methyldopa, hydralazine, guanethidine, ganglionic blockers, nitroglycerin, and peripheral vasodilators

TABLE 7.6. CNS MANIFESTATIONS OF ALCOHOL USE

CNS Manifestations	Proposed Mechanisms/Details
Alcohol Intoxication—maladaptive behavioral changes, slurred speech, lack of coordination, unsteady gait, nystagmus, or flushed face Conditions related to intoxication: Alcoholic coma Pathological intoxication Blackouts	Depressant action on CNS neurons by acting on cell membrane and membrane-associated proteins, which function as receptors and ion channels Biphasic physiologic effects at all levels of the nervous system. Low ethanol concentrations increase electrical excitability (increase frequency and regularity of spontaneous spikes); higher concentrations depress this excitability and finally suppress it completely
Alcohol withdrawal syndrome—tremor, nausea/vomiting, malaise/weakness, autonomic hyperactivity, anxiety, depressed mood/irritability, transient hallucinations/illusions, headache, insomnia, hyperreflexia and convulsions	CNS hyperexcitability—activated sympathetic nervous system; increased urinary and plasma catechol levels
Associated syndromes: **Alcoholic hallucinosis** **Withdrawal seizures** **Delirium tremens**	Hypomagnesemia causing neuromuscular irritability and convulsions, but not DTs Respiratory alkalosis caused by tachypnea and increased respiratory depth
Alcoholic dementia—short- and long-term memory impairment, impaired abstract thinking, impaired judgment, disturbed higher cortical functions (e.g., aphasia, apraxia, agnosia, and personality change)	Mental deterioration due to alcohol's direct toxic effects on the CNS, which persists for at least 3 weeks after alcohol ingestion ceases and excludes all causes of dementia except prolonged, heavy alcohol ingestion
Hepatic encephalopathy	Enlarged protoplasmic astrocytes in the basal ganglia, thalamus, red nucleus, pons, and cerebellum. Laminar necrosis in the cortex, patchy loss of neurons throughout the cortex, basal ganglia and cerebellum, and cavitation of the cortico-subcortical junction and superior pole of the putamen
CNS disorders with nutritional etiology	Primarily a thiamine deficiency
Wernicke's encephalopathy	Chronic lesions involve demyelination, gliosis, and loss of neuropil with relative preservation of neurons Atrophy of the mammary bodies
Korsakoff's psychosis	Lesions of the dorsomedial thalamus
Wernicke-Korsakoff syndrome	Loss of myelinated fibers in the mammary bodies, periaqueductal gray matter, inferior and superior colliculi, fornices, and the 4th ventricle floor near the dorsal motor nuclei of the vagi. Virtually complete tissue necrosis with only some surviving glial elements
Alcoholic cerebellar degeneration	Degeneration of the cerebellar cortex, usually confined to the anterior-superior vermis and lobes

TABLE 7.7. CARDIOVASCULAR MANIFESTATIONS OF ALCOHOL USE

Cardiovascular Manifestations	Proposed Mechanisms/Details
Alcoholic cardiomyopathy—dilation of all cardiac chambers with cardiomegaly, hypocontractility, and increased left ventricular end-diastolic pressure Thiamine-dependent, alcoholic beriberi Thiamine-independent, alcoholic cardiomyopathy	Fatty tissue infiltration—cells laden with lipid droplets, glycogen particles, abnormal pigmentation, lost myofibrils, dilated sarcoplasmic reticulum, dehisced intercalated disks, and abnormal clusters of abnormal mitochondria
Arrhythmias—Sudden Death	Modest amounts of alcohol or its metabolite, acetaldehyde, can alter calcium uptake by cardiac sarcolemma, impair oxidative phosphorylation in mitochondria, disrupt, the alignment of the contractile proteins (actin and myosin), and cause myofibrillar necrosis and patchy interstitial fibrosis, setting the stage for reentrant arrhythmias. Other causes include: nutritional and metabolic abnormalities—vitamin B deficiency, cobalt or lead overload, hypomagnesemia, hypophosphatemia, hypokalemia and respiratory alkalosis or increased circulating catecholamines
"Holiday Heart"	Shortened action potential duration due to alcohol's lipophilic properties. Neither alcohol nor its metabolites appears to affect sinoatrial node activity directly
Coronary artery disease—more susceptible to MI despite patent or minimally stenotic coronary arteries	Increased myocardial glycoprotein and coronary perivascular fibrosis lead to toxic cardiomyopathy-induced MI
Hypertension—systolic changes greater than diastolic	Increased sensitivity to alcohol's blood pressure-elevating effects; increased plasma cortisol
Myocardial depression—decreased cardiac output, it is often compensated by increased heart rate and changes in peripheral vascular resistance	Changes in cardiac lipid and protein metabolism impair mitochondrial function and sodium pump activity; alterations in the composition and properties of myocyte membrane
Ischemic and hemorrhagic strokes	Thrombus formation from alcohol-induced cardiac arrhythmias; hypertension
Changes in regional blood flow Increased—flushing and warmth of skin, increased splanchnic flow Decreased—to limbs and organs, ischemic heart is particularly susceptible	Changes in regional blood flow Vasodilator effects of alcohol Vasoconstrictive effects of alcohol metabolites acetate and acetaldehyde
Protective effects of alcohol (Red wine > beer > distilled spirits)	Dose-related increases in high density lipoprotein (HDL) cholesterols while decreasing the unfavorable low density lipoprotein (LDL) cholesterols; increases prostacyclin metabolite, 6-keto-PGF_1-α, that inhibits platelet function; inverse relation to plasma fibrinogen concentration; increases secretion of plasminogen activator from endothelial cells (exact clinical relevance unclear at this time)

TABLE 7.8 GASTROINTESTINAL AND ENDOCRINE MANIFESTATIONS OF ALCOHOL USE

System and Manifestations	Proposed Mechanisms/Details
Gastrointestinal	
Alcoholic liver disease	
• **Fatty liver**—usually asymptomatic, but occasionally presents as a severe illness with hepatic encephalopathy and jaundice	Centrilobular distribution of hepatocytes filled with fat. It can appear even after casual drinking
• **Alcoholic hepatitis**—liver enlargement, abdominal pain, jaundice, AST is usually higher than the ALT by about 2:1, and the AST is rarely greater than 300	Hepatocyte "ballooning"—hepatocytes swell to three times normal size—secondary to either the toxic metabolic by-product acetaldehyde, peroxidation of hepatic lipids, or direct stimulation of connective tissue deposition. It is a prelude to frank cell necrosis
• **Alcoholic cirrhosis**—destruction of normal hepatic architecture with regenerative nodules to replace lost hepatocytes. Increased resistance to microcirculation leads to portal hypertension	Central hyaline sclerosis—hepatocytes around the central vein are obliterated by extensive fibrous tissue. Alcohol causes lipocytes to transform and increases connective tissue deposition
Pancreatitis—abdominal pain during attacks precipitated by ingestion of either alcohol or large amounts of fat	High protein content of the basal pancreatic secretions predisposes to formation of proteinaceous plugs in pancreatic ducts, which may later calcify. Obstruction leads to local retention of pancreatic secretions, followed by autodigestion and inflammation
Gastritis—acute, hemorrhagic, and chronic (hyperemic gastric mucosa with patchy erosions and petechiae)	Stimulation of gastric acid secretion; delay in gastric emptying; disruption of the tight junctions between epithelial cells, allowing back diffusion of H^+ ions and malnutrition
Malabsorption (general and vitamin B12)	Intestinal changes; inadequate food intake
Diarrhea	Inhibition of the Na^+/K^+ ATPase causing decrease in active absorption of electrolytes and passive transport of water
Endocrine disturbances	Combination of alcoholism and liver disease alters ratio of androgens to estrogens (affects mostly males):
Hypogonadism—reduced libido, testicular atrophy, oligospermia, and reduced growth of secondary sexual hair	*Direct alcohol effects:* Supression of testosterone production; suppression of the hypothalamic-pituitary-gonadal axis; inhbition of the conversion of vitamin A to its active aldehyde form; increase in aromatase, which converts androgens to estrogens.
Feminization—gynecomastia and female distribution of body hair and body fat.	*Intrinsic liver damage:* Failure to clear estrogens

ment. Although abstinence leads to partial recovery within the first few weeks, about 10% of alcoholics have persistent cognitive dysfunction ranging from selective amnesia to dementia. Diverse clinical effects on the nervous system reflect alcohol's diverse mechanisms: direct toxic effects on nerve cells, withdrawal of alcohol after chronic intoxication, and secondary nutritional deficiencies, which affect the central and/or peripheral nervous systems (Table 7.6).

Alcohol Intoxication

Alcohol intoxication is characterized by recent ingestion of alcohol leading to behavioral changes, such as disinhibited sexual/aggressive impulses, labile mood, impaired judgment and social/occupational dysfunction, and at least one of the following five signs: slurred speech, reduced coordination, unsteady gait, nystagmus, or flushed face. An array of subjective experiences accompanies intoxication ranging from exhilaration, excitement, and loquacity to irritability, combativeness, drowsiness, stupor, and coma. Motor activities, including standing posture, speech control, and eye saccades become slow, muddled, less accurate, less effective, and more random during intoxication. Cognitive functions like learning, remembering, thinking, and judgment are also impaired.

Pathological (Idiosyncratic) Intoxication

In a small population of people, often with no history of alcoholism or psychiatric/neurological disease, small amounts of alcohol have extreme, excitatory effects, characterized by outbursts of blind fury, combativeness, and destructive behavior. Without sedation these outbursts are difficult to subdue. They usually end with spontaneous deep sleep. On awakening, patients have no memory of the outburst. This anecdotally-defined disorder must be distinguished from sociopathic rage and the occasional violent outbursts involved in temporal lobe epilepsy.

Blackouts

Blackouts are transient episodes of amnesia that occur during periods of intoxication, even when bystanders detect no altered state of consciousness. This amnesia represents intoxication to a degree that prevents memory formation.

Alcohol Withdrawal Syndromes

After a period of sustained, excessive alcohol consumption, discontinuation or a decrease in alcohol intake will produce withdrawal symptoms including tremors, hallucinations, seizures, and delirium. Uncomplicated alcohol withdrawal begins with a coarse tremor of the hands, tongue, or

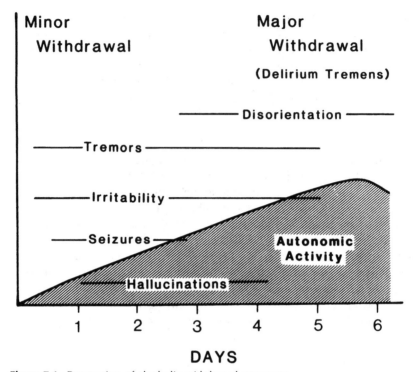

Figure 7.1. Progression of alcoholic withdrawal symptoms.

eyelids, and then proceeds to any of the following: nausea/vomiting, malaise/weakness, autonomic hyperactivity (tachycardia, sweating, elevated blood pressure), anxiety, depressed mood/irritability, transient hallucinations or illusions, headache, and insomnia (Figure 7.1 outlines the time course for withdrawal symptoms). Withdrawal carries a significant mortality and is often initiated by an illness, such as trauma, infection, pancreatitis, gastritis, or pneumonia. Illness interferes with the continued alcohol intake. This previous intake had prevented the alcohol withdrawal symptoms that become apparent upon hospitalization.

Alcoholic Hallucinosis

About 25% of patients with alcohol withdrawal symptoms experience some disordered sense of perception, such as "bad dreams" that are difficult to differentiate from reality, illusions, and visual and/or auditory hallucinations. Alcohol hallucinosis involves persistent hallucinations that develop about 48 hours after cessation or reduction of heavy alcohol ingestion in someone who has an alcohol use disorder.

Auditory hallucinations, which predominate, are characterized by either voices that are reproachful, threatening, or maligning, or unstructured sounds, like low-pitched humming, chants, buzzing, ringing, shots, and clicks. These hallucinations commonly begin the first night after the patient stops drinking and can continue intermittently and unceasingly for up to 6 days. A small proportion of these patients develop chronic auditory hallucinosis with symptoms resembling schizophrenia, including disjointed paranoid delusions, prominent ideas of reference and influence, illogical and vague thinking, and tangential associations.

Withdrawal Seizures ("Rum Fits")

Over 90% of withdrawal seizures occur within 6 to 48 hours after patients take their last drink following prolonged drinking bouts. Peak incidence occurs after 12 and 24 hours. About 3% of the cases develop status epilepticus. In about 28% of patients, the seizures precede delirium. "Rum fits" are distinct from delirium and other pre-existing seizure disorders that alcohol consumption can exacerbate or trigger. Focal seizures usually indicate a focal neurologic or systemic disease, such as head trauma, meningitis, or metabolic abnormalities, in addition to alcohol withdrawal.

Delirium Tremens (DTs):

The most serious alcohol withdrawal syndrome, the DTs, is characterized by autonomic hyperactivity—fever, tachycardia, profuse sweating, dilated pupils, flushing, nausea, confusion, disorientation, altered level of consciousness, disorganized thinking, agitation, delusions, hallucinations, tremors, and sleeplessness. These symptoms and delirium (a syndrome of growing confusion, disordered perception, and psychomotor and autonomic nervous system overactivity) usually peak 2 to 3 days after abstinence. In other cases, delirium appears after a known alcoholic begins to recover from other withdrawal symptoms (hallucinosis, seizures). Up to 10% of patients withdrawing from alcohol experience DTs.

Although the DTs usually resolve in 3–5 days, it is fatal in 5% of cases. Most cases of the DTs are benign and short-lived but can recur with varying degrees of severity amid intervals of complete lucidity over several days to weeks. In most fatal cases there may be concurrent infection, injury, hyperthermia, or peripheral circulatory collapse. A treatment protocol is outlined in Table 7.9.

Hepatic Encephalopathy

Hepatic encephalopathy develops in many alcoholics with liver disease and is characterized by altered sensorium, frontal release signs, asterixis, hyperreflexia, extensor plantar responses, and occasionally, seizures. While some patients progress from stupor to coma and death, others recover completely. Incomplete recovery causes progression of symp-

---

TABLE 7.9. SUGGESTED TREATMENT PROTOCOL FOR SEVERE DELIRIUM TREMENS

---

1. Make the diagnosis of delirium tremens based on the patient's history and a physical examination. Perform a lumbar puncture in febrile patients.
2. Search for infections, or other sequelae of alcohol abuse (such as gastrointestinal bleeding or pancreatitis) and treat as indicated.
3. Sedate the patient with 5–10 mg diazepam i.v. every 5 minutes until the patient is awake but calm. Use lorazepam 1–2 mg i.v. in place of diazepam in liver-impaired or elderly patients. Reduce the doses of benzodiazepines as the patient recovers
4. Administer 100 mg of thiamine p.o., i.v., or i.m. Give multivitamins daily.
5. Estimate the patient's fluid deficit and replace with normal saline if the serum sodium concentration is more than 120 mEq/L. If the serum sodium concentration is less than 120 mEq/L, raise the serum sodium to 125 mEq/L with 3% or 5% saline at a rate of 2 mEq/L/hr, then use normal saline. Monitor for fluid overload.
6. Replace potassium, magnesium, and phosphorus if the serum levels are low. Potassium may be given in the intravenous fluids at a rate of 20 mEq/hr. Give magnesium sulfate, 1 g i.v. or i.m. every 6–12 hours for 48 hours or give magnesium oxide. 250–500 mg p.o. q.i.d. for 48 hours. Give doses of 12–18 mM potassium phosphate in the intravenous fluids every 8 hours.
7. Load with Dilantin, 15 mg/kg, only if the patient has an untreated, non-alcohol-related seizure disorder, a history of previous withdrawal seizures, or multiple seizures during the current admission.
8. Consider giving a beta-blocker, p.o. or i.v. if the patient's systolic blood pressure is more than 180 mm Hg or the heart rate is more than 120/min.
9. Keep the patient in a quiet room. Restrain in bed if necessary, but avoid if possible since this may increase feelings of paranoia and agitation.
10. Provide frequent monitoring of the patient's status by a nurse and/or physician.

---

toms, including tremors, choreoathetosis, dysarthria, ataxia, and dementia.

Nutritional Deficiencies and CNS Pathology

Nutritional deficiencies most often occur when alcohol displaces food from the diet or when demands for B vitamins (especially thiamine) increase to handle alcohol metabolism. Alcoholics also exhibit a decreased capacity to absorb thiamine and folic acid, and have impaired pancreatic function, which hampers fat digestion. How thiamine deficiency causes brain lesions remains unclear.

Wernicke's Encephalopathy

General mental disturbances (global confusion, apathy, and drowsiness, which can progress to stupor and coma), acute or subacute onset of ophthalmoplegia (nystagmus, lateral rectus and conjugate gaze palsies), and gait ataxia characterize Wernicke's encephalopathy. In the almost always present global confusion state, the patient cannot sustain physical or mental activity, appears disoriented, inattentive, unable to concentrate, and suffers from deranged perceptions and memory.

Korsakoff's Psychosis

This mental disorder is most often associated with two abnormalities: retrograde and anterograde amnesia. Although confabulation may or may not be present, Korsakoff's patients tend to have limited insight into their own disability and may be apathetic to persons/events around them.

Wernicke-Korsakoff Syndrome (WKS)

This syndrome combines symptoms of both Wernicke's encephalopathy and Korsakoff's psychosis, as a result of thiamine deficiency. Although WKS can present with any of the abnormalities discussed above, global confusion, retrograde amnesia, and anterograde amnesia are nearly always present. Other common abnormalities include: nystagmus (horizontal and vertical), ataxia (ranging in severity from inability to stand or walk without support to a wide-based stance and slow, short-stepped, unsteady gait), mild peripheral neuropathy, and impaired vestibular function.

Although recovery is possible, the mortality rate among patients with WKS reaches 20% in early stages and 17% in chronic stages. The most common causes of death include decompensated liver disease or infection (pneumonia, pulmonary tuberculosis, pancreatitis, bacterial meningitis, or sepsis). Thiamine administration can begin to restore normal ocular movements within hours to days, with complete recovery in several weeks. Recovery from ataxia takes longer and is rarely complete. More than half of the WKS patients continue to walk with a slow, shuffling, wide-based gait and remain unable to tandem walk. In only 15% of WKS patients do the apathy and global confusion clear completely in about 2 weeks. Less than 20% of WKS patients completely regain their anterograde and retrograde memories.

Cardiovascular Manifestations (Table 7.7)

Alcoholic Cardiomyopathy

Chronic alcohol abuse produces two types of cardiomyopathy: (*a*) thiamine-dependent, alcoholic beriberi, and (*b*) thiamine-independent, alcoholic cardiomyopathy. Alcoholic cardiomyopathy occurs most often in men and in the Black population. Symptoms of the disease usually occur after 10 years of alcohol abuse. The most common, initial clinical presentation is shortness of breath, often out of proportion to the signs of heart failure. Patients may also complain of cough, especially at night, and describe the onset of an unabating "respiratory" illness as "flu-like"—without any respiratory infection. As the disease progresses, patients experience easy fatigability and complain of chest pain on exertion. In these cases they may have subendocardial myocardial ischemia. Congestive failure produces pulmonary congestion, cardiac arrhythmias, systemic edema, anorexia, and abdominal discomfort.

Hypertension

Alcohol use elevates systemic blood pressure independent of age, body weight, race, or cigarette smoking. There is a dose-dependent effect, altering systolic pressures more than diastolic. Even one to two drinks per day can elevate blood pressure, especially in those with underlying essential hypertension.

Coronary Artery Disease (CAD)

Knowledge about alcohol's effect on CAD is evolving, though it seems that the effect is dose-dependent. At low to moderate doses, alcohol has a protective benefit in terms of CAD. Alcohol contained in red wine exerts its "protective" effects against coronary artery atherosclerosis by increasing the favorable high-density lipoprotein (HDL) cholesterol while decreasing the unfavorable low-density lipoprotein (LDL) cholesterols (Table 7.7). However, at high doses, alcoholics are *more* susceptible to myocardial infarction (MI) despite patent or minimally stenotic coronary arteries.

Holiday Heart

Intermittent, disturbed cardiac rhythms and/or conductance usually occur after binge drinking in patients without clinical evidence of heart disease. These arrhythmias are primarily atrial fibrillation (AF), but also include atrial flutter, atrial tachycardia, multiple atrial premature contractions (APCs) or premature ventricular contractions (PVCs), junctional tachycardia, and ventricular tachycardia. This "holiday heart syndrome" can indicate early cardiomyopathy. While usually resolving with abstinence and having no residual effects, occasionally very rapid arrhythmias can cause sudden death.

Alcohol abuse and alcoholic cardiomyopathy are also on the differential diagnosis of paroxysmal atrial fibrillation. About one-third of patients presenting with new-onset AF have no recognizable heart disease, but about 30% of this group consume alcohol frequently.

Gastrointestinal Manifestations (Table 7.8)

Alcoholic Liver Disease

The spectrum of alcoholic liver disease includes fatty liver, alcoholic hepatitis, and alcoholic cirrhosis. While fatty liver is usually asymptomatic, hepatitis and cirrhosis can produce dire consequences. Alcoholic cirrhosis is the leading cause of death related to alcohol abuse and the eighth leading cause of death overall in the United States. Nevertheless, only 15–30% of heavy drinkers develop significant alcoholic liver disease.

The average male alcoholic consumes 150–200 grams of ethanol (10–13 drinks/day) for 10–20 years before onset of hepatitis or cirrhosis. Women seem more susceptible to alcoholic liver disease than men. The average woman with severe alcoholic liver disease has consumed 120–160 grams of ethanol (8–10 drinks/day) for 12–15 years by the time of diagnosis. Most patients with alcoholic hepatitis will progress to cirrhosis if they continue to drink, but it is not known whether alcoholic cirrhosis is *always* preceded by alcoholic hepatitis. Hepatic tenderness may indicate coexisting hepatitis or fatty liver. However, the liver then becomes hard, irregular, and nontender. Advanced cirrhosis classically produces a shrunken, fibrotic liver. Cirrhosis without acute hepatitis does not produce many symptoms until its late stages.

Severe alcoholic liver disease produces clinical problems secondary to hepatitis and cirrhosis, which include ascites, portal hypertension, bleeding esophageal varices, spontaneous bacterial peritonitis, functional renal failure, hepatic encephalopathy, hepatocellular carcinoma, hypersplenism, anemia, thrombocytopenia, and a variety of coagulopathies. In a study of the natural history of alcoholism, cirrhotic patients without ascites, jaundice, or bleeding had a 5-year survival rate of 89.9% if they abstained and 68.2% if they continued drinking. Patients with any of these complications on entry into the study did much worse, even those who ceased drinking had only a 60% 5-year survival rate.

Pancreatitis

Alcohol is the major cause of chronic, calcifying pancreatitis in temperate climates where up to 75% of patients with chronic pancreatitis have coincident alcoholism. To produce chronic pancreatitis, excessive consumption of alcohol on the order of 150–175 grams (equivalent to 10–15 drinks/day) for more than 6 years is generally required, though individual susceptibility varies widely.

Abdominal pain is the classic symptom of alcoholic pancreatitis. This pain is often epigastric, radiating to the back, unrelieved by antacids, and lasts for days (by comparison biliary pain lasts for only hours). Advanced disease can present with additional signs and symptoms, including steatorrhea and weight loss secondary to exocrine pancreatic insufficiency, and diabetes mellitus due to destruction of pancreatic islets.

TABLE 7.10. DIAGNOSTIC SIGNS OF ALCOHOL USE AND ABUSE

Physical Signs	Psychological Characteristics
Painful and painless liver enlargement	Clouded mental status
Severe, constant upper abdominal pain and tenderness radiating to the back	Preoccupation with alcohol
	Self-deception
Tremulousness	Guilt
Nausea	Anxiety
Diaphoresis	Depression
Weakness and diminished sensation in the feet and legs	
Heart murmurs and extra heart sounds	**Signs of Loss of Control**
Early arcus senilis (the fatty ring-like opacity of the cornea)	Complaints of increased upheaval in relationships
Acne rosacea (red nose)	Motor vehicle violations/accidents
Palmar erythema (red palms)	Absenteeism from work
Dupuytren's contractures	Trouble keeping appointments at work or with friends to the point of losing jobs, friends, and even family support
Telangiectasias	
Gynecomastia	
Asterixis	Injuries from trauma
Alcoholic ketoacidosis	Aggressive, violent outbursts
CNS depression ! respiratory alkalosis	
Protracted vomiting ! metabolic acidosis	
Evidence of dehydration (tachycardia, hypotension, dry mucous membranes, sunken eyeballs, poor skin turgor)	

CLINICAL PRESENTATION

Diagnostic Physical Signs

Clues to alcohol abuse can be found on physical examination and are summarized in Table 7.10.

Laboratory Tests

While no single laboratory test can adequately screen for alcoholism in the general population, clinicians often use a number of reliable tests to corroborate their clinical suspicions of alcoholism. Most commonly, serum markers, such as γ-glutamyl transpeptidase (GGT), mean corpuscular volume (MCV), liver enzymes, and high-density lipoproteins (HDL), are elevated. Alcoholics can also have elevated serum concentrations of uric acid, urea, and triglycerides.

Mean Corpuscular Volume (MCV)

MCV is the ratio of hematocrit to red cell count. An increased MCV (96–99) can be associated with ethanol's direct toxic effects and indirect alcohol-induced megaloblastic changes, such as nutritional deficiencies of B-12 or folic acid (other non-alcohol-related causes of elevated MCV include hypothyroidism, nonalcoholic liver disease, reticulocytosis, hematological malignancies, drugs, smoking, and aging). MCV can also be elevated in patients—alcoholic or not—with liver disease. The duration of macrocytosis in abstaining alcoholics is also prolonged and variable—high MCV can persist for several months despite abstinence and folate replacement.

Liver Enzymes

GGT

GGT is found in the liver, biliary tract, pancreas, and kidneys, and is an enzyme primarily involved in the hydrolysis of γ-glutamyl peptides, especially in glutathione metabolism. Most studies show that chronic doses of ethanol increase serum GGT, especially in alcohol drinkers with liver disease. Monitoring GGT during treatment may aid in detecting a relapse (denoted by a rise in serum GGT above baseline). Other microsomal-inducing agents (anticonvulsants, anticoagulants, and oral contraceptives) and other medical conditions (nonalcoholic liver or biliary tract diseases, hyperlipidemia, and hyperthyroidism) also increase serum GGT.

Transaminases

Aspartate amino or serum glutamic-oxaloacetic transferase (AST or SGOT) and alanine amino or serum glutamic-pyruvic transaminase (ALT or SGPT) are used as routine liver function screening tests. Hepatocellular injury increases the serum levels of the transaminases by altering cell membrane permeability. Elevation of AST and ALT in alcoholics tends to be associated with the severity of their liver disease. However, a ratio of AST:ALT greater than 2 can differentiate alcoholic liver disease from other, nonalcoholic liver disease (which produces an AST:ALT ratio less than 1) except advanced chronic viral hepatitis (with an AST:ALT ratio greater than 1).

Alkaline Phosphatase (AP)

Alkaline phosphatase (AP) catalyzes the hydrolysis of phosphate esters at optimal alkaline conditions and is found in liver, bone, intestine, placenta, kidney, and leukocytes. Elevated AP can result from alcoholism as well as cholestasis, cholangitis, infiltrative liver diseases, cirrhosis, hepatomas, and metastatic neoplasms. Although this makes AP an insensitive alcoholism marker, the ratio of serum GGT:AP has become useful in distinguishing alcoholic from nonalcoholic liver disease: a ratio greater than 1.4 suggests alcoholic liver disease while a GGT:AP ratio greater than 3.5 is considered diagnostic for this problem.

HDL

HDL has several roles in the body: it transports excess cholesterol from various tissues to the liver; it may play a protective role against atherosclerosis; and levels of it tend to increase with moderate ethanol consumption. However, many other factors can contribute to elevated HDL levels, including genetics, diet, exercise, and medications (bile acid-binding resins, estrogens, nicotinic acid, and gemfibrozil). The high variability of serum HDL cholesterol in the normal population and the complexity of alcohol's effects on HDL metabolism limit its use as a marker for alcohol consumption. Unlike the other markers, HDL is most sensitive in alcoholics without liver disease.

TREATMENT

Treatment of alcohol use disorders consists of managing the medical consequences of alcohol abuse, developing a treatment plan, monitoring recovery, clinically assessing the person and parameters of the problem constantly, and evaluating the treatment outcome. Motivating the patient to commit to treatment represents the clinician's first task. Flexibility in strategies and approaches is key since different types of interventions are more or less effective depending on the stage of a person's alcoholism and commitment to quitting. Perhaps the most daunting task for the physician, though, is the long-term management of an alcoholic who may need several rounds of detoxification/rehabilitation before finally achieving long-lasting sobriety.

Acute Intoxication

The treatment of acute alcohol intoxication combines support of vital functions, maintenance of physiologic homeostasis, and prevention of behavioral problems. All patients with suspected alcohol use should *always* receive thiamine and other B vitamins to prevent the development of Wernicke-Korsakoff syndrome.

Two sequelae of acute intoxication deserve special attention.

Coma

Alcoholic coma is treated like other drug-related comas: the patient's airway should be protected, toxicological screening of serum and urine performed, and meticulous supportive care given. Thiamine (100 mg intravenously) for prophylaxis against Wernicke's encephalopathy, and then 50 ml of 50% dextrose should be immediately administered intravenously (NOTE: Thiamine must be given first and dextrose second because dextrose alone further depletes the body's stores of thiamine.) Naloxone 0.4–2.0 mg should be given because of the possibility of concomitant opiate use, which would potentiate alcohol-induced CNS depression.

Behavioral Problems

The belligerent drinker has a high potential for violence. Behavioral measures to calm the patient include providing food and a quiet, comfortable environment, conducting the interview in a polite, nonthreatening manner, and having security guards present. Medications, such as lorazepam 1–2 mg orally and haloperidol 5 mg orally, can effectively supplement behavioral methods. If the patient becomes violent, then haloperidol can be administered intramuscularly and a second dose given as needed.

Alcohol Withdrawal Syndromes

The alcohol withdrawal syndrome must be promptly recognized and treated to provide relief from anxiety and hallucinations and, more importantly, to prevent withdrawal seizures or DTs. Alcohol withdrawal evolves over time, forming a continuum of severity from earlier, mild symptoms to the later, and more severe, physiologic consequences of delirium tremens (Figure 7.1). A previous history of withdrawal symptoms or DTs should alert the physician that they may happen again. Alcohol drinkers frequently present with volume depletion, acidosis, and a number of electrolyte disturbances (including hypomagnesemia, hypophosphatemia, and hypokalemia) which also need immediate attention.

A variety of pharmacological agents have been used to treat alcohol withdrawal. These agents include alcohol itself, adrenergic blocking agents, chlorate derivatives, paraldehyde, benzodiazepines, barbiturates, antihistamines, neuroleptics, antidepressants, lithium, and calcium channel blockers. Only the more commonly used medications are discussed here.

Benzodiazepines

Benzodiazepines are the cornerstone of withdrawal therapy in the United States. They have anticonvulsant effects and low toxicity, and attenuate the signs and symptoms of withdrawal. Furthermore, they have minimal respiratory and cardiac depression in comparison with other CNS depressants, and they can be given parenterally to an uncooperative patient.

Diazepam (Valium), chlordiazepoxide (Librium), lorazepam (Ativan), oxazepam (Serax), and clorazepate (Tranxene) are the benzodiazepines used most frequently in the treatment of alcohol withdrawal. Guidelines for their use appear in Table 7.11. Recent studies have suggested that benzodiazepines are optimally effective when the dose is titrated according to a withdrawal severity scale. The Clinical Institute

TABLE 7.11. GUIDELINES FOR USE OF BENZODIAZEPINES IN ALCOHOL WITHDRAWAL

	Dose[a]	Interval	Half-Life[b]	Comments
Diazepam (Valium)	5–20 mg, p.o. or i.v.	q 6h	30–60 hours	Lower doses required in liver failure
Chlordiazepoxide (Librium)	25–100 mg p.o. or i.v.	q 6h	5–15 hours	Effective half-life is 50–100 hours because of active metabolites
Lorazepam (Ativan)	1–2 mg p.o. i.v. or i.m.	q 4 h	10–20 hours	Recommended in liver failure and for the elderly
Oxazepam (Serax)	15–30 mg p.o.	q 4h	5–10 hours	Same as above
Clorazepate (Tranxene)	30 mg p.o.	q 12h	50–80 hours	May be less euphorogenic

[a]Doses should be reduced by approximately 25–50% each succeeding day.
[b]Half-life will be longer in hepatic failure.

Withdrawal Assessment for Alcohol—Revised (CIWA-Ar) is a highly accurate screening test for the need to treat withdrawal with benzodiazepines. An individual with a score of less than 10 on the CIWA-Ar may be adequately treated with supportive care alone. Individuals with scores higher than 10 require pharmacological interventions and should be reassessed every two hours (Figure 7.2).

No clear evidence supports the use of one benzodiazepine over another. However, lorazepam (Ativan) has an appealing profile: (*a*) good bioavailability in oral, intramuscular, and intravenous forms; (*b*) rapid and complete absorption intramuscularly in agitated patients without intravenous access; (*c*) intermediate half-life (14 ± 5 hours), an important consideration for convenience of administration *and* to avoid oversedation; (*d*) a much smaller increase in its half-life in patients with cirrhosis or liver failure than other benzodiazepines; and (*e*) relatively less abuse potential than many other benzodiazepines, e.g., diazepam.

Neuroleptics

Although haloperidol *may* be used with caution, the use of other neuroleptics is generally not recommended since they may lower the seizure threshold. Haloperidol is favored because it has less propensity to lower the seizure threshold, is more potent than chlorpromazine, and has little effect on myocardial function or respiratory drive. Combinations of a benzodiazepine and haloperidol can be used in difficult cases.

Anticonvulsants

Although 10 to 25% of withdrawing alcoholics will have a generalized grand mal seizure within the first 48 hours of alcohol withdrawal, single

Patient _____   Date I __ I __ I __ I   Time _____ : _____
                      y   m   d   (24 hour clock, midnight = 00:00)

Pulse or heart rate, taken for one minute: _____   Blood pressure: _____/_____

NAUSEA AND VOMITING—As "Do you feel sick to your stomach? Have you vomited?" Observation.
0 no nausea and no vomiting
1 mild nausea with no vomiting
2
3
4 intermittent nausea with dry heaves
5
6
7 constant nausea, frequent dry heaves and vomiting

TREMOR—Arms extended and fingers spread apart. Observation.
0 no tremor
1 not visible, but can be felt fingertip to fingertip
2
3
4 moderate, with patient's arms extended
5
6
7 severe, even with arms not extended

PAROXYSMAL SWEATS—Observation.
0 no sweat visible
1 barely perceptible sweating, palms moist
2
3
4 beads of sweat obvious on forehead
5
6
7 drenching sweats

ANXIETY—Ask "Do you feel nervous?" Observation.
0 no anxiety, at ease
1 mildly anxious
2
3
4 moderately anxious, or guarded, so anxiety is inferred
5
6
7 equivalent to acute panic states as seen in severe delirium or acute schizophrenic reactions

TACTILE DISTURBANCES—Ask "Have you any itching, pins and needles senations, any burning, any numbness or do you feel bugs crawling on or under your skin?" Observation.
0 none
1 very mild itching, pins and needles, burning or numbness
2 mild itching, pins and needles, burning or numbness
3 moderate itching, pins and needles, burning or numbness
4 moderately severe hallucinations
5 severe hallucinations
6 extremely severe hallucinations
7 continuous hallucinations

AUDITORY DISTURBANCES—Ask "Are you more aware of sounds around you? Are they harsh? Do they frighten you? Are you hearing anything that is disturbing to you? Are you hearing things you know are not there?" Observation.
0 not present
1 very mild harshness or ability to frighten
2 mild harshness or ability to frighten
3 moderate harshness or ability to frighten
4 moderately severe hallucinations
5 severe hallucinations
6 extremely severe hallucinations
7 continuous hallucinations

VISUAL DISTURBANCES—Ask "Does the light appear to be too bright? Is its colour different? Does it hurt your eyes? Are you seeing anything that is disturbing to you? Are you seeing things you know are not there?" Observation.
0 not present
1 very mild sensitivity
2 mild sensitivity
3 moderate sensitivity
4 moderately severe hallucinations
5 severe hallucinations
6 extremely severe hallucinations
7 continuous hallucinations

(continued on next page)

AGITATION—Observation.
0 normal activity
1 somewhat more than normal activity
2
3
4 moderately fidgety and restless
5
6
7 paces back and forth during most of the interview, or constantly thrashes about

HEADACHE, FULLNESS IN HEAD—Ask "Does your head feel different? Does it feel like there is a band around your head?" Do not rate for dizziness or lightheadedness. Otherwise, rate severity.
0 not present
1 very mild
2 mild
3 moderate
4 moderately severe
5 severe
6 very severe
7 extremely severe

ORIENTATION AND CLOUDING OF SENSORIUM—Ask "What day is this? Where are you? Who am I?"
0 oriented and can do serial additions
1 cannot do serial additions or is uncertain about date
2 disoriented for date by no more than 2 calendar days
3 disoriented for date by more than 2 calendar days
4 disoriented for place and/or person

Total CIWA-A Score _____
Rater's Initials _____
Maximum Possible Score 67

Figure 7.2. Clinical Institute Withdrawal Assessment for Alcohol—Revised (CIWA-Ar) scale and interpretation. An individual with a score of less than 10 on the CIWA-Ar may be adequately treated with support care alone. Individuals with scores higher than 10 require pharmacological intervention and should be reassessed every 2 hours.

seizures do not require chronic anticonvulsant treatment. For patients with multiple seizures during withdrawal, or who have a chronic seizure disorder, phenytoin is a useful adjunctive therapy to typical benzodiazepine therapy.

Other Medications

Beta blockers such as propranolol and atenolol and the α^2-adrenergic agonist clonidine can alleviate mild to moderate withdrawal symptoms by reducing the adrenergic signs of withdrawal—tachycardia, elevated blood pressure, and tremor. They have no effect on the duration of delirium. They should be considered as *adjunctive therapy* in benzodiazepine treatment of mild to moderate alcohol withdrawal.

In the future, clonidine may prove itself an effective alternative to benzodiazepines. Recent studies have found clonidine at least as effective

TABLE 7.12. GUIDELINES FOR HOSPITALIZATION FOR DETOXIFICATION

The presence of a medical or surgical condition requiring treatment

Hepatic decompensation
Infection
Dehydration
Malnutrition
Cardiovascular collapse
Cardiac arrhythmias
Trauma
Hallucinations
Tachycardia > 100/min
Severe tremor
Extreme agitation
History of severe alcohol withdrawal symptoms
Fever >38.5°C
Wernicke's encephalopathy
Confusion or delirium
Recent history of head injury with loss of consciousness
Social isolation

as chlordiazepoxide in improving the vital signs and subjective complaints of alcohol withdrawal. Advantages of clonidine over benzodiazepines include a greatly diminished risk of oversedation or dependency and lower abuse potential that makes it an ideal agent in the outpatient treatment of mild alcohol withdrawal.

Delirium Tremens

As described previously, DTs usually occur 48–72 hours after abstinence, and a comprehensive treatment protocol is detailed in Table 7.9.

Admission Guidelines and Disposition

While patients with mild alcohol withdrawal can be observed in the emergency room, patients with signs of major withdrawal (fever, hallucinations, confusion, extreme agitation) and/or new seizure activity require hospital admission. Typical guidelines for hospitalization appear in Table 7.12.

LONG-TERM MANAGEMENT OF THE RECOVERING ALCOHOLIC

The goals of long-term therapy for alcohol dependence are twofold: maintenance of sobriety and promotion of the healing of the individual and the family by psychological and social interventions. The two goals are intertwined since abstinence will occur more often if the emotional, social, and familial consequences of the illness are addressed.

Alcoholics Anonymous (AA) is the traditional foundation of recovery for many alcoholics. AA is a fellowship of recovering and recovered alcoholics who run discussion sessions and support groups for other recovering and active alcoholics. Few studies have assessed the actual, long-term efficacy of AA, but attendance at AA meetings has a good correlation with abstinence. AA is especially effective because it undermines the denial, which is part of the psychopathology of alcoholism. In many cities, a patient can attend an AA meeting at virtually any hour of the day, 7 days a week. Its sponsor program, in which a recovered alcoholic is paired with a newly recovering one, allows patients to seek help 24 hours a day to maintain sobriety. All physicians, regardless of specialty, should offer their alcoholic patients information on how and where to attend an AA meeting.

The clinician must remain aware of dysfunctional family dynamics and the denial, defensiveness, and hostility often present in family members. Families of alcoholics can seek education and support in organizations such as Al-Anon, Alateen, and Adult Children of Alcoholics (ACOA). These organizations have chapters in virtually every city in the United States.

For some patients, disulfiram (Antabuse) can help maintain abstinence by producing a deterrence effect. The drug inhibits acetaldehyde dehydrogenase, thereby causing an accumulation of the toxic metabolite acetaldehyde if alcohol is consumed in its presence. Acetaldehyde produces unpleasant symptoms, such as tachycardia, flushing of skin, dyspnea, nausea, and vomiting. Avoidance of the symptoms necessitates avoidance of alcohol, provided the patient complies with the treatment. The drawbacks of the medication include: dependence on patient compliance; the disulfiram reaction can occur with even the small amounts of alcohol found in mouthwashes or in topical application of alcohol in shaving lotions; and, finally, the drug is contraindicated in liver disease.

FURTHER READING

Adlaf EM, Smart RG, Tan SH. Ethnicity and drug use: a critical look. Int J Addict 1989;24:1–18.

Blum K, Payne TE. Alcohol and the Addictive Brain. New York: Free Press, 1991.

Brody GH, Forehand R. Prospective associations among family form, family processes and adolescents' alcohol and drug use. Behav Res Ther 1993; 31:587–593.

Charness ME. Brain lesions in alcoholics. Alcoholism (NY) 1993;17:2–11.

Ettinger PO, Wu CF, De La Cruz C Jr, et al. Arrhythmias and the holiday heart: alcohol-associated cardiac rhythm disorders. Am Heart J 1978;95:555–562.

Gupta KL. Alcoholism in the elderly. Postgrad Med 1993;93:203–206.

Halvorson MR, Campbell JL, Sprague G, et al. Comparative evaluation of the clinical utility of three markers of ethanol intake: the effect of gender. Alcohol Clin Exp Res 1993; 17:225–229.

Lieber CS. Medical and Nutritional Complications of Alcoholism—Mechanisms and Management. New York: Plenum, 1992.

Stoudemire A, Fogel B, eds. Alcohol and drug abuse in the medical setting. Psychiatric Care of the Medical Patient. New York: Oxford University Press 1993;139–153.

Mc Micken DB. Alcohol withdrawal syndromes. Emerg Med Clin North Am 1990;8:805–819.

Johnson B, Clark W. Alcoholism: a challenging physician-patient encounter. J Gen Intern Med 1989;4:445–452.

US Preventive Services Task Force. Guide to Clinical Preventive Services. An Assessment of the Effectiveness of 169 Interventions. Baltimore: Williams & Wilkins, 1989.

Chapter 8

Nicotine and Cigarette Smoking

Manish Bhandari and Shelley L. Sylvester with Nancy A. Rigotti

Although the use of tobacco predates the arrival of Columbus in the New World, cigarette smoking is largely a 20th century phenomenon. By 1918, cigarette consumption had surpassed all other forms of tobacco use, including chewing tobacco, cigars, pipes, and snuff. Social acceptance, technical advances in production leading to reduced cost, widespread advertising, government incentives to tobacco farmers (to maintain tax revenues from cigarettes), and the addictive character of nicotine account for the increase in the use of cigarettes. In 1962, an estimated 41% of the adult population of the United States smoked cigarettes. An increased number of lung cancer deaths paralleled this trend in cigarette consumption. By 1966, this previously rare disease had become the number one cause of cancer death, killing over 250,000 Americans per year.

After the Surgeon General alerted the public to the link between cigarette smoking and lung cancer in a landmark report in 1964, cigarette consumption declined to about 25% of the adult population of the United States by 1992. This fall in prevalence resulted primarily from smokers quitting, not from fewer people initiating cigarette use. Data that documented a decline in cigarette use after 1973 recently showed no change in cigarette use from 1990 to 1992, thereby underscoring the growing importance of smoking prevention efforts. Recently, data implicating secondhand smoke as a public health hazard have prompted smoking bans in public spaces, including federal offices, restaurants in certain towns, and all continental airline flights.

Cigarette use remains the most preventable cause of death in our society. The continued estimated annual mortality of more than 400,000 lives due to cigarette smoking represents one of the most important public health issues of our time.

EPIDEMIOLOGY

Data from the Centers for Disease Control estimate that 46.3 million adults (25.6% of the United States population) currently smoke cigarettes, including 24 million men (28.0%) and 22 million women (23.5%). The prevalence is highest among persons 25 to 44 years of age. The percentage of smokers who report that they smoke heavily (more than

20 cigarettes per day) has changed little from 1974 to 1985 (26.0 to 27.1%). In 1990, smoking-related illness accounted for one in five deaths and more than one-quarter of all deaths among people 35 to 64 years of age. Table 8.1 summarizes prevalence data for specific populations, and Table 8.2 lists some quick reference facts about nicotine and cigarette smoking. Chapters 2 and 3 provide additional epidemiological and cultural information about cigarette use.

The early age of initiation of cigarette use and the high percentage of illicit drug users who smoke cigarettes has prompted investigation of a connection between early cigarette use and future drug abuse. The data have revealed only that many substance abusers began using cigarettes, but that most cigarette smokers do not acquire other addictions.

As indicated by the data trends in Table 8.1, cigarette smoking has become increasingly a habit of poorly educated and socioeconomically disadvantaged people. Teenagers, especially teenage mothers, and minorities continue to smoke in disproportionately high numbers. Currently, cigarette companies focus advertising efforts on the young and minority groups, even though it is illegal to sell cigarettes to minors. Effective prevention and cessation interventions must increasingly focus on adolescents, minorities, and less-educated, young Americans to effect the greatest impact on smoking in the next century.

PHARMACOLOGY

Chemistry

Nicotine, the major addictive agent in tobacco, is a tertiary amine containing a pyridine and a pyrrolidine ring (Fig. 8.1). Nicotine is a weak base with a pK_a of 8.0, making it soluble in both water and lipids. According to Benowitz, at physiological pH, 31% of nicotine is unionized and able to cross cell membranes. The smoke from most cigarettes is slightly acidic, and therefore the nicotine in cigarette smoke does not readily traverse membranes, such as the buccal mucosa. The more alkaline characteristics of nicotine in pipe and cigar tobacco, smokeless tobacco, and nicotine gum facilitate absorption across the oral mucosa and cause a more gradual rise in serum levels of nicotine.

Absorption and Pharmacokinetics

Inhalation of cigarette smoke carries nicotine into the lungs on tar droplets and deposits it in small airways and alveoli. Rapid absorption into the circulation allows the drug to reach the brain within 8 seconds. Brain concentrations of nicotine decline within 20 to 30 minutes as the drug is distributed to other tissues in the body.

Although gastric absorption of swallowed nicotine is low (because of the acidic pH of stomach secretions), intestinal absorption is more

TABLE 8.1. EPIDEMIOLOGY OF CIGARETTE USE

Categories	Data
Cigarette use by women	• In 1992, 23.5% of women smoked cigarettes • Female smokers began to smoke at a younger age • They smoke more heavily than in the past. From 1965 to 1985, the percentage of women who smoke more than 25 cigarettes a day increased from 13 to 23% • Lung cancer, which caused an estimated 56,000 deaths in 1993, has surpassed breast cancer as the most prevalent cause of cancer death among women • Pregnant women who smoke have babies that weigh an average of 200 grams less than infants born to nonsmokers • Stillbirths and early neonatal deaths are increased by about 33% in the babies of smokers as compared with those of nonsmokers
Minority populations	• Disproportionately high prevalence of cigarette smoking among Native Americans (31.4%), Alaskan natives (29.2%), and Black men (35.1%) with lower than average prevalence for Hispanics (20.2%); the lowest rate is among Hispanic women (15.5%) • The proportion of heavy smokers (>20 cigarettes/day) in Blacks is considerably lower than in Whites • Smoking-related cancers (lung, oral cavity, pharynx, esophagus, and larynx) were highest among Black men despite lower rates of heavy smoking
Adolescents	• An estimated six million teenagers and another 100,000 adolescents under 13 years of age smoke, even though it is illegal to sell cigarettes to minors • 80 to 90% of smokers begin smoking before the age of 21 • 3000 teenagers start smoking each day • Approximately 1.1 billion packs of cigarettes a year are smoked by U.S. teenagers
The elderly	• Highest incidence of smoking for the over 65 population is among Black men (31.1%) • 24% of cerebrovascular disease in men over 65 and 6% in women over 65 is attributable to smoking • 20% of the cataracts in the U.S. are attributable to smoking
Educational status	• By 1987 large differences in smoking rates among educational levels replaced gender as the sociodemographic variable most highly predictive of differences in smoking prevalence rates • Smoking prevalence rates are inversely related to level of education
Passive cigarette smoke and children	• Major health hazard for children causing 150,000 to 300,000 cases of lower respiratory tract infections, such as pneumonia and bronchitis, annually in infants and young children up to 18 months of age • 200,000 to 1 million cases of asthma among children are worsened by exposure to environmental tobacco smoke • Infants of mothers who smoke are at an increased risk of sudden infant death syndrome

---

TABLE 8.2. FACTS ABOUT NICOTINE AND CIGARETTE SMOKING

- Smoking is the most preventable cause of death
- 90% of lung cancer is due to smoking
- More women die of smoking-related lung cancer than die of breast cancer
- Fires due to smoking are the leading cause of civilian fire deaths in the U.S.
- Six million teenagers and another 100,000 children under 13 years smoke regularly
- Nonsmoking spouses of smokers have a 20% higher incidence of lung cancer from secondhand smoke exposure, as compared to spouses of nonsmokers
- The estimated average lifetime medical costs for a smoker exceed those for a nonsmoker by more than $6000
- Cigarette smokers are absent from work approximately 6.5 days more per year than nonsmokers
- The estimated total cost of smoking to society in 1990 was $2.59 per pack of cigarettes
- Cost of smoking in terms of health care expenditure and lost productivity was a staggering $65 billion for the U.S. in 1985 and over $100 billion in 1994

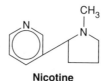

Nicotine

Figure 8.1. Chemical structure of nicotine.

efficient. However, high first-pass metabolism by the liver results in only 30% bioavailability. Normally, 80–90% of the drug is metabolized in the liver, lung, and kidney, and it has a half-life of approximately 2 hours. The drug and its metabolites, except cotinine, are rapidly eliminated by the kidney. Neither of the two main metabolites of nicotine, cotinine, nor nicotine-1'-N-oxide is pharmacologically active. Because of cotinine's long half-life (about 20 hours), it can be used as a marker for nicotine intake.

Mechanisms of Action

Nicotine's binding to cholinergic and nicotinic receptors in the central nervous system (CNS), adrenal medulla, neuromuscular junctions, and autonomic ganglia accounts for the addictive characteristics of the drug and the physical signs and symptoms of its use. Benowitz reports that in the brain, nicotine binding is greatest in the hypothalamus, hippocampus, thalamus, midbrain, brainstem, cortex, and nigrostriatal and mesolimbic dopaminergic neurons. Stimulation and neuroadaptation of dopaminergic neurons of the mesolimbic system appear to account for nicotine addiction, dependence, tolerance, and withdrawal. Difficulties in quitting smoking, the craving for a cigarette, and chain-smoking may all result from neuroadaptations of these brain regions.

Activity on other neuronal tissue is biphasic with an initial, brief stimulation preceding a depressive action. The autonomic ganglia are the primary targets for nicotine's action. Small doses cause ganglionic stimulation, while larger doses result in brief stimulation followed by ganglionic blockade. At neuromuscular junctions, the stimulatory component is minimal in comparison to the dopaminergic effects. Benowitz estimates that most smokers require at least 10 cigarettes (averaging 1–2 mg nicotine per cigarette smoked), or 10–40 mg nicotine per day to achieve these desired effects.

MEDICAL CONSEQUENCES OF USE

Acutely, nicotine has many systemic effects, affecting primarily the central nervous, cardiovascular, and endocrine systems. Overall, nicotine is a stimulant. Table 8.3 summarizes these acute effects.

Sequelae of Long-Term Cigarette Use

In addition to the acute physiological effects of nicotine, cigarette smoking is atherogenic and thrombogenic, causing cardiovascular disease, and carcinogenic, causing neoplastic disease. Presently, 420,000 (1 of 5) deaths per year in the United States are attributable to cigarette smoking. Neoplastic disease is one of the major sources of morbidity and mortality, and the percentages of individual cancers attributable to smoking appear in Figure 8.2. The health consequences of tobacco smoking are detailed in Table 8.4.

Passive Smoking

Passive smoke inhalation has deleterious effects on nonsmokers. The smoke drawn through the end of a cigarette a smoker inhales, called "mainstream" smoke, differs chemically from "sidestream" smoke produced between puffs by the burning cigarettes. Sidestream smoke contains more carbon monoxide, nitrosamines, and benzo [p] pyrene than mainstream smoke. In the company of heavy smokers, nonsmokers may passively inhale the equivalent of up to three actively smoked cigarettes per day.

Nonsmoking spouses of smokers have a 20% increased risk of developing lung cancer, which increases to 70% when the spouse is a heavy smoker. Nonsmokers exposed to passive smoke also have a greater risk for developing cardiovascular disease. Additionally, children under age two with smoking parents have an increased incidence of respiratory illness and abnormal lung function correlating with the parental cigarette smoking.

TABLE 8.3. MANIFESTATIONS OF NICOTINE USE

CNS/Behavioral	• Nausea and vomiting • Increased arousal • Relaxation in stressful situations • Enhanced short-term memory • Decreased reaction time • Increased attention and problem-solving abilities • Enhanced vigilance • Reduced hunger and body weight • Relaxation of skeletal muscles • Hand tremors
Cardiovascular	• Transient increase in heart rate, blood pressure, stroke volume, cardiac output, and coronary blood flow • Long-term decreased blood pressure and coronary blood flow • Decreased skin temperature • Systemic vasoconstriction • Increased blood flow to skeletal muscle • Increased circulating free fatty acids, lactate, and glycerol • Increased platelet activation
Endocrine	• Increased catecholamines, ACTH, GH, PRL, vasopressin, beta endorphin, cortisol • Earlier menopause • Increased risk of osteoporosis in women • Lower body weight • Increased metabolic rate during exercise and at rest
Respiratory	• Sputum production • Cough/wheeze

CLINICAL PRESENTATION

Dependence

Nicotine dependence and the dependence on cigarette smoking have three main features. First, cessation of nicotine intake initiates withdrawal symptoms, which peak within 24–48 hours of discontinuation of use and include anxiety, inadequate sleep, irritability, impatience, craving tobacco, restlessness, difficulty concentrating, drowsiness, increased appetite, and headache. Chronic smokers admitted to the hospital for any reason may experience signs and symptoms of nicotine withdrawal. The intensity of these symptoms usually diminishes after 2 weeks, but some symptoms, such as increased appetite and difficulty concentrating,

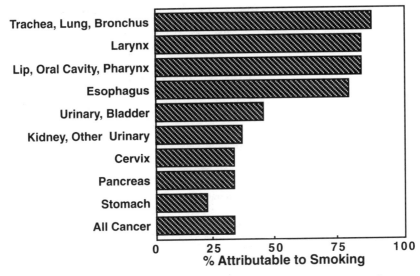

Figure 8.2. Proportion of cancer deaths attributable to smoking in the United States in 1985.

may persist for months. Since nicotine is addictive, smokers who cut down the number of cigarettes smoked may change the manner in which they smoke to maximize delivery of nicotine in the body. Deeper inhalation is one of these changes.

Second, cigarette smoking constitutes a habitual behavior, often used in response to stress or boredom. Dependence develops to holding a cigarette, moving the cigarette to the mouth, and inhaling the smoke. These behaviors are further reinforced by nicotine activating the brain reward circuitry.

Finally, the rapid alteration of nicotine levels in the brain after inhalation of smoke produces a pleasurable experience. These three aspects of dependence make discontinuation of cigarette use difficult to achieve. All three must be addressed in order for smokers to quit smoking and maintain abstinence. Table 8.5 discusses these components, their clinical relevance, and treatment strategies for them.

Tolerance

Limited tolerance develops to the effects of nicotine. After several cigarettes even a chronic smoker will continue to experience increased heart rate and blood pressure, hand tremors, decreased skin temperature, and increased levels of certain hormones. Tolerance to the symptoms dizziness, nausea, and vomiting occur quickly and do not affect chronic smokers without a large augmentation of their intake of nicotine. Benowitz has described a daily smoking cycle: after a 6–8-hour day of smoking,

TABLE 8.4. HEALTH CONSEQUENCES OF CIGARETTE SMOKING

System	Consequences of Smoking
Cardiovascular	Coronary artery disease/angina/myocardial infarction Peripheral vascular disease Aortic aneurysm Cardiac arrest Cerebrovascular disease Vasospasm Hypercoagulable states
Respiratory	Chronic bronchitis Emphysema Pneumonia
Neoplastic Disease	Lung Larynx and oral cavity Esophagus Bladder Cervix Pancreas Stomach
Gastrointestinal	Acute gastritis Peptic ulcer disease (PUD) Increased recurrence rate of PUD
Other Health Risks	Fires Osteoporosis Wrinkles Oral contraceptive pills contraindicated in smokers

most of the tolerance to the nicotine's effects wears off by morning. Hence, many smokers report feeling the greatest effect with the day's first cigarette. With each successive cigarette, tolerance increases and symptoms of withdrawal occur between cigarettes.

Nicotine Intoxication

Although adults rarely become acutely intoxicated from smoking cigarettes only, acute nicotine intoxication is a serious concern in children who orally consume cigarettes. Cutaneous absorption (nicotine patch, pesticides) alone or in combination with tobacco products is another cause of intoxication.

Symptoms of nicotine poisoning include nausea, vomiting, salivation, and abdominal pain; tachycardia and hypertension (early), bradycardia and hypotension (late), tachypnea (early) or respiratory depression (late), miosis, confusion, and agitation (early), and mydriasis, lethargy, seizure, and coma (late).

TABLE 8.5. MULTIPLE COMPONENTS OF TOBACCO DEPENDENCE WITH CORRESPONDING CLINICAL IMPLICATIONS AND INTERVENTIONS

Addictive Components	Clinical Relevance	Treatment Approaches
Habit (smoking cued by daily activities)	Smoking-associated activities and stimuli produce urges Smokers may relapse without awareness when performing smoking-associated activities (eg, talking on the phone, driving in a car)	1. Training to anticipate, modify, and avoid smoking-related activities 2. Training in cognitive and behavioral strategies to reduce urges, craving 3. Adoption of a substitute habit, eg, chewing gum, toothpicks, drinking water
Pleasure (smoking to increase pleasure)	Experiencing pleasure (eg, after a meal, at a party) may "prime" urges to heighten pleasure through smoking About 25% of relapses occur when smokers are happy	1. Identification and encouragement of alternative routes to enjoyment (eg, exercise, hobbies) 2. Anticipation of and/or preparation for high-risk pleasure situations (eg, partners, taverns)
Self-medication (smoking to reduce negative affect and physical symptoms)	Negative moods arising from stress or tobacco withdrawal produce powerful urges to smoke Craving may arise from withdrawal or stressors and is decreased rapidly by smoking Weight gain is a key withdrawal sign and causes many smokers to relapse About 65% of relapses occur when smokers are sad, angry, or anxious	1. Pharmacologic nicotine replacement to reduce withdrawal symptoms and stress reactions 2. Training to anticipate and cope with stressors 3. Healthy eating and exercise habits may reduce negative physical feelings and weight gain 4. Cognitive and behavioral strategies for coping with negative moods (eg, relaxation, using social support)

Absorption of nicotine can be reduced by gastric lavage, activated charcoal, and cathartics. Treatment of nicotine intoxication is primarily symptomatic with ventilatory support, anticonvulsants, antiarrhythmics, and if necessary, atropine.

TREATMENT STRATEGIES

Over 90% of adult smokers in the United States who quit successfully do so on their own. Some smokers will simply quit "cold turkey" using the "self-care" methods. Common reasons cited by those who attempt to stop smoking include specific and general health issues, limitation of health risks to family or fetus, desire to provide a positive role model for children, expense, freedom from addiction, social pressure, and cosmetic benefits of not smoking. Unfortunately, most attempts to quit end in relapse. Approximately 70% of smokers return to smoking after a quit attempt, most within 3 months of quitting. However, with each attempt to quit smoking the likelihood of successful cessation increases. Of those who continue to relapse, nonpharmacological and pharmacological therapies may help them finally quit.

For smokers who have never made a quit attempt, physicians should provide advice and self-help material to promote quitting on their own. Table 8.6 presents a smoking cessation protocol. The health care worker can play an instrumental role in helping patients quit smoking, serving as a source of information and an assistant in establishing goals for quitting. The National Cancer Institute (NCI) (1 (800) 4-CANCER) can provide informative materials such as *Why do I smoke?* and *Quit for Good*. See Table 8.7 for a list of other resources for smoking cessation materials.

Patients often have many questions related to smoking cessation. Table 8.8 summarizes the most frequently asked questions and provides answers and advice for the patient. Assisting a patient in quitting smoking can be a source of extreme frustration. High relapse rates in the face of overwhelming evidence that smoking is detrimental to the patient's health demonstrates the highly addictive nature of nicotine and cigarette smoking. The recognition that cigarette smoking is an addiction and that it is difficult to stop, coupled with the information that each attempt at quitting increases success rates, helps alleviate some of this frustration for the patient and the doctor.

Smoking Cessation and Patient Assessment

Behavioral scientists have recognized that smokers pass through five stages as they prepare to quit smoking and eventually do. Assessing the patient's readiness to quit helps the physician tailor his/her efforts to the needs of the particular smoker. The first phase is *precontemplation*, during which a smoker does not consider quitting. Overly forceful urging

TABLE 8.6. SYNOPSIS FOR PHYSICIANS: HOW TO HELP PATIENTS STOP SMOKING

Ask about smoking at every opportunity
- Do you smoke?
- Are you interested in stopping smoking?
- Have you ever tried to stop before? What happened?

Advise all smokers to stop
- State your advice clearly, for example—"Stopping smoking is the most important action you can take to stay healthy"
- Personalize the message to quit. Refer to the patient's clinical condition, history, family history, personal interest, or social roles

Assist the smoker in quitting

For smokers ready to quit
- Set a quit date. Help the patient pick a date in the next 1–2 weeks, acknowledging that no date is ideal. Calling the patient to remind him/her about the quit date will help reinforce the decision to quit
- Provide self-help materials to take home
- Consider nicotine replacement therapy (if previous quit attempts have been unsuccessful)
- Consider referral to a formal cessation program (if previous quit attempts have been unsuccessful)

For smokers not ready to quit
- Discuss advantages and barriers to cessation from the smoker's viewpoint
- Provide motivating literature to take home
- Advise smoker to avoid exposing family members to passive smoke
- Indicate willingness to help when the smoker is ready
- Ask about smoking at each subsequent visit

Arrange follow-up visits
- Make follow-up appointment within 1–2 weeks after the quit date
- At the follow-up visit, ask about the patient's smoking status; provide support and help prevent relapse
- Set a second follow-up visit in 1–2 months

For smokers who have quit
- Congratulate!!
- Ask smoker to identify high-risk situations
- Rehearse coping strategies for future high-risk situations

For smokers who have relapsed or been unable to quit
- Ask: "What were you doing when you had the first cigarette?"
- Ask: "What did you learn from the experience?"
- Ask smoker to set a new quit date

TABLE 8.7. RESOURCES FOR SMOKING CESSATION MATERIALS

American Academy of Family Physicians
(800) 274-2237

American Cancer Society
(800) 227-2345

American Heart Association
7320 Greenville Avenue, Dallas, TX 75231

American Dental Association
211 E. Chicago, Chicago, IL 60611

National Cancer Institute
Office of Cancer Communications, National Institutes of Health, Bldg. 31, Room 4B-43, Bethesda, MD 20892
(800) 4-CANCER

National Heart, Lung and Blood Institute
Smoking Education Program, National Institutes of Health, Bldg. 31, Room 4A-18, Dept. A-1, Bethesda, MD 20892
(202) 783-3238, (301) 951-3260

National Audio-Visual Center
Customer Services Section, 8700 Edgeworth Drive, Capital Heights, MD 20743-3701

Health Promotion Group, Inc.
PO Box 59687, Homewood, AL 35259

Warner Brothers
Attn.: Lorimar Home Video, 4000 Warner Boulevard, Burbank, CA 91522
(800) 323-5275

of the patient to quit at this stage may result in increased resistance to the idea of quitting. The patient should simply be presented with information at this stage. The next stage is *contemplation,* when the smoker considers quitting but is not ready to do so. At this time, the smoker becomes more receptive to smoking cessation messages. Table 8.9 lists the benefits of cessation of smoking, which can be presented to the patient. During the *preparation to quit* stage, the smoker convinces himself/herself to quit. In the next stage, the *action* stage, a smoker actually attempts to quit. Finally, after successfully quitting, the smoker tries to abstain from cigarettes—the *maintenance* phase.

Nonpharmacological Therapy

The American Cancer Society (ACS) and American Lung Association (ALA), as well as numerous other groups, have established multiple smoking cessation programs across the country. These programs focus on behavior modification. One type of behavioral modification involves

TABLE 8.8. RESPONSES TO COMMON QUESTIONS ABOUT SMOKING CESSATION

Won't I gain weight if I stop smoking?
- Not every person who stops smoking gains weight
- Average weight gains are small for people who do gain (5–10 lbs)
- Don't diet now—there will be time after you are an established nonsmoker
- Exercise is an effective technique to cope with withdrawal and to avoid weight gain
- Avoid high-calorie snacks. Vegetables and fruits are good snacks
- The risks to health from smoking are far greater than the risks to health from a small weight gain
- A small increase in weight may not hurt your appearance. Smoking is unattractive, and causes yellow teeth, bad breath, stale clothing odors, and wrinkled skin.

I don't have the willpower to stop smoking.
- More than 3 million Americans stop smoking every year
- Not everyone succeeds the first time, but many people are successful after several attempts
- I will give you all the support I can

I smoke only low-tar/low-nicotine cigarettes, so I don't need to stop
- There is no such thing as a safe cigarette
- Many smokers inhale more often and more deeply to compensate for low nicotine levels in these cigarettes

Is it better to stop "cold turkey" or over a long period of time?
- There is no "best way"
- Most successful former smokers quit "cold turkey"

What about insomnia?
- Many smokers report having problems sleeping after they stop smoking. If these symptoms are related to nicotine dependence, they should disappear within 2–3 weeks

Why do I cough more now that I have stopped?
- About 20% of former smokers report an increase in coughing after they stop smoking. This is a temporary response thought to be caused by an increase in the lung's ability to remove phlegm, so it actually represents recovery of the lung's defense mechanism

Now that I've stopped, can I smoke a cigarette occasionally?
- NO! Nicotine addiction seems to be retriggered quickly in most former smokers. Don't risk getting hooked again

Will my body recover from the effects of smoking?
- Some of the damage may be permanent, such as loss of lung tissue in emphysema
- Other functions are recovered, such as the lung's ability to remove phlegm

---

TABLE 8.9. BENEFITS OF SMOKING CESSATION

Mortality: Overall mortality of ex-smokers nears nonsmoker rate 10–15 years after smoking cessation

Cardiovascular risks: A relatively early reduction in the risk of coronary heart disease, particularly myocardial infarction (MI), occurs with smoking cessation. Compared to nonsmokers, smokers have a 3-fold increased relative risk of MI, which drops by 50% within 1 year of smoking cessation

Respiratory problems: After smoking cessation, a fairly prompt alleviation of coughing wheezing, and production of excess sputum occurs. Importantly, after a delay of years, the morality rates from COPD falls. Besides, it is never too late to quit since benefits accrue even at older ages after development of COPD

Lung cancer: A fall in mortality rate from bronchogenic carcinoma begins to appear in 5 to 9 years after smoking cessation and approaches basal nonsmokers' levels after 15 years of abstinence.

Multiple diseases: There is a decreased predisposition to all other smoking-related diseases like other cancers, peptic ulcers, obstetrical complications, etc. after smoking cessation. Some report that even skin wrinkles get better!

Fires: 25% of residential fire deaths are caused by a lighted cigarette. These are entirely preventable day after smoking cessation!

Contraceptive pills: Women can use oral contraceptive pills with less risk of thrombotic disease if they stop smoking

---

"self-management," in which the patient practices "self-monitoring," making a record of smoking and the environmental cues that seem to trigger the desire to smoke. The patient also practices "stimulus control," where a certain number of these cues is eliminated from the patient's environment. Some approaches use "nicotine fading," or cutting back gradually on the consumption of nicotine, by cutting back on the number of cigarettes smoked or changing to brands with lower nicotine content. Other strategies include learning to cope without cigarettes, relapse prevention strategies, and aversion conditioning (rarely used today).

The different methods described above have similar success rates of approximately 30% not relapsing at 1 year. Although physician counseling alone has only a 5% success rate, when it is combined with adjunctive interventions, success ranges from 22 to 43% in cardiac patients at 1 year. Self-help alone had a quit rate at 1 year of about 18%. Combination programs using a variety of cessation approaches are more effective than interventions using a single strategy, with successful quit rates of approximately 35% at 1 year.

Pharmacological Therapies

Nicotine Replacement Therapy

Rationale and Patient Selection

As described above, continued cigarette smoking involves a pharmaco-logical dependence on nicotine, and psychological dependence on the habitual behaviors and the pleasure derived from smoking (Table 8.5). The powerful craving associated with nicotine withdrawal is a frequently cited reason for a failed quit attempt. Consequently, adequate nicotine replacement over the course of acute nicotine withdrawal allows smokers to focus on coping strategies for other aspects of cigarette dependence.

Patients who benefit most from nicotine replacement therapy are those with the greatest dependency on nicotine, including smokers who smoke more than 20 cigarettes daily, those who smoke a cigarette within 30 minutes of waking up, and those who have failed quit attempts pre-viously because of strong cigarette craving in the first week of withdrawal. Additionally, smokers who are highly motivated to quit, but do not necessarily meet the criteria above, may also benefit from nicotine replacement therapy.

The Nicotine Patch (Table 8.10)

Available in the United States since 1991, transdermal nicotine delivery systems provide constant serum nicotine levels for 16 to 24 hours. This method provides good absorption of nicotine, a short half-life of it, and constant serum levels that significantly reduce the drug craving associated with nicotine withdrawal. An 8-week therapy is recommended and requires patients to change their patches daily. Additionally, many patch users must participate in an adjunctive smoking cessation counsel-ing program in order to receive reimbursement for the patches.

Patch therapy is indicated in the circumstances discussed above. Patients who also have known coronary artery disease can receive it as long as they do not smoke while on the patch. When nonpharmacological smoking cessation attempts fail for pregnant women, they may also receive nicotine replacement via the patch. While the exact effects of the nicotine patch on the fetus are not known, the potential benefits must be weighed against the known harm of continued cigarette use during pregnancy. Finally, since inpatient hospitalization gives health care providers the opportunity to motivate and educate patients while they are in smoke-free institutions, withdrawing/symptomatic, hospital-ized patients are also good patch candidates.

The main adverse effects of nicotine patches involve skin irritation, requiring either changing the patch location daily, or medical therapy involving over-the-counter hydrocortisone cream or prescription steroid

TABLE 8.10. NICOTINE REPLACEMENT OPTIONS

Brand Name (Manufacturer)	Nicotine Content (mg)	Dosage per Day	Recommended Duration of Use
Transdermal Nicotine Patch			
Habitrol (*Ciba-Geigy*)			
21 mg	52.6	21 mg/24 hr	4–8 weeks
14 mg	35.0	14 mg/24 hr	2–4 weeks
7 mg	17.5	7 mg/24 hr	2–4 weeks
Nicoderm (*Marion Merrell Dow*)			
21 mg	114.0	21 mg/24 hr	4–8 weeks
14 mg	78.0	14 mg/24 hr	2–4 weeks
7 mg	36.0	7 mg/24 hr	2–4 weeks
Nicotrol (*Parke-Davis*)			
15 mg	24.9	15 mg/16 hr	4–12 weeks
10 mg	16.6	10 mg/16 hr	2–4 weeks
5 mg	8.3	5 mg/16 hr	2–4 weeks
Prostep (*Lederle*)			
22 mg	30.0	22 mg/24 hr	4–8 weeks
11 mg	15.0	11 mg/24 hr	2–4 weeks
Nicotine Gum			
Nicorette 2 mg (*Marion Merrell Dow*)	2.0	9–12 pieces/day[a] (maximum 30)	2–3 months (maximum 6)
Nicorette DS (*Marion Merrell Dow*)	4.0	9–12 pieces/day[a] (maximum 20)	2–3 months (maximum 6)

[a]Chew as needed or 1 piece every 1–2 hours while awake.

creams. Although the 24 hour patch does prevent early morning nicotine craving, some users report adverse effects on sleep, including insomnia and nightmares.

Efficacy of the Patch

Studies of the patch have indicated that patch users are twice as likely to both quit smoking by the end of the treatment period and remain abstinent at 6 months. On average, smoking cessation rates for the patch are 27% at the end of treatment and 22% at 6 months, versus 13% and 9% for the placebo group. The 16 and 24 hour patches have similar efficacy in terms of overall quit rates. Meta-analysis of numerous double-blind, placebo-controlled studies has demonstrated no additional efficacy for either more than 8 weeks of treatment or for weaning of patients off the patches. Notably, several studies indicated added efficacy of adjunctive counseling and behavior modification programs.

As a result, nicotine replacement by patch can be incorporated into the primary care setting as an adjunct to asking about smoking, advising to quit, providing information and coping strategies, and following up with telephone or office visit contacts.

Nicotine Gum (Table 8.10)

Available since 1984, nicotine gum has 2 or 4 mg of nicotine bound to a resin at a pH that allows for maximal absorption across the oral mucosa. Since 85–90% of orally ingested nicotine is metabolized on first pass by the liver, nicotine delivery by gum is inefficient without correct chewing style (chew-park-chew-park). With correct use, chewers can achieve serum nicotine levels of 30–60% of those associated with smoking. Additionally, chewing gum can provide nicotine replacement on demand (much like smoking a cigarette in stressful situations) and a habitual behavior to compete with the need to smoke cigarettes. Unfortunately, compliance with gum therapy requires that patients chew a significant amount, follow a specific chewing style, and be aware that nicotine absorption is decreased by some foods and acidic beverages.

Average quit rates for gum use as part of an intense smoking cessation program are 27%, versus 18% for placebo, at 6 months. Unfortunately, the quit rates drop significantly when the gum is used in a general medical practice setting. The gum is used less frequently today given the clear need for adjunctive counseling, the difficulties in use, the lack of compliance, and the popularity of the patch therapy.

Other Pharmacological Therapies

Clonidine, a non-receptor antagonist of nicotine, has been reported to reduce nicotine withdrawal symptoms, but it does not affect smoking cessation rates long-term. Mecamylamine, a nicotine receptor antagonist, and various antidepressant agents, such as doxepin, and anxiolytics, such as buspirone, are also being evaluated as adjuncts to smoking cessation programs.

FURTHER READING

Benowitz NL. Cigarette smoking and nicotine addiction. Med Clin North Am 1992;76:415–437

Benowitz NL. Pharmacologic aspects of cigarette smoking and nicotine addiction. N Engl J Med 1988;319:1318–1330.

Blott WJ, Fraumeni JF Jr. Passive smoking and lung cancer. J Natl Cancer Inst 1986;77:993.

Cancer facts and figures—1993. New York: American Cancer Society, 1993.

CDC. Cigarette smoking—attributable mortality and years of potential life lost— United States, 1990. MMWR 1993;42:645–649.

Environmental Protection Agency. Respiratory health effects of passive smoking: lung cancer and other disorders. Washington, DC: Office of Health and Environmental Assessment, 1992.

Fielding JE. Smoking and women: tragedy of the majority. N Engl J Med 1987;317:1343–1345.

Fiore MC. Trends in cigarette smoking in the United States: the epidemiology of tobacco use. Med Clin North Am 1992;76:289–303.

Lee EW, D'Alonzo GE. Cigarette smoking, nicotine addiction, and its pharmacologic treatment. Arch Intern Med 1993;153:34–48.

MacKenzie T, Bartecchi CE, Schrier R. The human costs of tobacco use (Two Parts) N Engl J Med 1994;330:907–912; 330:975–980.

National Cancer Institues. How to Help Your Patients Stop Smoking: An NCI Manual for Physicians. Rockville, MD: US Dept. of Health and Human Services, 1992.

Pomerleau OF. Nicotine and the central nervous system: biobehavioral effects of cigarette smoking. Am J Med 1992;93(suppl 1A):2S–7S.

Reducing the health consequences of smoking: 25 years of progress. A report of the Surgeon General: executive summary. DHHS publication no. (CDC) 89-8411. Rockville, MD: Dept. of Health and Human Services, 1989.

Schwartz JL. Methods of smoking cessation. Med Clin North Am 1992; 76:451–475.

Chapter 9

Cocaine

B. Price Kerfoot and George Sakoulas with Steven E. Hyman

Cocaine has a long and colorful history dating from the time of the Aztecs to the present day (Table 9.1). Although initially hailed as an ideal drug without adverse effects, widespread use of cocaine in the late 1800s and early 1900s revealed its dangers. Use declined significantly in the 1930s, primarily due to government restrictions that made its price soar. By the 1950s, the level of cocaine use fell so low that law enforcement authorities cited this trend as a notable success of their drug policy.

When the United States entered an era of drug tolerance in the late 1960s, cocaine resurfaced as an expensive, "sophisticated" euphoriant believed to provide a harmless lift for everyday life. Little public memory remained of cocaine's addictive effects during the previous epidemic, and the lack of an obvious physical withdrawal syndrome supported the misinterpretation that cocaine was not addictive.

An explosion of South American cocaine production and distribution more than met the increasing demand for the drug, prompting the cost to drop from $150 per gram in 1980 to less than half that in most cities in 1993. The introduction of crack cocaine, a highly addictive, smokeable, and inexpensive form of cocaine, into the American market in 1985 further increased the drug's availability to a much broader cross section of society.

EPIDEMIOLOGY

The cocaine epidemic, with the possible exception of crack smoking, appeared to peak in the mid-1980s and was in decline by 1990. Unfortunately, as the following statements indicate, early data from the 1990s suggest that use rates may be in a state of flux rather than absolute decline:

- Cocaine use in the United States has fallen from its peak of 5.8 million current users (someone who has used the drug within the last 30 days) in 1985 to 1.9 million current users in 1991.
- The number of daily users of cocaine increased from 246,000 in 1985 to 336,000 in 1990, suggesting fewer users, but more intense use.
- Casual use peaked in 1986, as measured by the National Household Survey. High school senior use, as measured by the NIDA Survey, peaked even earlier.

TABLE 9.1. EARLY HISTORY OF COCAINE

6th century AD	Peruvians bury coca leaves as a "necessity" for the afterlife, likely indicating use at that time
16th century AD	Spaniards pay gold/silver mine slaves with coca leaves to improve performance
1859	Alkaloid cocaine isolated from coca leaves
1884	Freud publishes "Uber Coca" describing cocaine as a CNS stimulant useful in treatment of numerous ailments
1886	Coca-Cola produced by Georgia pharmacist Pemberton as "brain tonic" drink (caffeine substituted for cocaine in 1906)
1906/1914	Federal Acts require cocaine listed as an ingredient in patent medicines and registration of those involved in trade of coca products

- Statistics of intense cocaine use, including cocaine-related deaths and emergency room visits, suggest that cocaine use peaked in 1989.
- The number of current cocaine users actually increased to 1.9 million in 1991 from 1.6 million in 1990, most likely attributable to increased crack use.
- More than 20% of babies born in some inner-city hospitals have been found with cocaine in their bodies from maternal cocaine use of the drug during pregnancy.

PHARMACOLOGY

Chemistry

Illicit cocaine has two common forms: cocaine hydrochloride (cocaine HCl) and freebase, which is derived from the former by alkali extraction. Cocaine HCl has a slightly bitter taste and is more soluble in water (1 gram in 0.4 mL) than the freebase form. A variety of adulterants usually contaminate cocaine HCl powder. Sugars (e.g., mannitol, lactose) increase the volume of the final product, and cheaper stimulants (e.g., caffeine, amphetamine) or local anesthetics (e.g., lidocaine, procaine) add to the "freezing" or numbing effect, which many buyers mistakenly believe indicates the purity of the cocaine. The "cocaine" bought on the street may contain as little as 10% pure drug. The remaining adulterants may contribute significantly to the substance's toxicity.

Freebase cocaine (Figure 9.1) forms odorless, colorless crystals or a white crystalline powder, and has a bitter taste. It has a stability at temperatures required for vaporization, making it smokeable. Freebase cocaine can be prepared from cocaine HCl by mixing it with water and

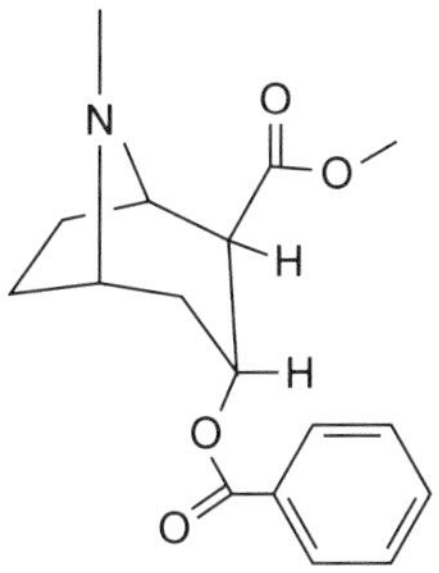

Cocaine

Figure 9.1. Chemical structure of cocaine.

sodium bicarbonate (baking soda) and then heating the mixture until all of the water has evaporated, producing crystals of alkaloidal cocaine. Development of an extraction procedure, which does not use volatile chemicals like ether, explains the recent increase in crack availability and popularity. Crack is the slang name for smokeable, freebase cocaine, derived from the popping sounds the crystals make as they are heated. Although extraction rids the cocaine of hydrochloride most of the original adulterants and any contaminants of the extraction process remain. In other words, crack is not pure cocaine.

Administration and Pharmacokinetics

Cocaine HCl is usually administered intravenously or by nasal insufflation. Upon "snorting" cocaine, peak plasma levels occur after 30 minutes. This route causes vasoconstriction of the nasal mucous membranes, thus limiting the absorptive bioavailability of the drug to 60%. Taken intravenously, cocaine effects have a very rapid onset of action, with an intense rush of euphoria reported within the first two minutes of injection. Elimination half-life of the drug is approximately 40 to 60 minutes.

Freebase cocaine is generally smoked in marijuana or tobacco cigarettes or in freebase pipes, such as special glass water pipes or even a disposable ball-point pen in the side of a plastic bottle.

Crack cocaine allows the drug taker to experience the rush of intravenous cocaine use without an injection. The intravenous and smoked routes of administration have virtually identical peak effect and dissipation of plasma levels. Blood levels peak rapidly, but the effect is relatively short. The euphoric effect of smoking cocaine occurs in about 8 to 10 seconds compared to 30 to 45 seconds intravenously, but usually lasts no more than 20 minutes. By contrast, the effects of intranasal administration may last 1 to 1.5 hours, due to the prolonged absorption of the drug.

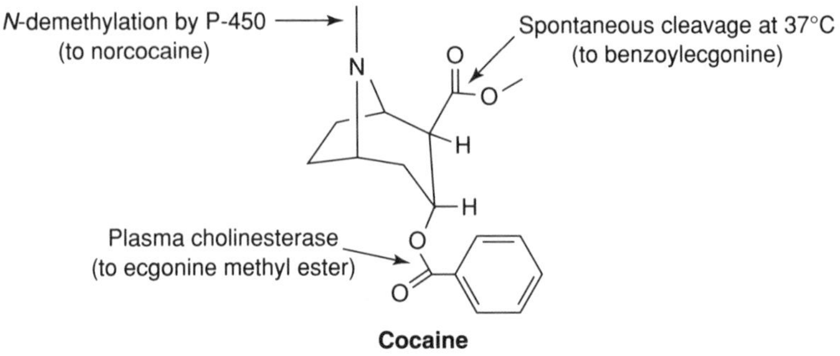

N-demethylation by P-450 ⟶ (to norcocaine)

Spontaneous cleavage at 37°C (to benzoylecgonine)

Plasma cholinesterase (to ecgonine methyl ester)

Cocaine

Figure 9.2. Sites of major metabolic reactions on the cocaine molecule.

Oral ingestion of cocaine is another route of administration especially common among frequent users of cocaine. Oral ingestion of the drug results in a prolonged absorption over 30–60 minutes with a bioavailability of 30–40%, the remaining 60–70% is eliminated by first-pass metabolism in the liver.

Polysubstance abuse occurs in cocaine users, primarily to reduce the anxiety that can accompany the cocaine high ("to smooth the highs") and to buffer the post-use "cocaine crash." Alcohol, benzodiazepines, and opiates are used for this purpose. "Speedballing" refers to the practice of injecting cocaine and heroin together to "mellow out" the stimulant effects of the cocaine with the more sedating, relaxing effects of heroin, and to guard against the depression that can frequently follow cocaine use. The use of these drugs together is significantly more dangerous than when used alone, because the cocaine potentiates the opiate's tendency to depress respiration.

Liver and plasma cholinesterases metabolize 90–95% of cocaine to water-soluble metabolites that are excreted in the urine. Ecgonine methyl ester and benzoylecgonine are the major metabolites; smaller amounts of norcocaine, ecgonine, and various hydroxylated products appear in the urine (Figure 9.2). Renal excretion of unmodified cocaine eliminates only 5–10% of the dose.

Mechanism of Action

Central Nervous System Effects

Cocaine and other related central nervous system (CNS) stimulants increase synaptic levels of dopamine, norepinephrine, and serotonin by inhibiting their reuptake. Chronic use alters the sensitivity of dopamine signal transduction mechanisms. This change may result in the development of tolerance and withdrawal. Blocking reuptake probably causes the acute behavioral and psychological effects of cocaine.

TABLE 9.2 SIGNS OF ADRENERGIC AROUSAL IN COCAINE USERS

Rise in arterial pressure
Tachycardia
Peripheral vasoconstriction
Mydriasis
Hyperglycemia
Hyperthermia
Tachypnea
Diaphoresis
Mental stimulation
Urinary and bowel retention
Decreased hunger
Increased basal metabolism
More rapid brain electrical activity
Increased myocardial contractility

Activation of Sympathetic Nervous System

Among its many actions, cocaine blocks the reuptake of norepinephrine at presynaptic nerve endings, causing it to accumulate at postsynaptic receptor sites. This accumulation potently activates the adrenergic system, accounting for many of the acute effects of the drug (Table 9.2).

Local Anesthesia and Vasoconstriction

Cocaine blocks the initiation and conduction of nerve impulses in peripheral nerves by preventing the necessary increase in cell membrane permeability to sodium ions. Topical application results in local anesthesia, which peaks within 2 to 5 minutes and lasts for 30 to 45 minutes. Since cocaine also produces vasoconstriction by activating the adrenergic system, it is extremely useful in surgeries, such as otolaryngeal procedures, which require the shrinking of mucous membranes, a concomitant decrease in bleeding, and increased visualization of the surgical field.

Cocaine has served as the prototype for a series of synthetic local anesthetic agents without the side effects of cocaine, but which require the coadministration of epinephrine for vasoconstrictive effects (e.g., procaine and lidocaine). Cocaine itself is rarely used for local anesthesia.

MEDICAL CONSEQUENCES OF USE

Cocaine has numerous systemic complications provoked by acute and chronic use. Table 9.3 summarizes these complications. The most common manifestations receive further discussion in this section.

TABLE 9.3. COMPLICATIONS OF COCAINE USE

System	Acute	Chronic
CNS	Euphoria, seldom dysphoria Increased sense of energy Enhanced mental acuity Increased sensory awareness Decreased appetite Increased anxiety Decreased need for sleep Increased self-confidence Delirium	Headaches Seizures Cerebral hemorrhage Cerebral infarctions Cerebral atrophy Cerebral vasculitis Depression Paranoia Psychosis Suicide Delusional disorder
Cardiovascular (also Table 9.4)	Chest pain Myocardial infarction Arrhythmia/sudden death Deep vein thrombosis	Cardiomyopathy Myocarditis
Respiratory	Pneumothorax Pneumomediastinum Pneumopericardium Pulmonary edema Pulmonary hemorrhage	"Crack lung" Bronchiolitis obliterans Asthma exacerbation
Gastrointestinal	Intestinal ischemia Gastroduodenal perforation Colitis	
Head and neck	Gingival ulceration Keratitis Perforated nasal septum Altered olfaction Retinal artery occlusion Epistaxis	Dental enamel erosion Corneal epithelial defects Chronic rhinitis Midline granuloma Optic neuropathy Osteolytic sinusitis
Renal	Rhabdomyolysis Acute tubular necrosis	
Endocrine		Hyperprolactinemia
Hematologic	Methemoglobinemia Sickle-cell crisis precipitation	
Obstetric (also Chapter 17)	Placental abruption Lower infant weight Prematurity Microcephaly	
Other	Sexual dysfunction Hyperpyrexia Decreased appetite Retinal artery occlusion	Weight loss Association with homicide Association with accidents Muscle and skin infarction

Effects of Cocaine on Brain Function

Consciousness/Arousal

Cocaine causes increased alertness, enhanced mental acuity when first administered, and altered electrical activity of the brain. Cocaine's actions on norepinephrine and serotonin in the reticular activating system mediate these effects.

Euphoria

Cocaine appears to induce euphoria by enhancing dopamine action in the nucleus accumbens. The reinforcing effects of cocaine cause animals to repetitively press a lever to receive injections of cocaine. They will even choose cocaine over food and water, and will continue to use cocaine if its access is unlimited, to the point of fatal toxicity and death.

Conditioning

Environmental conditioning develops with the administration of cocaine in the presence of nonpharmacologic stimuli or cues. Eventually, conditioning incites responses to the stimuli similar to the administration of cocaine alone. Dopamine appears essential to the acquisition of conditioned behaviors since dopamine antagonists, such as neuroleptics, diminish these behaviors. Commonly, after a period of abstinence, patients are confronted by external cues of their cocaine use—companions with whom they used cocaine, drug paraphernalia—and then feel a sudden powerful urge to use cocaine again.

Neurologic/Psychiatric Complications

Neurologic complications are the most common manifestations of cocaine toxicity in patients presenting to the emergency rooms of hospitals. However, cocaine-mediated neurologic pathology remains poorly understood.

Cerebral Infarction and Hemorrhage

The etiology of cerebral vascular accidents related to cocaine use is equally divided between infarction and hemorrhage. Most cases occur in patients in their mid-30s. Most infarctions occur in the cerebral hemispheres, although brainstem and spinal cord infarctions have been reported. Although cocaine users with dilated cardiomyopathies have an increased risk for embolic strokes, the etiology of most cocaine-associated strokes includes vasospasm of the cerebral blood vessels induced either by cocaine directly or by secondary catecholamine elevation.

Approximately 50% of strokes secondary to cocaine abuse are due to either subarachnoid or intracerebral hemorrhage. In 80% of the subarachnoid hemorrhages, saccular aneurysms have been documented by angiography. The link between hypertension and the formation and rupture of saccular aneurysms in cocaine-associated subarachnoid hemorrhage is still unclear. In cases of intracerebral hemorrhages, underlying lesions were evident in only about half of the cases; the most common lesion was an arteriovenous malformation (AVM). Transient elevations in blood pressure generated by cocaine use could lead to rupture of pre-existing AVMs or bleeding into a tumor. Hemorrhage in individuals without underlying lesions remains unexplained.

Seizures

A major nervous system complication and well-known presentation of acute cocaine toxicity is seizure activity. The seizure is usually generalized in nature. Most seizures occur in association with smoking crack or intravenous injection of cocaine. Intranasal cocaine use is more likely to precipitate seizures in patients with a previous history of a seizure disorder.

Behavioral Complications of Cocaine Use

Depression

After repeated, long-term use, many cocaine users experience depression and anxiety, effects seen with other CNS stimulants such as amphetamine or methylphenidate. Some long-term cocaine users simultaneously use CNS depressants such as barbiturates, benzodiazepines, opiates, or alcohol, in order to reduce dysphoria and anxiety. Cocaine withdrawal is characterized by depression.

Cocaine Delirium

Cocaine delirium begins 24 hours after drug use and is marked by sensory misinterpretation (tactile or olfactory hallucinations), disorganized thinking, and disorientation. Affect is labile and restraint is often required to control violent or aggressive behavior. The delirium usually disappears once the cocaine wears off.

Cocaine Delusional Disorder

Cocaine delusional disorder involves persecutory delusions developing shortly after cocaine use. The patient may experience feelings of suspiciousness and curiosity as a source of pleasure or entertainment at first. In the latter stages the suspiciousness, anxiety, and paranoia may evoke violence or aggression with hallucinations. Delusions may remain up to 1 year after use of cocaine.

Psychosis

Cocaine psychosis is typically preceded by a period of increased suspiciousness, compulsive behavior, and dysphoria that last 3 to 5 days after cocaine cessation. Users also become increasingly irritable and paranoid. Auditory and/or visual hallucinations can lead to violent, self-defensive behavior. Some individuals may experience tactile hallucinations, for example, "cocaine bugs" crawling under their skin (formication). Up to two-thirds of cocaine-dependent patients develop some degree of paranoia during cocaine binges. Increased dopamine activity appears to mediate these behaviors.

Other Central Nervous System Effects of Cocaine

Central nervous system stimulants such as cocaine may also produce tics, persistent mechanical repetitions of speech or movement, ataxia, and disturbed gait, which usually disappear after drug use is stopped.

Individuals with obsessive-compulsive disorder may experience a worsening of their compulsive behaviors when using cocaine.

Cardiovascular Complications

Cocaine causes vascular disease that involves vessels throughout the body. However, the heart is the most severely affected element of the cardiovascular system (Table 9.4).

Myocardial Ischemia/Infarction

Myocardial infarction (MI) is a frequent complication of cocaine use. Patients with cocaine-related MIs are, on average, in their early 30s. The nechanisms of cocaine-related MI involve coronary vasospasm (which has been documented angiographically after intranasal cocaine administration), enhanced platelet aggregation leading to thrombosis, accelerated coronary artery atherosclerosis, increased myocardial oxygen demand because of tachycardia and afterload increase, and medial and intimal hyperplasia of the coronary arteries (secondary to catecholamine excesses). The intimal hyperplasia and medial thickening produce ischemia suffered in multiple organs. Recent work has shown that cocaine and nicotine may have an additive effect on coronary artery vasospasm. Consequently, cigarette smoking may amplify cocaine-related cardiac ischemia.

Myocardial ischemia from cocaine use may occur from several minutes to 18 hours after drug intake. Holter electrocardiographic studies have documented a high incidence of silent ischemia during cocaine withdrawal, especially during the first week of abstinence.

In summary, cocaine makes the myocardium susceptible to ischemia by increasing myocardial oxygen demand and work, while simultaneously decreasing oxygen supply by diminishing blood flow. If asymptomatic, fixed lesions already exist; the increased myocardial work may lead to ischemia or infarction even without vasospasm. In the absence of fixed lesions, coronary vasospasm can still induce infarction. In young patients

---

TABLE 9.4. CARDIOVASCULAR COMPLICATIONS OF COCAINE ABUSE

Cardiac
  Coronary artery disease/myocardial infarction
    coronary artery vasospasm
    thrombosis (increased platelet aggregation)
    accelerated atherosclerosis
    medial and intimal hyperplasia in coronary arteries
    afterload increase
      systemic vasoconstriction
      hypertension
    left ventricular hypertrophy
  Arrhythmias
    ventricular tachycardia/ventricular fibrillation
    sinus bradycardia
    premature ventricular contractions
    asystole
  Myocarditis (2 types)
    toxic (catecholamine-mediated; dose-dependent)
    hypersensitivity (rare; not dose-dependent)
  Endocarditis

Vascular
  Aortic dissection
    hypertension
    medial disease
  Thrombophlebitis
    superficial (water-insoluble precipiants in vessels)
    deep
      increased platelet aggregation
      increased thromboxane
      water-insoluble precipitants in blood vessels

---

with few cardiac risk factors, cocaine use should be high on the differential diagnosis in cases of MI and chest pain.

Arrhythmias

Use of cocaine can result in various cardiac arrhythmias: ventricular tachycardia, ventricular fibrillation, sinus bradycardia, premature ventricular contractions, and asystole. Lethal arrhythmias are the most common cause of sudden death secondary to cocaine use. Sudden death occurs among both long-term and first-time users of cocaine. Cocaine may cause arrhythmias by slowing impulse conduction through sodium channel blockade, blocking potassium efflux, and indirectly stimulating α-adrenergic neurons. Myocardial fibrosis and channel-blocking properties of cocaine alter the electrophysiology of the myocardium. The probability of arrhythmia is increased further by cardiomegaly.

Myocardial Diseases

Cocaine users are susceptible to the development of left ventricular hypertrophy with increases in both muscle mass and thickness. Intermittent increases in sympathetic tone increase afterload enough to cause hypertrophy. This contributes to the development of ischemia and arrhythmias associated with cocaine use. Long-term cocaine users may also develop dilated cardiomyopathies.

Catecholamine-induced, toxic myocarditis may also occur in patients who severely abuse cocaine. Similar to patients with a pheochromocytoma, the catecholamines induce inflammation, necrosis, and fibrosis, which is histologically distinct from ischemic necrosis. Cellular infiltrates in the hearts of cocaine users have some degree of eosinophilia, suggesting that cocaine may also induce a rare hypersensitivity myocarditis (6 per 10,000).

Aorta and Peripheral Vessels

Hypertension and aortic medial disease are primary factors involved in the pathogenesis of aortic dissection, and both are increased by cocaine abuse. Both superficial and deep thrombophlebitis occur secondary to cocaine abuse. There is a particular risk of deep vein thrombosis of the upper extremity (Paget-von Schrötter's syndrome). Water-insoluble adulterants, cocaine-enhanced platelet aggregation, and increased thromboxane production cause the deep vein thrombosis.

Respiratory Tract Complications

Cocaine-related pulmonary disease is mostly associated with smoking the drug. The types of complications can be grouped into four categories: local inflammation/infection, barotrauma, parenchymal disease, and vascular disease.

Renal Complications

Acute renal failure secondary to rhabdomyolysis is the most common renal complication of cocaine abuse. The mechanism is clear only in cases involving seizure activity. Pressure-related injury may explain other cases, while necrosis of myocytes secondary to ischemia/anoxia caused by arterial vasospasm is proposed as yet another mechanism. Many cases of cocaine-induced rhabdomyolysis involve hyperthermia. Patients with rhabdomyolysis often have few neuromuscular symptoms, and hypocalcemia predicts more severe rhabdomyolysis. Acute tubular necrosis associated with cocaine use has a multifactorial etiology involving hypovolemia, renal artery constriction, and myoglobinuria.

Gastrointestinal Complications

Several gastrointestinal disorders, including intestinal ischemia, gastro-duodenal perforations, and colitis are associated with cocaine use. Most problems are secondary to effects of catecholamines on blood vessels.

Endocrine Complications

Adrenergic effects of cocaine can produce symptoms similar to hyperthyroidism. However, thyroid function tests are usually normal in cocaine users. Decreased prolactin levels seen during initial cocaine use result from the increases in dopamine, an inhibitor of prolactin release. However, in long-term cocaine use and withdrawal, dopaminergic depletion in the basal hypothalamus leads to hyperprolactinemia.

Hematologic Complications

Street cocaine is frequently diluted with drugs such as benzocaine, which cause the oxidation of ferrous to ferric hemoglobin and, occasionally, lead to methemoglobinemia. Additionally, cocaine abuse can secondarily precipitate a sickle-cell crisis in patients with sickle-cell disease. Cocaine-induced vasospasm can decrease oxygen tension in tissues, resulting in sickling of red blood cells.

Obstetric Complications—See Chapter 17

Sexual Dysfunction

Users of cocaine claim that the drug acts as an aphrodisiac. Feelings of sexual excitement that sometimes accompany cocaine may result from actions of cocaine on the dopaminergic neurons of the CNS. Cocaine users experience greater sexual arousal and prolonged stamina during intercourse while high. Cocaine use has also been associated with a "sexual addiction," meaning excessive preoccupation with and continuation of sexual behavior, despite adverse effects. These factors, along with the propensity of substance abusers to engage in unsafe sex, may explain the higher incidence of sexually transmitted diseases in cocaine users.

Chronic cocaine use causes sexual dysfunction, including impotence, secondary to cocaine's physiologic effects. These symptoms may persist for extended periods of time after abstinence. Men who use high doses of cocaine have difficulty maintaining an erection and ejaculating, and many report periods of decreased libido. In women, cocaine can cause irregular menstrual cycles, galactorrhea, amenorrhea, anorgasmia, and infertility.

Head and Neck Complications

Cocaine produces multiple otolaryngological changes that can help identify a cocaine addict. Cocaine HCl that has trickled down the sinuses and posterior oropharynx bathes the teeth in acid, leading to dental enamel erosion. Oral cocaine causes gingival ulceration at the site of application secondary to necrosis from vasoconstriction.

Keratitis and defects in the corneal epithelium are some of the ocular complications of cocaine abuse. There is evidence that crack smokers may be less able to resist corneal infection, resulting in infected corneal ulcers and corneal clouding.

Infectious Complications

Cocaine use carries an increased risk of certain infections because of the setting in which it is used and, although far less characterized, because of immune system alterations. The increased, unsafe sexual activity, both as the result of cocaine-induced compulsive sexuality and the exchange of sex for money or drugs, has increased the risk for sexually transmitted diseases (STDs). The STDs include HIV, gonorrhea, syphilis, and chlamydia.

As with all intravenous drug abuse, intravenous administration of cocaine is associated with HIV transmission, hepatitis B, foreign particle embolization, osteomyelitis, and endocarditis.

Miscellaneous

As a result of cocaine's effect on the primary eating drive center in the hypothalamus, many cocaine users show decreased appetite and experience significant weight loss and malnutrition.

Hyperpyrexia secondary to cocaine use can contribute to sudden death from seizures and cardiac arrhythmias. Body temperatures may elevate secondary to increased metabolism, severe peripheral vasoconstriction, and cocaine's impairment of the thalamus' ability to control body temperature. Treatment is total body immersion in cold water.

Despite the long list of medical complications of cocaine, the most common forms of death associated with cocaine are homicide, suicide, and accidents. Cocaine abuse is associated with violent behavior: in 1989, 40% of homicide victims in Fulton County, Georgia tested positive for cocaine metabolites in their blood; and in 1985, 21% of suicide deaths in New York City of persons less than 60 years of age involved persons who tested positive for cocaine at autopsy.

CLINICAL PRESENTATION

Addiction

Individuals in treatment for cocaine abuse report that development of their addiction takes about 2 to 4 years from initial exposure. The delayed addiction has reduced reports of cocaine's adverse effects during periods of increased cocaine consumption, and has contributed to the illusion that cocaine is not addictive.

In essence, cocaine magnifies the intensity of almost all pleasurable feelings without distorting them. Emotions and sexual feelings are enhanced; self-confidence and self-perception of mastery are increased; anxiety is initially decreased; social inhibition is reduced; interpersonal communication is enhanced; and satiation of appetite occurs.

On the basis of data by the National Institute of Drug Abuse, only 10–15% of those who initially try cocaine intranasally become regular users. The major reasons for discontinuation of use include anxiety, expense, difficult availability, and fear of loss of self-control.

A pattern of high-dose, extended binges during which the pleasurable effects occur without the negative ones classically marks addiction. Users compulsively ingest the drug every 10 to 30 minutes, an act often enhanced by increased availability of the drug and by high-intensity routes of administration. During these binges, feelings of extreme euphoria contrast with the dysphoria of the postbinge period, resulting in further craving of the drug. Addicts average one to seven binges per week, each lasting from 4 to 24 hours with virtually all thoughts focused on cocaine.

A person's susceptibility to addiction depends in part on the route of administration as well as the speed, degree, and duration of psychological and physical changes. Cocaine tends to be less addictive in small doses— the peak plasma levels are low, the onset of activity is slow, the duration of action is long, and the unpleasant withdrawal symptoms are minimal. This pattern occurs with chewing coca leaves, oral ingestion, and intranasal use.

Intravenous cocaine has a higher addictive potential than administration routes necessitating absorption through gastrointestinal or nasal mucosa. Given unlimited access to the drug, intravenous cocaine users will escalate the doses they administer until they undergo severe mental and physical deterioration, or until death.

Smoking cocaine has the highest addictive potential. Although the bioavailability of this route is less than by the intravenous route, smoked cocaine produces a potent, intense high that has an extremely quick onset. A brief euphoric effect is followed by a period of paranoia, depression, and anxiety. The user then craves the drug even more to prevent the recurrence of such feelings.

Withdrawal

Depression following cocaine abstinence occurs most often after long-term use. During the first one to three days of abstinence, users experience a "crash"—depression, irritability, anxiety, confusion, insomnia, and a gradually diminishing desire for cocaine. This is followed by a 1-

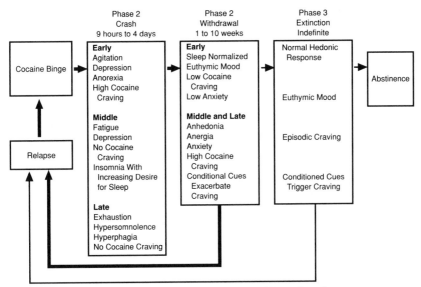

Figure 9.3. Cocaine abstinence phases. Duration and intensity of symptoms vary on the basis of binge characteristics and diagnosis. Binges range in duration from under 4 hours to 6 or more days. High cocaine craving in phase 1 usually lasts less than 6 hours and is followed by a period of noncraving with similar duration in the next subphase (middle phase 1). Substantial craving then returns only after a lag of 0.5 to 5 days during phase 2.

to 3-day period of depression, apathy, lethargy, increased appetite, and a desire for sleep with an aversion to cocaine.

Following the initial crash, withdrawal begins with 1 to 5 days of good sleep, feeling good, and little cocaine craving. This period of tranquillity often precedes another bout of depression, anxiety, irritability, lethargy, boredom, and intense cocaine craving. Over 1 to 4 days, recollection of cocaine's euphoric effects makes patients susceptible to relapse. This period can last up to 2 months. The triphasic symptom pattern of cocaine withdrawal is outlined in Figure 9.3.

Diagnosis

External Physical Signs

Patients with cocaine intoxication may present with a variety of complaints, but several external markers of cocaine abuse appear with intense, repeated use (Table 9.5). The absence of these external signs has little if any significance, but their presence is a strong confirmation of chronic cocaine use. In acute cocaine overdose, vital signs demonstrate increased systemic sympathetic tone: tachycardia, hypertension, diaphoresis, and dilated pupils.

TABLE 9.5. EXTERNAL PHYSICAL SIGNS ASSOCIATED WITH COCAINE ABUSE

Physical Sign	Description
Perforated nasal septum	First described in the 1900s when snorting cocaine became popular. Nasal drops containing vasoconstricting agents cause a similar finding
Cocaine "tracks"	Recent injection sites appear as salmon-colored bruises, sometimes with a clear central zone around the needle puncture site Aging lesions turn yellow and blue, eventually healing without scarring Slowly healing cutaneous ulcers have red to gray bases and blanched margins
Crack keratitis	Crack smoke anesthetizes the corneas of smokers. Decreased sensation can result in too much pressure being applied to the eye when rubbed, resulting in corneal abrasion or keratitis with ulcers and infection
"Crack thumb"	A callus may result from repeated contact of the thumb with a lighter wheel, usually on the ulnar aspect of the thumb
"Crack hand"	Blackened, hyperkeratotic, and burn lesions on the palmar aspects of the hands resulting from repeated handling of hot crack pipes
Dental erosions	Oral/nasal cocaine use bathes the teeth in acid, which erodes the tooth enamel. Gingival ulceration also occurs at the site of application

Toxicological Analysis

Urine tests for cocaine have limited usefulness because of their inability to detect drug use occurring more than 7 days before testing. Low concentrations of cocaine appear in the urine hours after the initial administration, and may be measurable for up to 36 hours. While detectable, these levels are inadequate for routine urine screening. By comparison, benzoylecgonine, a metabolite of cocaine, remains at detectable levels for 5 to 7 days after administration. It is the primary marker of cocaine use in urine toxicological screens.

TREATMENT ISSUES

Acute Cocaine Abuse

The choice of treatment for acute cocaine intoxication depends on the signs and symptoms. Supportive therapy is the first priority. Hyperthermia may be treated by vigorous body cooling. Cardiac and neurologic

TABLE 9.6. PHARMACOLOGIC MANAGEMENT OF SYMPTOMS OF COCAINE INTOXICATION

Sign or Symptom	Treatment
Anxiety, agitation, psychosis	Benzodiazepines (midazolam, lorazepam, or diazepam)
Seizure	Intravenous diazepam; if refractory, short-acting barbiturates (amobarbital) with neuromuscular paralysis if necessary
Hyperthermia	Cooling blanket, fan, ice-water sponging, or ice-water bath; monitor core temperature, and control any seizure activity (paralysis and sedation if necessary)
Tachycardia, severe or associated with chest pain	Beta blocker (propanolol, esmolol); or alpha plus beta blockers (labetalol)
Chest pain[a]	Calcium channel blockers, nitrates, beta blockers, or alpha plus beta blockers
Ventricular tachyarrhythmia	Lidocaine, beta blockers
Cocaine packet ingestion	Charcoal, mild laxatives, possible surgical removal

[a]Relief of myocardial ischemia with nitrates and/or calcium channel blockers is preferred over beta blockers as cocaine has very potent alpha-adrenergic activity; use of beta blockers in cocaine intoxication may result in unopposed alpha activity and cause increases in blood pressure.

status need close monitoring, with medical strategies aimed at relieving symptoms. Frequently, hospitalization for respiratory assistance may be necessary secondary to the concomitant use of sedative-hypnotics, alcohol, or opiates. Table 9.6 lists some pharmacologic interventions for many of the complications of cocaine intoxication.

Detoxification from cocaine requires only abstinence. However, medical treatment to prevent withdrawal will alleviate the drive to obtain cocaine. There is more evidence that bromocriptine, a dopamine agonist, may effectively reduce cocaine cravings as well as the withdrawal dysphoria, hyperprolactinemia, and tendency to develop seizures. The amino acid tyrosine and tricyclic antidepressants (desipramine and nortryptaline) may also diminish withdrawal symptoms.

Treatment of Cocaine Abuse

The treatment of cocaine abuse involves two major phases: (*a*) initiation of abstinence and (*b*) relapse prevention. Before treatment begins, the user must decide to seek help. Cocaine users rarely seek treatment because they feel their use is out of control, but rather because their abuse is creating problems in one or more aspects of their life.

The abuse may cause significant medical problems, a declining job performance, or a significant debt due to the huge expense of maintaining a cocaine dependency. Low-income users may prostitute themselves, steal, or deal drugs in order to support their habit. People come to treatment when the criminal justice system forces them into it, their abuse is scaring them, or family members give the patient an ultimatum. Since entering treatment does not mean that the patient is committed to it, a major goal of the initial treatment is to instill some motivation into the patient.

The first major decision in the treatment of a cocaine-abusing patient is whether the problem is best treated in an outpatient or inpatient environment. Some general rules to guide the treatment of cocaine users in either inpatient or outpatient setting include:

1. Cocaine use should stop all at once, not gradually; symptoms of cocaine withdrawal are not medically dangerous.
2. All other drugs of abuse, including marijuana and alcohol, should be stopped to avoid any decreases in inhibitions, which may lead to relapse.
3. A change in life-style will be necessary to break away from the behavior patterns that lead to the use of cocaine.
4. Other means of personal reward and enjoyment must be learned and substituted for the use of cocaine.
5. Avoid identified drug-using cues, such as the old neighborhood where drug use took place, drug dealers, etc.

Inpatient Treatment

Outpatient treatment is obviously preferable in terms of expense and the degree of interruption of the patient's life, but hospitalization is clearly indicated in the following circumstances:

1. Uncontrolled freebase or intravenous cocaine use;
2. Polysubstance abuse (e.g., alcohol, sedatives) requiring detoxification;
3. Serious medical or psychiatric problems requiring hospitalizations (e.g., systemic infections, cardiac events, psychosis, suicidal intent);
4. Severe psychosocial impairment, inadequate family or social supports;
5. Refusal to participate in outpatient treatment, including those mandated by court or employer;
6. Repeated failure in outpatient treatment;
7. Ready access to large amounts of cocaine;

8. Threatening harm to self or others.

Hospital treatment usually takes place in specialized substance abuse units. The hospital offers a safe refuge from cocaine and the stimuli associated with cocaine. At the initiation of treatment, when patients are least capable of resisting the drug on their own, other patients receiving treatment for substance abuse provide a supportive peer group. Family involvement is also critical. During inpatient treatment, patients can undergo extensive medical, psychiatric, and neurological evaluation while they are drug-free. This evaluation process facilitates the diagnosis and treatment of concomitant disorders, such as depression, anxiety, and insomnia, which are difficult to differentiate from the cocaine crash in the active user. The constant monitoring in the hospital also allows for the detection of subtle stresses or triggers of cocaine craving, which may then be targeted for therapy.

Therapeutic communities provide an inpatient alternative to hospitalization. These concept houses are self-help residential treatment programs that use highly confrontational techniques to rehabilitate drug users, especially those who have failed other types of treatment. A structured community allows the resident to rise through the hierarchy by demonstrating honesty, responsibility, and abstinence from drugs. While effective for some patients, these therapeutic communities are long-term, stressful, and psychologically difficult. Dropout rates are high, and such an approach is usually not recommended as a first treatment effort.

Since the highest relapse rates for cocaine users occur immediately after discharge, halfway houses offer individuals the opportunity to live in a structured environment while initiating and acclimating to a new life-style.

Outpatient Treatment

Outpatient treatment of cocaine abuse refers to a range of treatment modalities used with varying degrees of success. Often several modalities are used at once. This therapy allows the patient to confront the stimuli that triggered their drug abuse. The optimal frequency of outpatient sessions is undecided. A New York study found that over 80% of individuals receiving outpatient treatment once a week relapsed in their cocaine use within 1 year, strongly suggesting that more frequent treatment is needed.

Psychotherapy

Individual psychotherapy with an active or newly abstinent cocaine user examines current personal problems, including the patient's drug use, difficulties within relationships, and inner conflicts, in order to assist the individual in terminating drug use. As the patient achieves a stable abstinence and begins to master these problems, the psychotherapist can then explore the factors that precipitated drug use.

Group psychotherapy may involve one or two professional moderators and 6 to 12 cocaine-dependent patients who offer peer support, advice on such issues as vocational or marital difficulties, and confrontation if a group member relapses. While less open patients may have difficulties interacting effectively with the group, this approach allows drug-dependent patients to detect subtle signs of denial and self-deceit in others because of their own familiarity with these behaviors. Couples or families can enter psychotherapy as a unit to examine the impacts of cocaine use on family relationships and to work out anger and resentment between family members.

Relapse Prevention Therapy

By contrast, relapse prevention therapy helps the cocaine user develop practical strategies to avoid situations and settings in which relapse might occur, such as avoiding substance-abusing friends and even the streets on which they live. If a former cocaine user is tempted to buy drugs if she has $20 in her purse, arrangements can be made with family to ensure that she will only be given $15 at a time. Initial sessions address the ambivalence the cocaine user may have toward ending his/her substance abuse, while later meetings focus on the establishment of life-style changes to maintain cocaine abstinence.

Behavioral Therapy

Cocaine cue extinction, a type of behavioral therapy, focuses on diminishing addicts' classically conditioned responses to cocaine-related stimuli. By using repeated exposure to drug-related stimuli (e.g., drug paraphernalia, drug-buying location, drug-using friends) in the absence of cocaine use, the strength of the association between the drug-related cues and the actual use of cocaine is broken down.

In contingency contracting, a therapy based on operant conditioning models, patients agree to urine monitoring for a contracted period, with a negative contingency for a cocaine-positive urine sample or failure to provide urine when requested. A negative contingency might include a letter written by the patient detailing his/her drug use, which may be sent by the therapist to the patient's employer or licensing body. Drawbacks to this approach are that many patients will not enter into such a contract and that they often relapse once their contract period expires. Contingency contracting works best for patients who "still have something to lose," such as addicted doctors who risk loss of licensure.

Positive contingencies can also be negotiated, with, for instance, the therapist returning part of a sum of money taken at the start of treatment in exchange for each clean urine sample. Contracts that contain positive and negative rewards may be more attractive to the patient.

Self-Help Programs

Cocaine Anonymous (CA) is a self-help group that uses a 12-step model for establishing abstinence and recovery from all drugs. These worldwide organizations have regular meetings that allow recovering addicts to share their experiences and support each other's efforts to avoid relapse. Experienced group members (sponsors) support new members during the initial periods of abstinence when the risk of relapse is especially high. Unlike the help offered by health professionals, these organizations provide a social support system that is available around the clock. The deceivingly easy goal of staying drug-free "one day at a time" can be an effective stimulus in getting addicts to initially attempt to give up cocaine, and many drug-free members of these groups attend meetings daily to reaffirm their commitment to abstinence. While the emphasis on spirituality and a "higher power" in these 12-step groups makes some individuals uncomfortable, alternative approaches are available in organizations such as Rational Recovery.

Pharmacologic Therapies

The use of pharmacologic agents to facilitate the treatment of cocaine abuse as a primary disorder has been disappointing. There is no substance comparable to methadone for opiate addicts available for the treatment of cocaine addicts. The primary strategy of pharmacologic therapy attempts to reverse the known derangements in neurotransmission resulting from chronic cocaine use. The most widely used medications for these problems are tricyclic antidepressants. There is some evidence that desipramine, for example, may significantly decrease cocaine craving and reverse hypersomnolence related to cocaine abstinence. The 2- to 3-week period before the drug becomes effective after the initiation of treatment limits its usefulness, especially since this waiting period coincides with the period during which patients have the highest likelihood of relapsing into cocaine abuse.

Dopamine agonists such as bromocriptine and amantidine may alleviate cocaine craving in chronic users. However, the side effects of bromocriptine, such as nausea, headaches, dizziness, sedation, and hallucinations, reduce the usefulness of the drug. Amantidine may hold some promise since it has fewer side effects.

Treatment Summary

Given the large range of different approaches to the treatment of cocaine abuse, choosing which methods to incorporate for a given individual is difficult. No hard-and-fast rules apply. Certain doctors or treatment centers will have their own preferences based on what they have found effective. Cocaine abusers must be identified and immediately referred to competent practitioners of substance abuse treatment to negotiate with the user and to devise appropriate treatment strategies designed for the individual needs of the patient.

SUBSTANCE ABUSE JARGON

Cocaine

coke	lady	snow	nose candy
blow	toot	flake	

Crack Cocaine

crack	freebase
rock	base

FURTHER READING

Cregler LL. Medical complications of cocaine abuse. N Engl J Med 1986;315:1495–1500.

Gawin FH, Ellinwood EH. Cocaine and other stimulants: action, abuse, and treatment. N Engl J Med 1988;318:1173–1182.

Gold MS. Cocaine (and crack): clinical aspects. In: Lowinson JH, Ruiz P, Millman RB, eds. Substance Abuse: A Comprehensive Textbook. Philadelphia: Williams & Wilkins, 1992.

Johanson C, Fischman M. The pharmacology of cocaine related to its abuse. Pharmacol Rev 1989;41:3–42.

Karch SB. The Pathology of Drug Abuse. Boca Raton, FL: CRC Press, 1993;1–143.

Warner EA. Cocaine abuse. Ann Intern Med 1993;119:226–235.

Weiss RD, Mirin SM, Bartel RL. Cocaine. Washington, DC: American Psychiatric Press, 1994.

Chapter 10

Marijuana

Albert Losken and Saverio Maviglia with Lawrence S. Friedman

Marijuana has been used for at least 8,000 years, although it was initially spun into thread, made into rope, and woven into textiles. Approximately 5,000 years ago, the Chinese began to exploit its medicinal properties and the Greek historian Herodotus later documented its psychoactive properties. Like many psychoactive drugs, marijuana became extremely popular during the 1960s and 1970s as a method of self-exploration and experimentation by American youth. As drug use has become less socially acceptable in the last two decades, marijuana use has declined. However, marijuana continues to be associated with counter-cultural expression and adolescent experimentation.

EPIDEMIOLOGY

The 1992 National Household Survey on Drug Abuse revealed that 67.5 million persons had used marijuana at least once and that 8.6 million had used it in the last month. Figure 10.1 shows the incidence of marijuana use among high school seniors from 1975 through 1993. Although there is a noticeable decline in recent years after a peak in 1979–1980, use rates continue to remain high—greater than a third of high school students used marijuana at least once in 1992, while 18.8% used in the last month, and 2.6% used marijuana daily (see Chapter 2).

Chronic marijuana use has associations with dysfunctional family relationships (broken homes, marital break-ups), poor school performance (absenteeism), early sexual activity, and the use of other drugs (alcohol, cigarettes, stimulants, hallucinogens, narcotics, sedatives). Other factors motivating marijuana use include self-medication of anxiety, distress, or depression, widespread availability of marijuana, socialization of use among different age groups, and socially learned expectations or norms.

PHARMACOLOGY

Marijuana is the dried, crushed flowers and leaves of some strains of the cannabis hemp plant. Its intoxicating properties depend on several natural constituents of the cannabis resin. The three most abundant agents include isomers of tetrahydrocannabinol (THC), cannabinol, and cannabidiol. The concentration of THC determines the potency of the

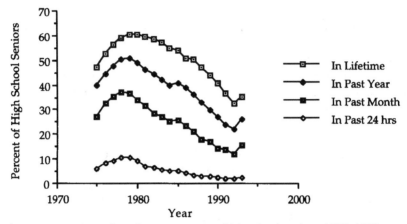

Figure 10.1. Estimated marijuana use among high school seniors, 1975–1993.

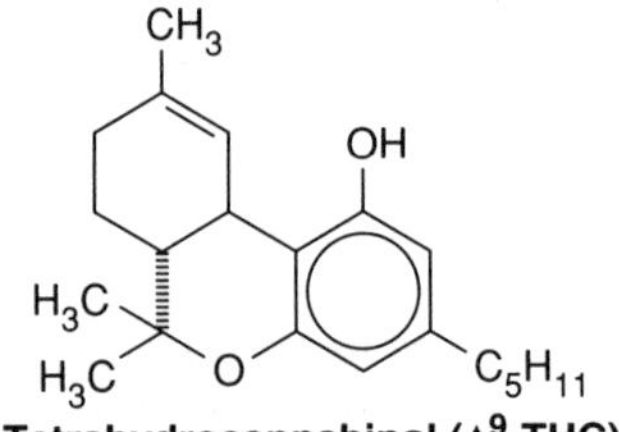

Tetrahydrocannabinol (Δ⁹-THC)

Figure 10.2. Chemical structure of tetrahydrocannabinol (Δ⁹-THC).

plant. The major psychoactive component of marijuana is Δ^9-tetrahydro-cannabinol (Fig. 10.2), whose potency is diminished by nonpsychoactive cannabinoids. In the United States, a 300–500 mg cigarette of marijuana has a THC content ranging between 0.5–11%. Hashish, a resin derived from the same plant as marijuana, is usually smoked in a compressed powder form and has similar pharmacologic properties.

Smoke inhalation is the most common route of administration, but cannabinoids may also be chewed, brewed as a tea, or eaten in baked foods. The absorbance of THC is variable and depends on the individual, the route of administration, and the efficiency of administration. Smoking delivers approximately 50% of absorbable THC to the bloodstream with peak plasma levels occurring within 70 minutes. The level then declines within an hour and subjective effects disappear after 6 hours. The maximum rise in plasma THC concentration for intravenous administration is similar to that of inhalation. By contrast, oral administration delivers approximately one-third less THC to the blood than smoking, with the effects appearing 30–120 minutes after ingestion.

TABLE 10.1. ACUTE EFFECTS OF MARIJUANA USE

System	Effect of Marijuana Use
General	Relaxation/euphoria
	Dilated pupils
	Congested conjunctiva
	Dry mucous membranes
	Dry mouth and throat
	Increased appetite
	Rhinitis/pharyngitis
Neurologic	Impaired cognitive ability
	Altered perception
	Impairment of skilled motor activity
	Slurred speech
Cardiovascular	Sinus tachycardia
	Increased systolic BP while supine
	Decreased systolic BP while standing
Psychiatric	Flashbacks
	Depersonalization
	Anxiety/confusion
	Hallucinations/illusions
	Loss of insight

From the bloodstream, THC either enters cells, remains bound to plasma proteins, or is deposited in fat where it may be found 2–3 weeks later. High-affinity binding sites for THC have been identified in the liver and brain. In the brain, cannabinoids bind to G-protein-coupled receptors in neurons and inhibit an adenyl cyclase/cAMP second messenger system. These interactions appear to be the biochemical basis for marijuana's central nervous system (CNS) effects. Since cannabinoids and their metabolites have high lipid solubility, THC may interact nonspecifically with cell membrane lipids, causing increased cell membrane fluidity. The liver metabolizes THC and then excretes it primarily via the biliary system and, to a lesser extent, via the kidneys. The half-life of THC in plasma is about 2 days.

CONSEQUENCES OF USE

Marijuana has stimulant, sedative, and hallucinogenic (at high doses) properties that are all dose-related. The most prominent effects occur in the central nervous and the cardiovascular systems (Tables 10.1 and 10.2).

Acute effects include impaired mental function, altered perception, and impaired skill performance. No evidence associates personality changes from marijuana use with irreversible changes to the nervous

TABLE 10.2. CONSEQUENCES OF MARIJUANA USE

System	Effects of Marijuana Use
General	Chronic fatigue and lethargy Chronic nausea or vomiting Headaches Irritability
Oropharyngeal	Discolored tongue Swollen uvula
Respiratory	Dry, nonproductive cough Chronic sore throat Nasal congestion Asthma exacerbation Frequent upper respiratory tract infections Chronic bronchitis Chronic obstructive pulmonary disease Lung cancer
Neurologic	Decreased muscular coordination Increased reaction time Impaired visual tracking (rapid eye test) Altered depth and color perception
Reproductive	Infertility Absent or abnormal menstruation Teratological abnormalities in progeny Impotence Diminished libido and sexual satisfaction
Psychiatric	Mood disorders (depression, anxiety) Rapid mood changes Panic attacks Personality changes Suicide attempts
Cognitive	Decreased short-term memory Impaired abstract reasoning Dementia Delirium
Social	Social withdrawal and isolation Change in peer-group identification Dropout from sports or other activities

system. However, long-term marijuana use does cause long-lasting structural and functional changes in hippocampal neurons of animals, suggesting it may have adverse effects on personality.

Marijuana is a relaxant that causes a feeling of well-being and/or euphoria that is dose-related. The immediate subjective effects—a sense of pleasure, a dreamy carefree state of relaxation, and an alteration of sensory perceptions—can give way to brief periods of anxiety and confusion with hallucinatory phenomena, such as "flashbacks," depersonalization, loss of insight, de-realization, marked cognitive and psychomotor impairment, and rare cases of acute toxic psychosis at high doses. The hallucinations and fantasies associated with high-dose THC can cause psychotomimetic phenomena such as distorted body image, loss of personal identity, and sensory and mental illusions.

Coupled with its alteration of mood and memory, marijuana impairs motor coordination and cognitive ability. Activation of marijuana-sensitive receptors in forebrain and cerebellum appear to mediate this action. Being "high" impairs the psychomotor skills needed to accomplish complex motor and cognitive functions, such as driving, perception, attention, and information processing. These effects persist for 4–8 hours—long after the subjective effects of the drug diminish. The usual postintoxication period is marked by calmness, clarity of mind, increased appetite, and restful sleep.

Marijuana increases heart rate and systolic blood pressure (SBP) while supine, and decreases standing SBP. In patients with hypertension, cerebrovascular disease, and coronary artery disease, increased cardiac workload induced by cannabinoids may be a potential risk.

CLINICAL PRESENTATION

Diagnostic Evaluation

Relatively few patients present specifically for treatment of acute marijuana use problems. Therefore, a thorough history will almost always reveal more than physical examinations or laboratory tests. Nevertheless, the clinician must actively seek out the signs and symptoms of marijuana use.

The signs of both acute and chronic marijuana use are, in general, nonspecific (Tables 10.1 and 10.2). Urine drug screening may be helpful, but false positive rates may be substantial. For instance, passive inhalation of THC smoke at a party may result in a positive drug screen. Other laboratory tests are neither sensitive nor specific for marijuana use.

Tolerance, Addiction, and Withdrawal

Tolerance develops to many of the effects of cannabinoids. In order to maintain a psychoactive response, chronic users must increase their doses and dosing frequency. Some experienced smokers report more subjective effects with fewer inhalations. This phenomenon may be explained by the slow release of accumulated THC stored in fatty tissue, coupled with the more efficient inhalation techniques of the experienced user.

TABLE 10.3. SIGNS AND SYMPTOMS OF MARIJUANA WITHDRAWAL

Insomnia	Anorexia
Nausea	Photophobia
Myalgia	Cannabis craving
Anxiety	Depression
Restlessness	Mental confusion
Irritability	Yawning
Chills	Weight loss
Sweating	Tremors
Diarrhea	

Marijuana can cause mild physical dependence and, consequently, a withdrawal syndrome with the following signs and symptoms: irritability, restlessness, nervousness, loss of appetite, weight loss, insomnia, rebound increase in REM sleep, chills, and tremors (Table 10.3). The symptoms can appear as early as a few hours after cessation of the drug and last up to 4–5 days. Chronic and periodic marijuana users often crave the euphoric effects of the drug, an effect probably mediated by THC-induced neuroadaptations in the brain.

Therapeutic Indications

Despite laws prohibiting the use of marijuana, government-grown marijuana was available by prescription until recently for therapeutic use. Several properties of THC help specific groups of patients: (a) its anti-emetic effects help cancer patients eat and be more comfortable; (b) in glaucoma patients it reduces eye pressure; and (c) in AIDS patients it stimulates appetite. However, in 1992 marijuana was switched from a Schedule 2 controlled substance (available for the treatment of certain specified conditions) to Schedule 1 (completely prohibited). The National Institutes of Health (NIH) determined that carcinogens and infectious agents in marijuana posed significant risks to AIDS patients and cancer patients with impaired immunity. Furthermore, safer, more effective therapies for these conditions became available.

Although marijuana is no longer available for medical use, its active ingredient (THC) has received approval for treatment of nausea, glaucoma, and decreased appetite. Case reports have described the use of marijuana to treat spasticity and ataxia in patients with multiple sclerosis, asthma, refractory childhood epilepsy, torsion dystonia, Tourette's syndrome, Huntington's disease, and Parkinson's disease. Although these effects may be related to the sedative, anxiolytic, or analgesic effects of marijuana, clinical trials still need to reveal if THC can be used therapeutically for these disorders.

TREATMENT

As with other types of drug use, denial is frequently a problem. The provider must present the need for intervention without accusations, blame, or excuses. In adolescent populations, in particular, the patient may feel that the use of marijuana helps him/her cope with life stresses, improve self-image, and give identity. Peer influence is strong and must be recognized as a potential barrier to successful treatment. For all patients, the provider must offer support and guidance throughout the entire process and ensure that appropriate follow-up care is provided.

Many treatment modalities for general substance abuse exist, but very few strategies have evolved for specific management of marijuana abuse. Treatment of marijuana abuse is currently divided into therapies for acute reactions and therapies for chronic complications.

Treatment of Acute Reaction

Acute reactions to marijuana use include panic attacks, drug toxicity, flashbacks, and withdrawal. Panic reactions are most commonly seen in naive users with hysterical, obsessional, or personality disorders. These patients receive supportive therapy—a quiet room with subdued lighting and a "talk down" approach without seclusion or physical restraints. Low-dose anxiolytics (chlordiazepoxide 10–50 mg) may be used in severe cases.

Toxic reactions usually follow ingestion of large oral doses and present as delirium, acute organic brain syndrome, or mutism. Therapy includes close observation and supportive measures. Pharmacotherapy should be avoided if possible.

Marijuana can trigger LSD-like flashback experiences, which usually last only a few minutes. If these reactions occur 6 months or more after abstinence or last for several hours, a psychiatric and neurologic evaluation is indicated. Otherwise the treatment includes reassurance and, if necessary, anxiolytics.

Withdrawal from marijuana may occur only in chronic, high-dose users. Unlike alcohol or opiate withdrawal, no pharmacological adjuncts are available specifically for marijuana withdrawal.

Treatment of Chronic Consequences of Use

Marijuana craving represents the most significant barrier to treatment. Treatment should focus on eliminating drug use and promoting increased physical, psychological, and social health. The first step is abstention from marijuana and all other nonprescribed substances. Since withdrawal symptoms may not occur for a week or more after abstinence, patients may not associate them with cessation of the drug. The addiction cycle often recurs at this point because the patient craves marijuana, but does not associate it with cessation of drug use. When initiating therapy, the patient should receive an outline of the symptoms and time course of the withdrawal. At this point, following the patient in a drug-free state and treating all medical problems are critical, so that the patient does not stray from the rehabilitation efforts.

Two controversial effects can accompany chronic marijuana use, *cannabis psychosis* and *amotivational syndrome*. It is unclear whether marijuana causes these effects or if use is coincident with preexisting disorders. Marijuana can intensify a preexisting schizophrenic condition and may antagonize the effects of neuroleptics. In any case, marijuana psychosis usually responds quickly to antipsychotic drugs. If psychosis persists, underlying primary schizophrenia should be considered. For amotivational syndrome, underlying depression must be ruled out.

SUBSTANCE ABUSE JARGON

Marijuana

pot	homegrown	ganga	chronic
reefer	roach	bone	hash
doobie	joint	weed	hash oil
smoke	grass	maryjane	
herb	dope	jay	

PCP with Marijuana

happy sticks	joy sticks	blunt

Getting High/Stoned

euphoric intoxication with marijuana

Joint, Roach, Bong

paraphernalia associated with smoking marijuana

FURTHER READING

Dewey WL. Cannabinoid pharmacology. Pharmacol Rev 1986;38:151–178.

Estroff TW, Gold MS. Psychiatric presentations of marijuana abuse. Psychiatric Annals 1986;16:221–224.

Sallen SE, Zinberg NE, Frei E, III. Antiemetic effect of Δ^9-tetrahydrocannabinol in patients receiving cancer chemotherapy. N Engl J Med 1975;293:795–797.

Schnoll SH, Daghestani AN. Treatment of marijuana abuse. Psychiatric Annals 1986:16:249–254.

Stenbacka M, Allebeck P, Romelsjo A. Initiation into drug abuse: the pathway from being offered drugs to trying cannabis and progression to intravenous drug abuse. Scand J Soc Med 1993;21:31–39.

Tennant FS. The clinical syndrome of marijuana dependence. Psychiatric Annals 1986;16:225–234.

Chapter 11

Opiates

David Hirsch and Jeffrey E. Paley with John A. Renner, Jr.

The term "opiate" refers specifically to the natural products of the opium poppy (*Papaver somniferum*), such as morphine and codeine. Narcotic is a broader classification of central nervous system (CNS) depressants with morphine-like effects. Narcotics include both the natural opiates and synthetic opiate-like compounds, such as methadone, heroin, and fentanyl.

The use of opiates dates back to Sumerian civilization and Arabic literature from as early as the 10th century documents its use. More recently, three events of the 19th century greatly affected opiate use and abuse: the isolation of morphine; the invention of the hypodermic syringe; and the synthesis of diacetylmorphine (heroin) in 1874. These events led to the widespread use of opiates for analgesia, but also increased the potential for opiate abuse. Higher serum concentrations of morphine or heroin could be achieved by injection than by smoking or chewing.

Public attitudes toward opiate use altered in the 1870s when it became apparent that many of the "medical" uses of opiates actually treated the symptoms of opiate dependence, not systemic illnesses. Legal, nonmedical use of opiates ultimately ended with the Harrison Act of 1914, which required registration of narcotic producers and distributors, taxed drug handlers, and banned narcotic use without a doctor's prescription. Despite these efforts, abuse of opiates remains an important social issue.

The potential for opiate abuse and their medical utility in problems ranging from pain control to diarrhea make an understanding of the distinction between addiction and dependence important.

EPIDEMIOLOGY

The epidemiology of opiate use affects many different populations. The following data highlight its widespread use:

- A 1992 screening study of newborn meconium revealed that only 25% of the mothers whose baby's meconium tested positive for opiates self-reported a history of opiate use.
- In a 1993 study of employed and insured individuals in New York, approximately 1% of the total subscriber population and 2% of the adult males used intravenous opiates.

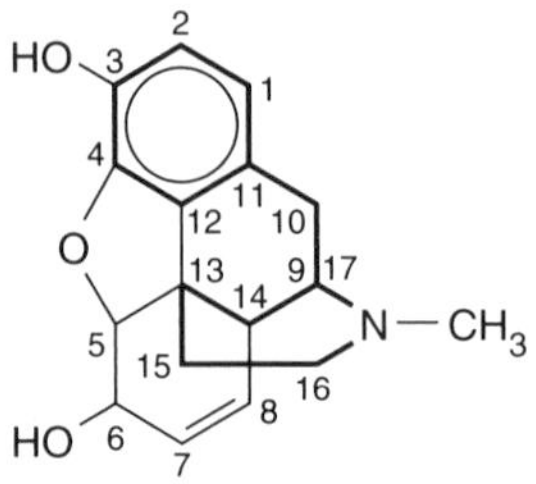

Morphine

Figure 11.1. Chemical structure of morphine.

- In a 1986 study, 21% of male New York prison inmates reported using heroin. Of that 21%, 81% were intravenous users and 3% were less than 21 years old.
- The rate of personality disorders among opiate-abusing individuals ranges between 65 and 90%, with antisocial personality disorder the most common diagnosis.

Since the late 19th century, importation, production, distribution, and use of narcotics have had strong connections with criminal behavior. No evidence demonstrates that opiate intoxication stimulates individuals to commit crimes. Rather, the link between opiate abuse and crime appears to be the money needed to maintain an opiate addiction.

PHARMACOLOGY

Formulation and Administration

The active ingredients of the poppy are obtained by opening the seed pod after the petals of the flower have dropped. A white latex oozes out, turns brown, and hardens upon standing. By weight, 75% of this resin is inert, consisting of various plant products. However, the remaining material is a mixture of 25 different alkaloids with morphine (Fig. 11.1) present in highest concentration.

Since the 1940s, several synthetic opioid agonists and antagonists have been developed (Table 11.1). In 1975 an entirely new field of molecular pharmacology began with the identification of the first endogenous opioid. Called enkephalins, these pentapeptides are opiate receptor agonists. The discovery of β-endorphin and dynorphin, each the degradation product of a larger precursor peptide, quickly followed. Current research has identified at least 18 endogenous peptides with opiate-like activity.

TABLE 11.1. COMMON NARCOTICS

Strong Agonists	Morphine
	Meperidine
	Methadone
	Fentanyl
	Heroin
Moderate Agonists	Propoxyphene
	Codeine
Partial Agonists	Pentazocine
Antagonists	Naloxone
	Naltrexone

Mechanism of Action and Pharmacokinetics

Three distinct opiate receptor subtypes, mu, kappa, and delta, exist. The mu-receptor preferentially binds morphine and is found mostly in areas involved with analgesia—the periaqueductal gray matter, rostroventral medulla, medial thalamus, and dorsal horn of the spinal cord. This receptor also mediates euphoria, miosis, and respiratory depression. The prototypic ligand for the kappa-receptor is ketocyclazocine and other benzomorphan drugs. The dorsal horn, deep cortical layers, and other regions of the brain have kappa-receptors. Activation of this receptor accounts for spinal analgesia, miosis, and sedation. The delta-receptor has a high affinity for enkephalins, such as deltorphins. The major locations for these receptors are the limbic system and the dorsal horn of the spinal cord. While kappa- and delta-receptors both function in analgesia at the dorsal horn, delta-receptors play a role in miosis and hypotension.

G-proteins coupled to opiate receptors link opiate, extracellular binding to intracellular actions. Mu- and delta-receptors inhibit adenlyate cyclase and activate inwardly-rectifying potassium channels (see Figure 1.2). Kappa- and delta-receptors inhibit the opening of voltage-dependent calcium channels through a pertussis toxin-sensitive mechanism. The locations of these receptors in the brain include the nucleus raphe magnus and the locus ceruleus in the brainstem, and the periaqueductal gray and mesolimbic dopamine system in the midbrain. In the spinal cord, opiates have inhibitory effects on spinothalamic nociceptive neurons. Naloxone can antagonize the actions of each of these receptors.

Opiates are absorbed subcutaneously, intramuscularly, and orally. However, first-pass metabolism reduces the blood plasma levels achieved by oral administration. Although they bind to plasma proteins, opioids rapidly leave the blood and concentrate in the lungs, liver, spleen, and kidneys. Due to its bulk, skeletal muscle can be a reservoir for the drugs.

TABLE 11.2. ACUTE AND CHRONIC SEQUELAE OF OPIATE USE

System	Acute Effects	Chronic Effects
CNS	Analgesia Euphoria Sedation to unconsciousness Suppression of the cough reflex	Dependence syndrome Peripheral neuropathy Myelopathy Amblyopia Mood instability
Respiratory	Respiratory depression	Increased respiratory disease (more pneumonia, more TB)

GI	Diminished propulsive
	  contractions
	Decreased biliary, pancreatic,
	  and intestinal secretions
		Constipation
		
		Impaired liver function
		
		Nausea and vomiting

Eyes	Miosis (except meperidine)	
Renal	Inhibition of urinary voiding reflex	Narcotic-induced nephropathy
Metabolic		Altered adrenal metabolism
Sexual	Reduced libido	Irregular menstruation

The hydrophobic quality of drugs, such as heroin and codeine, allow them to traverse the blood-brain barrier much more efficiently than morphine, thus augmenting their effect on the CNS. The liver metabolizes opioids into polar compounds, which are then excreted. Agents that contain free hydroxyl groups, such as morphine, are glucuronated. Esters, such as heroin, are acted upon by esterases and then conjugated.

CONSEQUENCES OF USE

Table 11.2 summarizes the physiological changes involved with acute and chronic opiate use.

Central Nervous System

Among the numerous physiologic effects of opiates, analgesia and euphoria are the most prominent. Opiate-induced analgesia occurs in supraspinal and spinal locations. Supraspinally, the opioids activate neurons in the periaqueductal gray matter (PAG) and nucleus raphe magnus (NRM). The major descending analgesic pathway involves PAG projections to the rostroventral medullary region (NRM) which then projects to the dorsal horn. Within the dorsal horn, serotonergic fibers from the NRM appear to activate enkephalinergic neurons, which release endogenous opioids. These opioids inhibit spinothalamic nociceptive neurons by making direct postsynaptic contact with them. Opioid-containing interneurons may exist that also inhibit the nociceptive fibers presynaptically. These interneurons probably play a role in the inhibition of nociceptive reflexes observed with opiate administration. Chapter 19 presents a more thorough discussion of pain management and the role of narcotics in the treatment of pain.

Respiratory

Opiates depress respiratory drive by decreasing the responsiveness of the brainstem respiratory centers to carbon dioxide. Furthermore, depression of pontine and medullary centers affects the rhythmicity of breathing. Respiratory depression is the most common cause of death in opiate overdoses and can occur 5–10 minutes after intravenous administration of morphine and within 30–90 minutes of intramusclar or subcutaneous administration.

Gastrointestinal

Opiate action on smooth muscle decreases motility, while it increases resting tone. The consequences of these actions are decreased biliary, pancreatic, and intestinal secretions, decreased propulsive contractions, and increased nonpropulsive segmental contractions (generally felt as cramps). For these reasons, opiates effectively treat diarrhea and dysentery, but by the same mechanism, opiates can also cause constipation.

CLINICAL PRESENTATION

Opiate compounds are used for analgesia and anesthesia, and to treat diarrhea and cough. Since opiates only treat the symptoms of underlying diseases, they may mask the progress of a disease. When prescribing them, opiate dependence must be weighed against the benefits of symptomatic relief. Though physiological dependence will eventually develop whenever opiates are given therapeutically for prolonged periods of time, the loss of control, compulsive drug use, and other social and behavioral patterns seen in addiction rarely develop in patients without a previous history of abuse. The consequences of dependence in both the addicted and nonaddicted patient are manifested systemically as tolerance and withdrawal symptoms upon cessation of drug intake. In treating patients on long-term opiate therapy, these syndromes must be addressed if discontinuation of the drug occurs.

For an addict, the drug-craving and withdrawal symptoms can lead to prostitution, theft, violent crimes, and other illegal activities in order to procure the funds needed for drugs. This egocentric drug-seeking behavior leads the addict to seek one type of security—a steady flow of the drug. To this end, users often develop only erratic social contacts, usually associated with opiates, and may steal from a friend to continue drug use.

TABLE 11.3. MEDICAL SYNDROMES ASSOCIATED WITH OPIATES

Syndrome	Characteristics
Opiate intoxication	Conscious Sedated "Nodding" Mood normal to euphoric Pinpoint pupils
Acute overdose	Unconsciousness Pinpoint pupils Slow, shallow respiration

Opiate Withdrawal	Objective Signs	Subjective Signs
Anticipatory (3–4 hours after last "fix")		Fear of withdrawal Anxiety Drug craving Drug-seeking behavior
Early (8–10 hours after last "fix")	Sweating Yawning Rhinorrhea Lacrimation Dilated pupils	Anxiety Restlessness Nasal stuffiness Drug-seeking behavior Stomach cramps
Fully developed (1–3 days after last "fix")	Tremor Piloerection Vomiting Diarrhea Fever Muscle spasms Increased BP Tachycardia	Severe anxiety Restlessness Muscle pain Impulse-driven, drug- seeking behavior Chills Headache Irritability
Protracted abstinence (may last up to 6 months)	Hypotension Bradycardia	Insomnia Loss of energy Loss of appetite Stimulus-driven opiate cravings

Categories of Opiate Use

Opiate use may be broadly categorized as dependence, abuse, or medicinal. Although the DSM-IV definitions of opiate dependence and abuse are similar to those for other classes of abused substances (see Chapter 1), opiate intoxication and opiate withdrawal have unique physiological manifestations (Table 11.3).

Opiate abuse generally presents in one of two basic clinical patterns: acute or chronic. Acute presentations that warrant prompt medical intervention include opiate overdose and the opiate withdrawal syndrome. Chronic opiate users, on the other hand, may present to the health professional for vague reasons without obvious evidence of substance abuse. Recognition of opiate abuse in this latter group of patients often requires a more detailed history and physical examination.

Clinical Assessment

Physical Examination

Symptoms of opiate abuse differ significantly depending on whether the patient presents with opiate overdose, withdrawal, or nonacute opiate dependence. Table 11.3 outlines the constellation of signs and symptoms characteristic of each presentation. When evaluating a patient for *withdrawal* the signs and symptoms may be characterized as either objective or subjective symptoms. The separation of the two will help differentiate physical withdrawal from drug-seeking behavior. Chapter 19 discusses pain-seeking behaviors.

Laboratory Tests and Diagnostic Procedures

1. Urine toxicology—this test will detect opiate use in the preceding 48 hours with about a 90% sensitivity, but a positive result is not diagnostic of opiate dependence.
2. Naloxone challenge—naloxone (Narcan), an opiate receptor antagonist, is used to determine the presence and severity of opiate intoxication. Because naloxone can precipitate acute withdrawal, careful administration should occur in the presence of an experienced physician. Given these side effects, the main use for this challenge is for an unconscious patient in the emergency room and it follows below:
   - A dosage of 0.2–0.4 mg of naloxone is administered intravenously over 5 minutes or, alternatively, by bolus injection subcutaneously or intramuscularly.
   - Observe closely for signs of early withdrawal such as pupillary dilatation, tachypnea, lacrimation, rhinorrhea, or sweating.
   - If no observable response develops over 15–30 minutes, a second dose of 0.4 mg intravenously or 0.4–0.8 mg subcutaneously can be administered and the response reassessed.
   - If no response is subsequently observed, then opiate dependence is virtually excluded.
   - Remember: If the patient is a polysubstance user, naloxone will not reverse symptoms of non-narcotic drugs.

TREATMENT

While management of the acute syndromes of opiate overdose and withdrawal is typically straightforward, the clinical approach to long-term management of the opiate-abusing patient represents a greater challenge. Many different treatment options exist for the treatment setting (inpatient versus outpatient), goal of treatment (abstinence versus stabilization), modality of treatment (pharmacotherapy versus psychotherapy), and duration of treatment.

Acute Treatment: Opiate Overdose

Opiate overdose is a medical emergency heralded classically by respiratory depression, miosis, and coma. The severely intoxicated patient may also present with marked bradycardia and/or hypotension. Patients who present with dysphoria, seizures, agitation, or tremors may have overdosed on meperidine, propoxyphone, or an agonist/antagonist. In addition to airway support, the treatment of choice is naloxone 0.4–0.8 mg intravenously (0.01 mg/kg; naloxone comes in 1-ampule vials with 0.4 mg/ampule) of naloxone, a pure opiate antagonist, which can reverse cardiorespiratory depression and restore the patient to consciousness within seconds. Treatment with naloxone follows the following guidelines:

- For likely addicts/opiate overdoses: Give 0.2–0.4 mg to minimize chance of putting the patient into acute withdrawal. Then titrate every hour or with an intravenous drip of naloxone until the patient regains consciousness.
- The half-life of naloxone is less than most opioids. Therefore, the patient needs continued reassessment and potential redosing after he/she has regained consciousness, especially if the overdose was due to long-acting drugs such as methadone, pentazocine, or levomethadyl.

Because of the possibility of a long-acting opiate overdose, patients should not be discharged after the initial response no matter how dramatic the improvement—they must be observed for at least 24 hours.

Transitional Treatment: Detoxification for Opiate Withdrawal

Abrupt opiate withdrawal is not life-threatening in otherwise healthy individuals, but can be extremely unpleasant. The treatment for patients experiencing acute withdrawal is detoxification, a process intended to eliminate the abused substance by tapering off use of that substance or another drug with similar, but longer-acting and less euphoric, qualities. Treatment may be administered on an inpatient (psychiatric hospital, substance abuse treatment center, or psychiatric/medical unit of a general hospital) or outpatient basis.

Pharmacologic Therapies

Methadone

Methadone hydrochloride, a synthetic long-acting opiate agonist, is the most commonly used and most effective pharmacologic agent for the treatment of opiate dependence. It is used as primary therapy in one of two clinical settings: short-term detoxification and long-term maintenance of opiate-dependent patients.

The underlying principle of methadone use in the detoxification setting is as follows: methadone, a long-acting agent, is substituted for the short-acting agents such as morphine or heroin, to stabilize the patient for several days with minimal symptoms of withdrawal, and fewer episodes of euphoria and sedation. Subsequently, the gradual withdrawal of methadone occurs over a period of days to weeks with careful monitoring of both subjective and objective symptoms of withdrawal. The final goal of detoxification is the attainment of a drug-free state.

A number of specific properties make methadone a safe and effective treatment. First, an adequate single dose (see below) of methadone in a stabilized patient has a 24–36-hour duration of action, providing relief of narcotic craving without causing euphoria, sedation, or analgesia. Second, patients on methadone can maintain entirely normal social function and perform mental and physical tasks without impairment. Third, methadone also provides cross-tolerance to other opiates by opiate-receptor blockade, thus minimizing the effects of short-acting narcotics and decreasing the likelihood of opiate overdose. Finally, methadone has minimal side effects.

Methadone is contraindicated for patients who are dependent on lower potency narcotics such as meperidine (Demerol) and codeine. In these patients methadone can actually increase the severity of opiate dependence. By contrast, in patients who are methadone-dependent, mixed agonists-antagonists, such as pentazocine (Talwin), can precipitate acute withdrawal.

Controversy surrounds the duration of methadone detoxification therapy. Although the Food and Drug Administration allows two different regimens of detoxification, a short-term (up to 30 days) course and a long-term (up to 180 days) course, most states still restrict methadone detoxification to 21 days. Studies have shown that the addicts most likely to achieve rehabilitation are those who have already undergone multiple episodes of treatment. A sample methadone detoxification protocol that takes into account the different patient profiles of opiate dependence is shown in Table 11.4.

Recent studies have shown that in long-term methadone maintenance programs, the provision of additional services, such as medical care and psychosocial services, markedly enhances the efficacy of treatment. Participants of short-term detoxification programs should also benefit significantly from comprehensive social services, although this has not yet been specifically studied. Many substance abuse professionals agree that methadone detoxification programs should, at minimum, offer fol-

TABLE 11.4. SAMPLE METHADONE DETOXIFICATION PROTOCOL

For Light Opiate Dependency:

(Light defined as heroin use of $50/day or less, nonprogram or "street" methadone use of 40 mg/day or less, or use of prescription opiates equivalent to these.)

First day (day of admission): Give methadone, 10–30 mg total, in divided doses. Take into account the amount that the patient has taken before arriving for admission

Second day and following: Reduce the total daily methadone dosage by 10 mg/day until a total daily dose of 10 mg/day is reached

Order methadone 5 mg/day for 1 or 2 days

Observed the patient for at least 48 hours after the last methadone dose and then discharge if there are no objective signs of opiate withdrawal

For Heavy Opiate Dependency:

(Heavy defined as heroin use of $50/day or more, "street" methadone use of more than 40 mg/day, or use of prescription opiates equivalent to these.)

First day (day of admission): Give methadone, 30–40 mg total, in divided doses. Take into account the amount that the patient has taken before arriving for admission

Second day and following: Reduce the total daily methadone dosage by 10 mg/day until a total daily dose of 10 mg/day is reached

Order methadone 5 mg/day for 1–3 days

Observed the patient for at least 48 hours after the last methadone dose and then discharge if there are no objective signs of opiate withdrawal

For patients from Methadone Maintenance Programs

Confirm the patient's regular methadone maintenance dose and the last day of administration, then:

First day (day of admission): Give the patient their regular maintenance amount of methadone, but in divided doses

Second day and following: Decrease the total daily dose by 10 mg/day until a total daily dose of 40 mg/day is reached.

From this point, reduce the total daily dose by no more than 5 mg/day until the total daily dose is 5 mg

Give a single dose of 5 mg for 2 or 3 days

Observe the patient for at least 48 hours and discharge if no objective withdrawal signs appear

low-up outpatient counseling to be at least moderately effective at preventing relapse.

Clonidine

Clonidine, an α_2-adrenergic receptor antagonist, is safe and effective for opiate detoxification. It alleviates the physiological symptoms of withdrawal, but does not significantly relieve psychological symptoms, such as drug craving. Advantages of clonidine are that it does not produce euphoria, is not subject to abuse, and may be easily discontinued. Clonidine therapy occurs over 10–14 days and is used most frequently in patients for whom methadone detoxification is temporarily unavailable.

The combination of clonidine and naltrexone, a long-acting opiate antagonist, has been shown to provide more rapid (5 days), yet still safe and effective, opiate detoxification.

Naltrexone

Naltrexone, a pure narcotic antagonist like naloxone, is a useful adjunct in the treatment of opiate dependence. It plays no role in the acute treatment of overdose because it precipitates acute withdrawal in patients with opiates still in their system. Additionally, its long duration of action makes control of the acute withdrawal more difficult and unpredictable.

Instead, among the pharmacotherapies for opiate use and abuse, naltrexone holds the unique position as a purely preventive drug. As a long-acting narcotic antagonist, it binds tightly to opiate receptors and can block the effects of subsequently administered narcotics for as long as 3 days with few side effects. Most dramatically, it sharply inhibits narcotic craving and can thus extinguish drug-seeking behavior in the short term.

Unfortunately, naltrexone has a number of important limitations. For those who start naltrexone, there is a high dropout rate because the drug provides no euphoric effect, and thus requires significant patient motivation for continued compliance. In addition, many patients do not succeed in achieving a drug-free state long enough to initiate naltrexone therapy. Usually they fail detoxification or succumb to early postdetoxification relapse. Many patients simply prefer methadone's mild euphoric effect to naltrexone and often return to methadone maintenance therapy (MMT). However, naltrexone is effective in highly motivated patients, especially those with extensive social and family support.

Investigational Pharmacological Therapies

Buprenorphine, a partial opiate agonist, acetorphan, a parenterally active inhibitor of enkephalinase, and Ibogaine, an alkaloid with hallucinogenic and stimulant properties, are several drugs being investigated for opiate intoxication and maintenance therapies. Levomethadyl acetate (LAAM) has been recently approved by the Food and Drug Administration for maintenance treatment of opiate-dependent individuals.

Long-Term Intervention

Short-term treatment for opiate abuse has had poor overall success regardless of the modality used or the setting in which it has been undertaken. Consequently, substance abuse professionals have recognized that for many patients, an opiate-free life-style may require years of treatment. Furthermore, since long-term treatment has emerged as the predominant mode of management of opiate addicts, an intense debate has developed over what constitutes a successful outcome of therapy: social stabilization with controlled opiate use ("maintenance") or an an absolutely drug-free state.

Three distinct modalities of long-term treatment are currently used in the United States: methadone maintenance treatment (MMT), therapeutic communities, and outpatient drug-free counseling. In general, MMT providers accept the notion of long-term or even permanent opiate maintenance, whereas advocates of the latter modalities espouse a drug-free state as the only acceptable treatment outcome. MMT is well documented as an effective therapy and has become the preferred treatment modality for opiate addicts.

Methadone Maintenance

In contrast to methadone detoxification, MMT is designed to support and stabilize opiate-dependent patients for months or even years. In this setting, methadone dramatically reduces narcotic craving, induces sufficient tolerance to block the euphoric effects of heroin, and produces few significant side effects. In addition to feeling better, patients also show marked improvement in social functioning: many return to school, obtain employment, or experience improved family relationships.

Eligibility for admission to MMT requires that a patient have a current physiological dependence on a narcotic with dependence beginning at least 1 year prior to application for admission. These requirements vary somewhat for pregnant patients, patients under 18 years of age, or those patients who have received previous treatment in an MMT program.

Appropriate dosing of methadone in maintenance treatment helps achieve effective patient rehabilitation. Nevertheless, studies suggest that many patients receive inadequate doses of methadone, perhaps because many health care professionals and regulators still seek to aggressively minimize narcotic use. Some states actually limit the maximum daily dose to levels many substance abuse professionals feel are grossly inappropriate. The proper dose of methadone prevents withdrawal symptoms, reduces drug craving, and blocks the effects of other narcotics. Although each patient's stabilization dose should be individually determined, higher methadone doses (60–80 mg daily) are generally more effective than lower doses (20–40 mg).

Monitoring the methadone-maintained patient for compliance with the MMT program rules is an important component of the treatment plan. For opiate addicts, simple accomplishments, such as maintaining an adequate attendance record, help establish self-discipline and foster the ability to recognize authority. Intermittent random monitoring of urine for illicit drug use helps insure that the patient is committed to the goals of the MMT regimen. Federal regulations require at least 8 urine samples a year although in most programs urine is evaluated more frequently, sometimes as often as weekly.

The MMT clinic is more than just a center for dispensing narcotics. Government regulations require that MMT programs provide a comprehensive range of medical and rehabilitative services. These services often consist of complete medical treatment, drug counseling, vocational training, and other psychosocial services. The following list details the successes of MMT in achieving these goals:

- Reduction of illicit opiate use and other criminal behavior
- Improvement of social productivity, such as the ability to pursue schooling or to obtain and maintain employment
- Improvement of overall health status
- Promotion of patient retention in drug treatment programs until life-style is significantly improved
- MMT has been shown consistently to be cost-effective

Therapeutic Communities

Therapeutic Communities (TC) are carefully structured residences that utilize behavior modification as the focus of an intense, long-term effort to treat addiction to opiates and other drugs. The TC plan promotes behavior modification by aggressively confronting addicts about their antisocial behavior, by enforcing strict discipline, and by providing individual and group psychotherapy. Though all patients initially undergo pharmacologic detoxification, nonpharmacologic therapy is emphasized. The most successful TC programs provide individualized treatment and are closely integrated with the health care network.

Outpatient Drug-Free Treatment

Outpatient drug-free treatment has historically represented services rendered by nonstandardized drug treatment programs whose unifying theme was their emphasis on outpatient, community-based, nonpharmacologic approaches. In the past, services have included such diverse efforts as: drop-in counseling, crisis-oriented medical services, legal counseling, and employment information. In recent years, more structured outpatient treatment models have developed, some specifically geared to addicts of particular classes of drugs. In general, opiate abusers have not responded as well to these programs as have other drug users. Only detoxified or otherwise nondependent opiate addicts are candidates for drug-free treatment.

Prognosis

Opiate addiction is often a chronic, relapsing illness. Long-term follow-up studies of narcotic addicts suggest that cessation of narcotic use is a slow process, and difficult to sustain for a large proportion of patients. Risk factors for persistent relapse to opiate abuse include: history of chronic psychopathology (particularly antisocial personality disorder), low socioeconomic class, weak social supports, and failure to pursue repeated treatment efforts. While methods to treat opiate addiction continue to improve, it is becoming clear that no single treatment modality will emerge as the answer for narcotic addicts. Rather, each patient should receive an individualized regimen with particular attention placed on comprehensive educational and vocational rehabilitation and treatment of any comorbid psychiatric illness.

SUBSTANCE ABUSE JARGON

Morphine

drugstore	dope	dreamer	gunk

Heroin

H	smack	horse	china white

Percocet

perks

Methadone

dollies	done

FURTHER READING

Dole VP, Nyswander M. A medical treatment for diacetylmorphine (heroin) addiction. JAMA 1965;193:646–650.

Ling W, Wesson DR. Drugs of abuse—opiates. In: Addiction Medicine and the Primary Care Physician [Special Issue]. West J Med 1990;152:565–572.

Lowinson JH, Ruiz P, Millman RB, Langrod JG, eds. Substance Abuse: A Comprehensive Textbook. Baltimore: Williams & Wilkins, 1992.

McLellan AT, Arndt IO, Metzger DS, Woody GE, O'Brien CP. The effects of psychosocial services in substance abuse treatment. JAMA 1993; 269: 1953–1959.

Rawson RA, Ling W. Opioid addiction treatment modalities and some guidelines to their optimal use. J Psychoactive Drugs 1991;23(2):151–163.

Renner JA Jr. Methadone maintenance: past, present and future. Adv Alcohol Subst Abuse 1984;3:75–90.

Zweben JE, Payte JT. Methadone maintenance in the treatment of opiate dependence—a current perspective. In: Addiction Medicine and the Primary Care Physician [Special Issue]. West J Med 1990;152:588–599.

Chapter 12

Sedative-Hypnotics and Anxiolytics

Stephen D. Wiviott and Lori Wiviott-Tishler with Steven E. Hyman

The sedative-hypnotics are central nervous system (CNS) depressants with anxiety-relieving properties at lower doses and sedative-hypnotic effects at higher doses. Use of these pharmacological agents began with the introduction of bromide in the 1850s. After the introduction of the first barbiturate (barbital) in 1903, the clinical and commercial success of this drug spurred the development of over two thousand barbiturates. The introduction of chlordiazepoxide (Librium) in 1961 marked the beginning of widespread use of benzodiazepines because of their advantages over barbiturates. These advantages include less potential for fatal CNS and respiratory depression, a greater dose margin between anxiolysis and sedation, less tendency to produce tolerance and dependence, and reduced abuse potential. The medical usefulness of this class of drugs has resulted in widespread use. For this class of drugs, the distinction between addiction and dependence becomes vitally important.

EPIDEMIOLOGY

The following epidemiological information on sedative-hypnotics reflects their use as therapeutic agents, but not as drugs of abuse.

- Since their introduction, benzodiazepines have been among the most commonly prescribed drugs of any kind—in 1988, approximately 88 million prescriptions were written, mostly for emotional distress disorders.
- Approximately 12.5% of the adult population uses a prescribed anxiolytic in the course of a year—about 2% of the population takes one on any given day.
- Primary care physicians write more than half of all the prescriptions in the United States for these drugs, prescribing mostly benzodiazepines.

TABLE 12.1 COMMONLY PRESCRIBED BENZODIAZEPINES

Higher-Potency/Shorter-Acting:

Dependence is most severe and most likely to be symptomatic with: alprazolam (Xanax), midazolam (Versed), lorazepam (Ativan), and triazolam (Halcion)

Higher-Potency/Longer-Acting:

Estazolam (ProSom)
Clonazepam (Klonipin)

Lower-Potency/Shorter-Acting:

These may be the most useful to prescribe as sleeping agents for hospitalized patients:
Oxazepam (Serax)
Temazepam (Restoril)

Lower-Potency/Longer-Acting:

Dependence is relatively uncommon in a therapeutic setting, but can occur with relatively higher doses in an abuse setting:
Chlordiazepoxide (Librium), clorazepate (Tranxene), diazepam (Valium), flurazepam (Dalmane), halazepam (Paxipam), prazepam (Centrax), and quazepam (Doral)

- The use of anxiolytics for medical purposes is most common for persons in the 6th and 7th decades of life, and twice as common in females as in males.
- 50% of patients using benzodiazepines receive them for treatment of a primary psychiatric disorder.
- Older patients, patients with more physical ailments, and patients with chronic mental illness more often require long-term therapy with benzodiazepines.
- Data from the National Household Survey of Drug Abuse (1991) estimate that annual and monthly nonmedical use rates range from 1.9% and 0.7% in the 18–25-year-old age group, to 0.7% and 0.3% in groups older than 35.
- Benzodiazepine overdose is most commonly seen in the setting of suicide attempts or suicidal gestures.

Although benzodiazepines have relatively low levels of abuse in the general population, long-term benzodiazepine users are at significant risk for tolerance and dependence, especially when using shorter-acting, higher-potency agents (midazolam, triazolam). Other risk factors for dependence on benzodiazepines include treatment for longer than 4 weeks, increased dosage, and previous substance abuse. Excessive fears about addicting patients to these drugs have led not only to a marked decline in prescriptions for sedative-hypnotics in the last decade, but also, in some cases, the withholding of appropriate therapy. Table 12.1

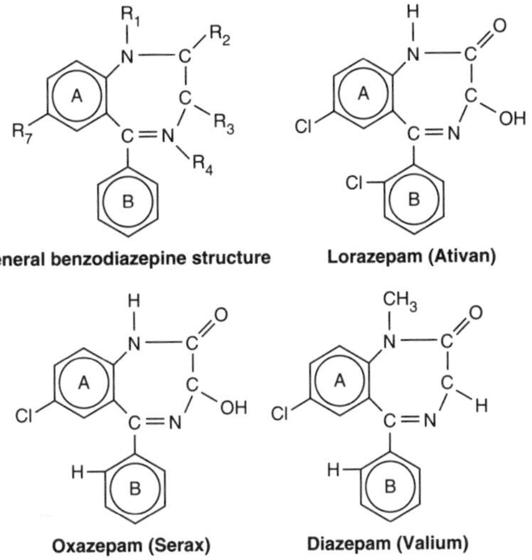

General benzodiazepine structure   Lorazepam (Ativan)

Oxazepam (Serax)   Diazepam (Valium)

Figure 12.1. Chemical structures of commonly used benzodiazepines.

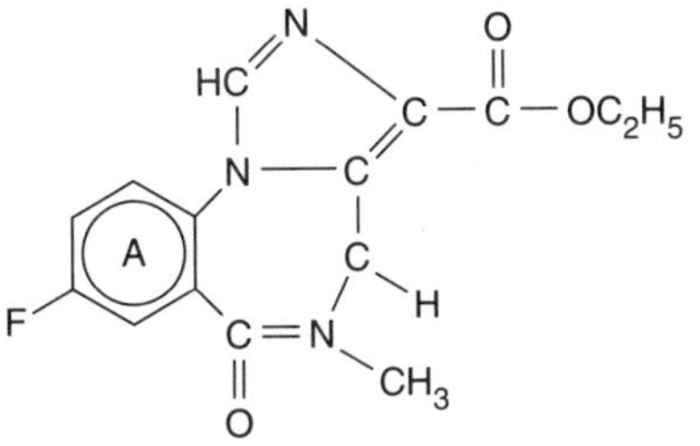

Flumazenil

Figure 12.2. Chemical structure of benzodiazepine antagonist flumazenil.

lists the commonly prescribed benzodiazepines by potency and duration of action.

PHARMACOLOGY

Structure and Pharmacokinetics

Benzodiazepines

The structure of the clinically important benzodiazepines consists of a benzene ring attached to a seven-membered 1,4-diazepine ring (Fig. 12.1). Substitute chemical groups at $R_1 - R_7$ and R_2 alter the potency and activity of the different agents. Flumazenil, a benzodiazepine antagonist, has a remarkably similar structure (Fig. 12.2).

Benzodiazepines have multiple routes of administration (oral, intravenous, and rectal), all of which provide high bioavailability. Once in the

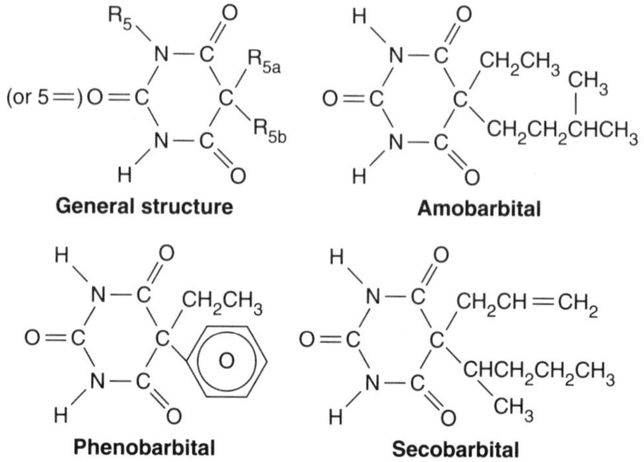

Figure 12.3. Chemical structures of commonly used barbiturates.

body, hepatic microsomal enzymes metabolize benzodiazepines to both active and inactive metabolites. Although the plasma half-life of flurazepam is only about 2–3 hours, its major metabolite, N-desalkylflurazepam, remains active for more than 50 hours. This type of active metabolite augments the duration of action of many of the benzodiazepines and plays a role in the development of dependence. Liver enzymes further metabolize benzodiazepines and their metabolites by conjugation before they are eventually excreted in the urine. In patients with hepatic failure, benzodiazepines such as oxazepam, which have relatively greater renal metabolism, should be the drug of choice.

The lipophilic qualities of benzodiazepines confer on them two important characteristics: First, benzodiazepines and their metabolites are highly bound to plasma proteins at levels ranging from 70% for alprazolam to 99% for diazepam; Second, the lipophilicity accelerates the passage of the drug across the blood-brain barrier and into the central nervous system, causing a more rapid onset of drug effects.

Barbiturates

The structure of the barbiturates is based on barbituric acid. Substitutes at the 5 position of the barbituric acid ring confers the specific actions of distinct agents on the CNS (Fig. 12.3).

Barbiturates can be administered orally, intramuscularly, or intravenously, resulting in high bioavailability in all cases. The intravenous route is useful for the rapid induction of anesthesia or treatment for status epilepticus. Similar to benzodiazepines, the degree of lipid solubility determines the characteristics of the different types of barbiturates. Shorter-acting barbiturates, such as pentobarbital and secobarbital, are highly lipid soluble and cross the blood-brain barrier rapidly. By contrast, the longer-acting barbiturates, such as phenobarbital, cross the blood-brain barrier more slowly.

Redistribution, hepatic metabolism, and urinary excretion diminish the actions of barbiturates. After administration, barbiturates are widely distributed to fat and muscle, decreasing blood levels of the drug. At the same time, hepatic metabolism by cytochrome P-450 enzymes and/or conjugation of barbiturates inactivates the drug and allows for subsequent renal excretion. The acute administration of barbiturates interferes with the biotransformation of other agents by microsomal enzymes. Following this initial phase of interference in the liver, barbiturates induce an increased quantity of microsomal enzymes that metabolize the drug. Consequently, the metabolism of barbiturates, ethanol, steroid hormones, fat soluble vitamins, and anticoagulants increases. This process explains the metabolic tolerance and cross-tolerance observed with barbiturate use.

Mechanism of Action

Both benzodiazepines and barbiturates interact with the γ-aminobutyric acid (GABA) receptor. GABA is a major inhibitory neurotransmitter of the CNS, which causes an allosteric change in the GABA receptor after it binds. This change induces an increased chloride flux that hyperpolarizes the cell (Fig. 12.4). Although benzodiazepines and barbiturates facilitate GABA actions at the GABA receptor, differences in their interaction with the receptor account for some of their clinically distinct actions.

Benzodiazepines potentiate the actions of GABA. Binding of the drug causes GABA to bind more tightly to the channel and increases the frequency of channel opening when GABA is present. However, benzodiazepines have no direct agonist activity at the GABA receptor.

Barbiturates also facilitate the actions of GABA by stabilizing the chloride channel in its open configuration. This stabilization keeps the channel open longer and increases the chloride flux. At high concentrations, barbiturates do have direct agonist activity at the GABA receptor. Barbiturate-induced neuronal inhibition may account for the increased dangers of CNS depression, coma, and death seen in barbiturate overdose. Barbiturates also inhibit rapid firing of voltage-dependent sodium channels. This action accounts for their ability to inhibit seizure activity.

Other Agents of Different Structure with Similar Effects

Methylprylon—Structurally distinct, but functionally similar to, secobarbital in terms of enzyme induction, intoxication, dependence, and tolerance.

Glutethimide—Actions of this agent are similar to those of the barbiturates. It has a high abuse potential.

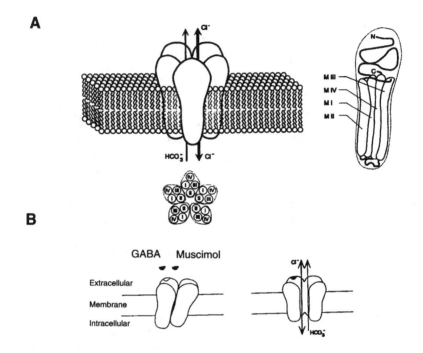

Figure 12.4. Molecular structure of the GABA$_A$ receptor channel. The GABA$_A$ receptor channel is a hetero-oligomeric protein molecule made up of two alpha, two beta, and one gamma or delta subunits that form an allosterically-controlled chloride channel. The alpha subunit is the site of GABA binding; the beta subunit binds barbiturates and benzodiazepines. Without a gamma subunit, the beta subunit will not bind benzodiazepines. **A.** The *left* part of the figure shows a complete pentameric receptor-channel complex partly embedded in the lipid matrix of the cell membrane. A single subunit with its four membrane-spanning domains (MI–MIV) is shown on the *right*. Note the critical positioning of MII in relation to the transmembrane channel depicted in the cross-sectional scheme on the *bottom*. **B.** This simplified scheme depicts the consequences of the activation of GABA$_A$ receptors. The ion-channel complex is an integral part of the receptor-channel complex. The *arrows* indicate the movements of the ions.

Meprobamate—Anxiolytic agent whose properties closely resemble those of the benzodiazepines. It may have a higher abuse potential.

Zolpidem—Chemically unrelated to benzodiazepines, but binds to benzodiazepine binding site on GABAa receptor and causes similar effects.

Methaqualone—(Quaalude, sopors, ludes)—A member of the sedative-hypnotic class of drugs, which is commonly abused. First synthesized in India as an antimalarial drug, methaqualone was introduced in the United States in 1965 as a nonaddictive sedative-hypnotic. The drug has pharmacological properties resembling barbiturates, but has greater euphoriant effects. Methaqualone has been reported to have additive

CNS depressant effects with other depressants. Finally, methaqualone sold on the streets commonly contains additives, such as barbiturates and benzodiazepines.

CONSEQUENCES OF USE

Sedative-hypnotics have few effects outside of the central nervous system, and these effects vary with the dose of the drug. Benzodiazepines and barbiturates have similar CNS depressant actions that progress in the following order with increasing dose:

1. Sedation, decreased anxiety, and disinhibition;
2. Hypnosis and the promotion of the onset of sleep and an increased duration of sleep;
3. Anesthesia with loss of consciousness, amnesia, and reduced reflex activity.

Nondepressant CNS effects of benzodiazepines include anticonvulsant activity and muscle relaxation. Respiratory depression may occur when benzodiazepines are taken in combination with other CNS depressants, such as ethanol or barbiturates.

By comparison, barbiturates alone can cause medullary depression leading to respiratory depression and coma. At doses three times hypnotic levels, neurogenic respiratory drive drastically diminishes. Chemoreceptor stimulation of respiration is affected at high doses with hypoxic drive failing at very high doses (lethal dose is 6 to 10 grams of phenobarbital acutely).

The two drugs demonstrate markedly different effects on the reward circuitry of the brain. At supratherapeutic doses, benzodiazepines cause only minimal reinforcing actions in the brain, while the barbiturates demonstrate reinforcing actions at therapeutic levels. These differences seem to explain the reduced abuse potential of benzodiazepines in comparison to barbiturates (Chapter 1 discusses the reward circuitry and reinforcing actions).

CLINICAL PRESENTATION

The actions of the sedative-hypnotics described above have made them important drugs in long-term treatment of panic disorders and anxiety disorders, and in short-term treatment of sleep disorders and alcohol withdrawal. As an unwanted side effect, these treatments may inadvertently lead to physical dependence. This dependence must be distinguished from addiction to sedative-hypnotics. Although discontinuation of benzodiazepine or barbiturate therapy in patients with dependence may produce a typical pattern of withdrawal, this person has *not* lost

---

TABLE 12.2 RATIONAL USE OF BENZODIAZEPINES

- Always treat the presence of a syndrome for which benzodiazepines are indicated
- Advantages of benzodiazepines over barbiturates include: greater dose margin between anxiolysis and sedation; less tendency to produce tolerance and dependence; less potential for abuse
- Use nonpharmacologic therapies when indicated
- Avoid open-ended treatment (insomnia/situation anxiety)
- Consider risks and benefits for each individual's treatment with benzodiazepines
- Adjust dose to optimize therapeutic effects and minimize side effects
- Monitor for abuse (unsupervised dosage acceleration or diversion to other individuals)
- Taper the drug after an appropriate trial in order to determine the need for any further therapy
- Reconsider the diagnosis if the patient is poorly responsive or if medication is needed longer or at higher doses than was originally estimated

---

control over use of the drug. Fears about the addictiveness of the drugs must be balanced with the potential benefit from the therapeutic actions of the drugs.

The sedative-hypnotics should neither be prescribed indiscriminately, nor withheld because of excessive fear about their abuse potentials. Table 12.2 presents guidelines for rational treatment with sedative-hypnotic drugs. Each of the following clinical presentations must be kept in mind both when there are fears that the patient has an addiction and when treating a patient maintained for a long period of time on benzodiazepines or barbiturates. The physician should reevaluate the need for the sedative-hypnotic at each visit and not indiscriminately refill prescriptions.

Dependence

Although dependence occurs infrequently in patients receiving short-term therapy, development of it is correlated with increased duration of treatment (longer than 4–6 weeks), increased dose of agents, a history of previous drug abuse, a higher potency, and shorter-acting agents. The therapeutic use of low-potency, long-acting drugs produces dependence relatively uncommonly. Discontinuation of the drug in dependent patients has three characteristic features (the first two features are more characteristic of benzodiazepine use):

Recurrence of the original symptoms—Over a period of time, previously treated symptoms, usually anxiety, will emerge as the patient is withdrawing from the drugs. The symptoms are indistinguishable from the ones for which the patient initially received treatment. Panic disorder commonly recurs once the benzodiazepines are discontinued. These recurrences usually require renewal of therapy.

TABLE 12.3. CHARACTERISTICS OF A SEDATIVE-HYPNOTIC WITHDRAWAL SYNDROME

Anxiety
Hallucinations
Delusions
Paranoia
Depersonalizations
Agoraphobia
Pain
Myoclonic jerks
Ataxia
Tinnitus
Panic
Delirium
Autonomic hyperactivity
Mood changes—irritability, emotional depression, dysphoria, apathy
Coarse tremor of hands, tongue, or eyelids
Nausea and vomiting
Malaise and weakness
Orthostatic hypotension
Sensory disturbances—double vision, hypersensitivity to light, sound, touch, and
    odors
Impaired memory and concentration
Insomnia
Grand mal seizures

Rebound symptoms—(especially anxiety)—After discontinuation, anxiety, insomnia, panic reactions, or other original symptoms return with greater intensity than before the commencement of the drug therapy. Some patients may experience this phenomenon while taking shorter-acting benzodiazepines, like triazolam.

Withdrawal—Although the withdrawal syndrome for all sedative-hypnotics is similar, the barbiturate-like drugs and the higher potency, shorter-acting benzodiazepines cause more severe symptoms. The withdrawal symptoms follow no specific pattern, but include any of the symptoms listed in Table 12.3. The degree of withdrawal depends on the dose of drug and the length of exposure to it. In the most extreme and complicated withdrawal syndromes, patients may experience delirium, an amnestic syndrome, seizures, hallucinations, hyperthermia, cardiovascular collapse, and death.

Withdrawal syndromes from shorter-acting barbiturates usually begin 12–24 hours after cessation of drug use, and peak in severity after 1 to 3 days. For shorter-acting benzodiazepines (e.g., alprazolam) the peak occurs 2 to 4 days after cessation of use. Withdrawal reactions from longer-acting barbiturates or benzodiazepines usually peak between the 5th to 8th day after cessation.

TABLE 12.4. SIGNS AND SYMPTOMS OF SEDATIVE-HYPNOTIC OVERDOSE

Slurred speech
Staggering gait
Sustained nystagmus (vertical or horizontal)
Pupillary constriction or dilatation
Slowed reaction time
Respiratory depression

TABLE 12.5. POTENTIAL SEQUELAE OF OVERDOSE

Pneumonia
Pulmonary edema
Hypotension
Renal failure
Cutaneous bullae

Tolerance

Pharmacokinetic and pharmacodynamic tolerance occurs in response to sedative-hypnotic administration. Particularly important is the cross-tolerance to other sedatives (benzodiazepines), ethanol, and gaseous anesthetics that develops. Tolerance and cross-tolerance require readjustment of therapeutic doses for efficacious management.

Overdose

Benzodiazepine Overdose

Benzodiazepines, when used alone, have minimal direct respiratory depressant effects and a much wider therapeutic index than barbiturates. For this reason, benzodiazepine overdose, without other drugs, is rarely fatal. Nevertheless, in conjunction with other drugs, particularly alcohol, the potential for overdose and mortality greatly increases. The signs and symptoms of benzodiazepine and barbiturate overdose are very similar: an initial excitement phase precedes drowsiness, dysarthria, or confusion (Table 12.4). Concomitant use of alcohol with benzodiazepines may evoke severe respiratory depression leading to coma.

In serious cases of sedative-hypnotic overdose, pneumonia or pulmonary edema (in patients with previously depressed myocardial function) may complicate the course. In addition, falling blood pressure may cause hypotensive shock and possible renal failure (Table 12.5). Occasionally, cutaneous bullae develop and can provide a nonspecific clue to the diagnosis.

Diagnosis

Laboratory Data

In any patient suspected of a drug overdose, toxicological screening of the urine and serum is helpful in diagnosing and determining the severity of the ingestion. The following guidelines will help determine the degree of the sedative-hypnotic danger:

- Toxic levels of shorter-acting barbiturates are 3 mg/dL or greater. For longer-acting barbiturates the toxic dose is 8–10 mg/dL, depending on the levels of tolerance to the drug.
- In benzodiazepine abuse, doses of 1–2 grams usually result in the need for supportive measures.
- Screen for other drugs, especially alcohol. If alcohol is involved, the patient has a greater risk of respiratory depression, need for supportive ventilation, and chronic treatment of alcohol withdrawal.
- Use other laboratory tests, such as liver function tests, kidney function, and arterial blood gases, to treat any acid-base disorder precipitated by the ingestion.

TREATMENT

Acute Treatment of Overdose

Acute treatment of an overdose requires a combination of therapies aimed at (*a*) diminishing the effect of the drug in the body; (*b*) reducing further absorption of the drug by the gastrointestinal tract; and (*c*) addressing long-term complications and nonemergent issues:

Step 1: Diminishing the effects of the sedative-hypnotic:
- The drug, flumazenil, a specific benzodiazepine antagonist, will counteract the effects of the benzodiazepines. Initially the drug is given at 0.2 mg intravenously (over 30 seconds), followed by a single 0.3-mg dose; the drug can then be given at 0.5-mg intervals (over 60 seconds) to a total of 3.0 mg, cumulatively. In dependent patients, flumazenil administration may precipitate withdrawal.
- For extremely high serum levels and severe symptoms, consider dialysis or charcoal resin hemoperfusion. These interventions may also help if there is severe intoxication from shorter-acting barbiturates.
- Supportive measures for overdose include: airway protection, mechanical ventilation, correction of acid-base disorders, alkalinization of the urine to a pH of 8 to improve renal clearance of the drug, and diuresis with furosemide 20–40 mg or mannitol 12.5–25 mg to maintain urine output at approximately 3–6 mL/kg/hour.

Step 2: Reducing further absorption of the drug:
- Induce emesis if the ingestion was recent. Otherwise, consider activated charcoal. Care must be given to avoid aspiration.

Step 3: Addressing complications of the overdose:
- Follow status for signs of respiratory depression, aspiration, and pulmonary edema. Antibiotics may be indicated if the patient has aspirated.
- If the patient made a clear suicide attempt, he or she should be placed on suicide precautions after initial, emergent care.

Chronic Treatment of Withdrawal

Long-term management usually depends on the level of drug dependence. For example, mild dependence may require only slow tapering of the drug over the course of a few weeks. The use of a long-acting benzodiazepine, such as clonazepam, may help with the discontinuation of short-acting, high-potency benzodiazepines. Conversely, more serious cases require a more comprehensive approach, directed not only at the physical detoxification, but also at rehabilitation.

Detoxification

In addition to the gradual tapering of the sedative-hypnotic suggested above, detoxification is often accomplished by initial drug substitution. In general, phenobarbital, a longer-acting barbiturate with a wider therapeutic index, is used. The dose of phenobarbital can be calculated by the dosage of barbiturate the patient was on previously. For example, a 100-mg dose of amobarbital can be converted into a 30-mg dose of phenobarbital (not to exceed 500 mg/day). Similar conversions can be used to manage patients abusing benzodiazepines. After stabilizing the patient for 2 days on a dose of phenobarbital, the patient is examined for signs and symptoms of overdose. In the absence of symptoms, the dose is decreased by 30 mg each day. The length of the withdrawal period varies from patient to patient. In uncomplicated cases, successful detoxification may occur within a few weeks. However, complicated patients—those with poor supports, high stress, or history of addictive disease—require a much longer detoxification period. Finally, rebound or recurring symptoms necessitate immediate attention, which may require institution of nonpharmacologic therapies or even use of a longer-acting, low-potency benzodiazepine.

SUBSTANCE ABUSE JARGON

Barbiturates

barbs	dolls	goof-balls	sleeping pills
candy	goofers	peanuts	downers

Amobarbital

blues	blue birds	blue heavens
blue velvet	blue devils	blue angels

Secobarbital

reds	red devils	pink lady
redbirds	seggy	

Pentobarbital/Nembutal

yellows	nembies	nebbies	yellow jackets

Secobarbital/Amobarbital

reds and blues	tooies	christmas trees
rainbows	double trouble	

Chloral Hydrate

mickey finn

Methaqualone

ludes

FURTHER READING

Farnsworth MG. Benzodiazepine abuse and dependence: misconceptions and facts. J Fam Pract 1990;31:393–400.

Smith DE, Landry MJ, Wesson DR. Barbiturates, sedatives, hypnotic agents. Treatments of psychiatric disorders: a task force of the American Psychiatric Association. Byram Toksoz, chairperson. Washington, DC: American Psychiatric Association, 1989.

Wetli CV. Changing patterns of methaqualone abuse. JAMA 1983;249:621–626.

Woods JH, Katz JL, Winger G. Abuse liability of benzodiazepines. Pharmacol Rev 1987;39:251–390.

Woolf DS. CNS depressants: other sedative hypnotics. In: Bennet G, Bourakis C, Woolf DS, eds. Substance Abuse: Pharmacological, Developmental, and Clinical Perspectives. New York: John Wiley & Sons, 1983.

Chapter 13

Hallucinogens and Phencyclidine

David Brendel and Howard West with Steven E. Hyman

Hallucinogens are drugs that induce hallucinations, illusions, and delusions. However, the feature that best distinguishes them from other drug classes is their ability to alter perception, mood, and thinking. Three of the most commonly used hallucinogens are *d*-lysergic acid diethylamide (LSD), psilocybin, and mescaline. Individuals taking these drugs often report a heightened awareness of sensory input, an increased clarity of thought, and a dissociation from the environment. Consequently, an alternative name proposed for this class of drugs is psychedelics. Most hallucinogens produce their effects by acting on serotonin neurotransmission in the brain. Although the chemically-unrelated drug phencyclidine (PCP) causes altered perception states, it should not be considered one of the hallucinogens since it acts primarily on glutaminergic receptors and is more addictive. For these reasons, this chapter will address LSD-related drugs and PCP separately.

⟲ LSD AND RELATED DRUGS

HISTORY

Hallucinogen use can be traced as far back as the Aztecs, who used psilocybin and peyote as part of religious practices. Since that time, the use of hallucinogens has continued in some Native American religions. More recently, Hofman, a research chemist working for Sandoz Laboratories, inadvertently discovered the profoundly mind-altering effects of LSD in 1943. While purifying and crystallizing LSD in an attempt to produce a circulatory and respiratory stimulant, he began to experience unusual sensations. Concluding that his experiences must have resulted from accidental ingestion of the compound, he repeated the experiment on himself, describing the effects in vivid detail.

LSD was then developed as a research tool for investigating and modeling psychosis. By the mid-1950s, however, the scientific community rejected the theory that the effects of LSD resembled psychosis, and its use as a psychomimetic rapidly disappeared. Nevertheless, the adjunctive use in psychotherapy to facilitate the breakdown of emotional and memory blocks and to shorten psychotherapy continued for several years. LSD therapy also demonstrated the potential to induce immediate behavioral change and was alleged to dramatically improve treatment of alcoholism.

Scientific and psychotherapeutic LSD use was soon overshadowed by its use as a "consciousness-expanding" drug. In 1957 Osmond documented LSD-induced, insightful and pleasurable experiences in research volunteers. He advocated the drug's use in the exploration of social, religious, and philosophical realms. In the early 1960s, Timothy Leary, at Harvard University, conducted studies with psilocybin and then LSD, taking hallucinogens with volunteers and recording experiences, until Harvard determined that nonmedical research with hallucinogenic drugs was too dangerous. Leary, consequently, left the university in 1962 to promote the use of psychedelic drugs for exploring thought and experience.

By 1965, the federal government decided that the use of psychedelic drugs was a public health risk and banned their sale or use. This action led to a rapid decline in the recreational use of LSD.

In the mid-1980s, use of a related compound, 3,4-methylenedioxymethamphetamine (MDMA) became very popular, especially among college students. Initially not listed in the Controlled Substances Act, MDMA was legal for a brief period, and some psychiatrists used it to facilitate psychotherapy. However, after MDMA was shown to kill serotonergic neurons in animal models, it was made illegal, and its therapeutic and recreational use declined.

Hallucinogenic drugs have no well-accepted, therapeutic use at the present time. The potential emotional devastation of negative experiences with drug use, central nervous system (CNS) toxicity, and somatic complaints that accompany hallucinogen use outweigh their ill-defined therapeutic potential for treating conditions that now have safer management modalities.

EPIDEMIOLOGY

The use rates of LSD and other hallucinogens have decreased markedly since a peak in the 1960s when they were used as part of the psychedelic movement. However, the annual (5.1%) and monthly (1.6%) LSD use rates among high school seniors increased slightly in 1991. Peak use rates occur in the 18–25-year-old age group, with males five times as likely to have used hallucinogens as females.

PHARMACOLOGY

Formulation and Administration

LSD and related drugs are usually taken orally. They are rarely smoked or injected. A common oral dose of LSD is 100–300 micrograms, usually ingested in pill form or absorbed across the oral mucosa from drug-impregnated blotting paper. However, doses as low as 20 μg can produce substantial effects in some susceptible users.

Psilocybin and mescaline are hallucinogens which, though much less potent than LSD, have clinical effects that are generally indistinguishable from those of LSD. Psilocybin and related drugs (e.g., psilocin) are found in a variety of hallucinogenic mushrooms and are usually ingested in doses of 250 μg/kg (which requires a varying number of mushrooms, depending on factors such as size and species). Mescaline, derived from the Mexican peyote cactus, is usually taken in doses of 5–6 mg/kg and is reported to cause more vomiting than related compounds. The drug is taken in the form of disk-shaped "mescal buttons," which are sun-dried pieces of the peyote cactus. In the United States, mescaline is rarely found in an unadulterated form outside the Southwest.

MDMA ("ecstasy") is the prototypical "designer" drug and has both hallucinogenic and amphetamine-like effects. Toxic effects of the drug, including perceptual distortion, attentional impairment, accommodation disturbance, polyopia, dysmegalopsia, and severe hypertension, are seen at doses exceeding 100 mg. In British and American cities, young people use MDMA at all-night dance parties called "raves." Fifteen people have reportedly died while participating in raves in England, presumably secondary to the hyperthermia and excessive physical exertion induced by the drug.

Mechanism of Action

Since the 1950s, LSD-like hallucinogens have been thought to interfere with the serotonergic neurotransmission involved in normal mental function. As seen in Figure 13.1, LSD and related drugs have molecular structures very similar to that of serotonin (5-hydroxytriptamine or 5-HT). LSD has a potent, pharmacologic action at doses of 20 to 25 μg, approximately 1/5000th the effective dose of mescaline.

The rank order of hallucinogenic potency correlates with binding affinity at the postsynaptic serotonin (5-HT$_2$) receptor. Animal subjects respond in a dose-dependent manner to different LSD-like hallucinogens, and this response is potently blocked by 5-HT$_2$ antagonists such as ketanserin.

Tolerance to the behavioral effects of LSD and other related hallucinogens may have a molecular correlate: after high doses or repeated administration of LSD, decreased binding of 5-HT$_2$ antagonists occurs after a period as short as several hours. Based on these findings, it has been suggested that LSD induces a down-regulation of receptors that may account for the rapid tolerance often seen with these drugs.

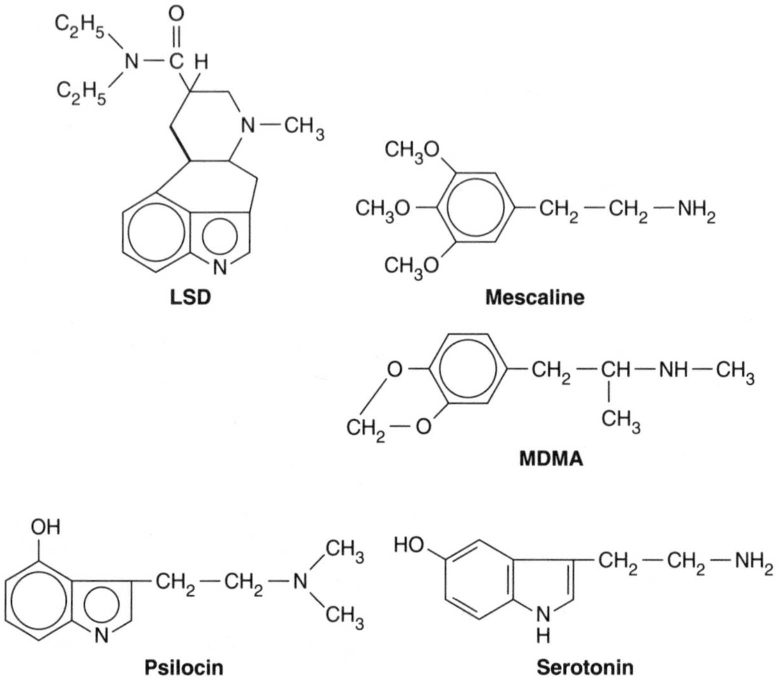

Figure 13.1. Chemical structure of commonly used hallucinogens and their analog serotonin.

Pharmacokinetics

LSD is quickly and completely absorbed from the gastrointestinal tract or the oral mucosa, and the onset of symptoms can occur within 10 minutes. The intensity of symptoms is most often a function of dose and tolerance. Although the plasma half-life of LSD is only 2–3 hours, acute symptoms can persist for as long as 12 hours, and a feeling of "psychic numbness" may even last for several days.

Metabolism of LSD by hydroxylation and glucuronidation occurs in the liver. While most of the drug is excreted in the bile, LSD may be detected in the urine up to 5 days after ingestion.

CONSEQUENCES OF USE

LSD induces a wide range of psychic and somatosensory changes in very low doses (Table 13.1 summarizes the effects). Within 5–10 minutes of ingestion, users experience significant sympathomimetic effects of the drug, including tachycardia, palpitations, blood pressure elevation, mydriasis, diaphoresis, and core body temperature increase. Other somatic effects, such as nausea, dizziness, tremors, weakness, and incoor-

TABLE 13.1 INTOXICATION STATES OF LSD-LIKE HALLUCINOGENS

Time of Reactions after Ingestion	Psychological	Physiological
5–10 Minutes	Uncontrollable laughing and/or crying	Tachycardia Palpitations BP elevation Mydriasis Sweating Elevated body temperature Nausea Dizziness Tremors Weakness Incoordination
15–20 Minutes	Mood changes Perceptual distortion Impaired thinking Behavioral disturbance Euphoria Feelings of invulnerability Detachment Paranoia Panic attacks Delusions Suicidal ideation	
2–3 Hours	Synesthesias (blurred boundaries between sensory modalities) Derealization Depersonalization Distorted sense of time and space	Visual hallucinations and illusions Blurring Visual perseveration
Chronic	Flashbacks	

dination, are also quite common at this time. The tension and anxiety produced by the rapid onset of these somatic symptoms may result in affective symptoms (e.g., laughing and crying).

The psychic effects of LSD usually begin about 15–20 minutes after ingestion and are characterized by mood changes, perceptual distortion, impaired thinking, and behavioral disturbance. The drug often causes a feeling of euphoria, ideas of reference, and feelings of transcendence, invulnerability, and detachment. Marked emotional lability and paranoia may result causing the user to have a panic attack. Vivid thoughts and memories may be evoked intentionally or occur unexpectedly. These thoughts can cause significant emotional distress, especially in inexperienced users. Some users have reactions that require immediate medical or psychiatric attention (see below), such as marked agitation, combativeness, suicidal ideation or attempt, or a dangerous delusional belief (such as the belief that one can fly).

The drug also causes a variety of visual transformations in the second or third hour after ingestion. These changes include visual illusions, formed hallucinations, blurring, visual perseveration, altered perception of light intensity, and qualitative transmutations of observed objects. Though common in schizophrenia and organic delirium, auditory hallucinations are not common with LSD use. However, the drug does frequently cause synesthesias, in which boundaries between the various sensory modalities are blurred—sounds may be felt or colors heard. Other common perceptual changes include depersonalization, derealization, altered body image, and distorted perception of space and time (clock time may seem slow).

The symptoms of LSD intoxication described above diminish after 8–12 hours. Most users experience no long-term changes in personality, level of functioning, or values. However, psychic numbness may last for many days after exposure. Some users who become floridly psychotic on LSD remain in this state even after their system has cleared the drug. It is unclear whether these individuals already had schizophrenia, bipolar disorder, or major depression before taking the LSD-like hallucinogens.

Flashbacks, the recurrence of images and feelings associated with prior use of a hallucinogen, occur in 16–57% of LSD users and are often induced by stress, use of another stimulant drug (such as PCP or marijuana), or illness. It is unknown whether flashbacks represent lasting CNS pathology caused by the drug or simply involve normal memory of an intense experience.

CLINICAL PRESENTATION

The differential diagnosis of LSD intoxication includes the entire grouping of diagnostic entities referred to as organic hallucinosis in the DSM-IV (Table 13.2). Hallucinations occurring in association with delirium, in which there is an impaired capacity to focus on external stimuli, and dementia, in which there is marked memory loss, must be considered. Schizophrenia or a severe mood disorder, like psychotic depression or bipolar disorder, may mimic LSD intoxication. Factors distinguishing these major psychiatric disturbances from hallucinogen intoxication include: the absence of organic factors, somatic symptoms and signs (such as sympathetic discharge), and acute onset and resolution of disturbance.

The differential diagnosis also encompasses hypnogogic hallucinations that occur in individuals with narcolepsy or in those who have no psychiatric disorder at all. Alcohol intoxication may produce visual

TABLE 13.2. DIFFERENTIAL DIAGNOSIS OF LSD INTOXICATION

Delirium
Dementia
Schizophrenia
Severe mood disorders
    Psychotic depression
    Bipolar disorder
Hypnogogic hallucinations
    Narcolepsy
Alcohol intoxication
PCP intoxication
Marijuana
Improper use of prescription medications
    antidepressants
Antiparkinsonian drugs

TABLE 13.3. ACUTE TREATMENT FOR LSD-LIKE HALLUCINOGEN OVERDOSE

Nonpharmacologic Intervention	Pharmacologic Intervention
Safe, supportive, quiet environment	Options for "bad trip" or panic attack:
Reassurance that drug is inducing	diazepam 10–30 mg p.o.
symptoms that will abate with time	lorazepam 1–2 mg IM
("talking down")	barbiturate to induce sleep

hallucinations, but has been associated more strongly with auditory hallucinations. PCP and marijuana are examples of illicit drugs whose signs and symptoms may be confused with those of LSD. Finally, a variety of prescription medications, when used improperly, also produce LSD-like effects; these drugs include tricyclic antidepressants and antiparkinsonian drugs with CNS anticholinergic activity (e.g., benztropine).

TREATMENT

Treatment of LSD intoxication always entails the provision of a safe, supportive, and quiet environment (Table 13.3). Continuous reassurance that the drug is responsible for the symptoms and that its effects will abate, ("talking down" the patient) often constitute adequate therapy. Calm, supportive friends are extremely helpful in facilitating the talking down process. However, a particularly bad trip, panic attack, or drug effects lasting greater than 12 hours may require pharmacological therapy. Benzodiazepines such as diazepam (10–30 mg orally) or lorazepam (1–2 mg intramuscularly) help reduce anxiety and agitation. No interventions can prevent bad trips, and individuals who have previously had good experiences with the drug are susceptible to bad trips with future

LSD use. Importantly, no evidence indicates that LSD-type hallucinogens produce dependence or withdrawal symptoms.

SUBSTANCE ABUSE JARGON

LSD

acid	flying saucers	blotter	purple haze
heavenly blue	blue cheer	electric kool-aid	window pane
pearly gates			

Psilocybin

magic mushrooms	mushrooms	'shrooms	purple passion

Mescaline

cactus	mesc	buttons	peyote

MDMA

ecstasy	XTC	adam

☙ PHENCYCLIDINE AND RELATED DRUGS

HISTORY

In contrast to LSD, PCP was quickly rejected by the scientific and medical community. Developed in the 1950s as an anesthetic agent, PCP produced analgesia and a dissociative anesthesia in animals and humans without cardiorespiratory depression. In clinical practice, however, it demonstrated a high incidence of postanesthetic reactions, which included blurred vision, confusion, and hallucinations. Its use was consequently abandoned in medicine. Ketamine, a related phenylcyclohexylamine, has been retained for anesthetic use despite its hallucinogenic effects.

PCP was used by psychedelic drug users because of its ease of synthesis and hallucinogen-like effects. It emerged in the mid-1960s in San Francisco as the PeaCePill. Users reported widely variable effects, including violence. These reports led to a decline in the popularity of the drug. Despite its continued popularity within isolated communities today, PCP use has declined appreciably over the past decade.

EPIDEMIOLOGY

PCP is far more likely to be involved in drug-related deaths than LSD or other hallucinogens. Overall, PCP accounts for 2.2% of national drug-related deaths; by comparison, cocaine causes 42% of drug-related deaths. The male-dominated usage patterns are reflected by the fact that 84% of these deaths occurred in males. Deaths related to hallucinogen

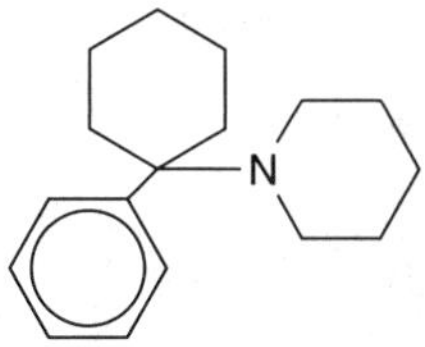

Figure 13.2. Chemical structure of phencyclidine.

or PCP use result from accidents, violence, toxicity of polypharmacy, and suicide, not from direct drug toxicity.

PHARMACOLOGY

Formulation and Administration

PCP can be snorted, smoked, taken orally, or injected intravenously. A large fraction of users smoke PCP, often in combination with marijuana. Drug effects are generally seen within 1 hour of oral ingestion, or within about 5 minutes if smoked, snorted, or injected. A typical high lasts 4–6 hours with a subsequent "coming down" period of variable length. Amnesia during the high is quite common.

Mechanism of Action and Pharmacokinetics

PCP and its congeners (Fig. 13.2) have effects on several different neurochemical systems. Early research focused on the binding of PCP to a receptor designated as the sigma opiate receptor. Currently, sigma receptors are not actually thought to be opiate receptors, and the behavioral effects of PCP are only weakly mediated by these receptors.

The major behavioral effects of PCP are mediated by receptors for excitatory amino acids, particularly the N-methyl-D-aspartate (NMDA) subtype of glutamate receptor. There is a high-affinity binding site for PCP within the NMDA receptor, which is the NMDA receptor channel. PCP blocks the normal cation flux in a voltage- and use-dependent manner, and acts as a noncompetitive antagonist with respect to NMDA (Fig. 13.3).

Significantly, PCP-like drugs have been tested for their potential neuroprotective ability as antagonists to the overexcitation of NMDA receptors which leads to neuronal death in cases of ischemia and seizures. Although PCP-like drugs can protect neurons from glutamate-induced excitotoxicity with an order of potency that parallels affinity at the PCP-binding site on the receptor, the potential for these drugs to produce psychosis has delayed their introduction into clinical use. PCP is hydroxylated by liver enzymes and conjugated with glucuronic acid. Only a small fraction of the drug is excreted in unmetabolized form.

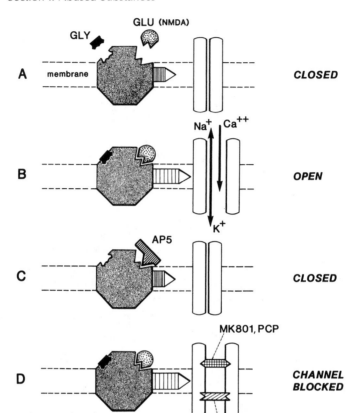

Figure 13.3. Model of proposed mechanisms of activation and deactivation of gluta-mate (GLU) N-methyl-D-aspartate (NMDA) receptor-channel complex. **A** and **B**. Gluta-mate attaches to receptor to cause opening of channel, first to Na$^+$ and K$^+$ and, after membrane depolarization, to Ca^{++}. Glycine (GLY) modulates effects of GLU. **C**. Competitive receptor antagonists, such as AP5, can prevent GLU activation. **D**. Other drugs and ions can block an opened channel by noncompetitive antagonism. These drugs include phencyclidine (PCP) and an experimental neuroprotective drug, MK801. Mg^{++} can also block the channel.

CONSEQUENCES OF USE (TABLE 13.4)

Small doses of PCP (less than 5 mg) can produce ataxia, dysarthria, nystagmus, blurry vision, numbness in the extremities, and blank staring. At doses of about 5–10 mg these symptoms become exaggerated, causing hypertonia, hyperreflexia, hypertension, and tachycardia. Diaphoresis, hypersalivation, fever, vomiting, repetitive movements, and muscle rigid-ity often accompany this clinical picture. An overdose of more than 20 mg may induce seizures, stupor, coma, and death.

TABLE 13.4. INTOXICATION STATES OF PCP-LIKE HALLUCINOGENS

Time of Reactions after Ingestion	Psychological	Physiological
Approx. 5 min (if smoked, snorted, or injected) or 1 hour (if ingested orally)	Disorientation Detachment Distorted body image Euphoria Auditory and/or visual hallucinations Depression Anxiety Paranoia Apathy Analgesia Belligerence Self-destructiveness	Ataxia Dysarthria Nystagmus Blurred vision Numbness in extremities Blank staring Hypertonia Hyperreflexia Hypertension Tachycardia Sweating Drooling Fever Vomiting Repetitive movements Muscular rigidity

Subjectively, disorientation, detachment, distorted body image, a "floaty" euphoria, and auditory or visual hallucinations characterize PCP intoxication. Feelings of depression, anxiety, paranoia, and apathy are also commonly reported. The behavioral effects of PCP overdose, however, make the drug dangerous to both the intoxicated individual and those around him. Behaviors associated with PCP intoxication include psychomotor agitation, belligerence, assaultiveness, impulsivity, poor judgment, and impaired social functioning.

Patients often arrive in the emergency room in the company of others who witnessed bizarre behavior, hostility, aggression, recklessness, or self-destructiveness. Due to their insensitivity to pain, individuals on PCP often display apparent superhuman strength, such as the ability to bend steel bars. These patients do not feel the pain of muscle tears and bone fractures, allowing them to perform these acts.

Even after the drug has been cleared from the body, some patients experience a phencyclidine-induced delirium, delusional disorder, or mood disorder. Additionally, PCP is more likely than any other hallucinogen to cause acute psychotic reactions, though these reactions occur more commonly in individuals already predisposed to psychosis. PCP does not precipitate a physical dependence or a physical withdrawal syndrome, but is more likely than LSD to produce psychological dependence.

CLINICAL PRESENTATION

The differential diagnosis of PCP intoxication includes intoxication with amphetamines or other hallucinogens. The most common presenting pattern is the following triad of signs: nystagmus, hypertension, and fluctuating level of consciousness. Additionally, since PCP use is often characterized by loosening of associations, depersonalization, and cognitive disturbances, acute schizophrenia must be considered. The diagnosis of PCP intoxication can often be made by the presence of phencyclidine or a related arylcyclohexylamine in the urine.

TREATMENT

Appropriate treatment of PCP intoxication differs from the treatment of overdose with other hallucinogens in that the "talking down" method may exacerbate the situation and should be avoided. Patients should be directed to a quiet isolation room and exposed to limited sensory stimulation; physical restraints may be used if the patient is unsafe to himself or others. Although the use of diazepam 10–20 mg orally will sedate the patient, caution should be used in case other CNS depressant drugs were used concomitantly with PCP.

For patients displaying a psychotic reaction to PCP use, which may last for as long as 2–3 weeks, hospitalization in a calm, quiet room may be indicated. Haloperidol, a dopamine receptor antagonist, may help alleviate PCP psychosis. The dose of haloperidol is generally 5 mg orally or intramuscularly twice a day, followed by desipramine (starting at 50 mg/day, then titrated upward to 200 mg/day) to prevent a postwithdrawal depressive reaction. PCP excretion is hastened by acidification of the urine to a pH less than 5. Giving ammonium chloride (2.75 mEq/kg in 60 ml normal saline every 6 hours per nasogastric tube) and ascorbic acid (2 gm in 500 ml normal saline every 6 hours per nasogastric tube) will facilitate PCP excretion by acidifying the urine. Table 13.5 summarizes the treatment modalities.

SUBSTANCE ABUSE JARGON

PCP

hog	sherman	whack	crystal
angel dust	magic mist	surfer	PeaCePill

PCP w/Marijuana

happy sticks	joy sticks	blunt

TABLE 13.5. ACUTE TREATMENT FOR PCP OVERDOSE

Nonpharmacologic Intervention	Pharmacologic Intervention
DO NOT "talk down" Isolation of patient and limited sensory stimulation +/− physical restraints	Diazepam 10–30 mg p.o. if no other CNS depressants abused
	Psychotic reaction: Haloperidol 5 mg p.o./IM b.i.d., then desipramine 50 mg q.d. titrated up to 200 mg q.d. to prevent postwithdrawal depression reaction
	Acidification of urine (and facilitated excretion) via ammonium chloride 2.75 mEq/kg in 60 mL/normal saline every 6 hours per nasogastric tube, or ascorbic acid 2 gm in 500 mL normal saline every 6 hours per nasogastric tube

FURTHER READING

Domino EF. Neurobiology of PCP (Sernyl), a drug with an unusual spectrum of pharmacological activity. Int Rev Neurobiol 1964;6:303–347.

Frederking Q. Intoxicant drugs (mescaline and lysergic acid diethylamide) in psychotherapy. J Nerv Ment Dis 1955;121:262–266.

Hoffer A. LSD: a review of its present status. Clin Pharmacol Ther 1965; 6:183–255.

Johnson KM, Jones SM. Neuropharmacology of phencyclidine: basic mechanisms and therapeutic potential. Annu Rev Pharmacol Toxicol 1990;30:707–750.

Leikin JB, Krantz AJ, Zell-Kanter M. Clinical features and management of intoxication due to hallucinogenic drugs. Med Toxicol Adverse Drug Exp 1989; 4:324–350.

Olney JW, Prince MT, Fuller TA, Labruyere J, Samson L, et al. The anti-excitotoxic effects of certain anesthetics, analgesics, and sedative-hypnotics. Neurosci Lett 1986;68:29–34.

Chapter 14

Stimulants: Amphetamines and Caffeine

Eugene Lit, Lori Wiviott-Tishler, and Suzanne Wong with Steven E. Hyman

AMPHETAMINES

The Chinese first described the properties of the stimulant ephedrine over 5000 years ago. Amphetamine, a synthetic analog of ephedrine, was introduced in 1932 as an appetite suppressant, and reports of its abuse appeared shortly thereafter. In the United States, widespread abuse occurred in the 1960s and early 1970s. Although some physicians in the 1970s actually prescribed amphetamines to increase alertness and productivity, their abuse potential has subsequently limited therapeutic use to the treatment of attention deficit-hyperactivity disorder (ADHD) and narcolepsy.

EPIDEMIOLOGY

Amphetamine users are twice as likely to be male, and most either ingest pills, inject the drug intravenously, or inhale smokeable forms. "Ice" is a smokeable form of *d*-methamphetamine, and has become popular, especially in California and Hawaii.

Categories of people who abuse amphetamines by oral administration include the following:

- Women initially prescribed amphetamines for weight reduction;
- Professionals, business executives, and other "high-achievers" who use amphetamines for their anti-fatigue, activity-sustaining effect, as well as for weight reduction;
- Students who initially used amphetamines to enhance school performance;
- Truck drivers who use the drugs to stay alert during long distance trips.

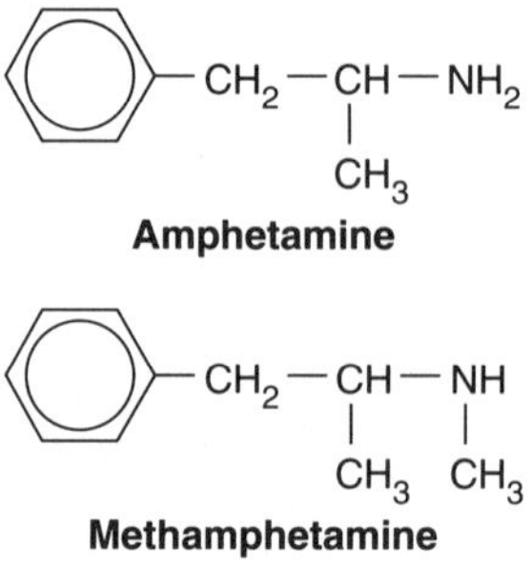

Figure 14.1. Chemical structure of amphetamine and methamphetamine.

Those who inject amphetamines intravenously or smoke "ice" include:

- Substance-abusing individuals who switched to amphetamines from other intravenous drugs;
- Polysubstance-abusing individuals;
- Those who previously used oral amphetamines;
- Experimenting adolescents and young adults.

PHARMACOLOGY

Chemistry and Pharmacokinetics

Amphetamine, a racemic phenylisopropylamine, is a synthetic congener of ephedrine. Methamphetamine, a chemically-related compound, is synthesized either by the reduction of ephedrine or by the condensation of phenylacetone and methylamine (Fig. 14.1).

Amphetamines are completely absorbed from the gastrointestinal (GI) tract and distributed throughout the body and the brain. Intravenous administration allows amphetamines to reach the brain within seconds; inhaled vapors first condense in the lungs and are then rapidly absorbed into the bloodstream.

The liver metabolizes amphetamines to active ephedrine derivatives and inactive forms. The half-lives of amphetamine and methamphetamine are 8 and 12 hours, respectively. Repeated dosing of amphetamines over several days, called "speed runs," keeps the serum concentration of the drug and its active metabolites elevated and prolongs effects. The metabolites are ultimately excreted in the urine, and may be detected by toxicology screens.

Mechanism of Action

Amphetamines, indirect monoamine agonists, produce actions both centrally and peripherally by causing norepinephrine, serotonin, and dopamine release from presynaptic terminals. These effects result from inter-

TABLE 14.1. CONSEQUENCES OF AMPHETAMINE/CAFFEINE USE

System	Amphetamines/Caffeine
CNS	increased alertness/vigilance decreased fatigue mood elevation increased concentration decreased appetite insomnia convulsions tremor psychosis
Cardiovascular	palpitations anginal pain premature contractions/arrhythmias
Respiratory	bronchodilation
Gastrointestinal	anorexia nausea/vomiting abdominal cramps diarrhea/increased gut motility metallic taste in mouth
Renal	diuretic effect similar to thiazides
Endocrine	breast tenderness (esp. w/fibrocystic breast disease)

actions of the drug with both the transporter involved in neurotransmitter re-uptake and the vesicular storage system, and from inhibition of the monoamine oxidase (MAO) system in the presynaptic nerve terminal.

Although amphetamines block the catecholamine re-uptake mechanism, the drug can be transported into the nerve terminal. Once inside the cells, they inhibit both the vesicular storage of dopamine and its breakdown by MAO. These two actions result in a buildup of catecholamines in the synaptic cleft and increased activation of the postsynaptic receptor. Long-term, repetitive use of amphetamines depletes the catecholamine supply. After the stores of catecholamines are depleted, the cell needs several days to synthesize more catecholamines. During this time, amphetamine users experience depressive symptoms.

CONSEQUENCES OF USE (TABLE 14.1)

Amphetamines are powerful central nervous system (CNS) stimulants with peripheral α- and β-adrenergic actions similar to those of the indirectly-acting sympathomimetic drugs. In the CNS, amphetamines stimulate the cerebral cortex, striatum, limbic system, and brainstem. With 10–30-mg doses of dextroamphetamine (the more potent isomer), this stimulation results in increased alertness and wakefulness, decreased fatigue, elevation of mood with increased initiative and self-confidence, a heightened ability to concentrate, decreased appetite, and insomnia. Increased release of norepinephrine and dopamine caused by the drug appears to mediate these effects. Higher doses can cause convulsions, stereotypic movements, or a psychosis mediated by the release of dopamine and possibly serotonin in the limbic system and cortex. Depression and fatigue almost always follow these behavioral changes when the drug is removed.

Dependence often occurs with chronic use of amphetamine. Regular users usually develop tolerance to the euphoric and anorectic effects of amphetamine within a few weeks. Some dependent individuals take 1700 mg per day without apparent ill effects. For unclear reasons, not all individuals develop tolerance to amphetamines. Some narcoleptics have been treated for years without increases in their initial effective dose.

Peripherally, amphetamine actions are mediated by the release of norepinephrine. They increase the systolic and diastolic blood pressure significantly by stimulating α-receptors in the vasculature and β-receptors in the heart. With the increased blood pressure, there is often a compensatory decrease in the heart rate. Cardiac arrhythmias can occur with large amphetamine doses. In contrast to caffeine, amphetamines have little effect on cerebral blood flow.

Adverse Effects

The most common CNS effects of amphetamines include restlessness, dizziness, tremor, irritability, insomnia, weakness, and hyperactive reflexes. Delirium, confusion, assaultiveness, panic states, and paranoia can occur even in individuals with no history of mental illness.

Chronic use can produce a state called "amphetamine psychosis" that resembles acute mania. In this state, individuals experience vivid hallucinations and paranoid delusions, followed by fatigue and depression. Chronic use may also result in nausea, vomiting, diarrhea, or weight loss. If the patient injects the stimulants, the risk of necrotizing angiitis or an intracerebral hemorrhage increases.

General effects of amphetamine use include headache, chills, pallor or flushing, excessive sweating, urticaria, impotence, and changes in libido. Palpitations, cardiac arrhythmias, anginal pain, hypertension or hypotension, and eventual circulatory collapse comprise specific cardiovascular effects. The GI system effects include anorexia, nausea, vomiting, abdominal cramps, diarrhea, and a metallic taste in the mouth. In fatal doses, amphetamines cause convulsions and coma, usually due to cerebral hemorrhage.

Stimulants, including the amphetamines, are thought to suppress growth in children who receive them for long-term treatment of ADHD.

Thus, periodic "drug holidays" are usually employed. Use of amphetamines is contraindicated in patients with known coronary artery disease, glaucoma, hyperthyroidism, and for patients concurrently being treated with MAO inhibitors.

CLINICAL PRESENTATION

Differential Diagnosis

The differential diagnosis of stimulant abuse includes organic and psychiatric disorders: hyperthyroidism, pheochromocytoma, anxiety disorder, mania, and paranoid schizophrenia. The following factors can quickly differentiate primary mental illness from amphetamine psychosis:

- Tactile and olfactory hallucinations occur with amphetamine overdose, but only rarely with schizophrenia.
- People with amphetamine overdose generally retain a clear sensorium and orientation.
- The patient on amphetamines does not generally have a formal thought disorder or a flat affect.
- Cocaine and amphetamine abuse can be easily confused.

Overdose Recognition

The physical signs of an overdose include seizure, hyperpyrexia, and cardiovascular compromise. The patient will likely have dilated pupils, tachycardia, and hypertension. The symptoms of amphetamine psychosis include paranoia, hypersexuality, delusional thinking, and visual, auditory, olfactory, and tactile hallucinations, but a preserved orientation and memory.

Treatment

Acute Overdose

Treatment is primarily symptomatic. For oral ingestion, emesis and activated charcoal are important. Otherwise, the following supportive measures may be necessary:

- Antipsychotic medication (e.g., haloperidol 2–5 mg or chlorpromazine 1 mg/kg every 4–6 hours);
- Medication for hypertension (alpha-blockers, such as phentolamine, or direct vasodilators, such as nitroprusside);
- Temperature control (cooling blankets and chlorpromazine to prevent further shivering and temperature elevation);
- Beta-receptor blockers may alleviate some of the catecholaminergic symptoms, and benzodiazepines may control anxiety;

- Seizures may be treated with intravenous diazepam, lorazepam, or phenytoin if benzodiazepine-resistant;
- Since life-threatening cardiac arrhythmias occur, cardiac monitoring may also be helpful; these arrhythmias may respond to propranolol;
- Acidifying the urine (ammonium chloride 2.75 mEq/kg or ascorbic acid 8 gm/day) to a pH of less than 5 hastens the excretion of the drug.

Chronic Amphetamine Addiction

Polysubstance abuse often complicates issues of stimulant withdrawal. Stimulants have strong addictive properties with specific withdrawal phases:

- The Crash (9 hours to 4 days)—This early phase of acute dysphoria can result in agitation, depression, and drug craving, later becoming fatigue and exhaustion with little drug craving.
- Withdrawal (1 to 10 weeks)—In this phase, there is less drug craving, more normal sleep, and a depressed or anxious mood. The phase tends to culminate with extreme drug craving.
- Extinction (Indefinite)—Mood normalizes, but episodic drug craving persists, especially when confronted by certain conditioned cues, such as alcohol use and its resultant disinhibition.

Therapy for chronic amphetamine abuse has two phases: disruption and relapse prevention.

Cycle *disruption* takes place during withdrawal and focuses on behavior modification. This phase of treatment seeks to magnify the harmful consequences of the drug and engage the patient in contingency contracting. In contingency contracting, a patient may choose to undergo regular urinalysis, with the understanding that an employer or professional licensing board will be notified if the patient has a positive urine screen. Establishing a support network composed of nonusing friends and relatives, support groups, and psychodynamic psychotherapy can help the user during the disruption phase of treatment.

For *relapse prevention,* long-term group therapy, contracts, and use of support groups such as Alcoholics Anonymous (AA) or Narcotics Anonymous (NA) are essential. At this stage, preventing relapses means learning to manage and decreasing drug craving. This process has three phases: (a) the initial removal of all conditioned cues, (b) the gradual reintroduction of these cues to help the patient develop methods of controlling cravings, and (c) further reintroduction of cues into the patient's life, and provision of long-term support and maintenance therapy.

TABLE 14.2. TYPICAL CAFFEINE DOSAGES

Substance	Dosage[a]
Brewed coffee	80–150 mg
Decaffeinated coffee	2–4 mg
Tea	30–75 mg
Anacin	32 mg
NoDoz	100 mg
Vivarin	200 mg

[a]Beverages are per 5 oz cup and pills are per tablet.

SUBSTANCE ABUSE JARGON

Amphetamines

speed	pep pills	bennies
uppers	crank	black beauties

Methamphetamine

crystal meth	ice (smokeable form)

CAFFEINE

The sources of caffeine in our society are coffee, teas, and the nuts of *Cola acuminata*. A legend proposes that caffeine was discovered in 850 AD by a goat herder in Abyssinia. Stories that his goats ate red berries from a dark-leafed shrub and then danced all night without sleep prompted curious monks to experiment with the berries. They found that the berries made a tasty drink that allowed them to stay awake during their lengthy prayer sessions. This news spread to other monasteries and coffee soon became a popular drink for elevating mood, decreasing fatigue, and increasing the capacity for work. Table 14.2 lists examples of caffeinated beverages and medications with their respective caffeine doses.

EPIDEMIOLOGY

Caffeine is the most widely used stimulant in the world and is consumed largely in the form of coffee. In 1983, 80% of the population of the United States regularly drank coffee, but this trend has been decreasing. Reports in 1991 showed that 53% of Americans drank coffee; increased amounts are consumed in areas of Central and South America and Western Europe. The highest consumption rates occur in the United Kingdom and Scandinavia. The average daily intake of caffeine in the United States is 200 mg—the equivalent to two cups of coffee per day. Regular use at this level would equal the consumption of 32 pounds of

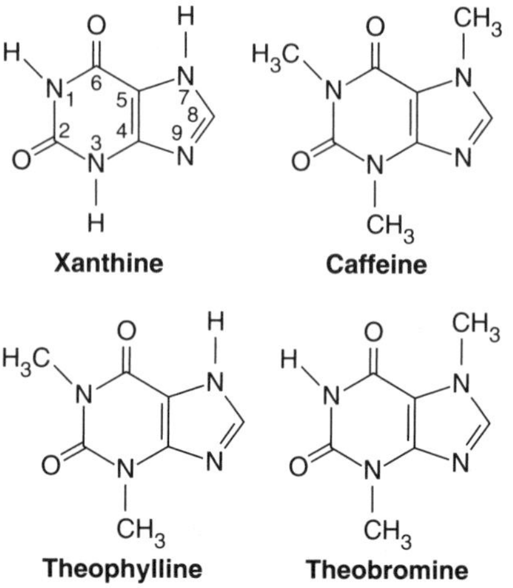

Figure 14.2. Chemical structures of caffeine and structurally similar methylxanthines.

coffee per year. In addition to coffee, caffeine is present in soft drinks, over-the-counter analgesics, antihistamines, stimulants, and weight loss aids.

PHARMACOLOGY

Chemistry and Pharmacokinetics

Caffeine, theobromine, and theophylline are related alkaloids found in plants. These methylated xanthines are structurally related to metabolically important compounds, such as purines (adenine, guanine), xanthine, and uric acid (Fig. 14.2).

Because of its lipophilic character, caffeine (1,3,7-trimethylxanthine) has a 99% absorption rate after oral ingestion and reaches peak serum concentrations in 30–60 minutes. After ingestion, it is rapidly distributed throughout the entire body, and crosses the blood-brain barrier by diffusion and a saturable transport system.

Caffeine and other methylxanthines are metabolized in the liver by the microsomal cytochrome P-450 reductase system and then excreted in the urine; 2–3% is excreted unchanged. The half-life for caffeine varies from 2–12 hours with a 4–6-hour average, depending on the individual. Pregnancy and chronic liver disease increase the half-life, while smoking decreases the half-life.

Mechanism of Action

Several hypotheses have attempted to explain the mechanism of caffeine's diverse array of actions on the body. The most important include:

(*a*) caffeine blocks adenosine receptors, (*b*) caffeine inhibits the enzyme phosphodiesterase, and (*c*) it induces a translocation of intracellular calcium.

As a neurotransmitter, adenosine acts on two kinds of receptors: (*a*) a high-affinity receptor (A1), which inhibits adenylate cyclase; and (*b*) a low-affinity receptor (A2), which stimulates adenylate cyclase. The interplay between the two is the topic of much study, and adenosine receptors are found in tissues all over the body, including the brain, heart and blood vessels, respiratory tract, kidneys, adipose tissue, and the GI tract.

Adenosine and its derivatives have central and peripheral actions. They cause depression of spontaneous electrical activity of neurons and inhibit the synaptic transmission of neurotransmitters, such as catecholamines and glutamate. Adenosine also influences behavior, such as inducing slow wave sleep and decreased vigilance. Adenosine and its derivatives decrease locomotor activity when administered, which can be reversed by a small dose of caffeine or theophylline. Finally, adenosine acts locally as a vasodilator, inhibits the release of renin, and reduces platelet aggregation in vitro. Caffeine and the other methylxanthines inhibit these actions.

In humans, caffeine acts as a competitive antagonist to adenosine receptors. The circulating plasma concentration of caffeine after drinking 1–3 cups of coffee (usually less than 100 μM) suppresses the effects of adenosine, but has no direct effect on cAMP levels or calcium shifts. Toxic levels (more than 200 μM) are required for caffeine-induced effects on calcium shift or cAMP levels. Caffeine plasma concentrations of more than 500 μM are lethal.

CONSEQUENCES OF USE (TABLE 14.1)

Central Nervous System

Drinking 1–2 cups of coffee (100–200 mg) increases alertness, heightens vigilance, maintains the capacity to perform complex motor functions, and decreases fatigue by stimulating the cortex and other areas of the brain. Higher doses of caffeine (1.5 grams or 12–15 cups of coffee) produce anxiety and tremors. The lethal dose of caffeine is 10 grams or 100 cups of coffee and causes emesis, convulsions, and cardiac arrhythmias. Contrary to popular belief, caffeine potentiates some effects of alcohol, making its reputation as an "antidote" for alcohol intoxication false.

Caffeine affects the brain in two main ways. First, caffeine-induced cerebral vasoconstriction decreases cerebral blood flow. Second, increased glucose consumption occurs in certain areas of hypoperfusion. These areas include the monoaminergic cells of the substantia nigra, ventral tegmental area, the medial and dorsal raphe, and the locus ceruleus. These physiologic changes correlate with the behavioral and physical changes seen during caffeine ingestion.

Caffeine ingestion 30–60 minutes before sleep increases sleep latency, decreases total sleep time, and decreases sleep quality. These effects vary between individuals depending on the regularity of coffee consumption.

Cardiovascular

The effects of caffeine on heart rate, blood pressure, and plasma catecholamines are disputed in the literature. Recent studies show that caffeine intake causes an abrupt increase in systolic blood pressure of 10 mm Hg, a decrease in heart rate for 1 hour, and a subsequent increase in heart rate for 2–3 hours. However, long-term use creates a tolerant state in which caffeine has little or no effect on heart rate, blood pressure, or catecholamine levels. Sensitive individuals may experience arrhythmias and premature contractions with caffeine ingestion.

Gastrointestinal

Caffeine, regular coffee, and decaffeinated coffee all increase gastric secretions and lower esophageal sphincter tone. Regular (caffeinated) and decaffeinated coffee cause more potent responses than caffeine alone. The additional active ingredients in coffee remain unidentified. Decaffeinated coffee, therefore, is not an appropriate alternative for people with peptic ulcer disease or gastroesophageal reflux disease.

Caffeine stimulates the bowel to secrete water and sodium, but coffee does not. On the other hand, coffee does cause increased motility of the distal colon and defecation, but this is seen with both caffeinated and decaffeinated beverages.

CLINICAL PRESENTATION

Caffeine Intoxication and Overdose

Table 14.3 presents the signs of mild and severe caffeine intoxication.

Patients with a caffeine overdose may present with wakefulness, restlessness, anorexia, vomiting, dehydration, and, at extreme doses, seizures. Sources of caffeine include both beverages and over-the-counter preparations of aspirin and diet pills, as well as drugs that are marketed as stimulants. The primary care provider should consider caffeine overuse in patients who complain of anxiety, irritability, heart palpitations, tremors, diarrhea, and insomnia. Caffeine may also cause painful breast tenderness in women with fibrocystic breast changes.

TABLE 14.3. PHYSICAL SIGNS OF CAFFEINE INTOXICATION

Mild toxicity:
  Tachycardia
  Palpitations
  Mild hypertension
  Slight tachypnea
  Dry mouth
  Hyperactivity
  Agitation
  Mild paranoia
  Anxiety

Severe toxicity:
  Serious tachyarrhythmias
  Marked hypertension
  High fever
  Seizures
  Delirium
  Paranoia
  Psychosis
  Cardiovascular collapse

TABLE 14.4. ACUTE TREATMENT OF AMPHETAMINE/CAFFEINE OVERDOSE

Emesis and activated charcoal if the drug has been taken orally
Cardiac monitor
Diuresis, acidification of urine
Symptomatic treatment (see text for details)
  Antipsychotic medications
  Antihypertensives
  Temperature control
  Beta blockers

The differential diagnosis of caffeine intoxication includes cocaine or amphetamine abuse, hyperthyroidism, pheochromocytoma, anxiety disorder, mania, and paranoid schizophrenia.

Treatment of Overdose

Although extremely rare, caffeine overdose can produce significant morbidity and even mortality. Therapy relies on supportive care that includes emesis and activated charcoal if the overdose is secondary to recent ingestion. Treatment guidelines for amphetamine overdose also apply to treatment of caffeine overdose (Table 14.4 outlines treatment options).

Long-Term Treatment

Although caffeine is rarely considered a drug of abuse, it produces a mild psychological and physical dependence. A caffeine withdrawal syndrome, consisting of nausea, lethargy, headache, and constipation, usually occurs upon discontinuation of the drug after several weeks of drinking five or more cups of coffee or tea daily.

Strategies for reducing caffeine consumption include a slow taper of use—decreasing intake of caffeinated beverages or mixing caffeinated coffee with decaffeinated beverages. Once the physical symptoms improve, patients who enjoy drinking caffeinated beverages may find it equally satisfying to switch to decaffeinated coffee, herbal or decaffeinated tea, or decaffeinated soft drinks.

FURTHER READING

Garattini S. Caffeine, Coffee, and Health. New York: Raven Press, 1993.

Gawin FH, Ellinwood EH Jr. Cocaine and other stimulants. New Engl J Med 1988;318:1173–1182.

Gross P. Toxicologic emergencies. In: Wilkins EW Jr, ed. Emergency Medicine: Scientific Foundations and Current Practice. 3rd Ed. Baltimore: Williams & Wilkins, 1989.

Holbrook JM. CNS stimulants. In: Bennet G, Bourakis C, Woolf DS, eds. Substance Abuse: Pharmacological, Developmental, and Clinical Perspectives. New York: John Wiley & Sons, 1983.

Smith D. Amphetamine Use, Misuse, and Abuse. Boston: GK Hall, 1979.

Chapter 15

Anabolic Steroids

David L. Kaufman with Lawrence S. Friedman

The anabolic effects of the "male hormone" were initially recognized by Kochakian and Murlin in 1935. They found that administration of this hormone, later identified as testosterone, induced a positive nitrogen balance in castrated dogs by improving the metabolism of ingested protein and increasing nitrogen retention. Testosterone acts on a wide variety of central and peripheral hormone-sensitive structures and produces both anabolic and androgenic effects. Initially, medical indication for testosterone use was limited to treatment for hypogonadism, but soon medical use expanded to include burns, malnutrition, and anemia. Anecdotal reports suggest that the German Army used testosterone to augment the aggressiveness of their combat troops in World War II.

Four years after the successful synthesis of testosterone, suggestions that it could enhance physical performance led to its widespread use by athletes. In the 1940s, bodybuilders introduced the use of anabolic steroids in the United States. Use by elite athletes competing in high-strength, short-endurance sports ensued in the early 1950s. In 1972 a survey of Olympic athletes from seven countries found that 68% admitted taking anabolic steroids. Since no reliable method for detecting illicit steroid use existed at the time, the International Olympic Committee (IOC) did not ban these drugs until 1976.

More recent studies reveal that the use of anabolic steroids is not confined to elite athletes. College, high school, and even middle school students—not all athletes—take these substances. These findings led to the classification of anabolic-androgenic steroids as controlled substances.

EPIDEMIOLOGY

There are more than one million current or former users of anabolic steroids, half of them under the age of 26. Steroids are often used concomitantly with illicit drugs, cigarettes, and alcohol.

In 1988, of 6765 United States male high school seniors, 6.6% used or had taken anabolic steroids; 67% of these began use prior to their 16th birthday. Moreover, a 1989 study of five high schools indicated 1.4% of females used steroids before graduating from high school.

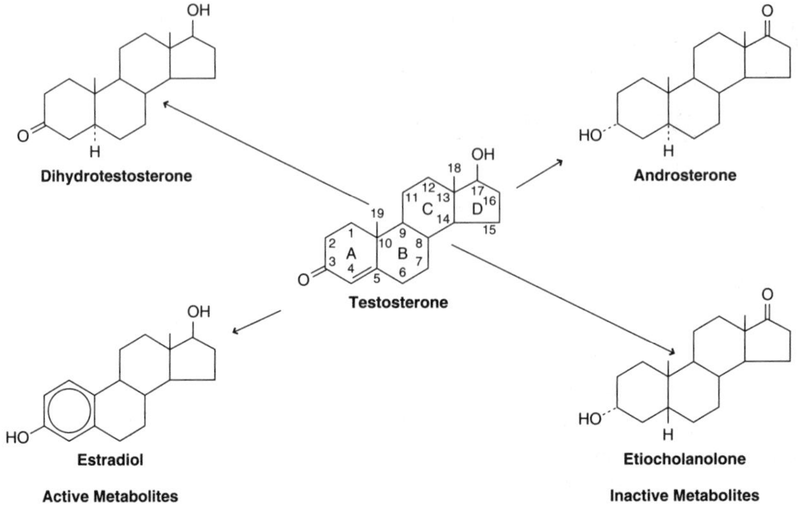

Figure 15.1. Testosterone metabolism.

Anabolic steroid use has increased over the past decade, and that use varies according to geographic location and population group. Young athletes involved in high-strength sports are the individuals most likely to take them. While competitive athletes report a higher prevalence of anabolic steroid use, a large number of recreational athletes, including women, also take these drugs.

Access to steroids is often via the black market, making purity and formulation suspect. The United States manufactures some steroids, but many are imported from Europe and Mexico. Moreover, illicit dosing may exceed the recommended therapeutic doses by 2 to 40 times. Generally, patterns of use consist of 1- to 4-month cycles "on" steroids, followed by intermittent "off" periods of 2 to 3 months. Change of drugs, dosing regimens, and/or supplementing with other drugs often occurs without scientific basis or physician consultation.

The cost of steroids ranges from $0.30/tablet, for stanozolol, to high-cost injectables like trebolone acetate, at $140.00/vial. Not all abused anabolic steroids were intended for human use. Equipoise (boldenone undecyclenate), Finiject 30 (bolasterone), and Winstrol (stanozolol), and mibolerone were developed initially for veterinary medicine.

PHARMACOLOGY

Synthetic, anabolic steroid production modifies testosterone to increase oral availability and half-life, to decrease androgenic effects, and to maximize anabolic effects. Testosterone's structure and metabolism is shown in Figure 15.1. Under normal physiological conditions, testoster-

TABLE 15.1. ORAL AND INJECTABLE STEROIDS

Oral		Injectable	
Trade name	*Generic*	*Trade name*	*Generic*
Anadrol	oxymethonone	Deca-Durabolin	nandrolone decanoate
Anavar	oxandrolone	Durabolin	nandrolone phenpropionate
Dianabol	methandrostenone	Depo-testosterone	testosterone cypionate
Maxibolin	ethylestrenol	Delatestryl	testosterone enanthate
Winstrol	stanozolol	Oreton	testosterone propionate
Halotestin	fluoxymestrone	Primabolin depot	methenolone enanthate
Nilevar	norethandrolone	Equipoise	boldenone undecyclenate
Primobolan	methanolone acetate	Finajet	trebolone acetate
Proviron	mesterolone	Parabolin	trebolone
Teslac	testolactone		

one is first metabolized in the liver by conjugation with glucuronic or sulfuric acid, and then excreted via the urine.

Alkylation at the 17-α position results in slower hepatic inactivation, a modification found in most oral agents. These agents are rapidly absorbed, but cause hepatotoxicity. Parenteral use requires carboxylic acid esterification at the 17-β position. 19-nortestosterone and testosterone ester derivatives, common parenteral agents, are administered intramuscularly. They have slow systemic absorption and long half-lives due to the greater hydrophobicity and greater lipid solubility generated by reduction of the molecule's polarity.

Although most testosterone is bound to plasma proteins, the unbound molecules exert its pharmacological action. In reproductive tissues and the brain, testosterone must undergo modification before it becomes biologically active. Intracellular enzymes convert testosterone to more potent metabolites, such as the 5-α-reductase modification of testosterone to dihydroxytestosterone (DHT). Testosterone acts via its metabolites on intracellular receptors, which regulate nuclear transcription. The net effect of this influence results in changes in protein production within the cell. These proteins affect the anabolic actions of the steroids.

Table 15.1 lists common oral and parenteral anabolic steroids used in athletics.

STEROID USE BY ATHLETES

From an athletic standpoint, anabolic steroids have four effects:

1. During training, steroids can competitively bind to glucocorticosteroid receptors, blocking their catabolic effects.
2. Retention of systemic nitrogen and enhanced utilization of ingested nitrogen convert a negative nitrogen balance to a positive one.

3. Anabolic steroids may induce protein synthesis in skeletal muscle.
4. Many athletes feel heightened aggression (termed " 'roid rages"), increased tolerance of more intense training periods, diminished fatigability, euphoria, and decreased recovery periods.
(NOTE: Anabolic steroid use does not increase aerobic capacity.)

Most athletes use anabolic steroids to gain strength and muscle mass. Considerable disagreement focuses on whether these drugs actually work. The American College of Sports Medicine believes that the use of anabolic steroids can result in small but significant increases in strength in some, but not all, athletes.

Some investigators have concluded that improved athletic performance may be observed only if certain criteria are met. These include steroid administration in highly trained athletes, diet supplementation with high-protein, high-calorie diets, high dosage levels for prolonged periods, and sensitive measurement of strength (single-rep, max-weight, multi-joint exercise). No studies have shown an increase in strength when nonathletes are administered anabolic steroids. In summary, although strength, muscle mass, or physical performance may be augmented by steroid usage in the eugonadal male, the change is small.

CONSEQUENCES OF USE

The pathophysiology of anabolic steroid abuse results from dosages at levels tens to hundreds of times greater than the intended therapeutic dose. In addition, the questionable purity of the drugs may contribute to pathological changes.

The major medical issues associated with anabolic-androgenic steroids reflect their effects on the endocrine system. Women taking anabolic steroids may develop acne, deepened voice, hirsutism, reduction in breast mass, male-pattern alopecia, clitoral hypertrophy, and amenorrhea or dysmenorrhea. While some of these changes may be temporary, baldness, facial hair, clitoral development, and voice alterations are generally permanent.

After a single month of anabolic steroid use, men experience a decrease in circulating testosterone levels. Chronic use may cause testicular atrophy, but notably, this is usually reversible.

As medical therapy, androgens and anabolic steroids have several appropriate indications (Table 15.2).

The major medical consequences of anabolic steroids are listed in Table 15.3.

TABLE 15.2. MEDICAL INDICATIONS FOR ANABOLIC STEROID USE

Anabolic
  Relief of bone pain accompanying osteoporosis
  Weight loss after surgery, trauma, or chronic infection
  Offset protein catabolism seen with extensive corticosteroid administration
  Anemia and blood disorders

Androgenic (Men)
  Oligospermia
  Impotence secondary to insufficient androgen production
  Replacement due to decreased testosterone resulting from hypogonadism,
    castration, or delayed puberty

Androgenic (Women)
  Premenopausal, hormone-sensitive breast cancer
  Postmenopausal, inoperable, metastatic breast cancer

TABLE 15.3. CONSEQUENCES OF STEROID USE

System	Consequences of Use
CNS/psychological	Increased aggression
Cardiovascular	Elevated blood pressure Coronary artery spasm/acute myocardial infarction Lipid profile changes (HDL down, LDL up)
Gastrointestinal	LFT abnormalities Cholestatic jaundice Peliosis hepatis (blood sacs in liver) Increased risk for hepatic tumors
Infectious disease	Sharing needles for i.m./i.v. increases risk for hepatitis and HIV
Endocrine	In women: acne, deepened voice, hirsutism, reduction in breast mass, male-pattern alopecia, clitoral hypertrophy, and amenorrhea/dysmenorrhea In men: decreased circulating testosterone and testicular atrophy
Dermatological	Sebaceous gland hyperplasia w/acne
Musculoskeletal	Premature epiphyseal fusion (adolescents) Overextension/training leads to muscular tears and injuries

CLINICAL PRESENTATION

History and Physical Examination

The clinical presentation of an anabolic steroid user is diverse. Physicians should not exclude anabolic steroid use from the differential diagnosis based on patient sex, age, or even athletic conditioning.

During history taking, questions must address factors associated with steroid use, such as participation in recreational athletics and/or weight lifting/bodybuilding. Additionally, patterns of unusual weight gain and/ or physical maturation should be questioned. In those patients who report use, it is important to ascertain duration, agents, route of administration, and dosage.

In conducting the physical examination, the physician looks for the following signs of steroid use: jaundice, acne, edematous face or extremities, yellow sclera, elevated blood pressure, testicular atrophy, gynecomastia, hirsutism, clitoral enlargement, hepatic enlargement, needle marks, and prostate hypertrophy.

Steroid users often use other medications to hide anabolic steroid abuse or reduce the associated side effects. Tamoxifen, an anti-estrogenic agent, and human chorionic gonadotropin (HCG) help reduce gynecomastia. Competitive athletes often attempt to dilute their urine samples by taking diuretics, such as furosemide (Lasix), or by using probenecid (Benemid), which blocks renal excretion of steroid metabolites.

Laboratory Studies

Potential laboratory abnormalities in a patient using anabolic steroids include any of the following: urine toxicology screen positive for anabolic steroids and their metabolites, elevated fasting glucose, low serum HDL and elevated serum LDL cholesterol concentrations, elevated BUN/ creatinine ratio (especially with diuretic use), and inappropriate bone age (especially in adolescents).

Additionally, there may be nonspecific elevation of liver function tests. Disagreement about the validity of enzyme tests to monitor hepatic dysfunction exists because strenuous exercise alone induces elevated serum levels of alanine and aspartate aminotransferases, lactate dehydrogenase, and phosphatases.

TREATMENT

The primary therapy for anabolic steroid use is discontinuation followed by abstinence from other drugs of the same or similar classes. Informing the patient of the dangerous side effects of steroid abuse, some of which are irreversible, may persuade users to quit or prevent other patients from initiating use.

SUBSTANCE ABUSE JARGON AND DEFINITIONS

Stacking: The concurrent administration of multiple agents, usually at least one oral and one injectable.

Pyramiding: Systematically increasing the dosages over a period of weeks to a previously determined level, and then decreasing the dose in the same fashion.

Plateau: The point at which strength gains are perceived to cease and often the agent is changed at this point.

Cycling: The technique of "on" and "off" steroid pattern usage.

Inverted pyramiding: Starting a cycle at high dosage and decreasing it toward a basal level, then increasing the dosage systematically until the initial level is reached.

'Roid Rages: Aggressive feelings associated with steroid use.

FURTHER READING

Celotti F, Cesi PN. Anabolic Steroids: A review of their effects on the muscles, of their possible mechanisms of action, and of their use in athletics. J Steroid Biochem Mol Biol 1992;43:469–477.

Haupt HA, Rovere GD. Anabolic steroids: a review of the literature. Am J Sports Med 1984;12:469–484.

Hickson RC, Ball KL, Falduto MT. Adverse effects of anabolic steroids. Med Toxicol Adverse Drug Exp 1989;4:254–271.

Johnson MD. Anabolic steroid use in adolescent athletes. Pediatr Clin North Am 1990;37:1111–1123.

Kennedy MC. Anabolic steroid abuse and toxicology. Aust N Z J Med 1992; 22:374–381.

Strauss RH, Yesalis CE. Anabolic steroids in the athlete. Annu Rev Med 1991; 42:449–457.

Yesalis CE, Kennedy NJ, Kopstein AN, Bahrke MS. Anabolic-androgenic steroid use in the United States. JAMA 1993;270:1217–1221.

Chapter 16

Inhalants

John T. Brooks and Gordon Leung with Michael Shannon

Inhalants comprise a diverse group of organic volatile liquids and gases that are intentionally inhaled to induce euphoria. A variety of factors make inhalants popular as substances of abuse including: low cost, lack of regulation (with the exception of anesthetic gases and some nitrites), availability in many commercial products or other easily accessible materials, capacity for direct use without specialized equipment, rapid intoxication, short duration of action, and rapid recovery with few acute side effects (Table 16.1).

These properties make inhalant abuse especially popular among adolescents and young adults first experimenting with intoxicating substance use, among people with restricted access to other drugs because of high cost or social isolation (e.g., prisoners, impoverished) and among people with special access to inhalants who cannot risk prolonged intoxication (e.g., health professionals, industrial workers). Employment history can often provide important clues concerning special access to inhalants.

Inhalants can be subdivided into three major pharmacologic groups: (*a*) general volatile organic compounds (VOCs), such as glues, aerosols, and solvents, (*b*) volatile nitrites, and (*c*) anesthetic gases (nitrous oxide). Nitrites and nitrous oxide comprise a small fraction of all inhalants with a waning frequency of abuse. Abuse of the more ubiquitous VOCs has steadily increased, with the most rapid rise among school-age adolescents. In 1993 roughly one in five 8th graders had inhaled a glue, aerosol, or solvent at least once for the purpose of becoming intoxicated, a 2% increase from the previous year. These data reflect the steady decline in the use of "hard drugs," such as LSD, amphetamines, barbiturates, and opiates, among adolescents with a concomitant rise in the abuse of more available, "softer" compounds like inhalants and alcohol.

Although inhalant abuse is universal, certain groups disproportionately abuse these substances. For example, while Native Americans and the impoverished people of developing nations inhale gasoline due to its low cost and ubiquity, nitrite inhalation occurs among sexually active gay men for the effects of enhanced sexual arousal.

TABLE 16.1. UNIQUE PROPERTIES OF INHALANTS

Low cost
Lack of regulation (with few exceptions)
Multitude of forms
Ubiquitous materials
No specialized equipment, technique, or preparation required for use
Rapid intoxication
Short duration of action
Rapid recovery
Few significant acute side effects

☺VOLATILE ORGANIC COMPOUNDS

EPIDEMIOLOGY

Use of VOCs encompasses all age groups and socioeconomic classes with a markedly higher prevalence among adolescents. This prevalence peaks between the ages of 11 and 13, then levels off and declines in young adulthood. In the United States during the 1980s, roughly 10% (range 3.5–15%) of high school students had used inhaled hydrocarbons at least once. By comparison, in 1993 and 1994, lifetime inhalant use among graduating high school seniors was around 17%. Most adolescents try VOCs a few times and quit; less than 3% become chronic users. However, VOCs are often characterized as one of a group of drugs (including alcohol, marijuana) with which teenagers first experiment before trying other drugs of abuse.

Men use VOCs about twice as often as women. Abuse levels among racial minorities and the economically disadvantaged are also elevated.

PHARMACOLOGY

VOCs comprise a diverse group of hydrocarbon liquids produced by distillation and fractionation of crude oil. Classification of the VOCs separates them according to their structure and chemistry (Table 16.2). Pure forms of VOCs are used as solvents (e.g., dry cleaning compounds, varnish removers), as solubilizers and dispersants for application of other compounds (e.g., paints, glues, sprays), as refrigerants (Freon), as fire extinguishers, and as anesthetic gases (e.g., ether). Mixed distillates are used mostly as fuels with retention of their solvent and anesthetic properties. Most VOCs are flammable and volatile at room temperature.

Formulation and Administration

VOCs are available in a multitude of forms: as fluids in cans or bottles; as aerosols in sprays (e.g., hairspray, pesticides, and fire extinguishers);

TABLE 16.2. CLASSIFICATION OF INHALED VOLATILE HYDROCARBONS (COMMON NAMES)

Aliphatic Hydrocarbons
    ethane
    propane
    n-butane, isobutane
    n-hexane
    acetylene

Aromatic/Alicyclic Hydrocarbons
    benzene
    toluene (methylbenzene)
    xylene (dimethylbenzene)
    tetramethylbenzenes (durene)
    isopropylbenzene (cumene)
    isopropyltoluene (cymene)
    styrene (vinylbenzene)

Halogenated Hydrocarbons
    dichloromethane (methylene chloride)
    trichloromethane (chloroform)
    carbon tetrachloride (tetrachloromethane)
    bromochlorodifluoromethane (BDF)
    1,1,1-trichloroethane (methyl chloroform)
    trichloroethylene (TCE, trichloroethene, Trilene, trike)
    tetrachloroethylene (perchloroethylene)
    dichlorodifluoromethane (Freon 12, propellant 12)

Ethers
    dimethyl ether (DME, methoxymethane)
    diethyl ether (ethoxyethane, "anesthetic ether")
    enflurane (2-chloro-1,1,2-trifluorethyl difluoromethyl ether)
    isoflurane (2-chloro-2,2,2,-triofluoroethyl difluoromethyl ether)
    methyl tert-butyl ether (MTBE)

Ketones/Acetates
    acetone (dimethyl ketone)
    methyl ethyl ketone (MEK, butanone, butan-2-one)
    methyl n-propyl ketone (MPK, 2-pentanone)
    methyl n-butyl ketone (MBK, 2-hexanone)
    ethyl acetate

Mixed Compounds
    gasoline (petrol)
    kerosene
    mineral spirits
    jet fuels

TABLE 16.3. PRODUCTS INHALED FOR VOC CONSTITUENTS

Product	Major Volatile Component
Adhesives/Glues	
balsa wood cement	ethyl acetate
contact adhesives	toluene, hexane, esters
bicycle tire repair kits	toluene, xylenes
Aerosols	
air freshener	butane, dimethyl ether
deodorant/antiperspirant	butane, dimethyl ether
fly spray	butane, dimethyl ether
hairspray	butane, dimethyl ether
paint	butane, esters
Cigarette lighters	butane, propane
Dry cleaners, spot removers, and degreasers (commercial and domestic)	1,1,1-trichloroethane, tetrachloroethylene
Fire extinguishers	bromochlorodifluoromethane
Nail polish removers	acetone, esters
Paints and paint thinners	toluene, xylene, hexane, butanone, esters
Paint strippers	toluene, dichloromethane
Typewriter correction fluids	1,1,1-trichloroethane

or as semisolid compounds in tubes or small bottles (e.g., adhesives, correction fluids). Table 16.3 lists some of the commercially available products containing VOCs and their common industrial applications.

Inhalation of VOCs requires volatilization of the substance, usually by one of the following methods:

In *sniffing*, the VOC container or a surface to which the VOC has been applied (e.g., painted on wood or poured on table top), is held near the user's mouth and nose. The user then inhales and exhales rapidly. Application of heat—warming the container between a user's palms or heating the VOC in a container (e.g., can or cooking pan) on a hotplate, stove burner, or open flame—facilitates volatilization. This latter practice exponentially increases the degree of volatilization, but is associated with much greater risk of fire or explosion.

In *huffing*, the VOC is spread on cloth through which the vapors are inhaled. Huffers often use parts of their own clothing, which become permeated with the odor of the VOC (a potential clue for health care providers). In one variant, seen in industrial settings where respiratory protective devices are used, users place VOC-soaked cotton balls or cloth inside the filters of dust or fume masks. Users often titrate a constant exposure by adjusting the amount of VOC-soaked material inserted into the mask piece. This practice can lead to toxic overexposure.

In *bagging*, the VOC is poured, sprayed, or applied to the inside of a bag (e.g., potato chip bag, sandwich bag, or garbage bag), which is held closed and shaken to concentrate and volatilize the fumes. The bag opening is then placed over the mouth and/or nose and the vapors are inhaled. Most users hold their breath after inhalation to maximize vapor absorption and breathe in and out of the bag without fresh air to maximize exposure. Using this method, 10–15 closed inhalations generally suffice to induce euphoria with many VOCs.

Mechanism of Action and Pharmacokinetics

In general, VOCs are central nervous system (CNS) depressants, acting first on the cortex, and then affecting brainstem function as blood levels increase. Although the precise biochemical mechanism of this effect remains unknown, their actions appear similar to those of anesthetic gases. Since many VOCs are denser than air, they also act, in part, as simple asphyxiants by decreasing the partial pressure of inhaled oxygen, and this hypoxia probably contributes to the CNS effects. However, the intoxicating effect of VOCs cannot be ascribed to hypoxia alone.

VOCs used for intoxication are lipid-soluble, facilitating rapid absorption across lung tissue into the bloodstream and delivery to the CNS. Although the CNS effects occur within seconds of inhalation, diffusion times into other body tissues are slow, with peak levels occurring 15–30 minutes later. Serum half-lives may vary from hours to days, depending on the VOC. Protein binding is minimal and elimination of most VOCs involves some combination of pulmonary exhalation, urinary excretion, and hepatic oxidative metabolism. Typically, metabolites of the VOC, not its original form, cause toxic damage to organs.

Consequences of Use

The major health risk of inhaled VOC use is sudden death (termed "sudden sniffing death"). The number of deaths from VOC use has slowly, but steadily, increased worldwide since the 1970s. Cardiopulmonary arrest secondary to either arrhythmia and/or respiratory depression is the cause of death in these cases. VOC abuse also increases patients' risk for trauma, for accidental death from falls and thermal burns, for fatal chemical pneumonitis secondary to aspiration, and for asphyxiation. The major medical effects associated with VOCs are outlined in Table 16.4.

The changes in the CNS represent the most common and most diverse pathology associated with chronic VOC use. Both central and peripheral nerve damage can occur. Permanent damage is associated with sustained

TABLE 16.4. ACUTE AND CHRONIC SEQUELAE OF VOLATILE HYDROCARBON USE

System	Acute Effects	Chronic Effects
CNS	euphoria	cognitive dysfunction, esp. memory and concentration
	disinhibition	ataxia and dysarthria
	disorientation	hyperreflexia
	dizziness	tremor
	syncope	paresthesias
	headache	peripheral neuropathy
	confusion (high dose)	anosmia
	impaired judgment (high dose)	psychosis with or without: audiovisual hallucinations and pseudohallucinations
	memory difficulties (high dose)	
	seizure (high dose)	delusions, esp. paranoia
	coma (high dose)	diffuse cerebellar and cranial nerve atrophy, esp. CN I and VII
		encephalopathy
		depression
Cardiovascular	arrhythmia (including ventricular tachycardia/ ventricular fibrillation)/ sudden death— exacerbated by catecholamine surge	
	hypotension/reflex tachycardia (low dose)	
	bradycardia/low cardiac output (high dose)	
Ophthalmologic	injected sclera and conjunctivae	
	lacrimation	
	decreased visual acuity	
	diplopia	
Respiratory/ENT	nasotrachial irritation (including "chilled larynx")	oropharyngeal ulceration
	wheezing, rales, rhonchi	epistaxis
	pneumonitis (from aspiration and aerosol)	halitosis
		rhinitis
		tinnitus
Skin	burn (chemical, thermal)	dermatitis ("huffer's rash")
	desiccation	

(Continued on next page)

Gastrointestinal	salivation
	nausea/vomiting
	diffuse abdominal pain
	hematemesis
	hepatitis w/liver enzyme
	   elevation
	fulminant hepatic necrosis
	   (carbon tetrachloride and
	   halothane)
		fatty liver changes
		cirrhosis

Renal	distal tubular acidosis (toluene) toxic nephropathy	glomerulopathies (rare) nephrolithiasis
Hematologic (Benzene only)	transient pancytopenia preleukemic leukocytosis	leukemia (esp. acute myeloblastic leukemia) aplastic anemia
Metabolic	hypokalemia hypophosphatemia hypocalcemia metabolic acidosis (non- anion gap)	
Musculoskeletal	rhabdomyolysis	myopathy (symmetrical, all major groups)

periods of exposure. The anatomic localization and nature of neurotoxic effects vary somewhat among VOCs.

Inhaled VOCs, especially aliphatic and halogenated hydrocarbons, are arrhythmogenic. Through an unknown mechanism, they potentiate the activity of endogenous catecholamines on myocardium, predisposing the person to arrhythmias, such as ventricular tachycardia and fibrillation.

SUBSTANCE ABUSE JARGON
The term "dope" originated in relation to the use of the solvent 1,1,2,2-tetrachloroethane in "doping," or waterproofing, fabric-covered aircraft during World War I.

NITRITES

Originally developed as antianginals, alkyl nitrites (Fig. 16.1) are currently sold predominantly for their intoxicating effect. While its ability to relieve angina pectoris was described as early as 1867, amyl nitrite was not licensed in the United States for this purpose until 1937. Butyl nitrites have similar angina-relieving properties. Today, solid or semisolid nitroglycerin formulations, easily packaged and safely dosed, have

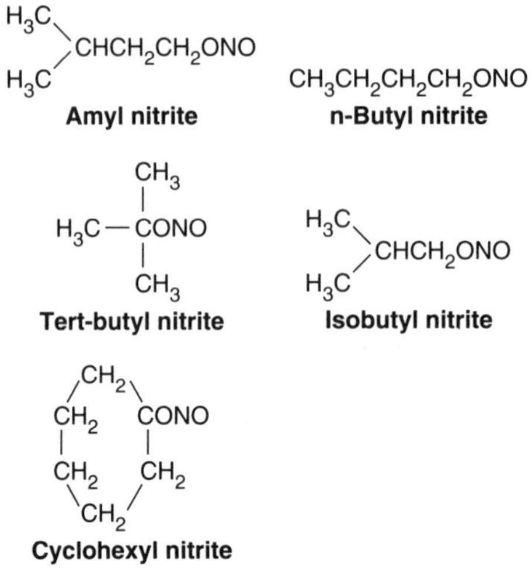

Figure 16.1. Chemical structures of the nitrites.

replaced liquid nitrite compounds. Amyl nitrite is also used as an antidote for cyanide poisoning.

EPIDEMIOLOGY

Gay Men

During the 1970s and 1980s many gay men used amyl and butyl nitrite to enhance sexual activity by creating a floating sensation of disinhibited euphoria, intense sexual arousal, and increased penile blood flow. A survey from the mid-1980s demonstrated that up to 70% of gay men had used inhaled nitrites. However, the false association of nitrite inhalation with AIDS and AIDS-related illness (see below), as well as increasing awareness of substance abuse issues within the gay community, has led to a rapid and steep decline in their use. Currently, estimates reveal that less than 20% of gay men use inhaled nitrites.

Adolescents

Inhaled nitrites are inexpensive, widely available, and can be rapidly intoxicating with a short duration of action—all factors that make them appealing to adolescents. A 1986 survey of American high school students demonstrated that approximately 10% of the students had used nitrites at least once, but only a small proportion, less than 1%, used them more than ten times per month. However, within the subpopulation of chemically-dependent adolescents, 74% (males more than females) reported regular abuse of nitrites.

TABLE 16.5. COMMERCIALLY AVAILABLE NITRITE-CONTAINING PRODUCTS

Aroma of Men
BlackJack
Bullet
Climax
D&E Video Head Cleaner
Dr. Bananas
Krypt Tonight
Lightning Bolt
Locker Room
Oz
Quick Silver
Rush
Satan's Scent
Sweat
Mama Popper's Olde Fashioned Fragrance

PHARMACOLOGY

Formulation and Administration

Nitrites are available as volatile liquids and, less commonly, as vaporizing semisolid "pearls." As an antianginal, amyl nitrite is sold in gauze-wrapped glass capsules, similar to the ammonia capsules used for fainting. Crushing the capsule releases the fluid into the gauze for volatilization and inhalation, and gives the drug its nicknames "popper" and "snapper."

Nitrites are usually inhaled directly from small screw cap bottles, but with their popularity, specialty jewelry, such as pendant vials, has appeared for carrying and inhaling nitrites. Inhalation requires that a thumb or finger be placed over the open top while the bottle is shaken and warmed in the palm. At this point the finger or thumb is retracted slightly, allowing the vapor to be inhaled.

While amyl nitrite is sold by prescription only, butyl and cyclohexyl nitrites are available over-the-counter as room deodorizers or electronic equipment cleaners (Table 16.5).

Mechanism of Action

Like the VOCs, nitrites have intoxicating effects, but they are also potent vasodilators. Nitrites, like most nitrogen oxide-containing substances, generate the reactive free radical nitric oxide (NO). NO activates intracellular guanylate cyclase, which in turn increases cyclic guanosine monophosphate (CGMP), leading to the dephosphorylation of myosin light chains. The resulting smooth muscle relaxation affects peripheral vasodilation and hypotension, GI sphincter relaxation (e.g., lower esophageal

TABLE 16.6. ACUTE AND CHRONIC SEQUELAE OF NITRITE INHALANT USE

System	Acute Effects	Chronic Effects
CNS	euphoria disinhibition disorientation dizziness syncope headache	
Cardiovascular	peripheral vasodilation syncope hypotension/tachycardia (low dose) hypertension/bradycardia (high dose)	
Eye/Ear	injected sclera and conjunctivae lacrimation tinnitus decreased visual acuity visual changes ("yellow haze")	
Respiratory	nasotrachial irritation tracheobronchitis respiratory allergic reaction (wheeze)	sinusitis
Skin	flushing (head, neck, chest) pruritic rash burn (chemical, thermal)	dermatitis
Gastrointestinal	relaxed sphincter tone (i.e. lower esophageal sphincter, anal) nausea/vomiting (ingestion)	
Hematologic	methemoglobinemia	hemolytic anemia

sphincter, internal anal sphincter), decreased rectal tone, and increased penile blood flow.

The mechanism of producing feelings of euphoria, disinhibition, and sexual excitement has not been elucidated. Like most inhalants, hypoxia may contribute to the effects, but is not the sole basis for the phenomenon.

CONSEQUENCES OF USE

Inhaled nitrites produce a variety of effects that, for the most part, resolve rapidly with discontinuation of use. The majority of these effects are not life-threatening. However, there are a few potentially lethal conditions associated with nitrite inhalation, in both the acute and chronic setting. The major medical effects associated with nitrite inhalants are outlined in Table 16.6.

SUBSTANCE ABUSE JARGON
The most common nicknames for nitrites are "poppers" or "snappers." Commercially available products include room deodorizers, liquid incense, or video head cleaner.

⑥⌒NITROUS OXIDE

EPIDEMIOLOGY

Like other inhalants, nitrous oxide abuse occurs mainly among adolescents and people with special access to the gas, particularly those who work in the fields of dentistry, anesthesia, supercharged automobile racing, and gaseous substance storage or distribution.

PHARMACOLOGY

Chemistry

Nitrous oxide was first discovered in 1772 by Joseph Priestly. Priestly combined iron disulfide with nitric acid to produce "nitrous air." First used in the early 19th century for its entertaining, pleasurable effects, the therapeutic and analgesic effects were recognized in the second half of the 19th century. While use as an inhalational anesthetic continues, it has also acquired commercial applications.

Nitrous oxide is a colorless, tasteless, odorless gas that is nonflammable, but does support combustion. It is synthesized commercially by heating ammonium nitrate to 245–270°C. In the heating process, various gaseous impurities, such as ammonia, nitric acid, nitrogen, nitric oxide, and nitrogen dioxide, are produced in addition to nitrous oxide. Subsequent cooling, scrubbing, compressing, drying, and liquefaction purify the gas mixture. Contamination of the nitrous oxide with higher oxides of nitrogen has caused deaths from pulmonary edema in the setting of both controlled anesthesia and homemade nitrous oxide administration.

Formulation and Administration

Pure nitrous oxide gas is available from chemical supply companies and racing supply stores in pressurized tanks, and is used most often for anesthetic purposes, analytic chemistry (e.g., atomic absorption spectroscopy), and race car supercharger tanks.

Tasteless, nonflammable, and bacteriostatic, nitrous oxide is used as a propellant gas in certain food products, especially whipped cream and nonstick cooking sprays, and in some fire extinguishers (Table 16.7).

In contrast to VOCs and nitrites, nitrous oxide does not require volatilization and is administered directly as a gas. Inhalation of the gas occurs

---

TABLE 16.7. ABUSED PRODUCTS CONTAINING NITROUS OXIDE

Whipped cream (preaerosolized, or self-prepared with specialized cartridges)
Nonstick cooking spray
Fire extinguishers
Race car supercharger tanks
Anesthesia tanks

---

either directly from commercial tanks, propellant devices, or balloons inflated with the gas. Small cartridges of compressed nitrous oxide and cans of prepressurized whipped cream can contain between 2 and 8 liters of gas.

Mechanism of Action and Pharmacokinetics

Nitrous oxide is a central nervous system (CNS) depressant, which acts via an incompletely understood alteration of CNS neuronal membranes.

Low blood solubility and consequent rapid rate of equilibration between alveolar and inspired concentrations of nitrous oxide cause a rapid onset of euphoric effects. Nitrous oxide does not undergo significant biotransformation and is eliminated by exhalation in an unchanged form.

Since nitrous oxide is 30 times more soluble than nitrogen, the predominant gas in closed gas spaces within our bodies, it will continue to diffuse into nitrogen-containing spaces.

CONSEQUENCES OF USE

Inhalation of 50–75% nitrous oxide produces an exhilarating "rush" within 15 to 30 seconds, followed by a sense of euphoria. Most effects of nitrous oxide inhalation disappear within 2 to 3 minutes. The major medical effects associated with nitrous oxide inhalation are outlined in Table 16.8.

The most significant acute risk of nitrous oxide inhalation is asphyxiation. Nitrous oxide rapidly displaces oxygen in enclosed spaces (e.g., bags over the head, fixed face masks), inducing a lethally low oxygen tension. The blunting effect of the gas on the respiratory drive exacerbates the risk of asphyxiation. Barotrauma and pneumomediastinum (especially from inhalation of pressurized nitrous oxide from cartridges), and oropharyngeal frostbite secondary to the cooling of the nitrous oxide gas as it expands from pressurized containers, may also occur acutely. After discontinuation of nitrous oxide inhalation, back diffusion of the gas into the lungs during elimination of the gas from the blood may significantly reduce the alveolar pO_2, extending the period of hypoxia.

TABLE 16.8. ACUTE AND CHRONIC SEQUELAE OF NITROUS OXIDE USE

System	Acute Effects	Chronic Effects
CNS	euphoria	peripheral and subacute combined degeneration of the spinal cord extremity paresthesias
	headache (high dose)	early symptoms: numbness, paresthesias, ataxia, clumsiness, weakness
	confusion (high dose)	late symptoms: gait disturbance, impotence, loss of sphincter control
	syncope (high dose) hallucinations (high dose) seizure (high dose) coma (high dose)	
Cardiovascular	myocardial depressant with simultaneous sympathetic stimulation. No significant hemodynamic changes unless preexisting high level of sympathetic stimulation or poor myocardial contractility	
Respiratory	asphyxiation	pneumonitis secondary to nitrous oxide contaminated by higher-order nitrogen oxides
	barotrauma pneumothorax/mediastinum air emboli oral frostbite respiratory depression diffusion hypoxia	
Hematologic	megaloblastic anemia	agranulocytosis aplastic anemia
Immune	depressed production, motility, and chemotaxis of leukocytes in vitro (in vivo effects inconclusive)	
Teratogenicity	spontaneous abortion	

DIAGNOSIS

No pathognomonic signs of inhalant abuse exist. History and/or self-disclosure guide diagnostic thoughts. Unless obvious by the presence of specific odors or inhalant paraphernalia, few clinicians immediately

---

TABLE 16.9. DIAGNOSIS AND TREATMENT OF METHEMOGLOBINEMIA

Bedside test: Place a drop of the patient's blood on white paper or gauze next to a drop of blood from a person with otherwise unaffected hemoglobin. When the methemoglobin concentration exceeds 10%, the patient's blood will remain chocolate-brown or dark colored in the presence of atmospheric oxygen, whereas unaffected blood will brighten slightly before coagulating.

Therapy: Give methylene blue 1–2 mg/kg in 1% solution i.v. over 5 minutes, repeat in 1 hour, then every 4 hours to a total dose of 7 mg/kg or 300 mg/day until symptoms abate.

---

suspect inhalant abuse. Persons presenting with recent, short-term mental status changes associated with a constellation of other diffuse constitutional complaints and signs (e.g., palpitations, syncope/dizziness, cyanosis, altered respiratory pattern, red eyes, distinctive breath odor, weakness) should receive special consideration for abuse of inhalants.

Abnormal liver function tests (e.g., elevated transaminases, reduced synthetic function) may suggest recent VOC abuse. Methemoglobinemia in the absence of identifiable pharmacologic or congenital causes should raise the possibility of nitrite inhalation (Table 16.9). Megaloblastic anemia in the context of a normal vitamin B_{12} level with or without the presence of neuropathy may also point to abuse of nitrous oxide.

Useful screening studies for patients suspected of abusing inhalants include a complete blood count (CBC) with blood smear and differential, serum toxicologies, arterial blood gas, liver function tests, and urinalysis with urine toxicologies.

TREATMENT

Interrupting use of the inhalant and restoring and maintaining oxygenation will usually lead to a resolution of symptoms within minutes. However, supplemental oxygen and ventilation assistance may be required in patients presenting with arrhythmia, seizure, or coma. No specific antidote or technique enhances elimination. Health care providers should anticipate complications and treat them accordingly. Conjunctivitis, headache, most respiratory tract irritation, and dermal inflammation can be treated symptomatically. Patients with significant neurologic findings, such as neuropathy or persistent ataxia, should receive formal evaluation with close follow-up.

DEFINITIONS AND SUBSTANCE ABUSE JARGON

Laughing Gas: due to giddy euphoria and spontaneous laughter produced
Whippets: chargers pressurized with nitrous oxide

EZ Whip: pressurized chargers like CO_2 cartridges used in carbonated water
Doing a Whippet: includes inhaling nitrous oxide gas from cans of preaerosolized whipped cream as well as from nitrous oxide cartridges.

FURTHER READING

Volatile Organic Compounds

Andrews LS, Snyder R. Toxic effects of solvents and vapors. In: Cassarett and Doull's Toxicology. 4th Ed. New York: McGraw-Hill, 1991.

Flanagan RJ, Ruprah M, Meredith TJ, et al. An introduction to the clinical toxicology of volatile substances. Drug Saf 1990;5:359–383.

Linden CH. Volatile substances of abuse. Emerg Med Clin North Am 1990;8: 559–578.

Nitrite Inhalants

Dax EM, Lange WR, Jaffe JH. Allergic reactions to amyl nitrite inhalation. Am J Med 1989;86:732.

Gowitt GT, Hanzlick RL. Atypical autoerotic deaths. Am J Forensic Med Pathol 1992;13:115–119.

Haley TJ. Review of the physiological effects of amyl, butyl, and isobutyl nitrites. Clin Toxicol 1980;16:317–329.

Haverkos HW, Dougherty J. Health hazards of nitrite inhalants. Am J Med 1988;84:479–482.

Nitrous Oxide

Crider RA, Rouse BA. Epidemiology of Inhalant Abuse: An Update. NIDA Research Monograph 85. US Department of Health and Human Services, 1988.

Flanagan RJ, Ruprah M, Meredith TJ, et al. An introduction to the clinical toxicology of volatile substances. Drug Saf 1990;5:359–383.

Messina FV, Wynne JW. Homemade nitrous oxide: no laughing matter. Ann Int Med 1982;96:333–334.

Sharp CW, Beauvis F, Spence R. Inhalant Abuse: A Volatile Research Agenda. NIDA Research Monograph 129. US Department of Health and Human Services, 1992.

Wagner SA, Clarck MA, Wesche DL, et al. Asphyxial deaths from the recreational use of nitrous oxide. J Forensic Sci 1992;37:1008–1015.

SECTION III

ISSUES

Chapter 17

Intrauterine Effects of Substance Abuse

Chandrajit P. Raut and Antonia Stephen with Barry Kosofsky

Recent estimates suggest that 19% of pregnant women use alcohol, 20% of pregnant women smoke cigarettes, and 5.5% of pregnant women use some illicit drug during pregnancy. In this population, detecting and treating substance abuse has critical importance because, in addition to the direct effects that drugs have on the expectant mother, substance abuse also affects fetal development and pregnancy outcome. The effect of prenatal drug exposure on the fetus depends on several factors including the type and form of drug used, timing of exposure during gestation, frequency of exposure (chronic use versus periodic binges), and actions of the drug on placental blood flow and fetal tissues. Obstetricians should look for both physical and behavioral evidence of drug use in their patients during each obstetric visit and counsel patients on the effects of substance abuse during pregnancy (Table 17.1).

DEVELOPMENTAL TIMELINE

Understanding the effects of a given drug on a fetus requires knowing the stage of development when the fetal exposure occurred. Gestation is divided into three trimesters. Most organogenesis transpires during the first 8 weeks of the first trimester. During this period, the fetal tissues are most susceptible to teratogens, like drugs. Consequently, first trimester drug use is associated with major malformations, birth defects, and spontaneous abortions. After formation during the first trimester, organ systems develop and grow during the remainder of the pregnancy. Hence, exposure during the second and third trimesters causes deformities, functional defects, intrauterine growth retardation, preterm labor, and premature rupture of membranes. Different organ systems are susceptible to transplacental drug effects at various times, based on developmental timetables specific for each organ system, as schematically illustrated in Figure 17.1.

TABLE 17.1. SIGNS OF SUBSTANCE ABUSE IN OBSTETRICAL PATIENTS

A. Physical Signs Consistent with Substance Abuse in Obstetrical Patients
   1. Maternal signs
      a. increased spotting/vaginal bleeding
      b. sexually transmitted diseases
      c. anemia
      d. subacute bacterial endocarditis/septic thrombosis
      e. seizures
      f. poor venous access
   2. Pregnancy and placental signs
      a. spontaneous abortion
      b. premature rupture of membranes
      c. precipitous labor
      d. preterm labor
      e. placental insufficiency
      f. abruptio placentae
   3. Fetal signs
      a. intrauterine growth retardation/small for gestational age
      b. low birth weight
      c. meconium staining
      d. stillbirth
      e. intrauterine fetal demise/neonatal death
      f. fetal tachycardia/abnormal fetal heart monitoring
      g. hyper, hypoactive fetus
      h. breech presentation
B. Behavioral Signs of Substance Abuse in Obstetrical Patients
   1. Late registration for prenatal care
   2. Poor compliance
   3. Reluctance to give urine specimen
   4. Altered physical appearance over the course of routine obstetrical visits
   5. Mood swings
   6. Agitation/anxiety/defensiveness about the topic of substance abuse

PLACENTAL STRUCTURE AND TRANSPLACENTAL PHYSIOLOGY

The interaction of maternal, placental, and fetal factors modulate fetal drug exposure by influencing the distribution, metabolism, and excretion of drugs (Table 17.2).

Pregnancy alters many of these processes and thereby drug disposition. While certain changes in pulmonary and gastrointestinal absorption affect the quantity of drug entering the maternal circulation, a variety of factors affect the distribution of drugs and their metabolites into tissues. During pregnancy there is an increase in intra and extravascular volume, a large accumulation of body fat, a decrease in drug binding to plasma proteins, and hemodynamic changes, like increased venous pressure, all of which alter the concentration of drugs. Fetal circulation

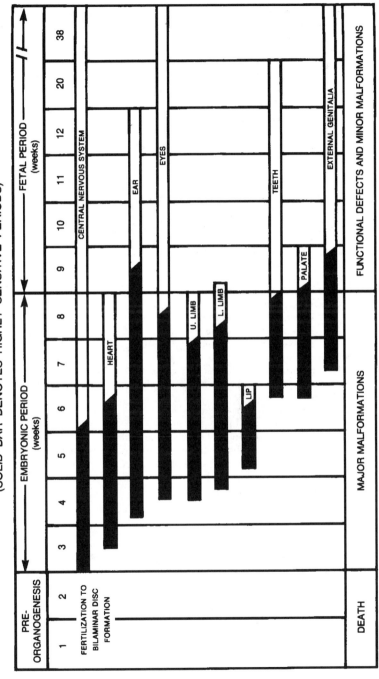

SUSCEPTIBILITY TO TERATOGENESIS FOR ORGAN SYSTEMS
(SOLID BAR DENOTES HIGHLY SENSITIVE PERIODS)

TABLE 17.2. FACTORS THAT AFFECT FETAL DRUG EXPOSURE

A. Maternal Factors
1. Drug absorption
   a. gastrointestinal absorption
      i. decreased GI motility
      ii. delayed gastric and intestinal emptying
      iii. reduced gastric acid secretion
      iv. increased mucous secretion
   b. pulmonary absorption due to increased alveolar ventilation
   c. intramuscular absorption due to increased venous pressure in lower limbs
2. Drug distribution
   a. increased intra and extravascular volume
   b. large accumulation of body fat
   c. decreased drug binding to plasma proteins
   d. hemodynamic changes
3. Drug metabolism (decreased albumin binding)
4. Drug excretion
   a. increased renal excretion due to
      i. increased renal plasma flow
      ii. increased GFR
      iii. decreased albumin binding
   b. increased pulmonary excretion due to
      i. increased respiratory rate
      ii. increased tidal volume
      iii. increased minute volume
B. Placental Factors
1. Placental structure
   a. diffusability of substances across the placenta is determined by
      i. size of the substance
      ii. lipid solubility of the substance
      iii. protein binding of the drug in plasma
      iv. degree of ionization of the drug molecule
      v. morphology and stage of development of the placental membranes
   b. rate of drug delivery across the placenta is greatly affected by uterine and umbilical blood flow rates
2. in vivo placental biotransformation
C. Fetal Factors
1. Fetal distribution
   a. hepatic metabolism partially bypassed
   b. lungs partially bypassed
   c. increased drug distribution to upper portions of the body
2. Delayed maturation of metabolic enzymes that inactivate drugs
3. Decreased renal excretion
   a. decreased fetal renal plasma flow
   b. decreased fetal glomerular filtration

then distributes substances acquired from the maternal circulation unequally. Approximately 55% of umbilical venous blood passes through the ductus venosus, thereby escaping hepatic metabolism and bypassing the lungs. The upper body organs may therefore receive blood that bypasses both the fetal liver and the lungs, with a higher concentration of drug. The distribution of drugs between maternal and fetal tissues affects the actual amount of exposure that the fetus receives.

Drug metabolism by mother, placenta, and fetus all have an impact on fetal drug exposure. For many drugs, decreased albumin concentration in pregnant women increases the plasma-free fraction of drugs. Since drug actions occur as a result of the "free" fraction of drug, a smaller dose results in a higher effective concentration, and requires increased drug metabolism by the liver. The effect of placental metabolism in mediating placental biotransformation, and thereby the fetotoxicity, of drugs must be considered.

Finally, fetal drug metabolism may also result in fetotoxic effects. While pregnancy induces increased rates of renal and pulmonary drug excretion in women, fetal renal excretion rates are low. As a result, the fetus experiences long elimination half-lives of polar, water soluble compounds and demonstrates a greater dependence on maternal detoxification and drug elimination for such polar compounds. Drugs also accumulate in the amniotic fluid because of renal excretion and the diffusion of drug across nonkeratinized fetal skin, chorioamnion, or respiratory epithelium. These substances may be reabsorbed through fetal swallowing of amniotic fluid. As the fetus develops, fetal renal and pulmonary drug excretion and hepatic metabolism mature.

In summary, maternal, placental, and fetal factors affect fetal exposure to toxic substances used by the mother. In the following sections, these anatomical and physiological factors are considered in relation to the different substances used and their effects on the developing fetus.

CONFOUNDERS AND MODIFIERS

Certain confounders, some associated with substance abuse in general and some specific to pregnant women, complicate attempts to assess the intrauterine effects of substance abuse. First, physicians can miss or underestimate actual drug intake for two main reasons: (a) **self-report:** women are likely to deny or underreport their drug use and (2) **laboratory report:** urinalysis often misses exposure since it screens women at a single point in time. Second, many women are polysubstance abusers, so epidemiological studies must be designed to distinguish the independent effects of particular drugs. Additional confounding variables found in the population of substance-abusing women include inadequate prenatal care, sexually transmitted diseases, poor nutrition, and lower socioeconomic status. Each factor is likely to have certain effects on the fetus, making it difficult to attribute a particular fetal outcome to specific drug use. For example, of those pregnant women who report use of both alcohol and cigarettes, 20% also use marijuana, and 9.5% also use cocaine.

Studies may underreport the fetotoxic effects of drug exposures due to delayed expression of toxicity. For example, prenatal exposure to substances such as alcohol and cocaine, which affect central nervous system development, can cause cognitive, affective, and adaptive deficits that are difficult to quantify, especially at birth. These deficits may manifest themselves later in life as altered attention span and poor social interaction.

Finally, the postnatal environment affects the expression of an intrauterine toxic insult. For example, a prenatal insult may manifest itself only slightly in a child raised in an appropriately stimulating and controlled environment. That same insult could be expressed as a more substantive deficit if that child grows up in a suboptimal environment. This is often the case when continued maternal drug abuse results in a chaotic life-style and environment for her children.

SPECIFIC DRUGS

Alcohol

Intrauterine alcohol exposure causes a spectrum of problems ranging from malformations to neurologic and growth disorders. The pattern of alcohol effects was first described by Lemoine in France in 1968, and subsequently labelled the fetal alcohol syndrome (FAS) by Jones in 1973. The quantity and duration of maternal alcohol ingestion have a direct impact on the severity and incidence of the physical and neurological features associated with FAS. Exposure to lower levels of alcohol results in a milder syndrome called fetal alcohol effects (FAE).

Reports estimate that a maternal daily consumption of 5 ounces of absolute alcohol (4–6 drinks, ⅓ pint of whiskey) will result in ⅓ of the children having FAS, ⅓ manifesting some toxic prenatal effects (FAE), and ⅓ being normal. Although the most obvious group of children likely to have FAS are born to late-stage, chronic alcoholic women, any pregnant woman, young or old, is at risk if she drinks during the pregnancy.

Mechanism

Though the effects of alcohol exposure are well recognized, the mechanisms by which alcohol (which crosses the placenta) and/or its metabolites produce these effects are uncertain.

TABLE 17.3. FEATURES OF FETAL ALCOHOL SYNDROME

1. Growth retardation (brain and body)
2. CNS impairment
   a. developmental delay
   b. long-term deficits
      i. attention deficit disorder
      ii. fine and gross motor function deficits
      iii. problems in visual perception
      iv. impaired reaction times
      v. subnormal intelligence and memory
      vi. poor concentration
      vii. poor organizational skills
      viii. cooperation difficulties
      ix. impaired socialization and adaptive skills
      x. difficulty with problem solving
3. Facial features (figure 17.2)
   a. microcephaly
   b. prominent epicanthal folds with short palpebral fissures
   c. low nasal bridge, short nose
   d. indistinct philtrum
   e. thin upper lip

- Ethanol accumulates in the amniotic fluid and is present even when there is none in the maternal circulation, suggesting that binge drinking may result in prolonged fetal exposure to alcohol.
- Binge drinking in the first trimester may influence fetal outcome, resulting in a significant frequency of learning and behavior problems in exposed offspring.
- Exposure to alcohol and moderate cigarette use synergistically diminishes and alters learning in newborns. However, it is not clear how nicotine or other drugs, including caffeine and diazepam, potentiate the effects of alcohol.
- Postnatal environmental factors can alter the expression of fetal alcohol exposure.

Pregnancy Complications

There is a 2–4-fold increased risk of miscarriage with maternal alcohol use.

Fetal Effects

FAS is characterized by a triad of growth retardation, mental retardation, and specific facial features (Table 17.3 and Fig. 17.2). In fact, alcohol is the most commonly identifiable and preventable cause of mental retardation, accounting for 1.7/1000 live births (compared to 1.3/1000 for Down's syndrome).

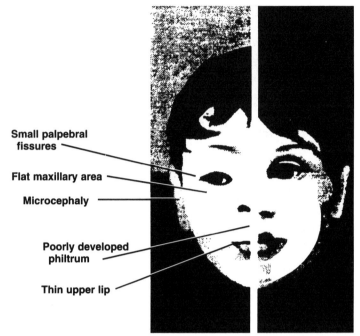

Figure 17.2. Facial features of fetal alcohol syndrome.

FAE and FAS represent a continuum of fetal exposure to maternal alcohol abuse as well as variability in fetal sensitivity. The effects of FAS do not diminish with time, although the specific manifestations vary with increasing maturity. Attention deficit-hyperactivity disorder, which affects 75–80% of patients with FAS and poor adaptive and social skills, contributes to difficulties in the classroom and problems with future employment in affected individuals. While growth deficits, such as microcephaly and short stature, tend to persist as the child matures, facial features become more difficult to recognize over time.

Even in the absence of these obvious features, prenatal alcohol exposure may adversely affect fetal development. The behavioral characteristics of FAE, which may include stubbornness, aggression, hyperactivity, and sleep disorders, may reflect either less alcohol exposure or a less sensitive fetus.

Withdrawal Effects

In the mother, withdrawal occurs within 48 hours of discontinuation of alcohol consumption, and in addition to the typical alcohol withdrawal symptoms, causes an increased risk of preterm labor. The effects of alcohol withdrawal in the fetus are not well understood. The safety of the use of disulfiram (Antabuse) during pregnancy has not been

TABLE 17.4. COMPLICATIONS ASSOCIATED WITH CIGARETTE USE BY PREGNANT WOMEN

A. Complications of Pregnancy
   1. Vaginal bleeding
   2. Spontaneous abortion
   3. Stillbirths
   4. Prematurity
B. Fetal Effects
   1. Growth retardation
      a. birth length decreased
      b. birth weight decreased
   2. Congenital anomalies
C. Effects Beyond the Perinatal Period
   1. Increased risk (2.5 times) for sudden infant death syndrome (SIDS)
   2. Increased neonatal apnea
   3. Developmental and intellectual delays
   4. Behavioral disorders
   5. Induction of mixed function oxidases ! altered drug metabolism

established. Finally, it is important to realize that alcohol can be passed to the infant through breast milk.

Cigarette Smoking/Nicotine

With increasing cigarette use by women in the United States, particularly among the 18–34-year-old age group (the main childbearing years), the effects of smoking on pregnancy outcomes have become an increasingly worrisome issue.

Mechanism

Constituents of inhaled cigarette smoke affect the development of the fetus.

- Nicotine diminishes oxygen and nutrient delivery to the fetus by inducing vasoconstriction.
- Carbon monoxide further decreases the oxygen-carrying capacity of maternal and fetal blood by binding to hemoglobin at the oxygen binding site.
- Polycyclic aromatic hydrocarbons in cigarettes alter placental and fetal handling of foreign organic compounds.

Pregnancy Complications

Smoking during pregnancy increases the risk of complications, especially the risk of premature birth; up to 14% of all births before 37 weeks of gestation are thought to be caused by smoking (Table 17.4).

Fetal Effects

Maternal cigarette use in general and individual components of cigarettes cause characteristic fetal effects:

- The lower birth weight is associated with lower survival rates of infants during the first year of life.
- Nicotine can cause atrophic and hypovascular changes in placental villi, impairing uteroplacental circulation, leading to retardation of fetal growth. Nicotine also concentrates in maternal milk where it has a half-life slightly exceeding that in the serum, and can affect the baby postpartum.
- Elevated thiocyanate levels may contribute to fetal growth retardation. Both cyanide and its principal metabolite may induce hypotension, inhibit cytochromes, interfere with vitamin B_{12} metabolism, cause degenerative neurological disease, and alter thyroid function. Maternal thiocyanate levels correlate directly with the number of cigarettes smoked daily by the mother, and thiocyanate has a 14-day half-life.
- Effects of passive smoking (i.e., the exposure of nonsmokers to air contaminated with cigarette smoke) on the fetus have not been well documented. Passive smoking in the home or workplace will increase the fetal thiocyanate levels in the fetus of a nonsmoking mother. However, the effect of this relatively minor increase in thiocyanate level is unclear.
- Exposure of infants to smoke may predispose such infants to respiratory infections and long-term lung damage.

Enumerating the sequelae of pre and postpregnancy smoking may further encourage a woman to quit before or during pregnancy, and to not smoke postpartum.

Cocaine

In the past decade, cocaine and crack use among pregnant women has become a major health issue. Recent studies illustrate the magnitude of the problem: 1.1% of pregnant women use cocaine, with higher rates of cocaine use documented in certain ethnic groups (e.g., 4.5% of pregnant African Americans use cocaine, with crack cocaine inhalation accounting for the higher rate of overall use in this population).

Mechanism

Cocaine is a stimulant that increases catecholamine concentrations at aminergic neural synapses. By inhibiting catecholamine reuptake,

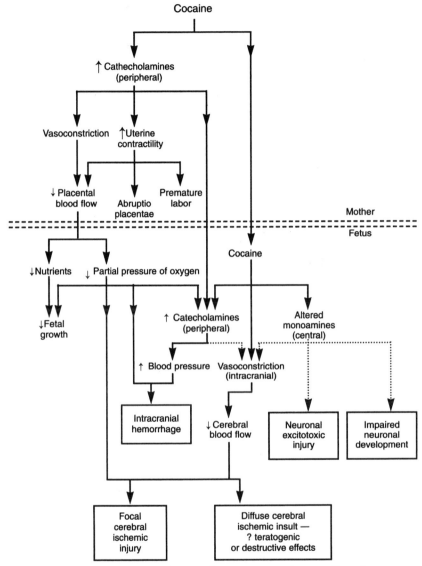

Figure 17.3. Deleterious effects of maternal cocaine use on fetuses. Effects that appear plausible on the basis of current information but whose confirmation requires more supporting evidence are indicated by dotted lines. " denotes increased, and # denotes decreased, effects.

cocaine has central and peripheral effects (Fig. 17.3). Higher peak blood levels and recurrent self-administration of cocaine, achieved most easily with intravenous administration and crack inhalation (smoking freebase cocaine), cause the most profound effects on the fetus.

TABLE 17.5. COMPLICATIONS ASSOCIATED WITH COCAINE USE BY PREGNANT WOMEN

A. Complications of Pregnancy
　1. Pretérm labor
　2. Abruptio placentae
　3. Fetal injury secondary to maternal convulsions, arrhythmias, and stroke
B. Fetal Effects
　1. Intrauterine growth retardation
　2. Decreased mean birth weight, length, head circumference
　3. Congenital urinary malformations
　4. Structural CNS changes
　5. Possible neurobehavioral abnormalities
　　a. selective language delay
　　b. impaired attention span

Pregnancy Complications

The use of cocaine has been associated with a number of pregnancy complications (Fig. 17.3 and Table 17.5). Cocaine use during the first trimester is associated with an increased rate of spontaneous abortion. While the pregnancies of 8% of cocaine-abusing women result in abruption and stillbirth, there is up to a 25% risk for premature births. In addition, cocaine can cause convulsions, life-threatening arrhythmias, stroke, and other conditions which, while potentially life-threatening to any adult, could also lead to fetal injury or death.

Fetal Effects

The direct effects of cocaine on the developing fetus are in Table 17.5.

- Decreased uterine and placental blood flow leads to fetal tachycardia and decreased fetal oxygenation.
- Cocaine-induced anorexia and weight loss in the mother is often compounded by poor maternal nutrition—another possible mechanism underlying fetal growth retardation.
- In addition to inducing malnutrition, cocaine exerts direct effects in reducing fetal brain and body growth.
- Focal, structural central nervous system (CNS) damage may be detected by cranial imaging, and may not be associated with any clinical abnormalities. Although the precise mechanism is unknown, these structural anomalies may arise secondary to either acute vascular compromise and/or more direct teratogenic effects of cocaine on the developing fetal brain.
- Cocaine use in the 48–72 hours preceding delivery has been associated in a limited number of cases with perinatal cerebral infarcts.

- Cocaine's actions at neural receptors, especially the dopaminergic system, may contribute to neurobehavioral abnormalities, which manifest themselves as difficulties in maintaining an oriented and alert state. Not only are exposed neonates physically small for their gestational age, but they also demonstrate more immature patterns of neuroelectrical activity, suggesting developmental immaturity for chronological age. These electrophysiological abnormalities will usually normalize, except in rare cases of severe vascular compromise, such as a large vessel infarction or perinatal asphyxia due to abruptio placentae. Delayed language acquisition and cognitive impairment may persist as clinically detectable deficits in some exposed infants.

Withdrawal Effects

Some neonates with positive urine tests for cocaine demonstrated certain symptoms, such as irritability and vigorous sucking, believed to be cocaine withdrawal. Recent studies have shown that these symptoms reflect the slow elimination of cocaine and/or its metabolites from the fetal circulation and more likely reflect cocaine toxicity, not withdrawal.

Opiates

By the end of the 19th century, reports described fetuses exposed to opium in utero who postnatally exhibited excessive nervousness, rapid breathing, and convulsive movements (neonatal withdrawal). In these cases, death often occurred within the first week of life. During this century, the opiate of choice has changed from morphine in the 1950s to heroin today. Recent studies estimate that 7000 infants born each year in the United States are exposed to opiates in utero.

Pregnancy Complications

The major complications of pregnancy associated with maternal opiate use and abrupt cessation are listed in Table 17.6. Despite distinct opiate effects, a lack of prenatal care and poor maternal nutrition often complicate these effects. Methadone provides more steady blood levels of drug, avoids cycles of craving and withdrawal, decreases maternal complications, improves fetal outcome, and may decrease possible maternal exposure to HIV—all advantages for opiate-abusing mothers. In comparison to the general population, infants born to women on opiates have an increased risk of neonatal seizures, neonatal withdrawal syndrome, prematurity, meconium aspiration syndrome, and intrauterine growth retardation. Infants whose mothers have been maintained on methadone, dependent on the amount of prenatal care, will clearly have better outcomes than those exposed to heroin in utero and no prenatal care.

TABLE 17.6. COMPLICATIONS ASSOCIATED WITH OPIATE USE BY PREGNANT WOMEN

A. Pregnancy Complications Secondary to Opiate Dependence
   1. Toxemia of pregnancy/preeclampsia
   2. Meconium-stained amniotic fluid
   3. Intrauterine growth retardation
   4. Preterm labor
B. Pregnancy Complications Secondary to Acute Cessation of Opiates
   1. Abruptio placentae
   2. Spontaneous abortion
   3. Preterm labor
   4. Fetal meconium passage/aspiration
C. Perinatal Physiological Effects
   1. Low-dose opiate usage
      a. CNS excitation
      b. EEG desynchronization
      c. increased body and eye movements
      d. continuous breathing movements
      e. increased heart rate
      f. increased metabolic demand consistent with increased oxygen consumption
      g. decreased pH and base excess in the fetus
   2. High-dose opiate usage
      a. CNS depression
      b. increased EEG synchronization
      c. decreased body, eye, and breathing movements
      d. decreased metabolic demand
D. Perinatal Anatomic and Pathophysiologic Effects
   1. Microcephaly
   2. Fetuses small for gestational age
   3. Low birthweight infants
   4. Increased incidence of sudden infant death syndrome
   5. Generally high morbidity and mortality among newborn infants
   6. Respiratory distress syndrome in the premature (with heroin)
   7. Increased incidence of breech presentation
E. Effects Beyond the Perinatal Period
   1. Fine motor coordination may be less advanced than other skills
   2. Delayed mental, motor, speech, and language development at 18 months of age
   3. Attention deficit-hyperactivity disorder
   4. Sleep disturbances
   5. Temper tantrums
   6. Small head circumference
   7. Strabismus and/or nystagmus
   8. Abnormal muscle tone
   9. Less than normal tactile, visual, and auditory skills
  10. Difficulties with social adjustment
  11. Poor language skills

However, infants born to methadone-maintained mothers generally have a mean birth weight that is lower than infants unexposed to drugs.

Fetal Effects

The effects of opiate exposure during fetal development are compounded by the insult that occurs postnatally during drug withdrawal or abstinence syndrome. Opiate exposure can cause an elevated systolic pressure and increased blood flow to the fetal brain, heart, and diaphragm, leading to prolonged periods of arousal, enhanced respiratory activity, and other consequences. Since intermittent and/or low-dose opiate exposure does not allow the fetus to develop a tolerance, metabolic demands remain high, resulting in unnecessary fetal consumption of energy substrates and subsequent intrauterine growth retardation. Higher opiate doses may have almost the opposite effects of exposure to lower doses (Table 17.6).

Opiate exposure may result in various anatomical and pathophysiological sequelae (Table 17.6). A number of deficits manifest themselves during infancy. Although few studies have looked at children beyond infancy, some long-term deficits have been documented (Table 17.6). Since a growing number of studies suggest that in utero opiate exposure may result in abnormal structural organization of the fetal brain, these structural changes may underlie the neurobehavioral abnormalities characteristic of fetal opiate exposure.

Meperidine (Demerol) is a synthetic opiate used since 1939 as an intravenous or intramuscular obstetric analgesic. Both mother and fetus metabolize the drug to the more toxic compound normeperidine. Administration of a single, small dose of meperidine to serve as a maternal analgesic is pharmacologically safe for the neonate if it is born within 1 hour. Nevertheless, general depression of fetal heart rate has been observed within 30 minutes of meperidine injection. Additionally, respiratory depression, subtle neurobehavioral deficits, and APGAR scores lower than controls have been associated with meperidine use.

Withdrawal Effects

Fetuses exposed to opiates develop a passive dependency. Sixty to 90% of infants chronically exposed to heroin, methadone, meperidine, morphine, codeine, or pentazocine suffer a withdrawal or abstinence syndrome at birth which, when not recognized or treated, has a neonatal mortality of 3–5%. Withdrawal from heroin occurs within 24–48 hours after birth, while that from methadone occurs several days later. Treatment of the withdrawal syndrome with paregoric or phenobarbital can last anywhere from a few days to several months. Characteristics of the neonatal withdrawal syndrome are described in Table 17.7.

TABLE 17.7. CHARACTERISTICS OF THE NEONATAL OPIATE WITHDRAWAL SYNDROME

A. Fetal Distress (secondary to intermittent intrauterine withdrawal)
    1. Meconium staining
    2. Increased amniotic fluid catecholamines
B. CNS Abnormalities
    1. Tremors
    2. Myoclonic jerks
    3. Hyperreflexia
    4. Seizures
    5. Increased eye movements
    6. Hypertonicity
    7. High-pitched cries
    8. Hyperactivity
    9. Sleep deficit
    10. Twitching
    11. Disorganized sucking reflex
C. Vasomotor/Respiratory Abnormalities
    1. Respiratory alkalosis
    2. Lacrimation
    3. Hiccups
    4. Sneezing
    5. Sweating
    6. Fever
    7. Frequent yawning
    8. Mottling
    9. Nasal stuffiness
    10. Nasal flaring
    11. Tachypnea
D. Gastrointestinal Abnormalities
    1. Diarrhea
    2. Poor feeding
    3. Regurgitation/vomiting
E. Possible Long-Term Sequelae
    1. Diminished adaptive behavior
    2. Hyperactivity
    3. Attention deficit disorder
    4. Decreased fine motor coordination
F. Other
    1. Irritability
    2. Skin excoriations
    3. Electrolyte imbalances

The pathogenesis of abstinence-related seizures may relate to the depletion of endogenous opioid neurotransmitters. Symptoms, which are worse for methadone than for heroin, begin during the first month of life and may persist for 4 to 6 months. Additionally, some residual deficits may persist into early school age.

Other substances consumed by the mother, including barbiturates, chlordiazepoxide, clomipramine, alcohol, meprobamate, glutethimide, hydroxyzine, and ethchlorvynol can elicit withdrawal symptoms secondary to fetal opiate exposure.

Women in methadone programs prior to conception should remain there during pregnancy. Opiate-addicted mothers in methadone programs generally receive more prenatal care, have better support systems, deliver larger and healthier infants with less long-term impairment, and are at reduced risk for HIV disease. In women who continue taking opiates postpregnancy, these compounds pass into their breast milk.

Amphetamines

No conclusive evidence demonstrates that amphetamines are teratogenic.

Benzodiazepines

While benzodiazepines are not considered teratogenic, some adults who were exposed to benzodiazepines during gestation may demonstrate a disturbed response to environmental stresses. This effect most likely arises from an effect on the developing brain's γ-aminobutyric acid (GABA) receptors, to which benzodiazepines bind. This mechanism implicates a developmental role for GABA in the organization of integrated stress responses. Prenatal exposure to ethanol and phenobarbital, both of which influence the function of the GABA receptor, may result in similar consequences.

The withdrawal syndrome for infants exposed to benzodiazepines in utero consists of hypertonicity, irritability, and poor temperature regulation.

Cannabinoids (Marijuana, Hashish)

Although Δ_9-tetrahydrocannabinol (THC) crosses the placenta and is a known teratogen in animals, there are no proven effects in humans. Smoking marijuana, like smoking tobacco, leads to fetal exposure to carbon monoxide and vaporized and particulate matter, resulting in impairment of fetal oxygenation and fetal growth retardation. One study suggests that use of marijuana during pregnancy results in more meconium staining and longer duration of labor. Another links dose-related cannabinoid use to nervous system and visual response abnormalities. THC can be found in the mother's milk in greater concentrations than in the plasma, and can thus be absorbed by the fetus.

Hallucinogens (LSD, Mescaline, Phencyclidine)

Some data show that LSD abuse may cause an increased risk for spontaneous abortion in humans.

Although few pregnant women use phencyclidine, most of these women are polysubstance abusers, making it difficult to determine the isolated effects of phencyclidine on fetal development. PCP crosses the placenta and can be found in breast milk.

In addition to known behavioral and neurological findings, phencyclidine may have teratogenic effects on facial development. The specific neurological and behavioral disturbances associated with phencyclidine use are hypertonic ankle and brachial reflexes, spasticity, depressed grasping and rooting reflexes, decreased joint mobility, miosis, attention deficits, sudden outbursts of agitation, rapid changes in level of consciousness, increased mood lability, and poor consolability. Use during the first 6 weeks of pregnancy may cause cerebellar malformations. The only anatomic anomaly in the fetus reported is microcephaly.

Barbiturates

Some data indicate that phenobarbital administered as monotherapy in the first trimester is associated with a twofold increase in the frequency of major malformations, microcephaly, and growth retardation as compared to unexposed controls. Neonates exposed to barbiturates may have respiratory depression and exhibit withdrawal symptoms of hyperactivity, hypertonicity, seizures, and poor feeding.

Solvents (Glue, Gasoline, Cleaning Solution)

Chronic sniffing of glue, gasoline, and other solvents is associated with a significant risk for major effects on fetal growth and neurologic development. Published accounts describe a "fetal solvent syndrome" similar to FAS.

Tranquilizers

Tranquilizers like ethchlorvynol (Placidyl), meprobamate (Miltown, Equanil), chloral hydrate (Noctec), and glutethimide (Doriden) may induce neonatal depression and withdrawal, but there are insufficient data to determine their toxicities on the developing fetus.

CONCLUSION

Despite the best efforts of physicians, nurses, and counselors, many women who abuse drugs, including tobacco, will not discontinue their use during pregnancy. In these cases, a focus on prenatal visits and good nutrition will improve the outcome of the pregnancy. Helping a mother discontinue use of a drug should be attempted, but not forced, at the expense of good prenatal care. Likewise, alienation of a pregnant substance-abusing patient denies that mother the personal and professional support of a physician, and thereby a relationship that is critical during pregnancy. Upon birth of a substance-exposed infant, the physician should prepare for withdrawal symptoms and treat appropriately. Postnatal monitoring and treatment of the medical and psychological needs of the mother-infant pair are essential for optimal outcomes.

FURTHER READING

Buchi KF, Varner MW, Chase RA. The prevalence of substance abuse among pregnant women in Utah. Obstet Gynecol 1993;81:239–242.

Castro LC, Azen C, Hobel C, Platt LD. Maternal tobacco use and substance abuse: reported prevalence rates and association with the delivery of small for gestational age neonates. Obstet Gynecol 1993;81:396–401.

Chang CN, Lee CC. Prenatal drug exposure: kinetics and dynamics. Research Monograph 60. Rockville, MD: National Institute on Drug Abuse, 1985.

Drug Abuse and Pregnancy. A technical bulletin of the American College of Obstetrics and Gynecology, no. 96. Sept. 1986.

Finnegan LP, Kandall SR. Maternal and neonatal effects of alcohol and drugs. In: Substance Abuse: A Comprehensive Textbook. 2nd Ed. Lowinson JH, Ruiz P, Millman RB, eds. Baltimore: Williams & Wilkins, 1992:628–656.

Kilbey MM, Asghar K. Methodological issues in controlled studies on effects of prenatal exposure to drug abuse. Rockville, MD: National Institute on Drug Abuse, 1991.

NIDA. National Pregnancy and Health Survey. National Institutes of Health, Department of Health and Human Services. Washington, DC: Government Printing Office, 1995.

Volpe JJ. Effects of cocaine use on the fetus. N Engl J Med 1992;327:399–407.

Zagan IS, Slotkin TA. Maternal Substance Abuse: The Developing Nervous System. San Diego: Academic Press, 1992.

RESOURCES

Teratogen Information Service: (800) 322-5014

National Association for Perinatal Addiction Reasearch and Education: (312) 541-1272

National Directory of Alcohol and Drug Abuse Programs: (301) 443-7931.

Chapter 18

Substance Abuse and Mental Illness

Sherry Tziporah Cohen with Roger Weiss

DUAL DIAGNOSIS CONCEPT

Screening substance using patients for concurrent psychiatric diagnoses often reveals a *dual diagnosis*. The dual diagnosis concept refers to the constellation of problems associated with an individual who has a substance use disorder *and* a coexisting psychiatric disorder. All patients with a history of multiple psychiatric admissions, many failed detoxification treatments, or frequent relapses need serious consideration for this diagnosis. Since many abused substances can cause psychiatric symptoms, such as depression, anxiety, and hallucinations, screening for a dual diagnosis problem should be performed when a patient is known to be drug-free for an extended period of time.

Although the term dual diagnosis seems unifying, it designates a special population with specific needs whose heterogeneity poses unique diagnostic, therapeutic, and prognostic challenges. Effective treatment of either disorder requires that both the psychiatric and the substance use disorder be identified and specifically addressed.

EPIDEMIOLOGY

The prevalence of psychiatric illness is statistically greater in substance using patients than in the general population. The Epidemiologic Catchment Area (ECA) Study of the National Institute of Mental Health (an extensive prevalence study of psychiatric disorders in the general population) indicated that more than 50% of individuals with any nonalcohol drug disorder had at least one other psychiatric disorder—26% had mood disorders, 28% had anxiety disorders, 18% had antisocial personality disorder, and 7% had schizophrenia. Among individuals with an alcohol use disorder, 37% had a comorbid psychiatric disorder.

APPROACH TO MAKING A DUAL DIAGNOSIS

Identification and recognition of psychiatric illness in the substance-using patient represent a crucial first step. When a substance use disorder and a psychiatric disorder occur concomitantly, diagnosis of either disorder becomes more complicated. Since psychiatric disorders cannot be reliably diagnosed until intoxication and withdrawal effects have resolved, timing of the psychiatric assessment is important. Controversy surrounds the debate about the length of the drug-free period before the diagnosis of a psychiatric disorder can be confirmed. While many experts generally recommend waiting for two to four weeks, the actual length of time a clinician should wait depends on both the substance of abuse and the psychiatric disorder. For example, major depression in a cocaine-dependent individual cannot be confirmed within two weeks of the last cocaine use, since the temporary "crash" state symptoms persist and confound diagnosis. Consequently, substance use patients should receive frequent reevaluation, especially after detoxification.

The determination of the primary and the secondary disorder is based on which symptom or disease developed first, the primary disorder, and which followed, the secondary disorder. While this distinction may be helpful in some dually-diagnosed patients, it may imply a false causality. Additionally, treatment of the primary disorder does not automatically treat the secondary disorder. However, a careful history and/or discussions with family members and other caregivers should attempt to expose any psychiatric symptoms prior to initiation of drug abuse.

ETIOLOGICAL LINKS BETWEEN SUBSTANCE ABUSE AND PSYCHOPATHOLOGY

While the correlation between substance abuse and mental illness is clear, the nature of that relationship is less clear. Six potential connections between psychopathology and substance abuse that help explain the relationship include:

- Psychopathology may serve as a risk factor for addictive disorders.
- Psychiatric symptoms may develop in the course of chronic intoxication with an abused substance.
- Psychiatric disorders may emerge as a consequence of substance use and persist after remission.
- Psychopathology may affect the course of an addictive disorder in terms of rapidity of course, response to treatment, symptom picture, and long-term outcome.
- Substance use and psychopathological symptoms may become meaningfully linked over time.
- Substance abuse and psychiatric disorders may occur in the same individual, but are not related.

Psychopathology as a Risk Factor for Addiction

The self-medication hypothesis proposes that substance abuse begins when an individual attempts to self-treat psychiatric symptoms as a coping mechanism. People do not abuse drugs randomly, instead, they discover a specific drug that relieves their "painful" state. Repetitive use of the drug for self-medication can then lead to dependence. The initial feelings of relief that drug use provides often become feelings of unhappiness, helplessness, and general dysfunction, followed by increased drug use, dependence, and addiction. Although this hypothesis is based on detailed study of small groups of drug abusing individuals and is not experimentally validated, many clinicians use it to conceptualize the role of alcohol and drugs in the lives of some dually-diagnosed individuals.

For example, a patient with panic disorder and agoraphobia may discover that alcohol helps relieve his anxiety. Frequent use leads to dependence, withdrawal symptoms lead to increased anxiety, and increased anxiety causes continued drinking, which exacerbates the pattern of dependence. In a study of 30 chronic cocaine abusers, those with comorbid cyclothymia initially used cocaine during dysthymic cycles to return to hypomanic functioning. Eventually, these subjects used cocaine continuously, regardless of mood state.

The self-medication hypothesis does not imply that treatment of the individual's psychiatric disorder alone cures chemical dependency. Rather, recognizing that self-medication can cause a full-fledged addiction, possibly persisting after treatment of the psychiatric disorder, enables physicians to focus on treating substance use independently. In the above example, treatment with imipramine and behavioral therapy may eliminate the patient's panic attacks, but the addiction to alcohol may persist, requiring detoxification and long-term abstinence support.

Psychiatric Symptoms Secondary to Substance Abuse

Chronic Intoxication

Long-term substance abuse or withdrawal can precipitate a spectrum of psychiatric symptoms (Table 18.1). Depressive symptoms, such as insomnia, decreased libido, guilt, anhedonia, and suicidal ideation, are often seen in chronic alcoholism and may be indistinguishable from a major depressive episode. In a majority of cases, however, these depressive symptoms remit spontaneously after several weeks of sobriety. Chronic alcoholism also has associated personality changes that may resemble having antisocial, immature, histrionic, narcissistic, and dependent personality disorders. Unlike personality disorders, however, these characteristics frequently fade with continued abstinence.

Chronic marijuana use can be accompanied by depressive symptoms, as well as feelings of anxiety and paranoia. Additionally, certain hallucino-

TABLE 18.1. PSYCHIATRIC SYMPTOMS ASSOCIATED WITH CHRONIC SUBSTANCE USE

Substance	Psychiatric Symptoms
Alcohol	Depression, anxiety, sudden mood changes, paranoia, memory loss, unreliability
Cocaine	Acute paranoid ideation, mania, depression, anxiety, panic attacks, anhedonia
Stimulants	Same as cocaine
Inhalants	Anxiety, depression, personality/intellectual changes, impaired performance
Marijuana	Memory loss, anxiety, amotivational syndrome
Opiates	Depression, panic reactions, lethargy, sociopathy or ASP (antisocial personality) disorder
Depressants	Depression, anxiety, paranoia, psychosis
Hallucinogens	Panic reactions, anxiety, depersonalization, paranoia, confusion, psychosis, mania, OBS (organic brain syndrome)

gens, such as LSD, can cause perceptual disturbances, psychosis, mania, mood swings, depression, and suicidal ideation.

Withdrawal

In other cases, symptoms of psychiatric illness or psychosis begin during withdrawal. In acute alcoholic hallucinosis individuals may experience hallucinations (primarily auditory), which usually remit after several weeks of abstinence. Additionally, insomnia, irritability, and psychomotor agitation may be seen in alcohol or sedative withdrawal. Withdrawal from amphetamines and cocaine can produce a severe dysphoric state that includes psychomotor retardation, depressed mood, irritability, guilt, and suicidal ideation.

Persistent Psychiatric Disorders Due to Substance Abuse

In addition to transient psychiatric symptoms, substance abuse may precipitate psychiatric syndromes such as depression, anxiety, and psychosis, which persist after remission of the substance use disorder. Cocaine can cause panic attacks in some individuals. Initially, these attacks occur only during cocaine use, but they can persist for years. Similarly, the spontaneous recurrence of LSD-like perceptual distortions or visual hallucinations, traditionally called flashbacks, can recur after LSD ingestion, giving rise to the descriptive term posthallucinogen perceptual disorder.

Psychopathology and Addiction: Detrimental Nature of Comorbidity

Psychopathological Effects on Addiction

If coexisting psychopathology is neither the cause nor the effect of substance abuse, it may, nonetheless, affect the course, response to treatment, symptomatology, and long-term outcome of substance abuse. In a series of studies examining psychiatric illness as a predictor of outcome in substance abuse treatment, increased severity of psychopathology predicted a decreased response to treatment and a worse outcome. During a manic episode an alcoholic has an increased risk of relapse. Cocaine-abusing patients with comorbid diagnoses of cyclothymia could refrain from cocaine during dysthymic phases when they learned that their cocaine use was detrimental. Many patients reported that during a hypomanic phase they began to underestimate cocaine's negative effects, and relapse.

Addiction Effects on Psychopathology

A substance-related disorder may also affect the course of a psychiatric disorder. A recent study of patients with schizophrenia and related disorders evaluated the role of marijuana abuse. Patients who used marijuana had more frequent, earlier psychotic relapses or exacerbations than those who did not. Several possible mechanisms can explain how abused substances affect the course of psychiatric illness: (*a*) a substance-abusing individual is less compliant with medication regimens, leading to relapse; (*b*) the abused substance has a direct biologic effect. For example, the substance may up-regulate hepatic enzymes, leading to more rapid metabolism of medications, and subsequent lower plasma drug levels and inadequate treatment of the psychiatric disorder; (*c*) there may be no direct effect; instead, patients drawn to drug abuse may be more vulnerable to life stress in general, making them more prone to psychiatric relapse.

Long-Term Links of Substance Abuse and Psychopathology

While the self-medication hypothesis suggests that individuals use drugs to ease painful emotional and physical symptoms, individuals may also consume drugs to achieve other goals. For example, patients with eating disorders sometimes find that stimulants, such as amphetamines and cocaine, help them lose weight. A musician with performance anxiety may discover that an anxiolytic, such as diazepam, has a calming effect and leads to a better performance. These drugs may be highly reinforcing, thereby increasing the vulnerability to dependence over time.

Unrelated Coexisting Substance Abuse and Psychopathology

The occurrence of both substance abuse and mental illness in an individual may be coincidental rather than a result of a meaningful association. Since both substance abuse and mental illness are common in the general population, they may occur in the same individual by chance, in the same way that an individual may have both diabetes and migraines.

Genetic Connections

Another possibility, not addressed in these six relationships, is the genetic component of both substance abuse and mental illness. Strong familial components exist in some substance-related disorders, such as alcoholism, and some mental illness, such as depression. A single, genetic factor might predispose some patients to both substance-related disorders and mental illness. The dual diagnosis concept provides some evidence for this connection.

Family linkages of certain substance-related disorders and psychiatric illness have been discovered. A family-based study of mood disorders examined the prevalence of alcoholism with depression and found this dual diagnosis to be more prevalent in relatives of probands with the same dual diagnosis. Other family studies have looked at antisocial personality disorder and alcoholism, and have found familial links between them. A study of hospitalized, chemically-dependent patients examined rates of psychiatric illness in the patients' first-degree relatives and 35% met DSM-III criteria for at least one Axis I disorder. The most common diagnoses were alcohol and drug abuse or dependence among male relatives and affective disorder in female relatives. The female relatives of cocaine abusers had a stronger history of affective disorder than opiate or sedative/hypnotic abusers. Alcohol abuse and depression appeared with equal frequency in all three groups.

TREATMENT STRATEGIES

Past treatment strategies for dual diagnosis dealt with the two disorders as separate entities. Some psychiatrists emphasized the treatment of the psychiatric and emotional components and minimized the substance abuse, assuming that the substance abuse would disappear with resolution of the mental illness. Conversely, the addiction treatment community minimized the psychiatric symptomatology and emphasized the treatment of chemical dependency. Minimizing the importance of either diagnosis leads to treatment failure and high rates of relapse, and currently more programs are specifically designed for dual diagnosis patients and have an emphasis on educating the patient about substance abuse, psychiatric disorders, and their interactions.

Treatment of dually-diagnosed individuals involves the following stages:

- Stabilization—Risk assessment and detoxification;
- Engagement—Convincing patients that immediate treatment is both helpful and necessary;
- Persuasion—Convincing patients that both their substance abuse and psychiatric illness interact and require ongoing treatment;
- Active therapy—Teaching the skills needed to deal with each disorder;
- Relapse prevention—Aimed specifically at each diagnosis.

Controversy exists as to whether treatment of dual diagnosis patients should have a sequential or integrated approach. Sequential treatment deals with each disorder separately, with abstinence as a precondition for psychiatric treatment. Integrated treatment involves simultaneous treatment of both substance abuse and comorbid psychiatric disorders, preferably in a single treatment setting.

The clinician's familiarity with the patient and the history will help determine the best treatment approach. If the patient is unknown to the clinician and reliable records are unavailable, accurate diagnosis of comorbid disorders while the patient is using the drug is difficult. In these cases the patient must be drug-free before any psychiatric treatment can begin, implying a sequential approach to the therapy. However, for a patient well-known to the clinician or a patient with a reliable history from family or other caregivers, an integrated approach may prove most beneficial.

Treatment settings for dually-diagnosed individuals include inpatient hospitalization—dual diagnosis treatment units, substance abuse treatment units, or psychiatric treatment units—or outpatient programs. Inpatient dual diagnosis treatment units are ideal for those patients who need hospitalization. Treatment involves a full medical, psychosocial, and psychiatric assessment including immediate evaluation for suicide risk, psychotic symptoms, and the presence of coexisting mental illness.

When dual diagnosis units are not available, hospitalization can take place in either a substance abuse or psychiatric treatment unit. In either case, clinicians with expertise in the treatment of dually-diagnosed patients should participate in the treatment plan as early and as often as possible.

In the rapidly changing world of health care, outpatient treatment of dually-diagnosed patients has become more popular. Short-term hospitalization followed by intensive outpatient treatment involving support groups, psychotherapy, medical management, self-help groups, such as Alcoholics Anonymous (AA) and Narcotics Anonymous (NA), and the use of disulfiram has improved the treatment outcomes of substance abusers with severe psychiatric impairment. Although intensive drug rehabilitation programs, which include medication and psychotherapy, are most appropriate, partial hospitalization and residential programs provide another option for the treatment of these patients.

Pharmacotherapy

In the treatment of comorbid substance abuse and mental illness, pharmacotherapy is generally guided by the psychiatric disorder. Several issues dominate the pharmacological treatment of psychiatric symptoms in chemically-dependent patients.

First, many drugs of abuse interact with psychotherapeutic medications, leading to decreased effectiveness or dangerous side effects (Table 18.2). For example, during a manic episode, bipolar patients may lack adequate judgment or impulse control to abstain from drinking while taking disulfiram. Additionally, abused substances may increase or decrease the metabolism of certain medications, resulting in either toxic or subtherapeutic plasma levels of a drug and ineffective treatment.

Second, certain medications, such as anxiolytics, have increased potential for abuse in patients with substance-related disorders. Consequently, whenever possible, the least addictive medications should be used for both detoxification and for treatment of psychiatric illness. Benzodiazepines are most often singled out as having a serious risk for dependence in patients with a history of drug dependence. This risk may be even greater in patients with dual diagnoses. For this reason, benzodiazepines with longer half-lives, such as clonazepam, are recommended for use only in the short-term or acute management of anxiety. Alternative techniques for management of anxiety, such as relaxation, self-hypnosis, exercise, and behavioral therapy can be helpful adjuncts.

Psychotherapy

Certain types of psychotherapy have value in treating both patients with substance abuse alone or dually-diagnosed patients. However, efficacy varies depending on the drug of abuse and the specific psychiatric disorder. Psychotherapy provides support for continued abstinence as well as adherence to medical regimens.

One study of psychotherapeutic treatment of substance use randomly assigned opiate-dependent patients to three, separate, 6-month treatment groups: methadone plus drug counseling (consisting of review of urinalysis reports, help with employment, social services, and medical treatment) or a combination of methadone, drug counseling, and either supportive-expressive or cognitive-behavioral therapy. All three groups showed significant improvement as measured by decreased drug use, fewer crime days, improved psychological functioning, and increased

TABLE 18.2. INTERACTIONS BETWEEN DRUGS OF ABUSE AND COMMON THERAPEUTIC AGENTS

Drug of Abuse	Therapeutic Agent	Possible Interactions
Alcohol	Disulfiram (Antabuse)	Produces flushing, hypotension, nausea, tachycardia. Fatal reactions possible.
	MAO inhibitors	Impaired hepatic metabolism of tyramine in some beverages produces dangerous, possibly fatal, hypertension.
	Tricyclic antidepressants	Additive CNS impairment.
	Antipsychotics	Increased CNS impairment on psychomotor skills, judgment, and behavior. Possible increased risk of akithesia and dystonia.
	Anticonvulsants	Chronic ETOH use results in induction of hepatic microsomal enzymes, reducing phenytoin levels. Possible seizure risk.
Barbiturates	Tricyclic antidepressants	Reduced efficacy of tricyclics. May potentiate respiratory depression.
	MAO inhibitors	Inhibited barbiturate metabolism, prolonging intoxication.
	Antipsychotics	Induced hepatic microsomal enzymes may reduce chlorpromazine levels.
	Anticonvulsants	Valproic acid increases phenobarbital levels and toxicity. Induced hepatic microsomal enzymes may reduce carbamazepine levels and unpredictable phenytoin levels.
Benzodiazepines	Disulfiram	Enhanced benzodiazepine effects (oxazepam and lorazepam not affected).
	MAO inhibitors	Rare reports of edema with chlordiazepoxide.
Opiates	MAO inhibitors	Meperidine may produce severe excitation, diaphoresis, rigidity, hyper/hypotension, coma, and death.
	Antipsychotics	Hypotension and excessive CNS depression possible with meperidine and chlorpromazine.
	Anticonvulsants	Propoxyphene increases carbamazepine levels with risk of toxicity. Methadone metabolism may be increased by carbamazepine or phenytoin, causing withdrawal.
Stimulants	MAO inhibitors	Hyperpyrexia, severe hypertension, death when used with cocaine or amphetamines.
	Antipsychotics	Positive symptoms of chronic psychosis exacerbated by cocaine and amphetamines.

employment. However, the patients receiving either type of psychotherapy showed greater improvement and required significantly lower methadone doses and fewer other medications. By contrast, another study examining the treatment of cocaine abusers with weekly psychotherapy reported no effectiveness of therapy on cocaine use or other associated symptoms.

Response to psychotherapy may depend on patients' comorbid diagnoses. In the above study of opiate dependence, patients with only an antisocial personality disorder showed little improvement, while subjects with a diagnosis of depression and antisocial personality disorder showed measurable improvement with psychotherapy. Weekly outpatient group therapy for substance abusing patients with schizophrenia is effective in decreasing days of hospitalization during treatment. Long-term treatment of alcoholic schizophrenic patients with integrated mental health and substance abuse treatment involving case management, antipsychotic medication, housing support, behavioral substance abuse counseling, and dual diagnosis support groups has successfully initiated and maintained cessation of drinking.

While 12-step programs such as AA, NA, and Cocaine Anonymous are successful for patients with only a substance-related disorder, they may not adequately serve the needs of dually-diagnosed patients. Some of the groups have especially negative attitudes toward psychiatrists, psychotherapy, and the use of psychotherapeutic medications. Patients with dual diagnoses may find that they do not have much in common with other members of these groups and get no benefit from them. However, many other patients find them invaluable, and the programs should be encouraged whenever appropriate.

There are important advantages to *combined* pharmacological and psychotherapeutic treatment of substance-related disorders. The interaction of pharmacotherapy and psychotherapy may be synergistic. For example, for opiate addicts in methadone programs, both methadone and psychotherapy are essential to good outcome. Without methadone, patients may not reliably attend therapy sessions or benefit from social service intervention. Without psychotherapy, comorbid psychiatric problems contributing to substance use may not receive attention. Psychotherapy provides much needed support and encouragement in the difficult task of recovery, which many drug abusers may not receive from their families or friends.

FURTHER READING

Andreasen NC, Rice J, Endicott J, Coryell W, Grove WM, Reich T. Familial rates of affective disorder: A report from the National Institute of Mental Health collaborative study. Arch Gen Psychiatry 1987;44:461.

Drake RE, McHugo GJ, Noordsy DL. Treatment of alcoholism among schizophrenic outpatients: four-year outcomes. Am J Psychiatry 1993;150:328–329.

Gold MS, Slaby AE, eds. Dual Diagnosis in Substance Abuse. New York: Marcel Dekker, 1991.

Khantzian EJ. The self-medication hypothesis of addictive disorders: focus on heroin and cocaine dependence. Am J Psychiatry 1985;142:1259.

McLellan AT. Psychiatric severity as a predictor of outcome from substance abuse treatments. In: Psychopathology and Addictive Disorders. New York: The Guilford Press, 1986.

Meyer RE. How to understand the relationship between psychopathology and addictive disorders: another example of the chicken and the egg. In: Psychopathology and Addictive Disorders. New York: The Guilford Press, 1986.

Regier DA, Farmer ME, Rae DS, Locke BZ, et al. Comorbidity of mental disorders with alcohol and other drug abuse: results from the epidemiologic catchment area study. JAMA 1990;264:2511.

Weiss RD, Collins DA. Substance abuse and psychiatric illness. Am J Addict 1992;1:93.

Weiss RD, Mirin SM. The dual diagnosis alcoholic: evaluation and treatment. Psychiatric Annals 1989;19:261–265.

Chapter 19

Inpatient Management Issues and Pain Treatment

David H. Roberts with Booker Bush

In emergency rooms and on general hospital wards, patients with active substance-related disorders require particular attention, especially in terms of withdrawal prevention, pain management, and long-term follow-up care. In these cases, physicians need to recognize addictive behaviors, use appropriate detoxification and pain management agents, and discuss management issues explicitly with patients.

INPATIENT MANAGEMENT ISSUES

Withdrawal Prevention

The details of how to diagnose, prevent, and acutely manage specific withdrawal syndromes can be found in Chapters 7–16 of this text for each of the major classes of drugs. General keys to patient management and withdrawal prevention include:

- Always consider substance abuse as an etiology for the patient's presentation.
- Screen for substance abuse (i.e., CAGE (see Chapter 6) questions and blood/urine toxicology screens).
- Treat known substance abuse adequately to prevent withdrawal.
- Monitor for signs of withdrawal (heart rate, blood pressure, tremor, irritability, pupils).
- Respond to acute or severe signs of withdrawal promptly

Patient-Staff Interactions

Patients with substance-related disorder need medical care like all other patients, and are due the same respect and standards of treatment. Unfortunately, anxiety and distrust can pervade both staff and patient attitudes and behaviors.

For example, staff prejudices about chemically-dependent patients and their addictive behaviors may result in a patient not receiving adequate pain medication. Additionally, the question of continued substance use while the patient is hospitalized may provoke further conflict. On the other hand, the patient's attitude is often shaped by previous disdainful treatment by physicians, staff refusals when medications are requested, inadequate medications for their needs, and the fear that they will withdraw and not receive adequate treatment.

Team cohesiveness and communication are the keys to patient management, especially with patients who may try to "split" and manipulate the team. Team meetings with discussions of the problematic issues surrounding patient management, the plan for treatment, and the regimen for pain medications augment the patient's perception of a uniform plan of care. One team member should be the final authority and decision maker, thereby providing a single figurehead who has the support of the whole team. Finally, the patients should know that regimens will not be changed by covering physicians (i.e., in the middle of the night). Instead, team decisions will be renegotiated at a set, predetermined time.

Staff should understand that tolerance, physical dependence, and withdrawal do not mean abuse or addiction, and that use does not mean abuse. The concept of *pseudoaddiction* should also be understood. Pseudoaddiction describes an iatrogenic syndrome of abnormal behavior that can be a direct consequence of inadequate pain management. This syndrome passes through three characteristic phases: first, pain medications are inadequately prescribed to meet the needs of the patient; second, there is an escalation in the analgesic demands of the patient, with concomitant behavioral changes to convince others of the severity of the pain; finally, a crisis of mistrust develops between the patient and the team administering care.

Patient Cooperation and Limit Setting

In cases where patient cooperation or behavior limits medical therapy, it is important to encourage the patient to work with the team, to be honest with the team, and to emphasize mutual respect via adequate explicit contracting and direct communication. Staff must set limits and establish explicit contracts at the beginning of hospitalizations, rather than in response to crises. At all times, the patients should be made to feel that they are part of the team. Additionally, control is a major issue, and patients need to feel that they have some control.

Patient contracts should include:

- Specifics of withdrawal prophylaxis and management, especially with choices, (i.e., methadone maintenance, methadone taper, or clonidine);
- Pain management regimen with the specifics of analgesics and doses;

- Discussion of the need for frequent, random blood and urine screens;
- Clearly delineated decision-makers (team physician/nurses, not coverage personnel);
- Criteria for re-negotiation of the contract (specific issues/problems/unmet needs);
- Plan in case of violation of the contract (including ceasing care/restricting privileges/re-contracting).

Discharge and Follow-up

On arrival to the medical wards, patients with substance abuse problems should receive a drug addiction counselor or a consultation by the drug addiction service. As patients who have heart attacks see cardiologists for follow-up care, substance-abusing patients should similarly have referrals for follow-up care and detoxification programs on discharge. This practice should become routine protocol, and failure to follow it considered negligent patient care. Medical teams must avoid waiting until the day before discharge to address these issues or call these consults.

Although failure rates for chronic treatment programs are high, there should be no reason to not enroll patients in such long-term care. For patients who have undergone multiple detoxification admissions, the standard of care is another attempt at detoxification. With improved support systems and careful monitoring, the chance of success should increase with each attempt at detoxification. Patients should have simultaneous evaluation of underlying psychiatric disorders, and guidance and counseling with a psychotherapist.

PAIN MANAGEMENT ISSUES

Clinical Assessment of Pain

A fundamental difficulty in pain management is the lack of an objective measure of pain. As a result, on first evaluation, all reports of pain must be taken seriously, evaluated fully for an underlying organic process causing discomfort, and treated appropriately. The signs of autonomic arousal (increased heart rate or blood pressure, writhing) are grossly nonspecific, but can be reasonably sensitive in cases of acute pain. It is important to realize that patients with chronic pain may not demonstrate these findings. In fact, chemically-dependent patients may describe their pain as having a much greater intensity than other patients.

Without an objective measure, clinicians must rely on their knowledge and experience to make judgments. In addition to measurement of vital signs and autonomic functions, several scales make pain description and evaluation more objective.

Pain Intensity Scales

Simple Descriptive Pain Intensity Scale*

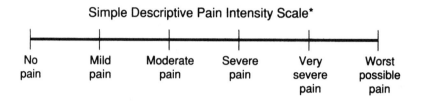

| No pain | Mild pain | Moderate pain | Severe pain | Very severe pain | Worst possible pain |

0 - 10 Numeric Pain Intensity Scale*

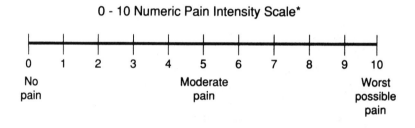

0 1 2 3 4 5 6 7 8 9 10

No pain   Moderate pain   Worst possible pain

Visual Analog Scale (VAS)**

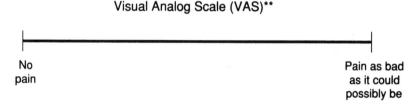

No pain   Pain as bad as it could possibly be

Figure 19.1. Examples of pain intensity scales. *, if used as a graphic rating scale, a 10-cm baseline is recommended. **, a 10-cm baseline is recommended for VAS scales.

- Visual-Analog Scale: Patient marks on line relative intensity of pain (Fig. 19.1);
- Verbal Nociceptive Scale: Patient reports pain as none, mild, moderate, severe, or excruciating, or rates pain on a scale from 1 to 10, with 1 being no pain and 10 being the worst pain ever;
- Functional Scale: Patient reports how pain limits activities;
- Monitored Activity Scale: Nurse/physician details patient's activities/functions;
- McGill Pain Questionnaire: 20 lists of words that describe definite somatic sensations (e.g., itchy, tingling, etc.), sensation in terms of a stimulus that might produce it (e.g., burning, pinching, tugging),

TABLE 19.1. WORDS COMMONLY USED BY PEOPLE TO DESCRIBE PAIN

1	2	3	4
1 Flickering	1 Jumping	1 Pricking	1 Sharp
2 Quivering	2 Flashing	2 Boring	2 Cutting
3 Pulsing	3 Shooting	3 Drilling	3 Lacerating
4 Throbbing		4 Stabbing	
5 Beating		5 Lancinating	
6 Pounding			

5	6	7	8
1 Pinching	1 Tugging	1 Hot	1 Tingling
2 Pressing	2 Pulling	2 Burning	2 Itchy
3 Gnawing	3 Wrenching	3 Scalding	3 Smarting
4 Cramping		4 Searing	4 Stinging
5 Crushing			

9	10	11	12
1 Dull	1 Tender	1 Tiring	1 Sickening
2 Sore	2 Taut	2 Exhausting	2 Suffocating
3 Hurting	3 Rasping		
4 Aching	4 Splitting		
5 Heavy			

13	14	15	16
1 Fearful	1 Punishing	1 Wretched	1 Annoying
2 Frightful	2 Gruelling	2 Blinding	2 Troublesome
3 Terrifying	3 Cruel		3 Miserable
	4 Vicious		4 Intense
	5 Killing		5 Unbearable

17	18	19	20
1 Spreading	1 Tight	1 Cool	1 Nagging
2 Radiating	2 Numb	2 Cold	2 Nauseating
3 Penetrating	3 Drawing	3 Freezing	3 Agonizing
4 Piercing	4 Squeezing		4 Dreadful
	5 Tearing		5 Torturing

and negative feelings that usually accompany pain, affective words (e.g., fearful, dreadful). It can assess the quality of pain and the effect that it has on the patient's life, and separate affective pain from sensory pain (Table 19.1).

These pain assessment scales can be completed at regular intervals, and then levels of pain medications adjusted appropriately. Discordance between patient claims of excruciating pain and nurse observations of a patient laughing and chatting comfortably on the telephone can help identify invalid pain complaints or pseudoaddictive behavior.

Strategies for Effective Pain Relief

Valid pain complaints require immediate treatment. Treatment for both the underlying organic process causing the painful stimulus and the patient's response to the pain (i.e., subjective response or anxiety) is necessary. In fact, as mentioned earlier, incomplete treatment of pain and secondary anxiety can produce a pseudoaddiction. The goal of an admission for inpatient management of pain must strike a balance among several issues: adequate treatment of the patient's illness or pain; limitations on pain medication; management of disruptive, confrontational behavior; and patient cooperation.

General Guidelines for Use of Pain Medications

A few general principles should guide the actual treatment of pain, particularly when dealing with chemically-dependent patients. In terms of the method of treatment, intramuscular injections should be avoided to prevent the association of needles and the relief of pain. Any intravenous injections should be given slowly. The faster the intravenous injection, the faster the serum level of medication rises. This quick escalation of drug level has an increased potential for inducing euphoric drug effects and subsequent addiction. Pain medication orders should not be written on an as-needed (p.r.n.) basis since such an order can stimulate clock-watching, pestering of nurses, or other disruptive behaviors. Similarly, for a medication order written "every three hours," staff must administer it on time to avoid these behaviors. Lastly, the pain medication regimen should be explicitly discussed with the patient. Discussing responses to inadequate pain relief or other problems helps avoid potentially disruptive behavior in the future.

Pain Medication Options

The choice of medications for pain relief is a difficult one, and allergies, side effects, or systemic illness often limit the options. The first line of pain relief medications should be nonnarcotic medications, including nonsteroidal antiinflammatory agents (NSAIDS), and other adjuvants. When these drugs alone have failed, then narcotics can be considered for pain relief. Usually, a combination of NSAIDS and opiates is initiated to decrease the dose of opiates necessary for pain relief. However, if no relief is attained, then the NSAIDS are discontinued and the dose of the opiates is increased.

Risk factors for poor opiate control and for development of addiction as an inpatient or an outpatient include:

- Active substance abuse;
- Prior abuse of pain medications;

- Lack of support systems;
- Lack of involvement in substance abuse therapy group (Alcoholics Anonymous/Narcotics Anonymous);
- Lack of insight, or denial of substance abuse.

Consequently, patients who do not have these risk factors, have a history of alcohol abuse only, or have substance abuse only in the remote past, have lower risks of addiction from narcotic pain medications. Once in treatment, the key is to treat pain fully and monitor efficacy by both patient report and staff assessment.

Chronic Pain Issues

Complaints in the Emergency Ward

Treating both chronic pain syndromes and systemic illness with acute pain flares, such as sickle cell anemia, in the emergency ward (EW) is challenging. As discussed previously, objective evaluation of pain complaints is extremely difficult, especially in a busy emergency ward. Additionally, patients with chronic pain syndromes may not demonstrate the typical findings of autonomic arousal, despite significant pain. Fundamentally, the evaluation begins by ruling out an organic etiology for the pain complaint. In addition to a regular evaluation with history, physical examination, and laboratory studies, a complete search through the patient's records should help avoid repeat imaging studies or expensive lab tests. If an organic etiology is discovered, the patient should be admitted or treated appropriately in the EW, and then sent to a primary care physician or pain management specialist for appropriate follow-up care.

If the patient's complaint has no obvious organic etiology and there have been numerous, similar EW presentations in the past, then the primary goal is to get the patient referred to a pain management clinic for treatment of chronic pain. Once connected with a pain management service, the covering pain management doctor can be called for help on the next presentation to the EW. This method of evaluation will help consolidate patient care with a physician who deals frequently with chronic pain issues, and prevent splitting and fragmenting the care.

In the EW the key is to treat adequately when required and to explain the reasoning when treatment is not felt to be indicated. Mistakes in diagnosis will be made, but encouraging patients to follow up with a physician outside the EW can increase the overall likelihood of adequate treatment.

Nonnarcotic Therapy Options

Once a medical evaluation has ruled out acute, untreated organic disease, then pain management should be offered. Pain management can include psychiatric evaluation, analysis of living situation and stresses, medical treatment, biofeedback, coping strategies, and relaxation techniques.

For medical management, the first step is to maximize nonnarcotic agents, such as nonsteroidal antiinflammatory drugs (NSAIDS). Next, adjuvant agents, such as tricyclic antidepressants (especially for pain at night), muscle relaxants, transcutaneous electrical nerve stimulation (TENS) units, ice/heat treatment, physical therapy, or regional anesthetic blocks (e.g., brachial plexus block for elbow pain), can be added to the patient's regimen. Other therapy modalities, such as biofeedback, relaxation, and self-hypnosis, also should be integrated into patient management. Finally, chronic pain can have an anxiety component. Although this anxiety can be treated with drugs (i.e., Percocet), which have dissociative effects, psychotherapy or anxiolytics (e.g., buspirone) may be more appropriate and efficacious.

Unconventional medicine, such as acupuncture, herbalism, or chiropractic therapy, represents another category of nonnarcotic therapies, which can provide important alternatives to traditional medical therapies for chronic pain. One recent study estimated that 34% of the population older than 18 years used at least one unconventional therapy in 1990, and that 83% of those people also sought traditional medical care for the same condition. The frequency of use of these therapies is much higher than previously thought. Furthermore, 72% of patients did not report these visits to their medical doctor. Communication with patients about their use of unconventional medicine may provide new insight into their chronic pain.

Treatment with Narcotic Medications

Once the decision to use narcotics has been made, then the goal becomes treatment of pain that maintains a high level of functioning with minimal side effects. Long-acting opiates, such as MS Contin, Methadone, Levorphenol, and Fentanyl, offer the best long-term pain management options. Additional, short-acting medications can be added for breakthrough pain management (Table 17.2).

The risks and benefits of narcotic pain management must be explained to patients, and they must give their consent to the therapy, as with other medical procedures. Risks include sedation, dysphoria, mood changes, dependence, and addiction. These side effects may have an insidious onset, and patients are often the last to recognize them. Although addiction in patients with acute pain is rare, the specific risk in those people with chronic pain syndromes is unknown, but may be slightly increased. In addition, chronic treatment can lead to endocrine and metabolic disturbances (see Chapter 11). The clear potential benefit is resolution and diminution of the pain syndrome.

TABLE 19.2. PRINCIPLES OF OPIOID ANALGESIC USE IN ACUTE AND CANCER PAIN

1. Individualize the route, dosage, and schedule.
2. Administer analgesics regularly (not p.r.n.) if pain is present most of the day.
3. Become familiar with the dose and time course of several strong opioids.
4. Give infants and children adequate opioid doses.
5. Follow patients closely, particularly when beginning or changing analgesic regimens.
6. When changing to a new opioid or different route, use an equianalgesic dosing table to estimate the new dose. Modify the estimate based on the clinical situation.
7. Recognize and treat side effects.
8. Be aware of the potential hazards of meperidine and mixed agonist-antagonists, particularly pentazocine.
9. Do not use placebos to assess the nature of pain.
10. Watch for the development of tolerance and treat appropriately.
11. Be aware of the development of physical dependence and prevent withdrawal.
12. Do not label a patient "addicted" (psychologically dependent) if you merely mean physically dependent on or tolerant to opioids.
13. Be alert to the psychological state of the patient.

The future standard of care for chronic pain management may include a trial treatment with narcotic medications. Pretreatment questionnaires evaluating sleep, pain level, systemic complaints, subjective analysis of patients by others, and interviews with family members, followed by a questionnaire during treatment (perhaps every 3 months), will be used to assess the success or failure of treatment.

If narcotics successfully treat the pain, then medication can be continued. However, if the posttreatment evaluation indicates no benefit or if addictive behaviors typical of substance abuse arise, discontinuation or tapering of the narcotic therapy is indicated. Examples of addictive behaviors include asking for replacements of lost or stolen prescriptions, asking for prescriptions from more than one physician, frequent phone calls to staff or physicians, showing up to physician's office without an appointment, not taking medications as directed, and asking for additional medications. Most patients for whom narcotic therapy is unsuccessful will demonstrate these behaviors within the first 2 months of treatment.

Postoperative Pain Management

Management of postoperative pain begins before surgery and continues until discharge (Fig. 19.2). Before the operation, a physician should explicitly discuss the plan for pain control with the patient, the availability and role of the pain management teams, how staff will work to avoid addiction to pain medication, and the low incidence of actual new addictions with postoperative pain medication.

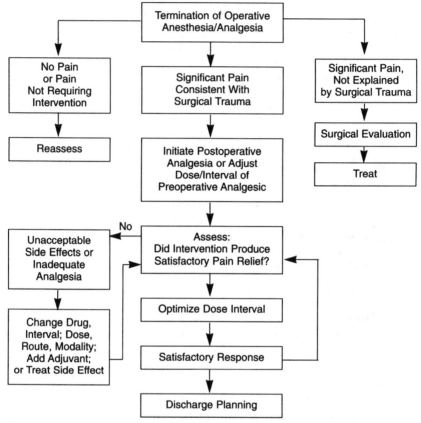

Figure 19.2. Postoperative pain management.

During the operation itself, anesthesia and analgesia should begin simultaneously. The administration of analgesia prior to incision can decrease the amount of postoperative pain by diminishing the central sensitization and "wind-up" phenomenon that occurs when nerves are cut or damaged.

Patient-Controlled Analgesia

Postoperative pain management involves maximizing nonnarcotic therapies, and then treating pain with narcotics for the reasons discussed previously. Patient-controlled analgesia (PCA) has been demonstrated to control pain better, decrease total medication used, and increase patient satisfaction. PCA initially involves a slow infusion of narcotic medication. The infusion rate parameters are established by a physician. Most notably, this slow infusion prevents a sudden elevation in serum drug levels, thereby preventing a euphoric rush. Patients then control the specific amount of medication they receive within those set parameters.

No literature exists on the use of PCA in the substance-abusing patient population, but anecdotally, there are three types of reactions to PCA. One group of patients will refuse PCA outright, realizing that they will not get a euphoric rush or mood elevation with the slow PCA infusion. Another population will use PCA correctly. It is important to remember that these patients may need higher infusion rates or higher doses because of tolerance. Finally, some patients will become dependent on the PCA. In addition to having little insight into their situation, they simply cannot resist their addiction and the temptation of narcotic use. Unable to differentiate between needing opiates for pain versus their addiction, these patients will fail PCA therapy.

Fears About Addiction to Pain Medications

Postoperative patients fear that use of pain medication leads to addictions, and need reassurance in regard to this risk. Unless patients have a history of substance abuse themselves or in their family, studies have indicated a low risk for addiction to pain medication for acute pain (on the order of 1 in 12–14,000).

One study of postoperative patients on PCA indicated that the most common reasons for using medication were pain, noisy neighbors preventing sleep, and anxiety. Consequently, patients might actually need two PCA-type pumps, one for analgesia and one for anxiolysis, to prevent inappropriate use of pain medication.

Patients also need to understand the common reasons for abuse of pain medications. If the patients understand the need for analgesia, and their low risk of addiction, they are less likely to use the pain medication incorrectly. Examples of reasons for abuse of pain medicines include:

- Psychiatric addiction to medication—needing the high;
- Self-medication for anxiety or sedation;
- Use of the medication as a dissociative tool;
- Use as a validating tool (e.g., my disease must be serious because my doctor gives me these strong medicines).

Consequences of Inadequate Treatment of Pain

The importance of adequate pain treatment can not be overemphasized. Patients deserve adequate treatment of acute, chronic, postoperative, and cancer pain. Inadequate treatment can lead to poor hospital care, frustration on the part of the patient and the treating team, disruptive behavior by the patient, pseudoaddictive behavior, a lack of trust between the team and the patient, and loss of the patient to follow-up.

SUMMARY

Inpatient management of chemically-dependent patients requires hospital staff cohesiveness, explicit discussions of therapies and pain management, appropriate and timely contracting, and prompt, unified responses to crises. Additionally, physicians and hospital staff need to recognize and attempt to prevent addictive behaviors and pseudoaddiction.

Important principles of pain management include: (*a*) patients with active or past substance abuse may require more pain medicine due to tolerance; (*b*) pain medicine regimens and the criteria for changing them should be explicitly discussed with patients; (*c*) certain patients may have little capacity to distinguish between their need for narcotics to treat pain, and their addiction.

Effective pain relief involves maximizing nonnarcotic therapy options before prescribing narcotic medications. When indicated, always treat pain with adequate doses of narcotics, even in the substance-abusing patient population. Specifically, use longer-acting, less euphoria-producing narcotic agents in therapy of both acute and chronic pain complaints.

FURTHER READING

Acute Pain Management: Operative or Medical Procedures and Trauma. Rockville, MD: US Department of Health and Human Services, 1992.

Eisenberg DM, Kessler RC, Foster C, Norlock FE, Calkins DR, Delbanco TL. Unconventional medicine in the United States. N Engl J Med 1993; 328:246–252.

Fields H. Pain. New York: McGraw-Hill, 1987.

Management of Cancer Pain. Rockville, MD: US Department of Health and Human Services, 1994.

Appendix 1

Summary Flow Chart of Screening Questions

Deborah Cohan

I. Children and Adolescents

Ask GENERAL QUESTIONS about the patient's life:
- school
- extracurricular activities
- friends and night-time activities
- neighborhood
- family life

Then, Ask ALCOHOL and DRUG Questions:
- Does anyone you know smoke? Drink alcohol? Use drugs?
- Does anyone in your family smoke, drink, or use drugs?
- Do any of your friends smoke, drink alcohol, or use drugs?
- Have you ever used tobacco, alcohol, or other drugs in the past? How about now?

Ask about any CONSEQUENCES of Alcohol and Drug use:
- Health – including suicidal ideation
- family/social relations – including sexual activity, physical and sexual abuse
- School work
- Financial/legal problems – including driving while intoxicated, arrests

II. Adults

A. Tobacco Screening Questions

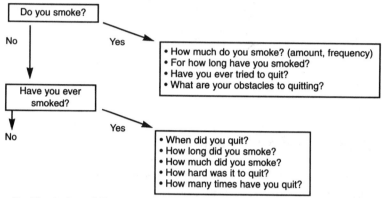

B. Alcohol and Drugs:

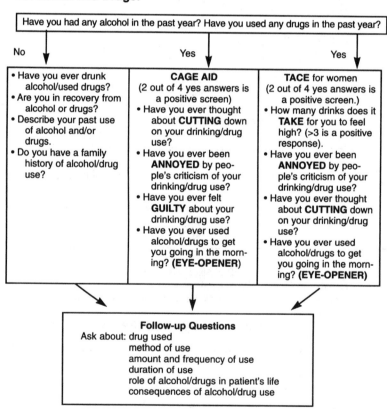

III. Elderly

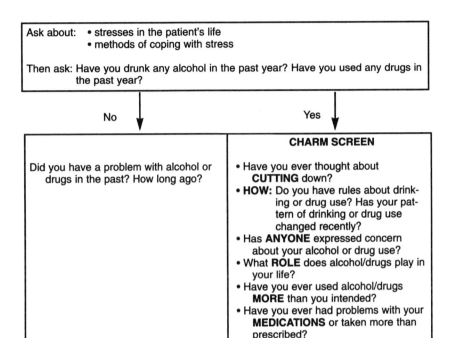

Ask about: • stresses in the patient's life
            • methods of coping with stress

Then ask: Have you drunk any alcohol in the past year? Have you used any drugs in
          the past year?

No

Yes

Did you have a problem with alcohol or
drugs in the past? How long ago?

CHARM SCREEN

• Have you ever thought about
  CUTTING down?
• **HOW:** Do you have rules about drink-
  ing or drug use? Has your pat-
  tern of drinking or drug use
  changed recently?
• Has **ANYONE** expressed concern
  about your alcohol or drug use?
• What **ROLE** does alcohol/drugs play in
  your life?
• Have you ever used alcohol/drugs
  MORE than you intended?
• Have you ever had problems with your
  MEDICATIONS or taken more than
  prescribed?

Quick Reference Substance Abuse Information Card

Courtesy of HMS Division on Addictions
From Friedman L, Hyman S, Fleming NF, Roberts DH, eds.
Source Book of Substance Abuse and Addiction. Baltimore:
Williams & Wilkins, 1996.

CAGE Test to Screen for Alcoholism: 1 positive = likely alcoholism

Have you ever:
· **C**ut back or **C**hanged your drinking pattern?
· felt **Annoyed** if people criticized your drinking?
· felt **Guilty** about drinking?
· needed a drink **E**arly in the day to steady yourself (**E**ye opener)?

ALCOHOL WITHDRAWAL

Mild Sxs: Tremor, anorexia, nausea, insomnia, anxiety, irritability, tachycardia, mild hypertension, hallucinosis, seizures.

Timing: Earliest onset 6–8 hours after abstinence; latest 5–7 days.

Rx: Benzodiazepines to achieve calm; model regimens: diazepam 10–20 mg or oxazepam (if liver diseases) 30–60 mg q2h p.o. prn aiming for calm, but not oversedation, q6h once stable; dosage requirements vary widely; decrease by 20% per day.

Low stimulation environment; thiamine 100 mg i.m. or i.v. qd × 3 days; folate 1 mg p.o. qd.

DTs: Marked hypertension, tachycardia, fever, hallucinosis, agitation, confusion, combativeness, seizures.

Timing: 24–72 hours after abstinence.

Rx: ICU monitoring, restraints, i.v. fluids, i.v. benzodiazepines, antipyretics if needed; diazepam 5–10 mg or lorazepam (if liver disease) 1–2 mg *slowly* i.v. q15–20 minutes until stabilized; then q2h prn.

Belligerent Patient: Security guards present; don't show anger; haloperidol 5 mg p.o. or i.m.; add lorazepam 1–2 mg if needed; restraints if violent.

Seizures

Sx: Generalized (focal gets a workup); often 2–6 closely spaced; status rare.

Timing: 12–48 hours after abstinence (late onset gets a workup).

DDX: R/O trauma, metabolic causes (incl low Mg^{++}), infection.

Rx: Benzodiazepines best; protect from falls.

Wernicke's Encephalopathy

Sx: Ataxia, nystagmus, ophthalmoplegia, confusion.
Prevention: Thiamine 100 mg i.m. or i.v. prior to any glucose.

OPIATE WITHDRAWAL

Mild Signs: Sweating, yawning, lacrimation, tremor, rhinorrhea, irritability,
   dilated pupils, respiratory rate, pulse >90.
Severe Signs: Insomnia, "HR, "BP, nausea, vomiting, abdominal cramps, diarrhea,
   muscle twitching, dilated pupils.
Course: (1) Heroin: onset in 8–12 hours, lasting 5–10 days, untreated. (2) Metha-
   done: onset in 30–48 hours, lasts 2–4 weeks.
Methadone: Methadone-maintained patient—confirm dose with methadone
   clinic.
· Analgesics: patient is tolerant to methadone's analgesia; always add analgesic
      Rx at conventional doses and frequency.
· Expect coping problems; don't dwell on dosage with patient.
· Monitor pulse, respiration, pupil size.

Dose (inpatient):
· Untreated street addict: at signs of withdrawal; Rx 20 mg p.o.
· Known heavy use: 30 mg p.o.; increase 5–10 mg q2–4 h to stabilize; rarely >40
      mg in first 24 hours, rarely >80 mg qd.
· If n.p.o.: 2/3 daily dose i.v., divided q6h and restart prior p.o. dose as tolerated.

Course: Onset 30–60 minutes; peak levels 2–6 hours; duration 24–36 hours.
Side Effects: Reduce 5–10 mg prn for lethargy.
Taper: If 1–14 days s/p admission, 10–20% qd; expect distress.
Discharge Planning: Initiate as quickly as possible.

REMEMBER: Patients may be withdrawing from mixed drug use,
including nicotine, so you may have to treat multiple withdrawal
syndromes simultaneously.

Appendix 3

CIWA-Ar As a Quick Reference Sheet in Pocket Form

Patient _____ Date |___|___|___| Time _____ : _____
y m d (24 hour clock, midnight = 00:00)

Pulse or heart rate, taken for one minute: _____ Blood pressure: ____/____

NAUSEA AND VOMITING—As "Do you feel sick to your stomach? Have you vomited?" Observation.
0 no nausea and no vomiting
1 mild nausea with no vomiting
2
3
4 intermittent nausea with dry heaves
5
6
7 constant nausea, frequent dry heaves and vomiting

TREMOR—Arms extended and fingers spread apart. Observation.
0 no tremor
1 not visible, but can be felt fingertip to fingertip
2
3
4 moderate, with patient's arms extended
5
6
7 severe, even with arms not extended

PAROXYSMAL SWEATS—Observation.
0 no sweat visible
1 barely perceptible sweating, palms moist
2
3
4 beads of sweat obvious on forehead
5
6
7 drenching sweats

TACTILE DISTURBANCES—Ask "Have you any itching, pins and needles senations, any burning, any numbness or do you feel bugs crawling on or under your skin?" Observation.
0 none
1 very mild itching, pins and needles, burning or numbness
2 mild itching, pins and needles, burning or numbness
3 moderate itching, pins and needles, burning or numbness
4 moderately severe hallucinations
5 severe hallucinations
6 extremely severe hallucinations
7 continuous hallucinations

AUDITORY DISTURBANCES—Ask "Are you more aware of sounds around you? Are they harsh? Do they frighten you? Are you hearing anything that is disturbing to you? Are you hearing things you know are not there?" Observation.
0 not present
1 very mild harshness or ability to frighten
2 mild harshness or ability to frighten
3 moderate harshness or ability to frighten
4 moderately severe hallucinations
5 severe hallucinations
6 extremely severe hallucinations
7 continuous hallucinations

(continued on next page)

ANXIETY—Ask "Do you feel nervous?"
Observation.
0 no anxiety, at ease
1 mildly anxious
2
3
4 moderately anxious, or guarded, so anxiety is inferred
5
6
7 equivalent to acute panic states as seen in severe delirium or acute schizophrenic reactions

AGITATION—Observation.
0 normal activity
1 somewhat more than normal activity
2
3
4 moderately fidgety and restless
5
6
7 paces back and forth during most of the interview, or constantly thrashes about

VISUAL DISTURBANCES—Ask "Does the light appear to be too bright? Is its colour different? Does it hurt your eyes? Are you seeing anything that is disturbing to you? Are you seeing things you know are not there?" Observation.
0 not present
1 very mild sensitivity
2 mild sensitivity
3 moderate sensitivity
4 moderately severe hallucinations
5 severe hallucinations
6 extremely severe hallucinations
7 continuous hallucinations

HEADACHE, FULLNESS IN HEAD—Ask "Does your head feel different? Does it feel like there is a band around your head?" Do not rate for dizziness or lightheadedness. Otherwise, rate severity.
0 not present
1 very mild
2 mild
3 moderate
4 moderately severe
5 severe
6 very severe
7 extremely severe

ORIENTATION AND CLOUDING OF SENSORIUM—Ask "What day is this? Where are you? Who am I?"
0 oriented and can do serial additions
1 cannot do serial additions or is uncertain about date
2 disoriented for date by no more than 2 calendar days
3 disoriented for date by more than 2 calendar days
4 disoriented for place and/or person

Total CIWA-A Score _____
Rater's Initials _____
Maximum Possible Score 67

Figure A3.1. Clinical Institute Withdrawal Assessment for Alcohol—Revised (CIWA-Ar) scale and interpretation. An individual with a score of less than 10 on the CIWA-Ar may be adequately treated with support care alone. Individuals with scores higher than 10 require pharmacological intervention and should be reassessed every 2 hours.

Substance Abuse Jargon

Arun J. Ramappa and David H. Roberts

Drug Name	Street Name	Drug Name	Street Name
Marijuana	pot	Methadone	dollies
	reefer		done
	doobie	Chloral Hydrate	mickey finn
	smoke		
	herb	Methaqualone	ludes
	homegrown	Nitrous oxide	laughing gas
	roach		whippet
	joint		
	grass	Nitrites	poppers
	dope		snappers
	ganga		pearls
	bone	Amyl nitrite	amy
	weed		
	Mary Jane	Butyl nitrite	bute
	jay	Barbiturates	barbs
	chronic		candy
	hash		dolls
	hash oil		goofers
Alcohol	booze		goof-balls
	sauce		peanuts
	juice		sleeping pills
	spirits		downers
	brew	Amobarbital	blues
Morphine	drugstore		blue velvet
	dope		blue birds
	dreamer		blue devils
	gunk		blue heavens
Heroin	H		blue angels
	smack	Secobarbital	reds
	horse		redbirds
	china white		red devils
Percocet	perks		seggy
			pink lady

Drug Name	Street Name	Drug Name	Street Name
Pentobarbital/ *Nembutal*	yellows nembies nebbies yellow jackets	*Cocaine*	coke blow lady toot snow flake nose candy
Secobarbital/ *Amobarbital*	reds and blues rainbows tooies double trouble christmas trees	*Crack Cocaine*	crack rock freebase base blotter
LSD	acid heavenly blue pearly gates flying saucers blue cheer		electric kool-aid purple haze window pane
		Psilocybin	magic mushrooms mushrooms 'shrooms purple passion
Amphetamines	speed uppers pep pills crank bennies black beauties	*Mescaline*	cactus mesc buttons peyote
		MDMA	ecstasy XTC adam
Methamphetamine	crystal meth ice (smokeable)	*PCP*	hog angel dust sherman magic mist whack surfer crystal PeaCePill
Caffeine	Java joe mud brew		
Nicotine	weeds butts chew dip	*PCP w/Marijuana*	happy sticks joy sticks blunt

General References for All Abused Substances

American Psychiatric Association. Diagnostic and Statistical Manual of Mental Disorders. 4th Ed. Washington, DC: American Psychiatric Association, 1993.

Balfour DJK. Psychotropic Drugs of Abuse. New York: Pergamon Press, 1990.

Goodman Gilman A, Rall TW, Nies AS, Taylor P. Goodman and Gilman's The Pharmacological Basis of Therapeutics. 8th Ed. Elmsford, NY: Pergamon Press, 1990.

Hyman SE, Tesar GE. Manual of Psychiatric Emergencies. Boston: Little, Brown, 1993.

Kandel ER, Schwartz JH, Jessel TM. Principles of Neural Science, 3rd Ed. New York: Elsevier, 1991.

Lowinson JH, Ruiz P, Millman RB. Substance Abuse: A Comprehensive Textbook. 2nd Ed. Baltimore: Williams & Wilkins, 1992.

NIDA. National Household Survey on Drug Abuse. Rockville, MD: National Institute on Drug Abuse 1991; 49–54.

Smith DE, Landry MJ. Psychoactive substance-related disorders: drugs and alcohol. In: Goldman H, ed. Review of General Psychiatry. Norwalk, CT: Appleton-Lange, 1992.

Viccellio P. Handbook of Medical Toxicology. Boston, Little, Brown, 1993.

Figure and Table Credits

Figures

Figure 1.1. Barnes DM. The biological tangle of drug addiction. Science 1988;241:415–417. Adapted from Bloom FE, ed. Brain, Mind, and Behavior. New York: Freeman, 1988.

Figure 1.2. Adapted from Nestler EJ, Hope BT, Widnell KL. Drug addiction: a model for the molecular basis of neural plasticity. Neuron 1993; 11: 995–1006.

Figure 7.1. From Turner RC, Lichstein PR, Busher JT, Waivers LE. Alcohol withdrawal syndromes: a review of pathophysiology, clinical presentation and treatment. J Gen Intern Med 1989;4:434.

Figure 8.2. Newcomb PA, Carbone PP. The health consequences of smoking. Med Clin North Am 1992;76:305–331. Adapted from US Department of Health and Human Services: The Health Consequences of Smoking: 25 years of progress. A report of the Surgeon General. USDHHS, PHS, CDC. Center for Chronic Disease Prevention and Health Promotion. Office on Smoking and Health DHHS publ. no. (CDC) 89-8411, 1989.

Figure 9.3. Adapted from Gawin FH, Kleber HD. Abstinence symptomatology and psychiatric diagnosis in cocaine abusers. Clinical Observations. Arch Gen Psychiatry 1986;43:107–113.

Figure 10.1. Source: Johnston LD, O'Malley PM, Bachman JG. Monitoring the Future: A Continuing Study of the Lifestyles and Values of Youth. University of Michigan, Institute for Social Research, 1994.

Figure 12.4. Adapted from Kaila K. Ionic basis of $GABA_A$ receptor channel function in the nervous system. Prog Neurobiol 1994;42:492, 494.

Figure 13.3. Wilson JD, Braunwald E, Isselbacher KJ, et al, eds. Harrison's Principles of Internal Medicine. 12th Ed. New York: McGraw-Hill, 1991; 1953.

Figure 15.1. From Goodman Gilman A. The Pharmacological Basis of Therapeutics. 8th Ed. New York: McGraw-Hill, 1990.

Figure 17.1. From Sadler TW. Langman's Medical Embryology. 6th Ed. Baltimore: Williams & Wilkins, 1990: inside front cover.

Figure 17.2. From Rosett HL, Weiner L, Morse BA. Identification and prevention of fetal alcohol syndrome. Brookline, MA: Fetal Alcohol Education Program, Boston University School of Medicine, 1985.

Figure 17.3. Volpe JJ. Effects of cocaine use on the fetus. N Engl J Med 1992;327:399–407.

Figure 19.1. Acute pain management: Operative or medical procedures and trauma. Rockville, MD: US Dept. of HHS, 1992:116.

Figure 19.2. Acute pain management: Operative or medical procedures and trauma. Rockville, MD: US Dept. of HHS, 1992:4.

Tables

Table 1.2. Adapted from Diagnostic and Statistical Manual. Ed. IV. Washington, DC: American Psychiatric Association, 181.

Table 1.3. Adapted from Diagnostic and Statistical Manual. Ed. IV. Washington, DC: American Psychiatric Association, 182–183.

Table 1.4. Adapted from Diagnostic and Statistical Manual. Ed. IV. Washington, DC: American Psychiatric Association, 185.

Table 2.1. Source: Substance Abuse and Mental Health Services Administration. National Household Survey on Drug Abuse: Main Findings 1992.

Table 2.3. Substance Abuse and Mental Health Services Administration. National Household Survey on Drug Abuse: Population Estimates 1992.

Table 2.4. Source: Substance Abuse and Mental Health Services Administration. Preliminary Estimates from the 1993 National Household Survey on Drug Abuse, July 1994.

Table 2.6. NIDA. "Monitoring the Future" Survey and National Household Survey on Drug Abuse. Rockville, MD: US Dept. of HHS, 1993.

Table 3.2. From: NIDA. Socioeconomic and Demographic Correlates of Drug and Alcohol Use: Findings from the 1988 and 1990 National Household Survey on Drug Abuse. Rockville, MD: US Dept of HHS, 1992; and Substance Abuse and Mental Health Services Administration (SAMHSA). National Household Survey on Drug Abuse:

Main Findings 1991. US Dept. of HHS, 1993.

Tables 3.4. and 3.5. Kleinman A. Rethinking Psychiatry: From Cultural Category to Personal Experience. New York: Free Press, 1988.

Table 4.1. Adapted from Graham AV, Berolzheimer N, Burge S. Alcohol abuse: a family disease. Prim Care 1993;20:121–130.

Table 4.2. Source: Graham AV, Berolzheimer N, Burge S. Alcohol abuse: a family disease. Prim Care 1993;20:129.

Tables 5.2. and 5.3. Drug Enforcement Administration. Physician's manual: an informal outline of the controlled substances act of 1970. Washington, DC: US Department of Justice, revised 1990.

Table 6.4. Source: Fact Sheet, 1993. Cleveland, OH:Alcoholism Services of Cleveland, Inc., 1993.

Table 6.5. Adapted from Selzer ML. The Michigan Alcoholism Screening Test (MAST): the quest for a new diagnostic instrument. Am J Psychiatry 1971;127:89–94.

Table 6.6. Adapted from Saunder JB, Aasland OG, Babor TF, et al. Development of the Alcohol Use Disorders Identification Test (AUDIT): WHO collaborative project on early detection of persons with harmful alcohol consumption–II. Addiction 1993; 88:791–804.

Table 7.9. Turner RC, Lichstein PR, Busher JT, Waivers LE. Alcohol withdrawal syndromes: a review of pathophysiology, clinical presentation and treatment. J Gen Intern Med 1989; 4:441.

Table 7.11. Turner RC, Lichstein PR, Busher JT, Waivers LE. Alcohol withdrawal syndromes: a review of pathophysiology, clinical presentation and treatment J Gen Intern Med 1989; 4:439.

Table 7.12. Data from Jacob MS, Sellers EM: Emergency management of alcohol withdrawal. Drug Ther 1977; 24:28.

Table 8.3. Adapted from Lee EW, D'Alonzo GE. Cigarette smoking, nicotine addiction, and its pharmacologic treatment. Arch Intern Med 1993; 153:34–48.

Table 8.5. Fiore MC, Jorenby DE, Baker TB. Tobacco dependence and the nicotine patch. JAMA 1992; 268:2687–2694.

Table 8.6. Adapted from Glynn TJ, Manley MW. How to help your patients stop smoking. NCI Institute Manual for Physicians. Rockville, MD: US Dept of Health and Human Services.

Table 8.7. Adapted from Lee EW, D'Alonzo GE. Cigarette smoking, nicotine addiction, and its pharmacologic treatment. Arch Intern Med 1993; 153:34–48.

Table 8.10. Abramowicz M, ed. Nicotine patches. Med Lett Drugs Ther 1992;34:37.

Table 9.3. Source: Warner EG. Cocaine Abuse. Ann Int Med 1993; 119:229.

Table 9.6. Adapted from Viccellio P, ed. Handbook of Medical Toxicology. Boston: Little, Brown, 1993;614.

Table 11.4. Adapted from: Lowinson JH, Ruiz P, Millman RB, Langrod JG (eds). Substance Abuse: A Comprehensive Textbook. Baltimore: Williams & Wilkins, 1992;408–409.

Table 15.1. Johnson MD. Anabolic steroid use in adolescent athletes. Pediatr Clin North Am 1990;37:1112.

Table 16.2. Adapted from Flanagan RJ, Ruprah M, Meredith TJ, et al. An introduction to the clinical toxicology of volatile substances. Drug Saf 1990;5:359–383; and from Linden CH. Volatile substances of abuse. Emerg Med Clin North Am 1990;8:559–578.

Table 16.3. Adapted from Flanagan RJ, Ruprah M, Meredith TJ, et al. An introduction to the clinical toxicology of volatile substances. Drug Saf 1990; 5:359–383.

Table 18.1. From Wartenberg A, Dubé CE, Lewis DC, Cyr MG. Diagnosing chronic substance use problems in the primary care setting. In: Dubé CE, Goldstein MG, Lewis DC, Myers EL, Zwick WR, eds. Projects ADEPT curriculum for primary care physicians training. I: Core modules. Providence, RI: Brown University, 1989.

Table 18.2. From Gastfriend DR. Pharmacotherapy of psychiatric syndromes with comorbid chemical dependence. J Addict Dis 1993; 12:155–170.

Table 19.1. Melzack R. The McGill pain questionnaire: major properties and scoring methods. Pain 1975; 1:277–299.

Table 19.2. Compiled from Principles of Analgesic Use in the Treatment of Acute Pain and Cancer Pain. Skokie, IL: American Pain Society, 1992.

Index

Page numbers followed by "f" represent figures; those followed by "t" represent tables.

42.95

DATE DUE